Preparing the Next Generation of Teacher Educators for Clinical Practice

A volume in
Advances in Teacher Education
Diane Yendol-Hoppey and David Hoppey, *Series Editors*

Preparing the
Next Generation
of Teacher Educators
for Clinical Practice

edited by

Diane Yendol-Hoppey
University of North Florida

Nancy Fichtman Dana
University of Florida

David Hoppey
University of North Florida

INFORMATION AGE PUBLISHING, INC.
Charlotte, NC • www.infoagepub.com

Library of Congress Cataloging-in-Publication Data

A CIP record for this book is available from the Library of Congress
http://www.loc.gov

ISBN: 978-1-64113-614-3 (Paperback)
         978-1-64113-615-0 (Hardcover)
         978-1-64113-616-7 (ebook)

This book is dedicated to teacher educators whose scholarship has focused on improving the preparation of teacher candidates and the next generation of teacher educators who will career this torch into the future.

CONTENTS

PART II

THE PREPARATION OF SCHOOL-BASED TEACHER EDUCATORS 137

PART III

INQUIRY AS A MECHANISM
FOR TEACHER EDUCATOR PREPARATION 193

PART IV

REFLECTIONS ON THE FUTURE
OF TEACHER EDUCATOR PREPARATION   273

PREFACE

As the landscape of teacher education continues to shift towards empha-sizing teacher preparation designs that require program coherence and highly integrated clinical practice, so too does the work of teacher educa-tors working in higher education. According to AACTE's, *A Pivot Toward Clinical Practice, Its Lexicon, and Renewing the Profession of Teaching* (2018), these clinical programs involve "practical experiences in school-based classrooms interwoven with academic coursework to make future teachers profession ready for the 21st century learner" (AACTE, 2018a, para. 1). These programs are designed to systematically and intentionally facilitate teacher candidates, practicing teachers, and teacher educators' linkage of theory, research, and practice. This preparation requires "mutually benefi-cial partnerships between educator preparation providers and PK–12 can successfully create laboratories of practice for both teacher candidates and practicing teachers, providing continuous improvement for all involved" (p. 2). The overarching belief is that clinical practice and partnership are essential to high-quality teacher preparation.

Although this movement is gaining attention from policy makers and educators around the world, the work of embedding clinical practice across teacher preparation programs began decades ago. During the last few de-cades, many educational organizations have called upon teacher educators to develop, implement, and sustain teacher preparation programs that more fully integrate clinical practice (AACTE, 2010; CAEP, 2015; Holmes Group, 1990, 1995; NAPDS, n.d.; NCATE, 2010; Goodlad, 1988). As a re-sult, many university-based teacher education programs have established

Preparing the Next Generation of Teacher Educators for Clinical Practice, pages xi–xvii
Copyright © 2019 by Information Age Publishing

strong partnerships with schools and reconceptualized teacher education resulting in pockets of program excellence.

Although pockets of excellence of clinically intensive preparation programs exist, today we continue to witness the implementation of teacher preparation programs that vary substantially in their commitment to teacher candidate learning within the context of practice and the level of programmatic coherence. This has been most recently noted in the AACTE Clinical Practice Commission's statement:

> Unfortunately, since the publication of the Blue Ribbon Panel report, reform and reinvention efforts have largely been scattered and with some haphazard attempts by programs and universities grappling with the idea of immersing teacher preparation in clinical practice. A unified professional structure with a shared understanding of clinical practice has yet to develop in teacher preparation. (2018b, p. 3)

We suggest that one reason that teacher preparation hasn't enacted nor sustained widespread shifts in the way we do teacher education is that we may not have prepared enough teacher educators with the interest in as well as the knowledge, skills, and dispositions to enact teacher education differently. This recognition begs the questions, to what extent have we intentionally prepared the next generation of teacher educators to enact teacher education that demonstrates these qualities of excellence? And, what must we do to systematically and intentionally prepare them to lead programs rich in clinical practice and partnership in the decades to come?

THE FOCUS ON TEACHER EDUCATORS

When we think about improving P–12 teaching and learning, we typically focus on how to improve the quality of teachers and teacher candidates. When one searches the literature on teacher education, there is an abundance of research focused on the preparation of teacher candidates and the importance of that preparation on P–12 student learning. Additionally, there is a great deal of attention paid to research focused on the professional learning of practicing teachers across their career span and the critical role their ongoing learning plays on P–12 student learning. That said, much less attention is given to the learning and development of those who prepare teacher candidates and support the professional learning of practicing teachers, the teacher educator. To date, too little research is available related to how to best support the development of the teacher educators who prepare teacher candidates for the profession. Zeichner (2005) noted, "Many universities today treat teacher education as a self-evident activity both for school- and university-based teacher educators who mentor prospective teachers in clinical experiences and for the instructors and faculty who teach courses in a teacher education program" (p. 118). In an effort to respond to this critique, *Preparing the Next Generation of Teacher Educators* begins to address this void by bringing together a compilation of research studies focused on the preparation of university and school-based teacher educators to develop and implement high quality, teacher preparation programs.

WHO ARE THESE TEACHER EDUCATORS?

Given the shift toward teacher preparation as a clinical practice, teacher educators today are required to do their work much differently than in the past and these teacher educators are emerging from a variety of contexts. This book focuses on both the preparation of university-based teacher educators as well as school-based teacher educators. Today, in teacher education programs with high quality clinical practices, we find district, school, and university personnel working together in hybrid roles across school and university contexts (Cosenza, & Buchanan, 2018; Polly, 2014). Drawing on the work of the AACTE Clinical Practice Commission (2018b), university-based teacher educators are defined as "Individuals involved in teacher preparation whose primary institutional home is a college or university. University-based teacher educators are a specific type of boundary-spanning teacher educator who engage in evaluation, coaching, instruction, and partnership. They assume expanded and multiple responsibilities within, and often across, each of these four domains" (p. 12). In the past, these individuals have often been referred to as university supervisor, clinical supervisor, and clinical faculty. Given the necessity of linking theory, research and practice, in high quality clinical programs these university-based teacher educators include non-tenure as well as tenure track faculty members. According to this same report, school-based teacher educators are defined as "Individuals involved in teacher preparation whose primary institutional home is a school. School-based teacher educators are a specific type of boundary-spanning teacher educators who assume mentoring and partnership responsibilities that are in addition to their school responsibilities" (p. 12). This role has often been referred to in the past by terms such as cooperating teacher, mentor teacher, collaborating teacher, and directing teacher.

As we begin this new era of teacher education, these new terms and titles suggest more robust and conceptually complex roles and responsibilities. Working together, these university and school-based teacher educators are collectively responsible for systematically and intentionally: (a) evaluating teacher candidates, (b) coaching teacher candidates, (c) developing and sustaining partnerships, (d) linking coursework to practice and practice to coursework, (e) providing program leadership that cultivates inter-organizational collaboration and partnership, and (f) conducting research to strengthen the scholarship of teacher education (Hoppey & Yendol-Hoppey, 2018). Together, university and school-based teacher educators actively support teacher candidate development throughout the teacher preparation continuum by bringing together the elements of theory, research, and practice that lead to quality instruction and PK–12 student learning.

WHAT WE HAVE LEARNED FROM THE PROCESS OF EDITING THIS BOOK

One of the most interesting parts about editing this book is what we have learned as we reviewed and discussed the manuscripts submitted. We were grateful for the opportunity to review so many manuscript submissions for this particular volume of *Advances in Teacher Education*. Although each of the submissions connected in some way to the increasing focus on the clinical component of teacher preparation, many of the submissions did not have anything to do with the preparation of teacher educators who would teach in clinically intensive teacher preparation programs. As we read the submissions and considered how those manuscripts fit within the call for proposals, we began to recognize that there continues to be confusion about *what the work of a teacher educator* is as well as *what research focused on preparing teacher educators includes*. Surprisingly, many of the manuscripts submitted focused on pedagogy related to the preparation of teacher candidates or the learning of practicing teachers. Other submissions focused on program configurations or some practices used to support candidate learning within clinical experiences. These manuscripts were submitted by those engaged in the preparation of teacher candidates, but many of them had little to do with research related to the preparation of teacher educators. The articles presented in the chapters that follow reflect a variety of genres including program descriptions, research, and thought pieces. Just as Zeichner expressed so many years ago, the field could benefit by developing a literature to inform the preparation and learning of teacher educators. The following chapters are intend to respond to Zeichner's challenge and encourage future conversation about how we can better prepare the next generation of teacher educators.

ORGANIZATION OF BOOK

In order to facilitate the reader's ease in looking across the chapters, this book is organized into three sections. The first section focuses on the preparation of *university-based teacher educators*. The section includes six chapters that provide insight into how we can better prepare university-based teacher educators during doctoral preparation:

Chapter 1: Purposeful Preparation for Roles in Boundary-Spanning Clinical Teacher Preparation

Chapter 2: Taking the Mentoring of New Teacher Educators Seriously: Lessons from a Clinically-Intensive Teacher Preparation Program

Chapter 3: The Pattern Emerges: Novice Teacher Educators Learn from Complexity

Chapter 4: Preparing the Teacher Educator: Negotiating the Tensions of Teacher Educator Preparation within the Research Institution

Chapter 5: The Changing Role of University-Based Teacher Educators: Lessons Learned in a Clinical Elementary Teacher Preparation Program

Chapter 6: How Did I Get to Where I Am? Turning Points in the Personal and Professional Lives of Literacy Teacher Educators

These chapters provide insights into how we can better prepare doctoral students to be successful university based teacher educators within teacher preparation programs committed to strong clinical practice.

The second section features two chapters that investigate the preparation of *school-based teacher educators*. This section includes:

Chapter 7: From Teacher Candidate to Teacher Educator: What It Means to "Grow Up" in a Professional Development School Partnership

Chapter 8: Collaborative Planning of Teacher Educators in a Professional Development School

Together, these chapters provide insight into how school-based teacher educators develop, shape their work, and thrive when working within the PDS.

In the third section of the book, we turn our attention to *how* current and future teacher educators are learning in and from their work as teacher educators. This section includes:

Chapter 9: Making the Case for Practitioner Inquiry in Doctoral Student Education: Supporting the Development of Future Teacher Educators

Chapter 10: Self-Study and Preparing the Next Generation of Teacher Educators

Chapter 11: Facing Practice: Teacher Educator Inquiry for Development Across the Professional Life Span

In combination, these chapters shed light on how teacher educators might continue to contribute to the knowledge base of teacher education while engaged in the work.

Finally, in Chapter 12, The Nomadic Teacher Educator: Teacher Educator's Emerging Role, Parkison provides an essay designed to complicate the work that is nestled within this text. He raises questions for teacher educators to ponder regarding who are the teacher candidates, where do they come from, what does the future hold for teacher education program design and how do teacher educators negotiate and cross borders to develop practice based communities that meets the needs of a variety of stakeholders.

Chapter 13, Concluding Thoughts: Looking Across the Chapters, provides commentary on the research collected in this volume and highlights the emerging themes identified around how teachers educators learn and what teachers educators need to be effective.

FINAL THOUGHTS

In combination, the chapters found within this book provide promising support to those interested in teacher education as a field of scholarship. To engage readers more deeply in some of the ideas shared in the text, at the end of each chapter the authors provide a series of discussion questions they believe can push our thinking about preparing the next generation of teacher educators. Together these chapters offer insight into the knowledge, skills, and dispositions needed to enact, support, sustain, and assess the work of teacher educators engaged in high quality clinical practice. We believe the book will be helpful to those interested in designing teacher education, supporting university and school-based educator preparation in teacher education, assessing the needs of and challenges faced by university- and school-based teacher educators, and providing support to those who engage in this work.

REFERENCES

American Association of Colleges of Teacher Education. (2018a, January). *Press conference by the AACTE Clinical Practice Commission.* Retrieved from https://www .aacte.org/professional-development-and-events/justec/eventdetail/119/-/ press-conference-by-the-aacte-clinical-practice-commission

American Association of Colleges for Teacher Education. (2018b). *A pivot toward clinical practice, it's lexicon, and the renewal of educator preparation: A report of the AACTE Clinical Practice Commission.* Washington, DC: Author.

American Association of Colleges for Teacher Education. (2018c). *A pivot toward clinical practice, it's lexicon, and the renewal of educator preparation: Summary brief.* Washington, DC: Author.

American Association of Colleges of Teacher Education. (2010). The clinical preparation of teachers: A policy brief. Washington, DC: Author. Retrieved from https://coe.uni.edu/sites/default/files/wysiwyg/AACTE_-_Clinical_Prep_Paper.pdf

Council for the Accreditation of Educator Preparation. (2015). *Accreditation standards.* Retrieved from http://caepnet.org/standards/standard-2

Cosenza, M., & Buchanan, M. (2018). *Visions from professional development school partners: Connecting professional development and clinical practice.* Charlotte, NC: Information Age.

Goodlad, J. I. (1988). *The national network for educational renewal: Past, present, future.* University of Washington, College of Education, Institute for the Study of Educational Policy, Center for Educational Renewal.

Holmes Group. (1990). *Tomorrow's schools: Principles for the design of professional development schools.* East Lansing, MI: Author.

Holmes Group. (1995). *Tomorrow's schools of education.* East Lansing, MI: Author.

Hoppey, D. T., & Yendol-Hoppey, D. (2018). *Outcomes of high-quality clinical practice in teacher education.* Charlotte, NC: Information Age.

National Association for Professional Development Schools. (n.d.). *Nine essentials.* Retrieved from https://napds.org/nine-essentials/

National Council for Accreditation of Teacher Education. (2010, November). *Transforming teacher education through clinical practice: A national strategy to prepare effective teachers.* Washington, DC: Blue Ribbon Panel on Clinical Preparation and Partnerships for Improved Student Learning.

Polly, D., Heafner, T., Chapman, M., & Spooner, M. (Eds.). (2015). *Professional development schools and transformative partnerships.* Hershey, PA: IGI Global.

Zeichner, K. (2005). Becoming a teacher educator: A personal perspective. *Teaching and Teacher Education, 21*(2), 117–124.

Zeichner, K. (2003). Teacher research as professional development for P–12 educators in the USA. *Educational Action Research, 11*(2), 301–326.

Zeichner, K. (1999). The new scholarship in teacher education. *Educational Researcher, 28*(9), 4–15.

PART I

THE PREPARATION OF UNIVERSITY-BASED TEACHER EDUCATORS

Recognizing the importance of the preparation of university-based teacher educators who are capable of building strong programs with quality clinical practice is central to the message found in the NCATE Blue Ribbon Panel Report (2010), the recent CAEP standards, and the new AACTE Clinical Practice Commission Report (2017). These reports continue to challenge teacher educators to rethink program design and the work of university-based teacher educators in order to strengthen and integrate the clinical components teacher candidates experience as they learn to teach. In order to engage in this reform work, we need to spend more time focusing on how to prepare the next generation of teacher educators to work differently and how to support them once they assume the role of university-based teacher educator. Just as Zeichner described decades ago, reforming teacher education today cannot remain "a tangential concern for most and the major concern of only a few" (1999, p. 11).

Today, we are in the process of creating a new cadre of teacher educators who will be responsible for conceptualizing teacher education beyond the traditional work of teaching a methods course to pivoting, reinventing, implementing, and researching how those methods courses are tied to clinical practice, supported in the field, and result in PK–12 student learning. This is the work of future teacher educators who will be responsible for high quality, clinically intensive teacher preparation.

Given the pressing shift to link closely with the clinical context, university-based teacher educators are facing ever-expanding responsibilities. For

Preparing the Next Generation of Teacher Educators for Clinical Practice, pages 1–6
Copyright © 2019 by Information Age Publishing

example, Cochran-Smith (2012) described the multifaceted and intensive work of the new teacher educator as including:

> Curriculum development; program evaluation; recruitment and admission of students; participation in professional and state-level accreditation reviews; establishment and maintenance of fieldwork sites; supervision of fieldwork experiences for teacher candidates in school and community settings; supervising and mentoring student teachers; providing professional development for experienced teachers; teaching courses with fieldwork components; collaborating with school-and community-based educators; providing career advice about teaching and other roles in schools; working in professional development or partnership schools; and developing, administering, and evaluating professional assessments (or assessment systems) for teacher candidates. (p. 100)

Actualizing these roles will require each teacher education program to cultivate a strong and collaborative team of teacher educators responsible for high quality program design and implementation.

Almost two decades ago, Zeichner (1999) problematized the field of teacher education when he stated that, "relatively few people who work in teacher education programs actually read the research literature and think about it in relation to their own teacher education programs" (p. 11). Today, the scholarship of teacher education is strengthening and a new breed of teacher educator is paying attention to their own learning.

About the same time period that Zeichner was noting this lack of attention to the teacher education research literature, Tom (1997) warned the field that the important shift towards clinical practice called for by reform groups such as Holmes and the National Network for Education Renewal would likely be met with resistance by faculty in colleges of education. In fact, he argued that teacher education reform would require teacher educators to make identity shifts that would be difficult for many as faculty expanded, renegotiated, and redefined their roles in teacher education. Today, Dinkelman (2011) describes the work of teacher educators as elusive. He depicts a teacher educator's professional identity as multiple, fluid, relational, always developing, shaped by a broad range of sociocultural power relationships and strongly influenced by contexts. Dinkelman suggests that these new teacher educator identities reflect an ever-shifting weave of personal and professional phenomena that can be claimed by teacher educators and/or given to them through the institutional roles that they assume. This multiplicity and fluidity often results in a role or identity that may not yet be aligned with traditional university rewards, structures, work assignments, and values.

Ultimately, the way university teacher educators learn to perceive themselves within their context influences their choices and actions.

University-based teacher educator expectations are complicated even more by the pressure within many universities to engage in research as well as tenure and promotion expectations. Murray and Male (2005) found that two of the main challenges new teacher educators faced were developing a pedagogy for teaching teachers while simultaneously becoming productive in research and scholarship.

Given the expanding roles associated with being a teacher educator, Zeichner (2003) argued that the preparation of the next generation of teacher educators must receive greater attention. He advocated that "the research universities that supply colleges and universities with the faculty who staff the vast number of teacher education programs throughout the United States need to take the preparation of teacher educators more seriously" (p. 335). Indeed, we still need more attention given to the preparation and support of teacher educators. For example, Kosnik, Cleovoulou, Fletcher, Harris, McGlynn-Stewart, and Beck (2011) noted that in the 2008 *Handbook of Teacher Education* there was only one chapter and commentary related to teacher educators. Similarly, Hollins, Luna, and Lopez (2014) reported that how teacher educators learn to facilitate teacher learning is not well understood.

Given the increasing complexity of teacher education, today it is even more important that we deepen our scholarship. In her recent reflections on teacher education from an international perspective, Rust (2017) described the complexity of the field of teacher education and the implications for those individuals who work within the field:

> ...the very complexity of the field requires a powerful shift in practice and in thinking—a shift that enables a commitment to experimentation at every level, a tolerance for multiple, even seemingly conflicting models, and the embrace of open communication that reaches beyond higher education and acknowledges and draws strength from the uncertainties that are inherent in a robust system. Systems theory embraces complexity. It does not allow for a single answer, a best system. Rather, it invites multiple visions of possibility, multiple enactments of theory, multiple perspectives on practice, multiple ways of learning, multiple forms of assessment—all in the service or toward the realization of the ideal of educating well both new and experienced teachers and teacher educators and ultimately all of those whom they teach. (p. 9)

Responding to these challenges will take a new type of teacher educator. Today, in many contexts colleges of education are seeking a critical mass of faculty who understand the current complexities of teacher education and are willing to collaborate together to learn from one another, engage in teacher education scholarship, and build high quality programs.

If the field is going to be successful in transitioning to clinically intensive teacher preparation, then we will need to re-tool current university-based teacher educators and build a strong cadre of future teacher educators who are positioned to carry out this work effectively. In Part I, we begin to address the important question of how we prepare the next generation of university-based teacher educators. These individuals will need to understand the complexity of the work of teacher educators involved in clinically intensive, teacher education reform. To these ends, we offer six chapters that provide insight into how we can cultivate university-based teacher educators through systematic and intentional preparation for the important work they will do. Together, these chapters offer insight into teacher education as a scholarly field.

In Chapter 1, "Purposeful Preparation for Roles in Boundary-Spanning Clinical Teacher Preparation," Audra Parker, Kristien Zenkov, and Seth Parsons respond to the recent calls for a shift towards clinical teacher education by offering insights related to the preparation of teacher educators. In this chapter, they describe their efforts to intentionally scaffold doctoral students into the changing world of teacher preparation through a paired course and internship experience. The course provides doctoral students a foundation in the historical, theoretical, and research trends related to clinical teacher preparation and is followed by a supervision internship with a boundary spanning university-based teacher educator. The structures introduced provide teacher educators insight into simultaneously re-thinking the training of our nation's teachers and the educators who will prepare them.

In Chapter 2, "Taking the Mentoring of New Teacher Educators Seriously: Lessons From a Clinically Intensive Teacher Preparation Program," Patricia Norman in collaboration with her colleagues Sara Sherwood, Rocio Delgado, and Melissa Siller, emphasize the importance of mentoring teacher educators into the important work they do related to clinical experiences. This chapter offers fine-grained descriptions of what serious mentoring efforts of new teacher educators look and sound like as well as their impact in helping field-based practitioners to develop critical aspects of their craft. The mentoring vignettes illustrate core field-based teacher education practices, including designing clinically based courses; establishing relationships in clinical settings; giving candidates feedback on their planning, teaching and progress; addressing significant concerns in candidates' practice and/or clinical placement; and supporting mentor development. Most importantly, the chapter points to the complexity of the work of teacher educators.

In Chapter 3, "The Pattern Emerges: Novice Teacher Educators Learn From Complexity," Janna Dresden, Katherine Thompson, Melissa Baker, Ashley Nylin, and Kajal Sinha address the question, "How is the preparation of teacher educators as practitioners, scholars and researchers facilitated, supported, challenged or enhanced by work in a clinically intensive setting?" The chapter begins with a review of clinically intensive teacher preparation and introduces complexity theory as a lens for understanding the challenges facing teacher education. Included in the chapter are narratives from a veteran teacher educator, two current doctoral students and a recent graduate of the doctoral program highlighting the rich complexity of clinically intensive programs and the importance of recognizing clinically intensive spaces as places for synergy between research and practice.

In Chapter 4, "Preparing The Teacher Educator: Negotiating The Tensions Of Teacher Educator Preparation Within The Research Institution," Lara Hebert, Lindsayanne Insana, Alexis Jones, and Meghan Kessler describe the preparation of the teacher educator as a complex and multifaceted field of practice and research. This chapter uses literature, self-study, and narrative to highlight the preparation experiences of these novice teacher educators within a research university. They identify four tensions that emerged as they wrestled with becoming teacher educators: (a) connecting research and teaching within teacher education, (b) navigating institutional expectations of expertise, (c) practicing what you preach, and (d) learning with and from others. Their narratives give voice to early career teacher educators and argue that the teaching of teachers is not an obvious, self-evident practice. They offer a series of recommendations that invite an opportunity for much needed change.

In Chapter 5, "The Changing Role Of University-Based Teacher Educators: Lessons Learned In A Clinical Elementary Teacher Preparation Program," Ann McCoy and Nicole Nickens discuss their work as teacher educators related to revising their elementary and early childhood teacher preparation programs to follow a clinical model. Although they expected much needed changes related to the preparedness of their teacher candidates, they did not anticipate that their role as university-based teacher educators would change to the degree they experienced. Their chapter provides an overview of their clinical model, a description of their new role as teacher educators, lessons learned about the knowledge, skills and dispositions required of teacher educators in their clinical program, as well as changes made in hiring practices and support for new teacher educators.

In Chapter 6, entitled "How did I get to where I am?: Turning points in the personal and professional lives of literacy teacher educators," Pooja Dharamshi, Clare Kosnik, and Lydia Menna examine the work of literacy teacher educators. This piece helps us better understand how key life experiences influenced literacy teacher educator efforts to engage in clinically intensive practices. Critical junctures were identified including early life experiences, classroom teaching, and doctoral studies. The deeply held beliefs about teacher education were rooted in personal experiences of classroom teachers, explored in doctoral research, and were central to their current research agenda. These turning points served as a form of preparation for the clinically intensive practices literacy teacher educators undertook as academics, carefully weaving theory and practice into courses, including involving teacher candidates in their field-based projects and research. This chapter brings our attention to an important point: For teacher educators, clinically intensive practice will "look" different because of what they teach, who they are, and what they bring to the program. Finally, these authors make clear that simply mandating more clinical-intensive practices is short-sighted and bound to fail if not intertwined thoughtfully into the entire program.

In sum, the chapters found within this section point to the complexity of the work of teacher education today. Each chapter contributes to a scholarship of teacher education by providing insight into how the next generation of teacher educators can be prepared for clinically intensive teacher education.

REFERENCES

American Association of Colleges for Teacher Education. (2018). *Report from the clinical practice commission: A pivot towards clinical practice, its lexicon and the renewal of educator preparation*. Washington, DC: Author.

Cochran-Smith, M. (2012). Composing a research life. *Action in Teacher Education, 34*(2), 99–110.

Dinkelman, T. (2011). Forming a teacher educator identity: Uncertain standards, practice and relationships. *Journal of Education for Teaching, 37*(3), 309–323.

Hollins, E. R., Luna, C., & Lopez, S. (2014). Learning to teach teachers. *Teaching Education, 25*(1), 99–124.

Kosnik, C., Cleovoulou, Y., Fletcher, T., Harris, T., McGlynn-Stewart, M., & Beck, C. (2011). Becoming teacher educators: An innovative approach to teacher educator preparation. *Journal of Education for Teaching, 37*(3), 351–363.

Murray, J., & Male, T. (2005). Becoming a teacher educator: Evidence from the field. *Teaching and Teacher Education, 21*(1), 125–142.

National Council for Accreditation of Teacher Education. (2010). *Report of the blue ribbon panel on clinical preparation and partnerships for improved learning*. Washington, DC: Author. Retrieved from http://caepnet.org/~/media/Files/caep/accreditation-resources/blue-ribbon-panel.pdf

Rust, F. (2017). Making teacher education matter. *Teachers and Teaching: Theory and Practice, 23*(4), 383–386.

Tom, A. (1997). *Redesigning Teacher Education*. Albany: State University of New York Press.

Zeichner, K. (1999). The new scholarship in teacher education. *Educational Researcher, 28*(9), 4–15.

Zeichner, K. (2006). Reflections of a university-based teacher educator on the future of college- and university-based teacher education, *Journal of Teacher Education, 57*(3), 326–340.

CHAPTER 1

PURPOSEFUL PREPARATION FOR ROLES IN BOUNDARY-SPANNING CLINICAL TEACHER PREPARATION

Audra Parker
George Mason University

Kristien Zenkov
George Mason University

Seth Parsons
George Mason University

The release of the 2010 National Council for Accreditation of Teacher Education Blue Ribbon Panel Report (NCATE, 2010) served as the impetus for a monumental, albeit much-needed, shift in teacher preparation in the United States—one that moved teacher preparation from isolated university settings to clinical PK–12 school partnerships. Similar movements are occurring across the globe, including Europe's "turn to the practical"

Preparing the Next Generation of Teacher Educators for Clinical Practice, pages 7–24
Copyright © 2019 by Information Age Publishing
7

(Furlong, 2013). This global reorientation allows for purposeful, scaffolded experiences with expert mentors—both school-based and university-based teacher educators—who facilitate the application of academic content in real world settings. It is to this third space—the intersection between university- and school-based teacher education that integrates theory and practice—that teacher education is increasingly moving (Zeichner, 2010).

In recent years professional organizations, policy-makers, and accrediting agencies have heeded this long-overdue call to resituate teacher preparation in clinical contexts. For example, the American Association of Colleges for Teacher Education (AACTE) and the Association of Teacher Educators (ATE) incorporated clinical practice into their membership agendas (see the Clinical Practice Commission of AACTE and the Clinical Fellows Institute of ATE, respectively). Similarly, the Council for the Accreditation of Educator Preparation (CAEP, 2014) acknowledged the growing importance of clinically intensive teacher preparation in their crafting of "Standard 2: Clinical Partnerships and Practice." While we recognize that clinical practice and school–university partnerships are not new ideas (Holmes Group, 1986; 1990), there is a growing expectation that clinically intensive teacher preparation should be the norm for all teacher education efforts, rather than the exception for a few, boutique programs.

Working within this new, clinically intensive orientation necessitates a shift in the work we do as teacher educators—both in schools and at universities. Yet the preparation and professional development required in doctoral programs for working in these contexts has not mirrored this move. In fact, the field of teacher education often functions under the premise that good classroom teachers will find their way to traditional doctoral programs in teacher education and that they will inherently possess the skills necessary for guiding teacher candidates as they learn the pedagogy of teaching. Many university-based teacher educators (UBTEs) obtained their positions by earning a doctoral degree in education, often in a discipline-specific area. Earning a PhD in curriculum and instruction with a specialization in math includes many courses in research and math teaching and learning, but it does not necessarily include any guidance in how to become an effective teacher educator. Likewise, many teacher educators are retired teachers (e.g., the university supervisors or coaches who work with most teacher education programs' student teachers), who undoubtedly have expansive knowledge to share with teacher candidates. However, extensive experience as a classroom teacher does not guarantee that one is adequately prepared to share knowledge about the science and art of teaching—rather than one's subject area content—in a new role as a teacher educator. Additionally, most teacher educators work in isolation to develop their pedagogy without support from peers or scaffolding from expert teacher educators.

The purpose of this chapter is to describe our efforts to break with these traditions and more systematically prepare future teacher educators for work in clinical contexts. In the sections that follow, we briefly highlight the research on teacher educator preparation. We then follow with a description of one example of how we have intentionally scaffolded doctoral candidates into experiences with an understanding of clinically intensive teacher education. We assert that any reforms to teacher preparation structures must simultaneously consider significant revisions to the training of the next generation of teacher educators. And that without attention to preparing these future teacher educators to work in clinical settings, the vision for teacher preparation set forth in the Blue Ribbon Panel Report (NCATE, 2010) and operationalized by the AACTE Clinical Practice Commission (AACTE, 2018) will not come to fruition.

PREPARING TEACHER EDUCATORS

Before delving into the research literature on teacher educator preparation, it is important to more clearly define who exactly we are referring to when we use the term "teacher educator." In fact, as a result of recent attention to a clinical orientation in teacher preparation, the term teacher educator is more complicated, contested, and all-encompassing than ever before. While we are accustomed to teacher educators who enter the profession through traditional doctoral routes, an increase in alternative certification routes that move teacher candidates directly into classrooms relies heavily on mentorship provided by classroom teachers. Given mentor teachers' roles as the primary link between theory and practice, these classroom teachers are often characterized as teacher educators (McNamara & Murray, 2013; Murray, 2014). Similarly, school-based teacher educators, much like those found in professional development school (PDS) contexts, take on increased responsibilities for mentorship and may serve in leadership and boundary-spanning roles across PK–12 and university contexts that lead some to include them under the umbrella term teacher educator (Van Velzen & Volman, 2009; Klein, Taylor, & Onore, 2012).

In university contexts, teacher educators are not simply those who work in colleges of education with teacher candidates. Rather, content specialists—those faculty who teach courses in the university that expressly serve teacher candidates—might also be considered teacher educators. To reflect these broad constructs, the AACTE Clinical Practice Commission, in its efforts to establish a common lexicon for clinical teacher preparation, determined that the phrase "teacher educator" should be included in reference to both university-based and school-based stakeholders engaged in work with teacher candidates (AACTE, 2018).

The majority of new teachers still enter the teaching profession through university-based teacher education programs, and tenure-track faculty members with PhDs in education remain the largest, most influential, and most commonly recognized single pool of teacher educators. Our chapter focuses generally on this demographic of teacher educators—or, more specifically, "university-based teacher educators" (UBTEs)—defined by the Clinical Practice Commission as "an individual involved in teacher preparation whose primary institutional home is a college or university" (AACTE, 2018, p. 12). This term encompasses those working as a "university supervisor, university liaison, clinical supervisor, or clinical faculty" (AACTE, 2018, p. 12). More specifically, our work centers on the preparation of "university-based doctoral prepared faculty who engage in teacher education—that is, the preparation of preservice or future teachers" (Goodwin et al., 2014, p. 300).

Understanding University-Based Teacher Educators

Historically, UBTEs have held low status and been among the most marginalized faculty in higher education (Furlong, 2013). This standing is likely due to a number of factors including the fact that teaching and teacher education have long existed as female-dominated fields (Murray & Maguire, 2007) that require significant clinical work—professional tasks and an aspect of higher education that are less frequently recognized or rewarded as consequential, particularly in research-intensive universities. In addition, teacher education roles, and more specifically those that are clinical in nature, have historically been filled by adjuncts and graduate students. As a result, faculty in these roles are often marginalized and do not have standing within institutions to participate in or guide decision-making, nor do they yet have the theoretical expertise to support teacher candidates' professional development (Furlong, 2013; Slick, 1998).

University-based teacher educators are also simultaneously marginalized from the PK–12 contexts within which their expertise also resides. Rarely are they consulted for curriculum and professional development support in the schools or school districts in which they spend significant amounts of time. Of course, full-time tenured or tenure-track university faculty operating as teacher educators have indeed historically been disconnected from practice, and as a result from the daily realities of PK–12 schools. But those faculty members—tenured, tenure-track, adjunct or short-term, or in clinical roles—whose positions require that they engage in clinical practice activities and spend substantial time in schools are neither situated firmly in the research traditions of the university nor in the daily workings of these schools. As a result they are generally overlooked in terms of policy-making decisions related to either preservice or in-service teacher education

(Murray, 2014). This positioning, as simultaneously "inside and outside the ivory tower" (Maguire, 1994, p. 24) means that they have little status in either. In fact, Arthur Levine, in his seminal 2006 report, *Education School Teachers*, described teacher educators as "more often inside rather than outside" and "out of date, more theoretical than practice" (p. 47).

Zeichner used the notion of *third space* as a means for addressing the disconnect between university and PK–12 programs. Zeichner (2010) posits a need for hybrid spaces in teacher education where expert knowledge, from both university and PK–12 settings, come together in ways that value and integrate the expertise of both practitioners and academics (Zeichner, 2010). But creating a third space is more complex than simply bringing university courses into PK–12 contexts (Norton-Meier & Drake, 2010). Rather, it is "a rejection of binaries such as practitioner and academic knowledge and theory and practice and involves the integration of what are often seen as competing discourses in new ways" (Zeichner, 2010, p. 92). It is within these hybrid spaces that boundary-spanning efforts of both university-based and school-based personnel can be situated. Such third-space activities continue to grow in number and range. They include integrating PK–12 teachers into positions such as "teachers in residence" where they may teach university courses, supervise field experiences, and engage in programmatic review/revision efforts. They also take the form of site-based course instruction where university faculty and students are thoroughly embedded in a PK–12 context (Gallagher et al., 2019). And they increasingly appear as critical, project-based clinical experiences where future teachers, veteran teachers, adolescents, and university faculty member collaborate as co-researchers (Zenkov, Parker, Parsons, Pellegrino, & Pytash, 2017) and *professors in residence* structures where university faculty members become formal members of a school community. While these boundary-spanning practices are becoming increasingly prevalent in the United States, the necessary preparation to work in these roles is less frequently present.

Becoming a Teacher Educator

We assert that the low status of teacher educators may be in part due to the varied and sometimes haphazard routes teacher educators take into the professoriate. Mayer and colleagues (2011) note teacher education is a "specialized field without specialists" (p. 258), and a career track from which teacher educators emerge from varied starting points (e.g., K–12 schools, the academy). As a result, teacher education lacks systematic preparation both within and across those entry routes. Goodwin and Kosnik (2013) suggest many academics hired in teacher education are neither prepared for nor qualified to do this work. This is particularly true of teacher educators who serve in boundary-spanning clinical roles such as university supervisors of student teachers and liaisons in school–university partnerships as there is often limited instruction for such roles in these individuals doctoral programs (Cuenca, 2010). Therefore, some teacher educators enter the profession circuitously or even accidentally, and the result is that they vary tremendously in their K–12 teaching experiences, theoretical preparation, research skills, and supervision skills (Mayer, Mitchell, Santoro, & White, 2011). More commonly, some teacher educators have extensive practical K–12 experience, while others have significant training as scholars and researchers, but less common are new UBTEs who have experience or preparation in both capacities. Our pathways into teacher preparation, then, serve to further cement the dichotomous nature of teacher preparation as focused on theory *or* practice, rather than uniting the two roles in such a way as required of *clinical* teacher preparation today: university-based theory, scholarship, research *and* school-based practice, pedagogical applications, and relationship-building.

An additional challenge to becoming a teacher educator is the profession's status as a "second order" practice (Loughran, 2006; Murray, 2002). In other words, teacher educators are not simply imparting content knowledge or expertise to students, they are teaching about pedagogy—about the very nature of *how* to teach. Loughran (2011; as cited in Hadar & Brody, 2017) noted, "...teaching about teaching must be informed by knowledge of practice that goes beyond recounting one's own teaching experiences or passing-on methods" (p. 1051). Rather, teacher educators must be able to model best practices while they simultaneously step outside of the act of teaching to discuss its complexities—this nuanced dance sheds light "on pedagogical reasoning, thoughts, and actions" (Loughran, 2006, p. 39). Thus, a theoretical look at the practical experiences of teaching content and PK–12 students is essential in becoming a teacher educator.

The lack of universal adherence to well-established professional pedagogies and the absence of a common lexicon for the preparation of teacher candidates are also complicating factors related to entry into teacher education. In fact, Goodwin and Kosnik (2013) suggest there is "little evidence of a curriculum for, or coherent codified pedagogy of, teacher education" (p. 298). Yet Shulman (2005) views professional pedagogies as essential in educating for a particular profession to the point that a given method of teaching ultimately becomes an inextricable part of preparation for a given field. According to Shulman, these habitual and visible pedagogies have three distinct characteristics: (a) They are unique/distinct to the given profession; (b) They are used consistently in preparation for the profession; and (c) They are essential for preparation for the profession. In other words, in order to teach and model best practices, there must be a consistent framework of pedagogies within which these practices are shared with future teachers. And, furthermore, in order for teacher educators' preparation to be effective, they must be well versed in the theoretical and practical applications of these pedagogies.

The recent focus on *signature pedagogies* by Yendol-Hoppey and Franco (2014) is providing some guidance as to emerging pedagogies that may guide the development of clinically intensive teacher education programs. Following a systematic review of articles published in *School–University Partnerships* and focusing specifically on PDS, these scholars identified inquiry, focused observation, mentoring and coaching, co-teaching, reflection on teaching, and integrated coursework and fieldwork as the foundational acts of effective instruction of teacher candidates in PDS contexts. Yendol-Hoppey and Franco acknowledge that while these pedagogies are emerging and need further exploration, they have the potential to reduce variation among and increase quality across teacher preparation programs. However, this potentially can only be achieved if our field builds up the knowledge and expertise of teacher educators tasked with preparing teachers to use these pedagogies.

Finally, yet perhaps most foundational in the challenges of preparing teacher educators is the lack of a common lexicon in teacher preparation. In their research on terminology used in teacher preparation programs (Parker, Zenkov & Dennis, in press), found as many as 18 different terms for a given role clinical practice. This variability contributes to confusion in communication and collaboration among school and UBTEs and serves to de-professionalize the field. Without clarity in how we define and discuss these roles, it is hard to imagine any consistency in how doctoral students are prepared to serve in them. A common lexicon of teacher preparation would provide consistency in how we speak of and prepare doctoral students to work in teacher education (AACTE, 2018).

Clinically intensive teacher education simultaneously addresses and augments the challenges teacher educators face both in their higher education contexts and in the view of the broader public. Conceptualized as "boundary spanners," clinically engaged teacher educators must embrace their roles both inside *and* outside the traditional, detached "ivory tower" because they are uniquely positioned to serve across contexts and in these dual capacities. However, the longstanding challenges described above complicate current efforts to prepare teacher educators for clinically intensive contexts. In an attempt to answer these challenges and effectively prepare the next generation of teacher educators, we have implemented a number of unique structures in our PhD program, which we introduce in the following section.

PREPARING FUTURE TEACHER EDUCATORS
FOR BOUNDARY-SPANNING ROLES

Our work is situated in a large, Research 1 institution that has a robust doctoral program in education and human development. One specialization within this doctoral program is "teaching and teacher education." Candidates in this specialization complete traditional doctoral coursework, accompanied by opportunities for teaching internships, at nonprofit agencies, in national organizations, and in school districts. Until recently, the program itself did not reflect the national turn toward clinical teacher preparation of our field. Because several faculty members affiliated with the specialization bring an orientation towards and expertise in boundary-spanning and clinical practice, efforts have been made to address this gap. In the next two sections we describe two of these efforts—related to course options and internship experiences—and some initial outcomes related to these efforts. Both of these revisions were designed to pivot our program toward preparing our PhD graduates for understanding and being able to operate in professional teacher education settings and with tasks that put clinical practice at the center of their work, with a specific focus on making theory to practice connections.

Course Overview: Working in Schools

While we have made a number of revisions to existing courses in our teaching and teacher education track, the most significant programmatic revision was the addition of a new course, Working in Schools: Spanning Boundaries/Expanding Roles.[1] Explicitly designed to address the gap between theory and practice in clinical teacher preparation in our existing teacher education doctoral program, we initially introduced the course as an elective, but after just two iterations it has already evolved into a required class in our 36-credit specialization. The course was designed to prepare future teacher educators and professional developers for their work in PK–12 settings by examining the principles of clinical field experiences, the foundations of school–university partnerships, and the roles and relationships of all stakeholders engaged in field-based teacher preparation and teacher professional development. The following learning outcomes guided course instruction:

- Increase understanding of the current contexts in teacher education as they relate to working with PK–12 school partners in field-based/clinical experiences.

- Examine the foundations of and appropriate models for clinical practice including school/university partnerships.
- Explore the various roles and responsibilities of the stakeholders engaged in boundary-spanning PK–12/university roles.
- Understand the tenets of culturally responsive pedagogy as it applies to boundary-spanning roles in cross-cultural settings.
- Examine the role of teacher education in school change.

The course was open to students from all doctoral specializations, and we encouraged those who saw themselves as either future university-based or school-based teacher educators to consider enrolling. After two versions of the course were offered, students in this course have primarily consisted of practicing teachers who were pursuing a doctoral degree with the intent of remaining in the classroom, entering district level positions, or transitioning into teacher preparation at the university level.

The course readings, assignments, and activities were organized around four themes: the *big picture* of clinical practice, boundary-spanning roles, culturally responsive collaboration, and models of partnership. Within the first theme, our readings focused on seminal publications such as the Blue Ribbon Panel Report (NCATE, 2010), various standards guiding clinical practice from leading teacher education organizations, including the Association for Teacher Educators (ATE) Field Standards, the National Association for Professional Development Schools (NAPDS) 9 Essentials, the Council for Accreditation in Educator Preparation (CAEP) Standard 2, and seminal pieces on field experiences and pedagogies of teacher preparation (Clift & Brady, 2005; Yendol-Hoppey & Franco, 2014; Zeichner, 2010). Within the second theme, we took a deeper dive into an exploration of the various stakeholders associated with clinical teacher preparation and professional development, including school- and UBTE and coaching roles (Burns & Badiali, 2016; Cuenca, 2010; Valencia, Martin, Place, & Grossman, 2009). In the third theme, we focused our efforts on examinations of culturally responsive collaborations, which included readings related to learning to teach in diverse contexts (Matsko & Hammerness, 2014; Ronfeldt, 2012). And, finally, with the fourth theme, we turned our efforts to models of partnerships, informed by readings related to professional development schools, teacher residencies, site-based course instruction, and the emerging clinical continuum—all in an effort to better define the contexts within which boundary spanners might expect to work (Dennis et al., 2017; Holmes, 1986; 1990; Zwart, Wubbels, Bergen, & Bolhuis, 2007).

Through the course assignments, we attempted to connect the theoretical readings with practical applications and experiences. For example, students constructed a *caselet* in which they described a problem, experience, or question they wanted our class to consider as it related to boundary-spanning roles. These often turned into therapy-like retellings of their own negative clinical experiences in learning to teach in their own teacher preparation programs or confessionals about their previous approaches to mentoring preservice, induction year, and even more veteran colleagues. These stories were shared early in the semester, and each week we considered how the readings might reshape or inform these doctoral students' reflections on these experiences. A summative writing at the end of the course explicitly required students to connect their practical, real world experiences with their theoretical readings so that they might see these "challenges" in a new, more informed light.

We also used "field trips" as unique assignments to connect theory to practice in this course. These "excursions" took on two different forms: face-to-face and virtual. For face-to-face field trips, students elected to shadow UBTEs in our elementary and secondary licensure programs as they engaged in their daily boundary-spanning work in school partnerships. The most recent iteration of these trips included an opportunity to observe any number of class sessions being held in collaboration with an elementary professional development school site.

This example of site-based course instruction provided students with a real world example of the power of PDS partnerships to create an opportunity to move a traditional university course into a clinical context. Students taking these field trip options also had a chance to observe faculty co-teaching at one of their elementary partnership sites, deep and rich collaborations with various stakeholders (including the principal, site facilitator, kindergarten teachers, and reading specialist), and students moving in and out of coursework/field activities fluidly. In another instance, students took field trips to observe a secondary faculty member engaged with partnership sites in critical, project-based clinical work. In this iteration, preservice teachers were leading a short-term photovoice writing intervention with high school students—with the young people, the adolescents' science teacher, and the university faculty member serving as co-researchers as they examined the question: "What makes an exceptional teacher?"

For students who were unable to attend face-to-face field trips, virtual options were provided. These required students to identify individuals, schools, partnership programs, PDS sites, or university programs that engaged in rich and interesting "work in schools." Their trip included an exploration of a relevant website and an attempt to connect and interview a key individual from the school or program they discovered on that website. Regardless of format, students summarized each field trip by making explicit connections between what they saw and their course readings and by suggesting implications for their current work and future teacher education or professional development roles.

Overall, this course served multiple purposes in our doctoral program. First, it addressed a glaring gap in our teaching and teacher education curriculum in terms of the clinical and teacher preparation aspects of teacher education. Furthermore, it exposed future teacher educators to the latest notions of clinically intensive teacher preparation and to the ways in which traditional teacher educator roles are rapidly and necessarily changing. Last but not least, the course connected the theoretical readings about clinical teacher preparation that we were encountering in our class session with practical experiences where these theories were being enacted. This included both a look at their own teacher preparation experiences and connections to traditional roles in teacher preparation and possibility seeing with field trips. Because the students were viewing teacher preparation and boundary-spanning roles from a multitude of perspectives, the theory to practice connections were of the utmost importance as we conceptualized what it meant to work in schools.

Internship Overview: A Scaffold Into Boundary-Spanning

In an effort to further scaffold future teacher educators into the profession, we designed an internship experience in boundary-spanning as a follow-up for the previously described course. Created in collaboration with two doctoral students, the experience was designed to purposefully connect theory and practice and gradually scaffold students into boundary-spanning roles. To study our collaborative efforts, we used an inquiry approach (Daoud, Parker, & Bruyning, 2019). The following assertion guided our approach to the internship: Without proper preparation or sufficient time to practice, novice university supervisors will struggle (Cuenca, 2010). The internship was structured around the doctoral students working weekly with a boundary-spanning UBTE who was immersed in a PDS.

A "gradual release of responsibility" philosophy framed the organization of the internship for the five elementary education preservice teachers who each completed a year-long internship in this PDS site. This approach mirrored doctoral students moving from theoretical understandings in the Working in Schools course, to engaging in an observer role with a boundary-spanning teacher educator—in this case a UBTE engaged in supervision at a PDS site—and culminating in practicing and leading some of the associated tasks that the UBTE completed weekly. Prior to the beginning of the experience, doctoral students and the UBTE read and discussed readings related to the role of a UBTE. During these discussions, the students and the UBTE set goals and expectations for the internship and developed a plan to ensure these were accomplished.

Because the UBTE was a facilitator at a PDS site, the students began the internship by immersing themselves in the school context, meeting stakeholders, and shadowing the UBTE. This shadowing created informal opportunities for the doctoral students to debrief and reflect throughout the experience with the UBTE. In these initial visits to the PDS site, the doctoral students had an opportunity to both observe the established relationship between the UBTE and the school site and work in building their own relationships within the partnership under the guidance of the UBTE. During this time students also shadowed the UBTE in observing and interacting with the each of the five PDS triads (UBTE, mentor teacher, and teacher candidate)—again, with the support of the UBTE. In the last phase of their mentored experiences, the doctoral students took on more responsibilities in this PDS context, including independently conducting observations. We hypothesize that the strategic use and progression of these activities allowed for optimal learning for these two doctoral students.

It is important to reiterate that as a result of the doctoral students and UBTE engaging at the PDS site together, there were multiple opportunities for shared reflection on the events of any given day. Furthermore, the activities that occurred during site visits expanded far beyond traditional observations. Rather, students in the internship with a UBTE participated in meetings with administrators, the site facilitator (a veteran teacher), groups of mentor teachers, groups of interns, etc. Each experience provided an opportunity for the doctoral students to learn, observe, participate, and reflect—all in a scaffolded manner. In addition, UBTE and doctoral students debriefed and reconsidered the experiences at regular monthly meetings and through written reflections at the end of the experience.

Perhaps most importantly, the internship projected the theoretical readings we encountered in our class meetings into practical applications. These applications were particularly important when we considered the work of UBTEs operating with a commitment to a clinical orientation as at the heart of the work of any boundary spanner is relationships. The authenticity of these relationships—whether new, developing, or established—in action was powerful, displaying the complexity of this boundary-spanning work, which is difficult to depict adequately in professional readings.

Our preliminary research findings (Daoud, Parker, & Brunying, 2019) indicate that internships in boundary-spanning roles support the acquisition of the unique technical and practical skills necessary for serving in these roles (Burns & Badiali, 2016). This further supports our choice to share this work as a description of a specific experience supporting doctoral students' professional development in the clinical practice realm. The technical skills addressed and practiced in the internship may include managing time and schedules, creating learning opportunities based on teacher candidates' needs, observing and conferring with teacher candidates and navigating interactions with partnership stakeholders. Similarly, practical skills that may be acquired during the internship included strategies for building and maintaining partnership relationships. In addition, the art and science of providing feedback to teacher candidates emerged as a practical skill learned in the internship. Learning this skill was particularly relevant as the doctoral students came to understand that such feedback exchanges included offering teacher candidates pedagogical advice during informal conversations and often spanned into topics such as confidence building, job counseling, and work–life balance. Ultimately, our initial findings indicate that internships in clinical contexts revealed the complexity of the role of boundary spanners that could not otherwise be conveyed and practiced in a traditional doctoral course experience.

DISCUSSION

It seems to us that teacher education is entering *new times*—times that bring an increased focus on clinically intensive educator preparation. Teacher educators have a unique history for many reasons. First, there are many types of teacher educators: school-based teacher educators like mentor teachers working with student teaching interns, UBTEs who are retired teachers or administrators, UBTEs who are academics trained through doctoral program, and others. Second, due to this variety and other factors, teacher educators are often marginalized at the university and often not seen as *real* scholars. Third, UBTEs are not always fully embraced by schools and teachers because of their affiliations with the university and their very part-time roles in the schools. Finally, unlike the training of future teachers, there exists no consistent preparation to become a teacher educator—a trainer of the trainers. The assumption in the field of teacher education seems to be that if you were a successful classroom teacher yourself or you completed a doctoral program in education, then you should be qualified to and knowledgeable about how to prepare future teachers. In this chapter, we have argued that the field of teacher education needs to move toward a more robust, rigorous, and perhaps even regulated preparation for teacher educators, especially in these new times. We have described two experiences that we designed in an attempt to achieve these ends.

Through the Working in Schools course we have been able to focus future teacher educators' gaze on the importance of and theory and scholarship surrounding clinically intensive teacher education. As a result of completing such a course, future teacher educators might enter the profession with a more nuanced understanding of why the field is moving the direction it is, and, more importantly, they might be better prepared to operate within these evolving contexts because they will be much better informed by current ideas and examples of effective practice in clinically based teacher education. Moreover, this course highlighted some key gaps in the teacher education literature—gaps that they as future scholars might address through rigorous research, and, thus, do the work to which all scholars aspire: to move the field forward.

Hosting doctoral students in internships in school–university partnerships is another way to intentionally introduce future teacher educators to the complex and difficult work of clinically intensive teacher education. In such an internship, doctoral students get to see how teacher educators build relationships with teachers, provide feedback to teacher candidates, negotiate university requirements with school pragmatics, initiate inquiries into researchable challenges, address poor teacher candidate performance, and more. This complex, multilayered and multifaceted experience cannot be adequately taught in a decontextualized setting like a university classroom. In addition, intentional and sustained school–university partnerships help to address some of the barriers to teacher educators' work described above. For example, working closely with a particular school over many years builds trust between teachers and teacher educators and helps to assuage educators' trepidation about collaborating with university faculty.

CONCLUSION

The two experiences we designed and on which we report in this chapter—the Working in Schools doctoral course and the school–university partnerships internship—are two structures the teacher education field might consider to better prepare future teacher educators for the work they one day hope to do. Together, the course and field experience created an opportunity for doctoral students in teacher education to make theory to practice connections, much like those we know and use in teacher preparation programs. This purposeful preparation assumes that those learning to teach teachers need intentional modeling and scaffolding into the work of teacher education.

However, we know that a more comprehensive approach to preparing UBTEs—and all teacher educators, not just those who enter through the academy—is needed to help combat the challenges described in the first part of this chapter. While our course and field structure is a start, comprehensive preparation of teacher educators necessitates a well-designed curriculum that addresses the many facets of working in clinical teacher preparation. This includes an examination of the seminal and current literature of the teacher education in terms of practice and policy, coursework related to supervision and teaching adult learners, and intentionally paired field work to scaffold new teacher educators into the role. Additionally comprehensive preparation should include a scholarly aspect to the work—one that prepares teacher educators to study their practice—so that they are prepared to work efficiently as scholars in boundary spanning roles.

We encourage all types of teacher educators and teacher education organizations to work together to continue to conceptualize empirically and theoretically informed guidance for a more intentional preparation of future teacher educators. If we count teaching as perhaps the most important of all professions in our society, then it follows that the teaching of teachers is not far behind.

Discussion Questions

1. Consider the various practical and pedagogical skills required of boundary-spanning teacher educators. In what ways were these skills scaffolded (or not) in your own preparation for work in clinical teacher education?
2. What opportunities and challenges exist in your current context with regards to purposefully preparing doctoral students for their future roles in clinical teacher education?
3. In what ways could school-based teacher educators play a role in preparing teacher education doctoral candidates for their future roles in clinical teacher preparation?
4. What are the pressures and traditions that are moving our field toward or away from boundary-spanning roles—in your institution, in the broader contexts of this work. What are these pressures and traditions and how would you respond to them?
5. What impact does the fact that teacher education is most often housed within a traditional university structure have on the movement of our field toward boundary-spanning roles?
6. If you had a chance to design the ideal program for preparing boundary-spanning teacher educators to do their important work, what program elements would you include?

NOTE

1. The design of Working in Schools: Spanning Boundaries and Expanding Roles was based on a course previously taught by the first author at the University of South Florida entitled Working in Schools.

REFERENCES

American Association of Colleges for Teacher Education. (2018). *Report from the Clinical Practice Commission: A pivot towards clinical practice, its lexicon and the renewal of educator preparation*. Washington, DC: Author.

Burns, R. W., & Badiali, B. (2016). Unearthing the complexities of clinical pedagogy in supervision: Identifying the pedagogical skills of supervisors. *Action in Teacher Education, 38*(2), 156–174. https://doi.org/10.1080/01626620.2016.1155097

Clift, R., & Brady, P. (2005). Research on methods courses and field experiences. In M. Cochran-Smith, & K. Zeichner (Eds.), *Studying teacher education: The Report of the American Educational Research Association panel on research and teacher education* (pp. 309–424). New York, NY: Routledge.

Council for Accreditation of Educator Preparation. (2014). *CAEP accreditation standards*. Washington, DC: Author.

Cuenca, A. (2010). In loco paedagogus: The pedagogy of a novice university supervisor. *Studying Teacher Education, 6*(1), 29–43.

Daoud, N., Parker, A. K., & Bruyning-Legget, A. (2019). *Extending clinical experiences: Supporting doctoral students' development as university supervisors*. Manuscript in preparation.

Dennis, D. V., Burns, R. W., Tricarico, K., vanIngen, S., Jacobs, J., & Davis, J. (2017). Problematizing clinical education: What is our future? In R. Flessner & D. R. Lecklider (Eds.), *The power of clinical preparation in teacher education* (pp. 1–20). Lanham, MD: Rowman & Littlefield.

Furlong, A. (2013). *Youth studies: An introduction*. New York, NY: Routledge.

Gallagher, M., Parsons, S. A., Parker, A. K., Groth, L., Brown. B. L., Baker, C., & Suh, J. (2019). Building critical, project-based clinical experiences across an elementary PDS program. In K. Zenkov & K. Pytash (Eds.), *Clinical experiences in teacher education: Critical, project-based interventions in diverse classrooms* (pp. 49–70). New York, NY: Routledge.

Goodwin, A. L., & Kosnik, C. (2013). Quality teacher educators = quality teachers? Conceptualizing essential domains of knowledge for those who teach teachers. *Teacher Development, 17*(3), 334–346.

Goodwin, A. L., Smith, L., Souto-Manning, M., Cheruvu, R., Tan, M. Y., Reed, R., & Taveras, L. (2014). What should teacher educators knows and be able to do? Perspectives from practicing teacher educators. *Journal of Teacher Education, 65*(4). 284–302. https://doi.org/10.1177/0022487114535266

Hadar, L. L., & Brody, D. L. (2017). Professional learning and development of teacher educators. In D. J. Clandinin & J. Husu (Eds.), *The SAGE handbook of research on teaching*. Thousand Oaks, CA: SAGE.

Holmes Group. (1986). *Tomorrow's teachers: A report of the Holmes group*. East Lansing, MI: Author.

Holmes Group. (1990). *Tomorrow's schools: Principles for the design of Professional Development Schools*. East Lansing, MI: Author.

Klein, E., Taylor, M., & Onore, C. (2012). Finding a third space in teacher education: Creating an urban residency. *Teacher Education, 24*(1), 27–57.

Levine, A. (2006). Educating school teachers. Washington, DC: The Education Schools Project.

Loughran, J. J. (2006). *Developing a pedagogy of teacher education: Understanding teaching and learning about teaching.* London, England: Routledge.

Maguire, M. (1994). *The job educating teachers.* (Unpublished doctoral dissertation). Kings College, University of London, England.

Matsko, K., & Hammerness, K. (2014). Unpacking the "urban" in urban teacher education: Making a case for context-specific preparation. *Journal of Teacher Education, 65*, 128–144. https://doi.org/10.1177/0022487113511645

Mayer, D., Mitchell, J., Santoro, N., & White, S. (2011). Teacher educators and 'accidental' careers in academe: An Australian perspective. *Journal of Education for Teaching, 37*(3), 247–260.

McNamara, O., & Murray, J. (2013). The school district direct programme and its implications for research-informed teacher education and teacher educators. In L. Florian & N. Pantic (Eds.), *Learning to teach: Part 1: Exploring the history and role of higher education in teacher education* (pp. 14–19). York, England: The Higher Education Academy.

Murray, J. (2002). Between the chalkface and the ivory towers? A study of the professionalism of teacher educators working on primary initial teacher education courses in the English education system. *Collected Original Resources in Education, 26*(3), 1–530.

Murray, J. (2014). Teacher educators' constructions of professionalism: Change and diversity in teacher education. *Asia-Pacific Journal of Teacher Education, 42*(1), 7–21.

Murray, J., & Maguire, M. (2007). Changes and continuities in teacher education: International perspective on a gendered field. *Gender and Education,* Special Edition, *19*(3), 283–296.

National Council for Accreditation of Teacher Education. (2010). *Report of the Blue Ribbon Panel on clinical preparation and partnerships for improved learning.* Washington, DC: Author. Retrieved from caepnet.org/~/media/Files/caep/accreditation-resources/blue-ribbon-panel.pdf

Norton-Meier, L., & Drake, C. (2010). When third space is more than the library: The complexities of theorizing and learning to use family and community resources to teach elementary literacy and mathematics. In V. Ellis, A. Edwards, & P. Smagorinsky (Eds.), *Cultural-historical perspectives on teacher education and development* (pp. 196–211). London, England: Routledge.

Parker, A. K., Zenkov, K., & Dennis, D.V. (in press). Exploring the lexicon or lack thereof in clinical teacher preparation. *Action in Teacher Education.*

Ronfeldt, M. (2012). Where should student teachers learn to teach? Effects of field placement school characteristics on teacher retention and effectiveness. *Educational Evaluation and Policy Analysis, 34*(1), 3–26. https://doi.org/10.3102/0162373711420865

Shulman, L. S. (2005). Signature pedagogies in the professions. *Deadalus, 134*(3), 52–59.

Slick, S. K. (1998). The university supervisor: A disenfranchised outsider. *Teaching and Teacher Education, 14*(8), 821–834.

Valencia, S. W., Martin, S. D., Place, N. A., & Grossman, P. (2009). Complex interactions in student teaching: Lost opportunities for learning. *Journal of Teacher Education, 60*, 304–322. https://doi.org/10.1177/0022487109336543

Van Velzen, C., & Volman, M. (2009). The activities of a school-based teacher educator: A theoretical and empirical exploration. *European Journal of Teacher Education, 32*(2), 345–367. https://doi.org/10.1080/02619760903005831

Yendol-Hoppey, D., & Franco, Y. (2014). In search of signature pedagogy for PDS teacher education: A review of articles published in School–University Partnerships. *School–University Partnerships, 7*(1), 17–34.

Zeichner, K. (2010). Rethinking the connections between campus courses and field experiences in college-and university-based teacher education. *Journal of teacher education, 61*(1–2), 89–99.

Zenkov, K., Parker, A. K., Parsons, S., Pellegrino, A., & Pytash, K. (2017). From project based clinical experiences to collaborative inquiries: Pathways to Professional Development Schools. In J. Ferrara, J. Nath, I. Guadarrama, & R. Beebe (Eds.), *Expanding opportunities to link research and clinical practice: A volume in research in professional development schools* (pp. 9–33). Charlotte, NC: Information Age.

Zwart, R. C., Wubbels, T., Bergen, T. C. M., & Bolhuis, S. (2007). Experienced teacher learning within the context of reciprocal peer coaching. *Teachers and Teaching. 13*(2), 165–187. https://doi.org/10.1080/13540600601152520

CHAPTER 2

TAKING THE MENTORING OF NEW TEACHER EDUCATORS SERIOUSLY

Lessons From a Clinically-Intensive Teacher Preparation Program

Patricia Norman
Trinity University

with
Sara A. S. Sherwood
Trinity University

Rocio Delgado
Trinity University

Melissa Siller
Trinity University

The challenges facing teacher educators entering their first faculty position in a clinically intensive teacher preparation program reflect similar difficulties that novice teachers encounter upon entry to their own classroom.

Preparing the Next Generation of Teacher Educators for Clinical Practice, pages 25–48

Just as new teachers must learn the ropes while performing the work of teaching (Feiman-Nemser, 2001; Wildman, Niles, Magliaro, & McLaughlin, 1989), so, too, must novice teacher educators learn to create clinically based learning opportunities for teacher candidates (American Association of Colleges for Teacher Education, 2018; Grossman, Hammerness, & McDonald, 2009) while learning to navigate the university system, establish their practice as field-based practitioners, earn strong student/course evaluations (Ramsden, 2003) and address the realities of "publish or perish" (Russell & Korthagen, 1995).

Numerous research studies indicate that novice classroom teachers benefit from being paired with a carefully selected and trained mentor who can help them make the transition to independent teaching (Hobson, Ashby, Malderez, & Tomlinson, 2009; Ingersoll & Strong, 2011; Stanulis, Brondyk, Little, & Wibbens, 2014). Although some within university settings have argued that university teacher educators must create structures and professional cultures that support new faculty's learning (Carroll, Featherstone, Featherstone, Feiman-Nemser, & Roosevelt, 2007), mentorship of faculty in higher education traditionally focuses on socialization, including learning the ins and outs of the institution (Cawyer, Simonds, & Davis, 2002) and integration into the campus community (Savage, Karp, & Logue, 2004). Missing from the literature are fine-grained descriptions and analyses of what serious mentoring efforts of new teacher educators look and sound like as well as their impact in helping field-based practitioners to develop critical aspects of their craft.

In this chapter, I first conceptualize educative mentoring. I then describe Trinity University's clinically intensive teacher preparation program that serves as the context for the mentoring vignettes that follow. The vignettes highlight core aspects of a field-based teacher educator's practice, including: designing clinically based courses; establishing relationships in clinical settings; giving candidates feedback on their planning, teaching, and progress; addressing significant concerns in candidates' practice and/or clinical placement; and supporting mentor development.

CONCEPTION OF EDUCATIVE MENTORING

A narrow view of mentoring focuses on assisting a novice's entry into teaching by answering immediate questions and offering psychological support. In contrast to a conception of mentoring as short-term socialization and technical assistance (Wang & Odell, 2002) lies the construct of "educative mentoring" (Feiman-Nemser, 1998). For an experience to be educative, it must result in growth (Dewey, 1938/1963). Educative mentoring is a form of individualized professional development designed to improve both the novice's performance as well as her students' learning. An "educative mentor" is a co-learner who also generates growth-producing experiences for the novice (Feiman-Nemser, 1998).

The concept of educative mentoring rests upon "social learning theories postulating that learning is situated, collaborative, and scaffolded" (Gardiner, 2017, p. 54). Vygotsky's notion of "assisted performance" is critical in clarifying the theoretical underpinnings of mentoring. Vygotsky (1978) first wrote about assisted performance in relation to working in a child's zone of proximal development where a learner is able to accomplish with a more knowledgeable help from others what she cannot accomplish alone. In other words, a learner engages in an activity to which she is committed. The teacher observes what the novice can do on her own then provides appropriate scaffolding so that the novice achieves the task. In the context of mentoring, the mentor must structure opportunities for the novice to take on the intellectual work of teaching under the mentor's support.

The scaffolding that a mentor provides the novice can occur both inside and outside of the novice's teaching (Schwille, 2008). Mentoring "inside the action" involves a mentor offering real-time coaching, co-teaching, or intervention *as* the novice engages in the work of teaching. Of course, other central tasks of teaching occur before or after instruction. "Outside the action" mentoring refers to support provided to a novice in preparation for or reflection on teaching.

CONTEXT

Educative mentoring and assisted performance play central roles in Trinity University's clinically intensive teacher preparation program. Trinity's Department of Education transitioned from a traditional 4-year education major to an intensive, 5-year, field-based model of teacher preparation, leading to a Master of Arts in Teaching (MAT) degree in 1990. Elementary teacher candidates complete any major offered at Trinity while taking 20 hours of undergraduate education courses that combine theoretical learning with clinically based experiences in our public partner schools. Table 2.1 provides the titles and brief descriptions of this coursework. Their undergraduate coursework equips candidates with foundational knowledge and skills to build on during their graduate program.

Upon entry to the MAT program, candidates complete a 5-week intensive summer program within an elementary or secondary cohort before beginning an 8-month, unpaid internship with a mentor teacher at one of our Professional Development Schools. We have sustained this MAT model for more than 25 years, creating long-term partnerships with a small number of urban schools that serve as the primary sites for teacher candidates' clinical

Course Number	Course Title	Description
TABLE 2.1 Trinity University Elementary Undergraduate Course Sequence		
EDUC 1331	Learners With Exceptionalities in School and Society	An introduction to the causes, characteristics, strategies, trends, and issues in teaching students with exceptionalities. Includes a field placement working with students with exceptionalities in a range of educational and community settings.
EDUC 3320	Child & Adolescent Development	The cognitive, emotional, and social factors influencing children and adolescents in contemporary society are explored. Emphases placed on practical application of current human development and learning theories related to the family, school, and peer groups.
EDUC 2201	Practicum: Early Childhood Teaching Exploration	An introduction to the developmental needs of young children in conjunction with a field placement in an early childhood classroom.
EDUC 3301	Field Seminar in Elementary Literacy	A study of literacy learning and instruction in the elementary school that integrates theory (seminars) and practice (field experiences).
EDUC 3341	Teaching Science in Elementary School	An introduction to principles of curriculum design and instruction for teaching science. Includes a field placement.
EDUC 3351	Mathematics in Elementary School	An examination of key content, strategies, and skills as well as methods of teaching and learning mathematics at the elementary level. Includes field placement.

experiences. Interns follow the public school calendar, completing all campus and district-level professional development alongside their mentor teacher and assist their mentor in setting up the classroom before students arrive. In the fall semester, elementary candidates are in their mentor's classroom 4 days a week, focusing on the planning, teaching, and assessment of reading and mathematics. They observe their mentors teach, co-plan and co-teach alongside their mentor, then complete 2 weeks of guided lead teaching where they plan, teach, and assess students' learning in math and reading with their mentor's support. In the spring semester, interns are in their clinical placement 5 days a week, entering into a period of "lead teaching" where they take primary responsibility for children's learning in all content areas for 5 consecutive weeks. In addition to their internship experience, candidates take graduate courses designed to help them prepare for and make sense of their clinical experiences. In addition, they complete key assessments such as the Praxis Performance Assessment for Teachers and projects including an action research investigation.

MENTORING VIGNETTES

I have assisted with the performance of my colleagues who, like me, are responsible for creating clinically intensive, learning-rich experiences for teacher candidates at the undergraduate and graduate levels. The following teacher education mentoring vignettes focus on core aspects of a field-based teacher educator's practice, including: (a) designing clinically based courses, (b) establishing relationships with key players in clinical settings, (c) providing feedback to candidates on their teaching, (d) addressing significant concerns in candidates' practice and/or clinical placement, and (e) supporting mentor development. Each is discussed in turn.

Designing Clinically Based Courses

New faculty members must learn how to design clinically based learning opportunities for their students. My colleague, Melissa, teaches an undergraduate clinically intensive course called Math in Elementary School. Melissa initially designed the field component of the course—an after-school math tutoring program—to reflect a structure I had created for candidates in a field-based literacy seminar in which they facilitate an after-school poetry club for elementary students. After using this structure for a semester, however, Melissa did not feel that the experience was as educative for the teacher candidates as she had hoped.

As we continued to discuss her reflections on the experience, I realized a key difference in the way we structured teacher candidates' clinical experiences. Melissa had asked each teacher candidate to tutor 1–3 students every week. Doing so left her feeling stretched thin in terms of giving timely feedback on their individual lesson plans and being available to observe and assist during the hour-long tutoring sessions. In contrast, I paired literacy field-seminar students up to co-teach a mini-lesson to all of the poetry club students while the rest of the candidates observed, then all Trinity candidates provided one-on-one support to students through writing conferences held during independent writing time. I encouraged Melissa to consider adopting this model. It would enable her to facilitate the first tutoring session herself, something that I do in the poetry club. Doing so allows the teacher educator to make the intellectual work of teaching visible to pre-service teachers by talking aloud about initial planning decisions, directing teacher candidates' observation of her teaching, then reflecting with the teacher candidates afterwards about challenges, surprises, and an assessment of whether learning goals were met.

Melissa followed suit when teaching the math methods course again. She structured the tutoring sessions to begin with a whole group mini-lesson—initially taught by her then later co-facilitated by pairs of teacher candidates—before then breaking up into smaller groups co-facilitated by all of her students. This structure enabled Melissa to give extensive feedback to each student pair *before* teaching the whole group mini-lesson. Moreover, she was available to "step in and out" of the mini-lesson to provide real-time support (Fieman-Nemser, 2012) *as* they taught. At semester's end, Melissa noted that scaffolding candidates' learning to teach in these ways significantly strengthened their ability to support elementary students' learning.

In a further example of mentoring, I supported Melissa in teaching a course I normally offer. While I was on leave last fall, Melissa stepped in to teach the literacy field-based seminar. I first offered her my syllabus and detailed teaching notes. After reading through them, we met so that Melissa could ask questions. I offered to serve as a guest teacher later in the course when teacher candidates use a protocol to analyze children's poems since Melissa was not familiar with this protocol. I then connected her to the after-school coordinator at our partner campus and explained some logistics of launching a poetry club—the clinical setting for teacher candidates.

Melissa and I checked in with each other periodically throughout the semester. Each time we spoke, Melissa shared how much she was enjoying the course. When I asked why, she said that she had gained a major insight. In the early days of the course, students first interviewed each other about their writing experiences and attitudes. They then wrote their writing autobiography and shared excerpts in class. They further got to know about each other by sharing poems they wrote about the meaning and impact of their own names. Rituals were established early on, including reviewing the agenda at the beginning of class, reading excerpts from their written reflections on the previous class, and sharing their writing in "compliment read arounds," all of which created a sense of predictability and community. On the fifth class, Melissa read in my teaching notes to invite her students to switch hats for a minute from writers to future teachers. She posed the question, "What have I done as the teacher so far to help us launch our classroom community and investigation of writing?" Doing so encourages the teacher candidates to unpack the deliberate choices that Melissa made in the early sessions to help them feel safe and begin taking risks in their writing and sharing. She told her students that just as they have benefited from the teaching moves she made, they, too, must do the same for their own students in classrooms.

Melissa realized that as a teacher educator, she needs to make explicit all that is implicit in her own teaching so that novices can learn in and from her practice. She explained to me that she never thought about creating a classroom learning community in an undergraduate course first, then using that work as a way to think about learning community in schools and candidates' role in developing it. In that same vein, Melissa felt a bit embarrassed as she shared that the notion of setting up the course to allow candidates to immerse themselves in writing beforehand then becoming teachers of writing had never occurred to her. She saw firsthand the benefits of doing so by using my teaching notes to guide her instruction. In her end-of-course evaluations, students stated how much they appreciated writing together beforehand, then structuring that experience to students in a school setting. She had not received such feedback before in previous courses she had taught.

Melissa's reflection on the literacy field-based seminar created opportunities to rethink the Math for Elementary Teachers course she teaches. She now plans to explicitly name aspects of her practice in the university-based portion of the course both to make transparent the intellectual work of teaching and to encourage them to use these teaching moves when tutoring students in the field. Moreover, when comparing her clinical role in her math course with the role she had just played in the literacy field-based seminar, she noted that she created a lot of time for teacher candidates to reflect on their instruction as well as students' learning, then she scaffolded them to use that understanding to inform future poetry club sessions. In past field experiences she supervised, Melissa focused more exclusively on planning and teaching, missing opportunities to engage candidates in student assessment and the provision of feedback to children. She now sees how she can structure clinical experiences in what she describes as a more authentic, seamless way so that candidates better understand the planning/teaching/assessment cycle.

Melissa also gained an appreciation for the importance of maintaining her practice in school settings, not just university settings. As the literacy seminar is structured, the teacher educator facilitates the first poetry club session rather than teacher candidates. As mentioned above, doing so gives candidates a vision of the possible and a framework to structure future sessions they will co-facilitate. It also sets up the expectation that the candidates, like Melissa herself did, reflect on their practice in front of classmates. When Melissa first read in my teaching notes that she would have to model teach the first poetry club lesson, she felt panicked. What if she failed? She recounted that this moment served as a valuable lesson for her to make sure that she is willing to do what she asks her own candidates to do. Remaining connected to her own classroom practices will keep her knowledge and expertise relevant in her teacher education practice.

Establishing Relationships With Key Players in Clinical Settings

Gaining access to clinical sites can feel like a daunting task when initially designing field-based experiences for teacher candidates. Part of my mentoring lies in connecting new faculty to key players in our clinical settings, including administrators and teachers. For instance, when Sara first taught an undergraduate early childhood practicum that I had taught in years past, I scaffolded her entry into the school that served as the site for her students' clinical experience. After giving her a tour of the building, I formally introduced her to school administrators in a pre-arranged meeting. During that session, we shared with the principal a written description of the practicum and how many early childhood teachers we hoped would serve as mentors to Trinity students. Keeping campus administrators informed and maintaining open lines of communication is central to creating strong clinical settings for novices.

I then set up and facilitated a meeting with identified teachers in order to walk them through course logistics, explain their role as mentors, and describe the two major projects that teacher candidates completed at the time (e.g., a semester-long study of a single child and an oral dictation/dramatization project). Sara sat in on this meeting which gave me the opportunity to introduce her to the teachers, many of whom I had worked with for several years. Sara later explained that this modeling was quite helpful to her. Getting to see an experienced teacher educator negotiate these opening moves with mentors who serve as school-based teacher educators gave her structures and language to draw on when she taught the course the following year and needed to partner with a different school. She felt well-equipped to establish relationships with administrators and teachers at the early childhood center. While I visited the new school with her and met with the principal for the first time to offer continued support, Sara facilitated mentor meetings on her own.

When I initially designed the early childhood practicum, I requested that mentors create space for teacher candidates to conduct the oral dictation/dramatization project in their classrooms. As curricular standards became more rigorous, however, a number of mentors began to push back on the project, noting that they expect their students to be writing on their own in pre-K and kindergarten by the time teacher candidates work with them in the spring semester. As Sara began to teach the course on her own, she was much more responsive to mentors' concerns than I had been. She gave up that particular project in order to create a much more open-ended expectation that candidates teach at least one literacy-based lesson that (a) meets a learning objective selected by the mentor, and (b) the candidate has time to fully plan and receive feedback before teaching. In that way, Sara reinforced for me the importance of insuring that field-based expectations for candidates support rather than thwart the mentor's teaching and children's learning.

In addition to helping my university colleagues establish initial lines of communication with mentors and administrators, I supported them in sustaining those relationships. For example, I had met twice a month with the principal at one of our professional development schools in the first year of our partnership. I encouraged my colleagues, Rocio and Sara, to join these meetings in Year 2 as soon as they began supervising teacher candidates at the school. Meeting regularly with school administrators is vitally important to ensuring a healthy university–school relationship. When I left the school a year later in order to establish a new partnership with another school, my peers were well-positioned to remain, coordinating the internship program at the initial school without me. And 3 years later when Trinity created yet another school partnership, Sara stepped into that role with full confidence of her own. She noted that these mentored experiences helped her quickly gain an appreciation for the importance of building respectful relationships. In her words, as teacher educators, we really are guests in a school that has graciously opened its classrooms and practices to us and our students. We must ensure that we are respectful of teachers' and administrators' time and maintain gratitude that our school partners are assuming additional responsibilities in order to support our teacher candidates.

Providing Feedback to Teacher Candidates

Novice teachers need feedback in order to learn from their teaching and make improvements. This happens in a variety of contexts: providing feedback on candidates' written plans, including individual lessons and curricular units; observing and debriefing individual lessons; supporting candidates' action research projects; and providing summative feedback on candidates' progress over time.

Feedback on Written Plans

Teacher educators need to give constructive, actionable feedback on teacher candidates' written plans. At Trinity, novices learn an approach to curricular design called Understanding by Design or UbD (Wiggins & McTighe, 2005). Sometimes known as "backward design," this approach to planning curricular units reverses the order in which teachers typically plan. Educators first identify desired learning results then determine acceptable evidence of those learning results before then designing learning activities. We support interns in developing two UbD units during the MAT program, one in the summer session as an introduction to UbD principles and one in early January to implement during lead teaching.

I have taught UbD principles and given formative feedback to candidates as they plan units in small teams and formally after submitting completed units for more than a decade. Our candidates sometimes struggle to clarify clear learning targets and assessments before planning a sequence of daily lessons. When Sara and I began co-teaching graduate courses in which candidates are given time in class to plan their UbD units, she was relatively new to UbD design principles. Knowing how to make sense of novices' early planning efforts in real time, to think on one's feet and to celebrate strengths while constructively addressing concerns is complex intellectual work. I initially offered to model how I give feedback. Sara quickly began to contribute her own questions and suggestions after a brief period of observation. Once she felt comfortable facilitating feedback sessions on her own, we thought it made sense to "divide and conquer," so we split ourselves up to work separately with teams under the assumption that we could provide more feedback. After doing so, however, both Sara and I realized that we prefer to remain together in order to jointly offer insights and suggestions to planning teams. While both of us are now adept at providing feedback on our own, we routinely continue to visit planning teams together. Doing so allows us to build off of each other's thinking and pedagogical moves in the moment, to debrief later what we're learning about the candidates as planners and to determine how to use our insights to inform next instructional steps. Moreover, it provides continued opportunities for us to learn with and from each other.

Observing and Debriefing Individual Lessons

While mentor teachers may debrief candidates' lessons after teaching, unless they have a clear focus or structure for such conversations, mentors can give unfocused or unreliable feedback that does not lead to significant learning (Hudson, 2014; Valencia, Martin, Place, & Grossman, 2009). This reality makes university teacher educators' feedback on candidates' teaching even more essential.

Before Sara began to assume responsibility for supervising graduate interns, I first suggested that she read *The School Mentor Handbook* (Hagger, Burn, & McIntyre, 1995), particularly the chapters on observation and assessment/supervision. We then met to discuss the text. During that conversation, I shared my own approach to observing novices' teaching by attending to the commonplaces (Schwab, 1978) which include the teacher and her teaching, the students and their learning, the curriculum, and the context. I also explained different approaches to taking notes while observing, including scripting (my preferred method), and dividing one's paper into two columns, using one side for descriptions and the other for questions/interpretations.

After developing some background knowledge, I then invited Sara to join me as I observed and debriefed a graduate intern's lesson. Both Sara and I took notes as we observed her. Before meeting with the intern, Sara and I first shared the notes we had taken with one another and discussed the intern's lesson in terms of the commonplaces. When I then asked her what role that she would feel most comfortable playing, Sara stated that she preferred to listen during the debriefing conference. After I debriefed the intern's lesson while Sara observed, she later shared how surprised she felt by the tone and tenor of the debriefing. Sara had expected the conference to be "super formal" but was struck by how conversational and coaching-oriented it was. I had asked many questions, using the intern's responses to determine what to focus on and what to highlight from my own observations. Sara felt prepared to then observe and debrief interns' teaching on her own.

Supporting Candidates' Action Research Projects

Beyond offering feedback to interns on their planning and teaching of individual lessons, university field-based teacher educators also need to provide support and guidance as candidates conduct action research projects. As novices move through this inquiry project, they

- draw on their classroom-based experiences to identify a question, puzzle, concern, dilemma, or problem of practice that they want to focus on;
- consult a range of human and textual resources to help them think about and explore their question;
- design and carry out a plan-of-action to address their question, adapting, or adjusting their plan as they proceed;
- keep track of the process by collecting information, data reflections, and examples that serve as evidence for them to assess their progress and support their learning;
- make sense of the data they collect, looking for insights into their question, taking stock of their progress, and making revisions to their question or data collection plan as needed; and
- summarize and report their findings at their Professional Development School campus so that their school-based colleagues can also benefit from their inquiry.

Interns benefit from feedback at every stage of this research project. At the outset, I help them craft a researchable question and offer feedback on their initial plan-of-action. In addition to supporting data collection by observing and providing feedback, I also meet individually with candidates during hour-long data analysis sessions. During these meetings, candidates share raw data and/or their initial findings. I review data with them, ask questions, offer my own analysis, and provide suggested next steps. Once interns draft their presentations, their peers and I use the Tuning Protocol (schoolreforminitiative.org) to identify strengths, ask probing questions, and offer suggestions for improvement. Finally, I formally assess their action research presentations when they give them at their school campus.

Although I take primary responsibility for offering these forms of feedback, I have mentored Sara around this action research project in several ways. First, Sara has observed me provide feedback during the half-day session when candidates explore initial ideas for their project and eventually narrow their focus to a researchable question. In addition, she recently began to observe me conduct individual data analysis sessions. Doing so allows her to see how I guide candidates through the process. Additionally, because Sara is strong at data analysis herself, she is able to make contributions during these conversations. Finally, both Sara and I now individually assess each intern's final presentation then jointly discuss our independent evaluations before determining final ratings and crafting narrative feedback.

Providing Summative Feedback

Beyond offering feedback on interns' action research projects, planning and instruction, university field-based teacher educators also need to provide summative feedback on candidates' progress over time. Trinity creates three occasions for interns to receive formal summative feedback from university teacher educators and their mentor teachers through 3-way assessment conferences held mid-semester in the fall, the end of the fall semester and the end of the spring semester. The conferences bring together university teacher educator, candidate, and mentor teacher in order for each to share his/her assessment of the candidate's progress toward meeting Trinity's Standards for Professional Practice.

Before Sara assumed responsibility for facilitating conferences on her own, she first sat in on nine end-of-fall semester conferences that I conducted. Beforehand, I showed her the detailed general written guidelines I use to structure the conference. I also shared with her the specific notes that I had created in preparation for each intern's conference. I explained that I constructed these notes by first reviewing the intern's written midpoint portfolio entries which each intern constructs to demonstrate progress toward the program's standards then reviewing my own observational/debriefing notes. I also explained the purposes of the fall end-of-semester conference: to celebrate progress/strengths in the novice's practice; to identify areas for continued growth and strategies to do so; and to look ahead to the upcoming semester when interns will assume increased responsibility for planning, teaching, and assessing students' learning. Observing the way that I structure the conference—including clarifying roles and expectations—then facilitate the conversation—including how to negotiate differences in ratings—gave Sara insights into this complex territory and left her feeling confident to facilitate spring conferences on her own.

Addressing Significant Concerns in Teacher Candidates' Practice

Although Trinity's Department of Education uses a rigorous admissions process, nearly every year at least one intern encounters significant difficulty during the year-long internship. Sometimes the causes of those concerns are internal, including significant mental health issues. Sometimes the causes are contextual, including a poor fit between the intern and clinical placement for any number of reasons. Sometimes the causes are pedagogical, including significant difficulty in developing specific core skills in assessment, instruction, and/or management.

The syllabi for Clinical Practice (Fall) and Advanced Clinical Practice (Spring) state that if at any point the university teacher educator, mentor teacher, or school administrator determines there is a significant problem with the intern's performance based on the professional teaching standards or any university or school-based guidelines, the intern will be placed on a professional growth plan that includes specific actions and/or behaviors as well as a reasonable timeframe for demonstrating adequate growth on the plan. If the Trinity faculty, mentor teacher, and administrator determine that the intern has failed to meet the terms of the growth plan within the predetermined time frame, the internship will be terminated and the intern will receive a failing grade for Clinical Practice or Advanced Clinical Practice.

Knowing how to identify interns' consistent versus short-term difficulties, to consider possible underlying causes, and to address the concerns constructively—including crafting professional growth plans that clearly state area(s) of concern and identify an actionable plan for addressing those concerns within a specified time period—are all skills that teacher educators must develop. Making informed decisions about whether, how, and when to address those concerns are rarely straightforward.

As a case in point, my colleague, Rocio, supervised an intern who showed signs of struggle early on in her year-long internship. The intern, Beth, was placed in a first grade Spanish immersion classroom with a mentor who was new to Trinity's MAT program. The Spanish immersion program at this school begins in first grade. English-dominant students are taught in Spanish the entire school day. Rocio felt confident that as a Spanish major, Beth possessed the Spanish language skills needed to teach in this context. Deeply committed to becoming a bilingual educator, Beth was really happy with her placement.

Beth thoroughly enjoyed her placement but experienced significant and consistent difficulty engaging children in learning and managing their behavior. Rocio and Beth's mentor offered numerous strategies to Beth for gaining students' attention. They encouraged Beth to use more nonverbal cues and to incorporate more songs with movement opportunities. The more Beth taught, however, the worse her students' behavior seemed to become. The mentor grew increasingly concerned that students were not learning.

Early in the spring semester, Rocio asked me to observe Beth teach in hopes that I might be able to offer additional suggestions to Beth, Rocio, and/or her mentor in how to strengthen Beth's instruction. What struck me most from that observation was how emboldened the students had become in ignoring Beth's directions and instruction. Beth seemed to struggle to find the language to communicate effectively. I strongly encouraged Rocio to place Beth on a professional growth plan and change Beth's placement to a general education classroom, arguing that learning to teach is difficult under the best of circumstances. Doing so in a second language seemed to have created insurmountable challenges for Beth.

To support Rocio in drafting the growth plan, I first walked her through several examples I'd previously written. I explained the importance of referencing the language from the syllabus about the growth plan process. I encouraged Rocio to organize the concerns she had about Beth's performance around Trinity's Standards for Professional Practice. I expressed the importance of providing 1–2 very clear examples for each concern using descriptive language. Rocio drafted a plan laying out the concerns then I provided extensive written feedback to her. Once we had clarified what Beth needed to improve in her practice, I thought aloud about how Rocio and I might structure a new placement in a different school so that Beth would have opportunities to develop key aspects of her teaching. For example, because Beth had struggled to establish her authority and manage students' behavior, I listed the following tasks for Beth to accomplish in the first week of her new placement:

- Describe currently established classroom procedures.
- Describe in detail the established behavior management system, including consequences for children's misbehavior.
- Describe several strategies your mentor uses to gain students' attention.
- Begin to establish yourself as an authority figure in the classroom, someone who is friendly but firm with students.

I explained to Rocio that if Beth could name these aspects of her new mentor's practice, she could then begin to use some of those strategies that she had observed when beginning to plan and teach her own lessons in subsequent weeks. I identified a new placement with a new mentor who was an alum of Trinity's MAT program, met with the mentor, then drafted a week-by-week structure for Beth's new placement.

Because Rocio had not yet conducted a professional growth conference, I offered to take the lead in facilitating Beth's conference with Rocio. My intent was to provide some modeling, but I privately worried that Rocio might feel that I was asserting myself too much. Fortunately, Rocio explained to me that looking back on the experience, she felt that my offer had been supportive, and she appreciated watching me facilitate the conference. I also took the lead in explaining the reasoning for changing Beth's placement with both the mentor and building principal, making sure that the decision was not a reflection on them but on the need for Beth to teach in English while establishing her moral authority. Rocio explained that she benefited from hearing the language I used to navigate those conversations. Happily, Beth experienced significant growth and success in her second placement and has become an accomplished teacher in a bilingual program.

Two years later, Rocio again found herself supervising an intern who encountered significant difficulty. The intern, Lisa, had been placed in a first grade general education classroom with a mentor who graduated from Trinity's MAT program and had successfully supported previous Trinity teacher candidates. Both Rocio and the mentor felt that Lisa's written lesson plans lacked sufficient detail. Sometimes Lisa failed to address an aspect of the reading or math block in her plans entirely. Other times Lisa hadn't sufficiently thought through key details in her plans. Both issues resulted in pacing difficulties as well as a lack of student engagement while teaching.

Rocio and the mentor mentioned these concerns at Lisa's fall mid-semester conference in October. Lisa demonstrated slow progress in the quality of her written planning following their feedback. Rocio continued to observe Lisa regularly but relied on her mentor to help Rocio know what was happening since the mentor was in the classroom everyday with Lisa. Unbeknownst to Rocio, the mentor grew increasingly concerned with the quality of Lisa's teaching but held off on sharing those concerns with Rocio because the mentor thought that Lisa's challenges would diminish with more teaching practice.

Rocio vividly remembers the mentor breaking her silence after Lisa really struggled to move students from their classroom to the library. The mentor sought Rocio out, described the incident then said, "I don't know how to address it. I'm such a conflict avoider." Rocio laughed and replied, "So am I! Both of us are conflict avoiders, but the more we let this go on, the more not only are we not helping Lisa but also her students are suffering." Rocio offered to talk directly with Lisa, something the mentor felt that she herself had not yet done. In addition to this one-on-one conversation, Rocio and the mentor reiterated their concern about some aspects of Lisa's planning and teaching at her end-of-semester assessment conference in December. Lisa voiced her need for more planning support. In response, Rocio set up weekly meetings with Lisa and her mentor so that the three of them could look ahead to the following week, identify resources that Lisa could share, and brainstorm activities given specific lesson goals.

Rocio and the mentor had privately discussed the possibility of placing Lisa on a professional growth plan, but since they had seen some improvement, they backed off, remaining hopeful that Lisa would demonstrate increasing competence. In January, however, Lisa continued to struggle. As she assumed increased responsibility for planning and teaching, the quality of her lesson plans grew inconsistent. She had difficulty submitting her lesson plans on time. More and more challenges surfaced in her instruction, including pacing and management. She found herself missing key materials in the middle of a lesson. She had difficulty keeping the classroom clean and organized as she entered into Lead Teaching.

The situation came to a head in February when Lisa arrived at school Monday morning without having developed or submitted written lesson plans for that day or week ahead of time. The mentor happened to see me in the hallway before the start of school and shared her concern that Lisa had no written plans. I reminded the mentor of the MAT program policy—interns cannot teach without written plans—and suggested that Lisa begin working on her plans while the mentor herself taught. I didn't want to step in and directly interact with Lisa without Rocio being there, fearing that doing so might undermine Rocio's authority.

When Rocio arrived soon after, the two of us consulted outside of the classroom. Together we brainstormed how to structure a conversation that Rocio would facilitate with Lisa. I encouraged Rocio first to ask Lisa why she did not have written plans for the week. Once she elicited that information, she could then explain to Lisa that she was being placed on a professional growth plan given the serious, unresolved concerns that Rocio and the mentor had. I also suggested that Rocio tell Lisa to step out of the classroom for the day to work on her missing lesson plans in the school library. Doing so would create time for Rocio to craft Lisa's growth plan. Rocio could then meet with Lisa (and hopefully the mentor) after school to share the plan.

I remained with Rocio as we spoke to Lisa privately. After confirming that Lisa hadn't submitted written plans, we asked why. Lisa broke into tears, explaining that she had suffered from a debilitating migraine all weekend that kept her from being able to work or sleep. Realizing just how exhausted she was, we sent Lisa home to rest, explaining that we would meet with her the next morning. Rocio used the growth plan that we had developed for Beth as a reference to craft Lisa's plan, and she felt confident to facilitate the professional growth conference on her own.

When developing this vignette, Rocio mentioned to me that she is sometimes "afraid to lay down the law" through a professional growth plan. When I asked her what she meant by that, she explained that when she creates a growth plan, it "unbalances the relationship—I become the know-it-all. But

I'm not the one in the classroom there every day, eight hours a day, like the mentor. It creates an imbalance of power." I offered an alternative way of viewing growth plans. First, doing so supports the mentor rather than diminishes her power. Typically, a mentor and clinical faculty have already tried many strategies to support a novice before a growth plan is warranted. In contrast to taking over, the university teacher educator is presenting a united front with the mentor. Moreover, taking responsibility for the physical drafting of the plan is not a power move but rather taking on a task that the mentor most likely does not have time to do herself.

In addition, I referenced Peter Elbow (1983) who argues that teachers face two seemingly contradictory obligations in their role as educators. On the one hand, we must support students in every way possible, doing whatever we can to ensure that they are successful. On the other hand, we must also be the gatekeeper, making hard decisions about whether our students sufficiently meet our goals for their learning. Elbow posits that while both commitments to support and evaluate are essential, we cannot enact them simultaneously. Rather, we must be clear with students from the outset about our expectations then do everything we can to make sure that they meet them. If, however, students are not successful, we must be willing to hold them accountable. I explained to Rocio that I strongly maintain this stance in my role as a field-based teacher educator. I also noted, however, that Elbow explains that many teachers avoid the tension between these obligations by focusing on one obligation at the expense of the other.

As Rocio and I talked further, Rocio mentioned that she sometimes continues to hope that simply giving a novice more opportunities to practice—be it planning, teaching, or assessing—will provide more opportunities to experience success. This is an assumption she wants to continue to question. She also noted that when drafting a growth plan, it is much easier for her to identify the areas of concern. Linking that set of underdeveloped knowledge and skills to subsequent learning opportunities is not so clear cut. As Rocio looked back at Lisa's plan, she felt that she needed to make her expectations for growth clearer and to develop a much more detailed plan for *how* Lisa could make that growth over time.

Our conversation clarified for me just how complicated this aspect of a clinically based teacher educator's practice truly is. At the same time that the teacher educator is negotiating her relationship with the teacher candidate, she is also managing her relationship with the mentor and supporting the mentor–novice relationship, too. Ensuring that the professional growth plan creates educative learning opportunities for all involved is the goal, but knowing how to do so requires great insight and skill. The teacher educator must be able to assess the situation from multiple stakeholder's points of view. She must be willing to step into this evaluative role. She must collaborate closely with the mentor to ensure that both are on the same page.

She must draft a coherent growth plan that clearly lays out concerns *and* lays a path forward for how to strengthen those aspects of the novice's practice. She must simultaneously support and stretch the intern, helping the novice remain open to learning rather than shutting her down.

Supporting Mentor Development

Another critically important component of a university field-based teacher educator's practice lies in supporting experienced classroom teachers to develop their mentoring practice (Carroll, 2007; Norman, 2011). Teacher candidates identify mentors as the single biggest influence on their learning (Clarke, Triggs, & Nielsen, 2014). The success of field-based internships rest on the mentors' ability to view their intern as a learner of teaching and themselves as teachers of teaching (Feiman-Nemser, 1998). This means that mentors not only understand the content to be taught—the learning to teach "curriculum"—but also are able to design learning opportunities based on knowledge of their intern and what she needs to learn (Gareis & Grant, 2014).

My own doctoral studies extensively focused on mentor development. As soon as I began supervising graduate interns at Trinity, I established mentor teacher study groups where mentors and I regularly meet to check in on how mentors and their interns are doing; focus on a single aspect of mentoring practice such as co-planning, observing/debriefing, co-teaching, or assessing interns' progress; and review expectations for interns' clinical responsibilities in the month ahead.

During mentor study group sessions, I regularly bring mentoring artifacts of practice for our collective examination. Sometimes the artifacts grow out of my own work with an intern (e.g., a videotape of a debriefing conference or co-planning session). Other times I will bring a video excerpt of a novice's teaching, inviting mentors to use different tools to observe then make decisions about what to discuss in a subsequent debriefing session as well as how and why. Still other times I ask mentors to bring an artifact of their own mentoring practice to the session or to identify mentoring challenges for joint problem-solving through the use of protocols.

As soon as my colleagues began supervising interns, I encouraged them to attend mentor study group sessions with me. I took responsibility for facilitating these sessions for nearly two years then later met with them to co-plan and co-facilitate subsequent sessions. Over time, they have assumed the role of facilitating mentor study groups on their own.

Sara noticed both in her observation and co-facilitation of mentor study group sessions that mentors may initially feel uncomfortable discussing interns without them being present. Doing so can feel like gossiping. As one mentor once said, "I wouldn't appreciate my colleagues sitting around talking about me. I've developed a sense of trust with my intern and I just don't feel comfortable at this point sharing something unless that person were here." Mentors need help understanding that their intern is their *student* of teaching. The teacher educator can help mentors to understand that just as they wouldn't hesitate to seek a colleague's support if they were struggling to support a *child* in their classroom, they should view mentor study group sessions as an opportunity to gain insights into how they can better support their novice's teaching and learning.

This is sometimes easier said than done. Openly discussing challenges that an intern is experiencing can lead a mentor to feel like she is tattling. The mentor might also feel inadequate in front of his/her teaching peers. Mentors need support in coming to see such conversations as an opportunity to clarify an intern's areas for learning and growth. More clearly understanding where interns' growing edges lie better positions all of us—mentors and university clinical supervisors—to better support their learning to teach. Creating a trusting learning community where all members of the study group view each other as co-learners of mentoring is an important skill that field-based teacher educators must develop and hone over time (Norman, 2011).

From these mentored experiences, Sara gained a deeper appreciation for the importance of supporting new and veteran mentors. Serving as a mentor in Trinity's program requires a host of knowledge and skills, including:

- programmatic knowledge (e.g., structure of the internship; roles/responsibilities of mentor, intern, and university clinical faculty);
- foundational knowledge/skill (e.g., knowledge of the developmental learning to teach continuum, knowledge of, and skill in the core tasks of teaching); and
- practical knowledge/skill (e.g., use the mentor's practice as a site for intern's learning; scaffold opportunities for intern to take on core tasks of teaching in ways that lead to further growth; provide feedback on intern's planning, teaching, and progress over time).

Mentors can really benefit from university teacher educators' support in developing their practice as teachers of teaching.

DISCUSSION

As the vignettes above illustrate, the serious and sustained support of novice teacher educators through assisted performance can take several forms.

Some of my mentoring efforts take the form of *demonstration* (as when Sara observed me conduct assessment conferences or Sara and Rocio initially sat in on mentor study group sessions). Some mentoring efforts occur through *guided practice* where together we perform a core aspect of the teacher educator's role (as Sara and I do when jointly providing feedback on candidates' UbD plans, or as Rocio and I co-conducted a difficult conversation with an intern in preparation for placing her on a professional growth plan). Still other mentoring efforts transpires after the novice teacher educator engages in *independent practice*, we come together to jointly problem solve (such as Melissa and I did when determining how to adjust the structure of the clinically based tutoring component of her math methods course).

The vignettes also illustrate that just as teacher candidates vary in the amount and forms of support needed to grow their teaching practice, so too does the quantity and kinds of assistance that teacher educators need to grow their field-based practice. Unlike Rocio who came to Trinity having served as a university supervisor while completing her doctoral program, Sara's graduate studies did not include teacher candidate field supervision. Reading the needs of my colleagues and checking my understanding by offering choices about whether/how to assist helped ensure that my mentoring efforts felt supportive. Offering my assistance by asking, "Would it feel helpful if I...?" helped me determine whether to step in, coach, co-conduct, or fade.

I have taught in Trinity's elementary MAT program for 17 years. I have regularly mentored department colleagues, both as newcomers to field-based teacher education and later as they have established an impressive practice themselves. In this way, I have come to understand that my role as mentor does not end once my colleagues have taught in the teacher preparation program for a certain number of months or years. Rather, mentoring is an iterative process where the more we collaborate, jointly problem solve, and assist each other, the more we find new ways to continue supporting each other's ongoing growth (Hanson & Moir, 2008; Nilsson & van Driel, 2010).

The benefits of taking the mentoring of teacher educators seriously are many. First, the teacher educator is immediately assisted in her practice. She is able to do with support what she could not successfully do on her own. By strengthening her practice, teacher candidates also directly benefit. Better supporting teacher candidates in turn benefits the children they teach. And of course, the mentor herself benefits greatly as well. As Clandinin (1995) notes, developing her practice as a teacher educator requires her to continually learn how to teach, regardless of how many years she has served in the role. This is true for me as well. Supporting my colleagues' field-based practices brings me new insights into the role and practice, positions them to support *me* when I encounter a thorny issue related to novices' clinical experiences, and creates incredibly rich and engaging opportunities to develop shared beliefs about teaching and learning. Constructing these shared beliefs better assures curricular and pedagogical coherence across Trinity's teacher preparation program.

IMPLICATIONS

Just as support for classroom-based mentor teachers must rest on a clear vision of teaching and the teacher's role, so, too, must support for university teacher educators rest on a clear understanding of the role and practice of clinically based teacher education. I offer one such conception which includes designing clinically based courses; establishing relationships in clinical settings; giving candidates feedback on their planning, teaching, and progress; addressing significant concerns in candidates' practice and/ or clinical placement; and supporting mentor development.

As noted earlier, many colleges and universities assign a faculty member outside of the department or school to help new faculty learn what it means to "do" the university. If we took more seriously a systematic means of supporting and guiding new faculty within schools and departments of education, we really would create stronger cadres of emerging field-based teacher educators who can create powerful clinical experiences for teacher candidates.

I recognize that Trinity is a unique, small-scale program and that larger institutions will have many more new faculty to mentor. I also recognize that teacher educators in large teacher preparation programs likely are required to supervise many more students than we do within our program. That said, whether meeting with a candidate for 15 times across a year or three times during a traditional student teaching placement, the educative quality of those interactions can be strengthened through serious, sustained efforts to mentor the teacher educators responsible for providing them.

Of course, this support and guidance needs to begin *before* they enter the professoriate. Doctoral studies in teacher education should give candidates significant opportunities to use best clinical practices as well. I was fortunate to complete my graduate work at Michigan State University under the guidance of Sharon Feiman-Nemser. Her deep interest in designing strong clinical experiences for teacher candidates also extended into providing support to doctoral candidates who served as university field supervisors. Sharon and I designed and co-taught a doctoral seminar on learning the work of field-based teacher education. Graduate students examined their own efforts to support teacher candidates' clinical experiences while simultaneously reading and discussing core texts in clinical supervision. Every doctoral candidate—including those who supervise student teachers during their graduate studies and those who will do so later on once in faculty positions themselves—deserves coordinated, mentored support in learning the practice of field-based teacher education. Doing so would provide essential initial preparation to support candidates' transition into clinical faculty roles.

Discussion Questions

1. Of the five core aspects of a field-based teacher educator's practice, which ones do you consider your strengths and which ones need further development?
   - Design clinically based courses.
   - Establish relationships with key players in clinical settings.
   - Provide feedback to candidates on their teaching.
   - Address significant concerns in candidates' practice and/or clinical placement.
   - Support mentor development.
2. Drawing on the vignettes, what mentored experiences might you pursue in order to deepen aspects of your clinical practice? Would you benefit from demonstration, guided practice, and/or independent practice?
3. In the "Designing Field-Based Courses" vignette, Melissa realized that she needs to make explicit all that is implicit in her own teaching so that novices can learn in and from her practice. Consider a recent teaching experience you had with teacher candidates. In what ways did you use your practice to support candidates' learning? In the future, how can you make even more explicit what is implicit in your teaching?
4. When observing a teacher candidate, how do you approach that observation? What do you look for? attend to? hope to see? How do you structure the debriefing conversation and why?
5. In the "Addressing Significant Concerns" vignette, the field supervisor and mentor both acknowledged that they were conflict avoiders. This trait created a real challenge in helping the intern work through her planning and teaching difficulties. What dispositional and interpersonal strengths do you already possess that will aide you in addressing significant concerns in candidates' teaching? What is a dispositional and/or interpersonal vulnerability that you will need to work on over time in order to help candidates work through challenges they encounter?

REFERENCES

American Association of Colleges for Teacher Education. (2018). A pivot toward clinical practice, its lexicon and the renewal of educator preparation: A report of the AACTE Clinical Practice Commission. New York, NY: Author.

Carroll, D. (2007). Helping teachers become teacher educators. In D. Carroll, H. Featherstone, J. Featherstone, & D. Roosevelt (Eds.), *Transforming teacher education: Reflections from the field* (pp. 181–202). Cambridge, MA: Harvard Education Press.

Carroll, D., Featherstone, H., Featherstone, J., Feiman-Nemser, S., & Roosevelt, D. (Eds.). (2007). *Transforming teacher education: Reflections from the field.* Cambridge, MA: Harvard Education Press.

Cawyer, C. S., Simonds, C., & Davis, S. (2002). Mentoring to facilitate socialization: The case of the new faculty member. *International Journal of Qualitative Studies in Education, 15*(2), 225–242.

Clandinin, D. J. (1995). Still learning to teach. In T. Russell & F. Korthagan (Eds.), *Teachers who teach teachers: Reflections on teacher education* (pp. 25–32). London, England: Routledge.

Clarke, A., Triggs, V., & Nielsen, W. (2014). Cooperating teacher participation in teacher education: A review of the literature. *Review of Educational Research, 84*(2), 163–202.

Dewey, J. (1963). *Education and Experience.* New York, NY: Collier Books. (Originally published in 1938).

Elbow, P. (1983). Embracing contraries in the teaching process. *College English, 45*(4), 327–339.

Feiman-Nemser, S. (1998). Teachers as teacher educators. *European Journal of Teacher Education, 21*(1), 63–74.

Feiman-Nemser, S. (2001). From preparation to practice: Designing a continuum to strengthen and sustain teaching. *Teachers College Record, 103*(6), 1013–1055.

Feiman-Nemser, S. (2012). Helping novices learn to teach: Lessons from an exemplary support teacher. In S. Feiman-Nemser (Ed.), *Teachers as learners* (pp. 253–276). Cambridge, MA: Harvard Education Press.

Gardiner, W. (2017). Mentoring "inside" and "outside" the action of teaching: A professional framework for mentoring. *The New Educator, 13*(1), 53–71.

Gareis, C. R., & Grant, L. W. (2014). The efficacy of training cooperating teachers. *Teaching and Teacher Education, 39,* 77–88.

Grossman, P., Hammerness, K., & McDonald, M. (2009). Redefining teaching, reimagining teacher education. *Teachers and Teaching: Theory and Practice, 15*(2), 273–289.

Hagger, H., Burns, K., & McIntyre, D. (1995). *The school mentor handbook: Essential skills and strategies for working with student teachers.* Abingdon, England: Routledge.

Hanson, S., & Moir, E. (2008). Beyond mentoring: Influencing the professional practice and careers of experienced teachers. *Phi Delta Kappan, 89*(6), 453–458.

Hobson, A. J., Ashby, P., Malderez, A., & Tomlinson, P. D. (2009). Mentoring beginning teachers: What we know and what we don't. *Teaching and Teacher Education: An International Journal of Research and Studies, 25*(1), 207–216.

Hudson, P. (2014). Feedback consistencies and inconsistencies. *European Journal of Teacher Education, 37*(1), 63–73.

Ingersoll, R. M., & Strong, M. (2011). The impact of induction and mentoring programs for beginning teachers: A critical review of the research. *Review of Educational Research, 81*(2), 201–233.

Nilsson, P., & van Driel, J. (2010). Teaching together and learning together—Primary science student teachers' and their mentors' joint teaching and learning in the primary classroom. *Teaching and Teacher Education, 26*(6), 1309–1318.

Norman, P. (2011). Planning for what kind of teaching? Supporting mentors as teachers of planning. *Teacher Education Quarterly, 38*(3), 49–68.

Ramsden, P. (2003). *Learning to teach in higher education* (2nd ed.). New York, NY: RoutledgeFalmer.

Russell, T., & Korthagen, F. (Eds.). (1995). *Teachers who teach teachers.* London, England: Routledge.

Savage, H. E., Karp, R. S., & Logue, R. (2004). Faculty mentorship at colleges and universities. *College Teaching, 52*(1), 21–24.

Schwab, J. J. (1978). The practical 3: Translation into curriculum. In I. Westbury & N. J. Wilkof (Eds.), *Science, curriculum and liberal education: Selected essays* (pp. 365–383). Chicago, IL: University of Chicago Press.

Schwille, S. (2008). The professional practice of mentoring. *American Journal of Education, 115*, 139–167.

Stanulis, R. N., Brondyk, S. K., Little, S., & Wibbens, E. (2014). Mentoring beginning teachers to enact discussion-based teaching. *Mentoring & Tutoring: Partnership in Learning, 22*(2), 127–145.

Valencia, S., Martin, S., Place, N., & Grossman, P. (2009). Complex interactions in student teaching. *Journal of Teacher Education, 60*(3), 304–322.

Vygotsky, L. (1978). *Mind in society: The development of higher psychological processes.* Cambridge, MA: Harvard University Press.

Wang, J., & Odell, S. J. (2002). Mentored learning to teach according to standards-based reform: A critical review. *Review of Educational Research, 72*, 481–546.

Wiggins, G., & McTighe, J. (2005). *Understanding by design* (2nd ed.). Alexandria, VA: Association for Supervision and Curriculum Development.

Wildman, T., Niles, J., Magliaro, S., & McLaughlin, R. (1989). Teaching and learning to teach: The two roles of beginning teachers. *Elementary School Journal, 89*(4), 471–492.

CHAPTER 3

THE PATTERN EMERGES

Novice Teacher Educators Learn From Complexity

Janna Dresden
University of Georgia

Katherine F. Thompson
University of Georgia

Melissa A. Baker
University of South Carolina

Ashley S. Nylin
University of Georgia

Kajal Sinha
University of Georgia

Our goal in this chapter is to recognize, understand, and problematize our work as experienced and novice teacher educators. In our role as teacher educators, we are responsible for preparing university students to take their place in the workforce as competent and capable teachers. As members of

Preparing the Next Generation of Teacher Educators for Clinical Practice, pages 49–72
Copyright © 2019 by Information Age Publishing
All rights of reproduction in any form reserved.

a university faculty, we are obliged to serve on committees to support the work of our programs, department, college, and university. As teacher educators in a department with a doctoral program, we are also charged with supporting the development of those doctoral students. Finally, as teacher educators at a research university, we are expected to have a coherent and productive line of scholarly inquiry (Murray & Male, 2005). Those of us who are doctoral students and novice teacher educators are expected to assist, observe, and learn. This wide array of responsibilities can cause teacher educators (and future teacher educators) to "experience their daily work lives as a kind of patchwork of disparate and discontinuous activities" (Cochran-Smith, 2012, p. 100).

We have found that our shared experience in a clinically intensive setting has enabled us to see the connections among these disparate pieces, in much the same way that the pattern of a quilt emerges from the intentional placement of otherwise random bits of cloth. In this chapter, we will describe the context within which we enact our myriad roles and responsibilities and explore the following question: How is the preparation of teacher educators as practitioners, scholars, and researchers facilitated, supported, challenged, or enhanced by work in a clinically intensive setting like a professional development school (PDS) or school district? Subsequent sections of the chapter will briefly address the background on clinically intensive programs of teacher preparation, explain the need for prospective teacher educators to engage in these types of programs during their time in graduate school, describe the context within which we work as individuals and as a group, and consider the theoretical framework that helps us understand that work before sharing narratives from several different perspectives. The chapter will conclude with a consideration of emergent themes and some tentative answers to the question that began our inquiry.

CLINICALLY INTENSIVE TEACHER PREPARATION

Interest in clinically intensive programs of teacher preparation has been increasing for the last 20 years or more and has become commonly accepted as a "best practice" with the 2010 publication of the *NCATE Report of the Blue Ribbon Panel on Clinical Preparation and Partnerships*. Situating teacher preparation programs in the day-to-day life of schools is believed to foster the development of exemplary teachers because in these types of programs teacher candidates have more frequent and substantive interactions with students and practicing teachers. These interactions then provide teacher candidates with the opportunity to flesh out the one-dimensional pedagogical strategies they have studied and apply the theories they have learned (Darling-Hammond, 2005; Rust & Clift, 2015). The centrality of action and application in all professional education is evident in the fact that publications from the Institute of Medicine (e.g., 2010) begin with the following quote from Goethe: "Knowing is not enough, we must apply. Willing is not enough, we must do." Both novice teachers and novice physicians benefit from situations in which they are required to act and apply the academic knowledge they have gained. Thus, using the teaching hospital as an analogy for teacher preparation, though frequently associated with PDSs, is appropriate for all clinically intensive programs of teacher preparation.

The teaching and learning process is also frequently characterized as complex (Ball & Forzani, 2009; Cochran-Smith, Ell, Ludlow, Grudnoff, & Aitken, 2014; Cochran-Smith, Ell, Grudnoff, et al., 2014; Grossman et al., 2009; Hollins, 2011; Stairs, 2011) and a second advantage of clinically intensive programs of teacher preparation is that this complexity can be neither ignored nor avoided. When teacher candidates have ongoing interactions with children and teachers, and when those interactions are facilitated and interrogated by university faculty, the complexities which result from factors such as varying personalities, temperaments, cultural backgrounds, physical settings, and subject matter are readily apparent.

A third benefit of clinically intensive teacher preparation is that such programs serve as fertile ground for the development of reflective practitioners. The idea, proposed by major scholars in the field of teacher education, that increased competence as a teacher is the result of engaging in and reflecting on practice (Cochran-Smith & Lytle, 2009; Darling-Hammond, 2006; Zeichner & Liston, 2014) demands that teachers be trained within a practical, clinically intensive context. It is simply not possible to reflect on experiences one has not had, and thus active engagement is a necessary prerequisite for becoming a reflective practitioner (Schon, 1983).

Finally, the supervision of teacher candidates by university faculty and doctoral students in a clinically intensive context alleviates a common problem noted in the literature about student teaching experiences. Classroom teachers who serve as mentors to teacher candidates during student teaching experiences often comment that there is a lack of clarity about university expectations (Bullough, 2005; Caruso, 1998). When faculty and/or doctoral student supervisors have a consistent and frequent presence in a classroom or school setting, as is more common in programs utilizing a clinically intensive approach, the communication tends to be more direct and clear.

PROSPECTIVE TEACHER EDUCATORS

If teacher candidates ought to be prepared to teach in clinically intensive settings, then doctoral students who are preparing to become teacher educators should also, by logical extension, be prepared in clinically intensive settings. If practice is to be at the center of teacher preparation, as suggested by the NCATE 2010 report, then future teacher educators must be at the heart of this endeavor. Like teacher candidates, novice teacher educators learn by doing. Active engagement within clinically intensive settings enables novice teacher educators to experience the foundational value of an inquiry stance (Cochran-Smith & Lytle, 2009), participate in a community of practice, as well as begin to craft an identity as a teacher educator, scholar, and researcher.

Future teacher educators are often advised, if not admonished, to develop an inquiry stance towards their work. Therefore, it is important to recognize that a clinically intensive program of teacher preparation is the primary context within which an inquiry stance towards teacher education can be enacted. Without the press of immediate experience, there is a tendency to simplify situations and gloss over tensions. In contrast, an inquiry stance "involves a continual process of making current arrangements problematic; [and] questioning the ways knowledge and practice are constructed, evaluated, and used" (Cochran-Smith & Lytle, 2009, p. 121). This level of questioning, re-evaluating, and reconstructing can only occur within a real-world setting with real people and real consequences.

Participation in communities of practice and the construction of an identity as a teacher educator are mutually constitutive activities. That is, communities of practice are sites for the social construction of identity (Cochran-Smith & Lytle, 2009; Dinkelman, 2011) and communities of practice are created through the gathering of individuals with shared purpose and common experiences (Dinkelman, 2011). In addition, communities of practice are the birthplace of an inquiry stance, fundamental to the enactment of reflective teaching practice and the preparation of thoughtful teachers and teacher educators (Cochran-Smith & Lytle, 2009).

Though there may be a variety of definitions for the term "teacher educator" and various locations for the work of preparing future teachers, an identity as a teacher educator is always actively constructed over time (Murray & Male, 2005) and in a particular context. The title *teacher educator* is typically reserved for individuals who work in higher education settings with teacher candidates (e.g., Murray & Male, 2005). However, classroom teachers who serve as mentors to teacher candidates may also be regarded, and consider themselves to be, teacher educators (Korth, Erickson, & Hall, 2009). It is interesting to note that in one study, classroom teachers who served as mentors to teacher candidates in schools where there was a strong and established partnership with a university were more likely to consider themselves to be teacher educators, defined as teachers of teachers, than were mentor teachers from schools without such strong partnerships (Korth et al., 2009). Thus, it would appear that the availability of a community of practice (through a partnership with a university) encourages a broader view of the role of classroom teacher and a more inclusive view of those who can fulfill the role of teacher educator.

For those working in higher education settings, an identity as teacher educator results from interactions with peers in a community of practice and from the quality of interactions one has with teacher candidates (Dinkelman, 2011). In addition, this identity grows from a sense of confidence about one's ability to teach teacher candidates effectively and is strengthened by the credibility derived from years of experience as a classroom teacher (Murray & Male, 2005). It would, therefore, appear that doctoral students are likely to develop stronger identities as teacher educators when they have sustained opportunities to interact with teacher candidates in settings of practice such as those found in clinically intensive programs of teacher preparation.

Future teacher educators also benefit from attending meetings in which the ethos of a community of practice is paramount. In these settings, the "day-to-day decision-making of teacher educators" can be known by others (Dinkelman, 2011) thus strengthening the commitment and identity of the group as well as the individual identities of the members of the group. And finally, these meetings make it possible to enact "a commitment to shared inquiry about the work of teacher education programmes [that] sends powerful messages to those just entering the profession about what it means to be a teacher educator" (p. 320).

The formation of identity as a teacher educator is supported by the communities of practice within which people work but is also challenged by the perceived tension between the demands of teacher preparation and the exigencies of a productive research agenda (Murray & Male, 2005). In their interviews with teacher educators, Murray and Male found that most could not conceive of ways in which teaching and research might be productively connected. This construction of research and practice as separate and distinct aspects of the work of teacher educators is potentially threatening to the quality of teacher preparation (Dinkelman, 2011; Zeichner, 1999) because it inhibits the crucial interplay of ideas, actions, questions, and goals. Future teacher educators prepared in clinically intensive setting are likely to benefit from the many and varied activities with which they are engaged. In addition, their interactions with peers and professors place them within a community of practice and give them space to craft their identities as teacher educators. On the other hand, all teacher educators, veterans as well as novices, may be challenged by the perceived tension between doing the work of preparing future teachers and conducting research in the field (Murray & Male, 2005; Zeichner, 1999).

COMPLEXITY THEORY AS A THEORETICAL FRAMEWORK

Our work is grounded in an appreciation of complexity, so we begin with the premise that complexity is not only unavoidable, but intellectually sustaining and ultimately useful. As Duckworth (2006) has pointed out, when we acknowledge and affirm the complexity of an enterprise or subject or set of concepts we make it "more accessible by opening a multiplicity of paths into it" (p. 135). When ideas are articulated with all their rich, and sometimes messy, complications and complexities, they are often surprisingly, if not ironically, easier to understand. When the complex nature of an idea is left intact, rather than reduced to a flat and superficial dictum, it enables people with varying backgrounds and ways of knowing to understand it (Duckworth, 2006). Thus, we should not eschew complexity, but embrace it. Similarly, Kennedy (2016) suggested that the field of teacher education should focus less on a debate between the value of understanding content versus the value of mastering pedagogical strategies, and instead be more insistent that teacher candidates recognize the complex challenges that will confront them daily and learn to approach these challenges analytically, or as Cochran-Smith and Lytle (2009) would say, from an inquiry stance.

Cochran-Smith, Ell, Ludlow, Grudnoff, et al. (2014) have further explored these ideas and considered the ways in which complexity theory can be used to understand and grapple with some of the profound issues in teacher education. Complexity theory would suggest that clinically intensive programs are beneficial because they are dependent upon relationships, highlight the variety and unpredictability of the teaching and learning processes, make evident the lack of linear mechanisms of change and still enable us to learn from and support one another. The major contribution of complexity theory is that it can guide researchers and practitioners towards the development of more powerful and productive questions (Cochran-Smith, Ell, Ludlow, Grudnoff, et al., 2014). Rather than searching for simple answers and definitive "best practices," complexity theory guides us to collectively consider alternatives and options that move us towards a richer and more nuanced understanding and a new set of generative questions about the world of teaching and learning.

OUR CONTEXT

In response to the call for clinically intensive experiences in teacher education (e.g., NCATE, 2010), the University of Georgia and the Clarke County School District established a PDS district partnership beginning in 2009. The partnership now consists of 21 schools, 20–25 College of Education (COE) courses taught at local schools each semester, and approximately 20 affiliate faculty, including nine professors-in-residence who devote at least 50% of their budgeted time to PDS-related work in their designated schools or at the district level.

The work of the PDS is accomplished through informal conversations, numerous e-mail communications, and a set of regularly scheduled meetings including an executive committee, a coordinating council, and local steering committees at each school. In addition, monthly meetings of our PDS collaborative (all faculty and doctoral students working within our PDS) serve as sites for substantive conversations that are the "visible indicators of the care, attention, and seriousness of purpose surrounding teacher education" (Dinkelman, 2011). In these meetings, we share ideas, support each other, and more importantly, strive to both problematize our work and seek ways to make the value of our endeavors evident to the surrounding academic and public school communities.

Although the broad categories of teacher educator preparation activities (e.g., teaching, scholarship, & mentoring) that occur in a traditional approach to preparing teacher educators also occur in our PDS model, the *way* that doctoral students experience teacher education in a public school context can be, and arguably *should be*, significantly and qualitatively different from university-based experiences. Dewey (1938) noted that education is not just about providing experiences but ensuring the quality of those experiences, as well. While the UGA-CCSD PDS partnership has naturally centered on the experiences of university teacher candidates, in-service teachers, and P–12 students, university faculty have also thoughtfully and intentionally created opportunities for graduate students to participate in PDS-related teaching, scholarship, program innovation, and professional learning, as well as many other activities associated with the partnership. Teacher educator preparation within a clinically intensive setting also provides graduate students with experiences that cannot easily occur in a university setting, such as arranging for university students to observe exemplary teachers and for public school practitioners to participate in course-based activities during the school day.

FOUR NARRATIVES: PERSPECTIVES ON WORKING WITHIN A CLINICALLY INTENSIVE PREPARATION PROGRAM

This section is devoted to four narratives, each of which exemplifies a unique perspective on the intricate pattern that is our PDS network. Appreciating the complexity of teaching and learning within a clinically intensive environment requires that we listen to multiple voices and examine problems from varying perspectives. In the first narrative, a university faculty member serving as a professor-in-residence in a local middle school describes how she integrates doctoral students into the work of the PDS. Next, a recent graduate, in her first year as a university faculty member, shares her perspective on the teacher educator preparation she experienced as a doctoral student in the PDS and how her experiences impacted her development as a teacher educator. Finally, two current doctoral students from different teacher education programs (middle grades education and early childhood education) describe their experiences living in the center of practice and discuss how the PDS model of teacher education is influencing their identity as teacher educators, their level of understanding and confidence, and how they perceive that they benefit from a PDS context.

Perspective of a Veteran University Faculty Member

For nearly a decade, my (Kathy) position as a teacher educator involved the roles and responsibilities one might typically expect of a professor preparing doctoral students for a future in teacher education. I involved graduate teaching assistants (GTAs) in the challenging work of developing course syllabi for and teaching undergraduate methods courses; I worked with doctoral students as they supervised teacher candidates during practicum experiences; and I mentored graduate students in developing scholarship to disseminate to colleagues in national and international contexts.

The model of teacher education described above is likely a familiar one to educators in higher education; graduate students work alongside faculty, emulating their mentors, as they prepare to become teacher educators themselves in a traditional university-centered context. In recent years, however, as attention has focused on the necessity for and benefits of a clinically intensive education for teacher candidates, so too must attention shift to the preparation of the teacher educators responsible for providing meaningful teacher preparation in school-based settings. When I took on the role of PDS professor-in-residence (PIR) in a local middle school 7 years ago, I committed to providing doctoral students with clinically intensive teacher educator experiences via the structure and possibilities of a PDS.

One of my primary responsibilities as a PIR, among others as described in Andrews and Thompson (2016), is teaching university courses on-site at a local middle school. Teaching undergraduate on-site courses affords numerous opportunities for GTAs to experience teacher education in authentic contexts. Not only do GTAs gain experience co-teaching teacher candidates on-site with university faculty, they also learn how to draw on the wisdom and expertise of practitioners in the school. For example, we invite teachers to model lessons that highlight the concepts teacher candidates are studying in their on-site methods courses. At other times, we arrange for teacher candidates to observe a strategy or concept being implemented in a teachers' classroom and then invite the teacher to debrief with the teacher candidates during his/her planning period in our school-based PDS classroom. GTAs do not have to wait for teacher candidates to go into their respective field placements before discussing the connections or tensions between theory and practice. Instead, they experience "real time" teacher education as teacher candidates examine their assumptions, identify misconceptions, and discover possibilities. In these communities of practice, GTAs learn how to connect theoretical concepts to classroom application, establish relationships with teachers in a PDS, and negotiate the logistical aspects (e.g., communication and scheduling) of providing these kinds of activities for teacher candidates.

In the PDS on-site preservice methods courses I teach, doctoral students also gain experience in guiding teacher candidates' development of an inquiry stance (Cochran-Smith & Lytle, 2009). Using a variety of inquiry models (Dana & Yendol-Hoppey, 2014; Juliani, 2015; Maiers, 2010), we lead teacher candidates in investigating problems of practice in middle grades classrooms through an inquiry project. GTAs help teacher candidates identify an inquiry question to investigate (e.g., "How can I incorporate movement in my middle grades classroom?"), explore the literature related to the question, develop a plan for examining the question, collect and analyze data, and share the results with PDS faculty and other teacher candidates. Working with teacher candidates to establish an inquiry approach to teaching and learning gives doctoral students experience in incorporating inquiry into teacher education and provides a vision for how these processes can be implemented in future contexts.

An added benefit of teaching on-site in a PDS is the opportunity for graduate students and teacher candidates to be involved in the life of the school beyond the classroom. GTAs and I work with school staff to identify school community service opportunities for which teacher candidates can volunteer. Examples of school community service at which teacher candidates have typically volunteered include curriculum nights, Halloween carnivals, back-to-school open house, student–faculty basketball games, science/social studies fairs, academic competitions, book fairs, tutoring, school dances, clubs, and sporting events. These school-based student and family engagement activities provide opportunities for teacher candidates to see children not simply as students in a particular period or class, but as multidimensional people with interests and talents and lives that matter (Andrews & Thompson, 2016). These insights regarding the complexities of students' lives are less likely to happen when teacher education is contained within the bounds of a university campus.

Guiding doctoral students in developing their own scholarship is one of the primary tasks of a university professor. As a PIR in a PDS, I have created some unique opportunities to engage doctoral students in research-related tasks. For example, doctoral students have collected and analyzed on-site course data and conducted focus groups related to teacher candidates' experiences in the PDS. What did teacher candidates learn about young adolescents? What did they learn about the role of the teacher inside and outside the classroom? What did they learn about families and communities? What did they learn about the importance of teachers knowing and connecting with students? As a result of these PDS-related research tasks, doctoral students are challenged to consider the impact of the PDS on pre-service teacher education and what role they will play as future teacher educators in providing clinically intensive experiences for teacher candidates.

In addition to teaching undergraduate initial certification courses on-site in a PDS middle school, I have also taught graduate courses on-site. These courses provide opportunities for doctoral students—and future teacher educators—to make connections between course curricula, their research interests, and the needs of the local school. For example, in response to sixth grade teachers' desire to improve relationships with students and families, Melissa, a student in one of the on-site graduate courses and also one of this chapter's authors, developed a needs assessment administered to sixth grade students, families, and teachers. The course project eventually led to the development of Melissa's dissertation study on parent perspectives of their students' transition from elementary school to middle school. Melissa's familiarity and involvement with the PDS proved beneficial as she conducted her study. She had developed trusting relationships with key school faculty, which opened lines of communication to teachers and parents. Melissa was not seen as an outsider conducting research; she was considered a partner providing the school with much needed information about family engagement.

A critical component of engaging in scholarly work is sharing one's findings, so I seek out opportunities for doctoral students to disseminate information related to our PDS efforts. To model for doctoral students the collaborative nature of PDS endeavors, I frequently submit conference and manuscript proposals in collaboration with in-service teachers and teacher candidates. Presenting and publishing with both novice and veteran educators gives voice to a variety of experiences and perspectives and provides an example to doctoral students of how university and school partners can collaboratively engage in intellectual work. I am thrilled when I hear doctoral students comment on how remarkable our teacher candidates are during conference presentations, as they realize the potential of these novice teachers and how much they themselves, as teacher educators, can learn from teacher candidates.

Professional learning for both in-service teachers and teacher candidates is a key aspect of PDSs (NAPDS, 2008). In my PDS work in a local middle school, we have developed an innovative way to combine professional learning for these two groups, and GTAs are integrally involved in these efforts. After examining a concept throughout the semester that relates to educating young adolescents, teacher candidates develop projects and products to share with the school's teachers that they can use as resources in their own classrooms. The sharing occurs in the form of a professional learning fair in the school's media center, and teachers participate during their planning periods (Andrews & Thompson, 2016; Andrews, Thompson, Naughton, & Waters, 2017). During the fair, in-service teachers and teacher candidates experience authentic, job-embedded professional learning (Zepeda, 2015) as they engage in lively discussions about research and instructional resources. By assisting in the implementation of these professional learning fairs, doctoral students who serve as on-site GTAs learn how to develop course assignments for teacher candidates that have a professional purpose and are intended for an authentic audience. GTAs also benefit from engaging in conversations with fair participants and observing the interactions between teacher candidates and in-service teachers.

During the past 7 years, my work as a teacher educator and mentor to doctoral students has taken on a richer, more nuanced dimension as a result of my involvement in a PDS partnership between my university and a local school district. Now, I am no longer mentoring graduate students in the isolated context of a university setting but instead immersing them in the complexities of real schools with real challenges and real possibilities. Through the PDS partnership, doctoral students see a public school teacher's classroom become the university classroom as the teacher models grouping strategies, transitions, or differentiation for teacher candidates. These future teacher educators witness practitioners and teacher candidates sitting side by side learning from one another while exploring challenging topics, such as classroom management, meeting the needs of every student, and integrating social justice issues into the curriculum. The doctoral students working on-site in the PDS also observe teacher candidates interacting with students and their families at a variety of school events and activities, demonstrating that being a teacher is more than delivering content in 50-minute segments throughout the day; it is about connecting with students beyond the classroom. By experiencing teacher education in a PDS setting, doctoral students begin to understand that effective teacher preparation should not be comprised of distinctly disparate settings and experiences with little meaningful connection to one another—coursework in a university setting and fieldwork in an unrelated school setting. Instead, these future teacher educators see university course content and school-based field experiences as being inextricably linked within the PDS, where they experience communities of practice among P–16 faculty, establish an inquiry stance toward teacher education and scholarship, and develop their own identities as teacher educators.

Perspective of a Recent Graduate and Novice Teacher Educator

My (Melissa) path to becoming a teacher educator was centered on the use of clinically intensive practices in a sustained school–university partnership. Having the opportunity to be a part of the UGA–CCSD PDS partnership as a doctoral student and graduate assistant greatly impacted not just how I viewed teacher education, but truly centered who I have become as a teacher educator. The PDS opportunities I experienced as a doctoral student showed me how sustained partnerships with P–12 schools can strengthen teacher education programs.

During my time at UGA in the Middle Grades Education program, I took multiple doctoral level courses on-site at a local middle school. One course allowed me to work with middle school teachers to develop interdisciplinary curriculum, and a service-learning course eventually led to my dissertation research. Taking on-site courses allowed me to grow relationships with local school faculty while opening the door to research, writing, and conference presentation opportunities. Aside from on-site doctoral courses, I also took a campus-based doctoral course about school–university partnerships. In this course, I learned more about the history, models, benefits, and challenges of school–university partnerships, which helped me to ground the work that was being done in the UGA–CCSD partnership within existing partnership research. It was then that I, as a future teacher educator, realized I could conduct research within the partnership that would support the schools, my own research agenda, and the field of school–university partnerships.

While taking an on-site doctoral level service-learning course, I met with the middle school's principal and sixth grade teachers to determine whether the school's needs also aligned with my own research interests. From these discussions, I learned that the sixth grade teachers had been struggling to engage students' families. The teachers believed there was a disconnect between school personnel and parents and expressed a need to improve relations. As a result, I constructed, collected, and analyzed quantitative data related to perspectives and experiences of students, parents, and teachers. The data were used to assess the school's current family engagement activities for students and parents transitioning from fifth to sixth grade and make changes to family engagement activities based on the needs, wants, and concerns of students, parents, and teachers. Follow-up conversations with the faculty and administration resulted in my conducting further research on family engagement across the school transition from elementary school to middle school. Taking graduate courses on-site at a local middle school as part of the PDS helped me to form stronger relationships with the school, thereby allowing me easier access to a research site where my dissertation research was supported and valued by the school's faculty.

During my time as doctoral student, I also served as a graduate assistant in the Middle Grades Education program and later in the Office of School Engagement (OSE). The first assistantship provided opportunities to teach undergraduate courses at UGA, observe undergraduate courses taught on-site at a local middle school, and support research being conducted about teacher candidates' experiences in PDSs. The assistantship with the OSE primarily focused on supporting the UGA–CCSD PDS partnership as a whole. My OSE assistantship included working with partnership faculty at both the university and in the local school district, helping to conduct research on the PDS, facilitating state-wide PDS workshops, and observing on-site courses in P–12 settings. Through these experiences, I learned how to initiate successful school–university partnerships and came to understand the immense effort and time needed to build trust and meaningful relationships within those partnerships.

The combined experiences from my assistantships and coursework fostered a strong belief that clinically intensive experiences are vital for pre-service teacher education. This understanding of what teacher education should look like led me to focus my job search on university postings that included building and sustaining school–university partnerships. By focusing on job calls with a school–university partnership component, I knew I would set myself up professionally to teach and conduct teacher education research using an approach in which I believed.

During each job interview, I specifically targeted what I envisioned my role in the partnership to be and identified work that I could be a part of within each partnership based on where each school–university partnership was in its development. While my goal had always been to be a teacher educator who established partnerships with local middle schools, I was able to speak expertly and confidently in job interviews as to how long it could take to develop a successful and sustainable partnership, the steps involved in developing partnerships, and ways to enhance existing partnerships. Without being a part of UGA's PDS, I would not have had a clear vision of what it takes to work in different stages of a partnership as a teacher educator.

After 1 year as a clinically focused, on-site teacher educator, I appreciate even more the coursework, assistantships, and relationship building I experienced as a doctoral student at the University of Georgia. Being a part of a PDS allowed me to hit the ground running as a teacher educator, facilitating the development of equitable school–university partnerships, and teaching on-site courses at a local middle school, while capitalizing on the assets of the site and school community members. As a novice teacher educator, I would not be able to do what I am doing now if I had not been exposed to the many rich, meaningful school–university partnership experiences teacher educators purposefully put in place at the University of Georgia.

Graduate Student Perspectives

Ashley

Like many teacher candidates, my own teacher preparation included fieldwork, but not something I would consider to be clinically intensive or intensive. I experienced a few different school contexts as designated by my program, but I was very much an outsider in each of these. Now, though, as a doctoral student preparing to become a teacher educator, I have been immersed in a program that is clinically intensive by design, as our COE is part of a system-wide PDS. The partnership that exists between the university and the school system provides greater exposure to undergraduate teaching than I ever imagined possible. Through this experience with the partnership, pieces of my own teacher education that may resemble "a kind of patchwork of disparate and discontinuous activities" to some, as discussed by Cochran-Smith (2012), appear more like a beautiful, meticulously pieced quilt from my vantage point.

What better way to prepare teacher educators to engage in clinically intensive teacher preparation than to prepare them clinically, as well? Being in a doctoral program engaged in PDS work provided me the opportunity to assist two professors-in-residence with an on-site course, as well as to engage in field instruction for teacher candidates at schools both inside and outside of our partnership. Preparing for and carrying out class sessions on-site was different from anything I had ever experienced, and is not comparable to the experience of being a graduate assistant for a course on campus. The realities of being in a public school, where middle grades students, practitioners, teacher candidates, and university professors shared common spaces, were addressed in real time rather than hypothetically in the cinder block rooms of the COE. Negotiating the school's bell schedule, district and state testing calendars, and even the weather—we sat through an extended tornado warning as a class, right next to the sixth graders— were all real-time school experiences that impacted not only the teacher candidates I worked with, but me as well. Being on-site on a regular basis highlighted both the challenges and benefits of working in a school. Much like the teacher candidates who want to know how to handle every situation before entering their field placement classrooms, doctoral students want reassurances as well. Sometimes, however, the best way to learn how to be an effective teacher educator is simply "to do," and being in a clinical space afforded me opportunities time and again to eyewitness teacher education in action.

Although working with teacher candidates as part of an on-site course was meaningful, my identity as a teacher educator interested in clinically intensive teacher preparation was first defined in my work with a summer learning program that grew from the partnership work of the university and the school district. Before working with this summer program, I was unaware of the term "professional development school" and agreeing to support the program as my assistantship was a bit of baptism by fire. I learned, much like when I was a classroom teacher, that great flexibility and creativity were required for the success of the program. Working with the camp thrust me into an environment where I worked with professors, teachers, teacher candidates, university personnel, vendors, and camp parents. I existed within the experience completely—there was no classroom time for me to step aside and digest. Being in this environment all the time required me to make decisions with real consequences every second of the day. It was exhausting, and it was exhilarating. With this experience came a crystal-clear vision for my future as a teacher and teacher educator. I know my desire as a future teacher educator is to work where a PDS partnership either exists or is desired.

What solidified my passion for work in the PDS is the community of educators within which I work each day. I am surrounded by people committed to simultaneously working with P–12 and university students on an ongoing basis. These people remain "in the trenches" of public education and stay connected to what is going on in our partnership schools. Beyond assisting with on-site courses, field instruction, and supporting programs, I have worked as a graduate assistant for the OSE. Every day, my work supports our partnership in one way or another, and I feel being part of this team is preparing me for my future work as a teacher educator beyond teaching classes. As a graduate assistant I have engaged in logistical planning, negotiated with faculty members to volunteer their time, communicated our mission to the community, and maintained communication with our affiliated school district. The many skills I have developed through these experiences all help to support the clinical preparation of teachers. Without my varied responsibilities as a graduate assistant I would enter the field of clinically intensive teacher education as naïvely as a first-year teacher who enters the teaching profession with little to no field experience. Unlike those suffering from the anxiety that comes with imposter syndrome, my experiences in the field learning to be a teacher educator help to ameliorate those fears (Murray & Male, 2005). Thanks to my own clinical preparation as a teacher educator, I will be better prepared to provide clinically based experiences for my future teacher candidates, and I have a solid community of colleagues on whom I can rely for advice and support.

My work as a graduate assistant may seem a bit piecemeal to some—like mismatched fabric samples on the floor of the cutting room. However, the context of our PDS has made each of my roles an important component of the quilt of my preparation as a teacher educator. Each conversation acts as a stitch, binding one piece to the next. Up close, the fabric pieces may not seem to coordinate well, but when I take a step back and see the entirety of the quilt, I see the richness that only exists when something is handcrafted, piece by piece, with purpose.

Kajal

On an afternoon in August, a university professor, an experienced elementary school teacher, an advanced doctoral candidate, and I, a new international PhD student, sat together in a classroom in one of the partnership schools. The agenda for our meeting was to collaboratively plan the coming semester's course for a group of teacher candidates. The elementary teacher and advanced doctoral student had already spent the day together planning for their elementary class and now they were brainstorming about how each one could bring their expertise to the on-site teacher education class. Hearing them talk gave me a window into multiple aspects of school systems and universities as institutions. As a new international PhD student and a teaching assistant for the course being discussed, I was conscious of my rich experiences in teacher education in a different country as well as my newness in this school–university–community context. My prior experiences and outsider status made me very intentional about my apprenticeship in learning to teach teachers (Lave & Wenger, 1991) by partnering with schools.

This initiative was a new venture—and I was participating in the making of it, though unsure about how it would unfold. The PDS model is one example of building on the expertise of schools (and community) and university to prepare educators who will teach the children in a variety of specific contexts. These experiences are educative in forging partnerships that are transformational to teacher education (Zeichner, Payne, & Brayko, 2015), and clarify that there are risks worth taking, risks that needed to be pursued and investigated.

Like other graduate students, I was offered many diverse opportunities to work with teacher candidates in this program as a graduate assistant— these opportunities included many complex facets of learning to teach teachers (Cochran-Smith, 2012) such as supporting their work with children in schools, with children in communities, and with their peers in university classrooms.

I have several examples that describe my growth as a teacher educator. First, I had the opportunity to observe, work with, and decompose the practices of the university professor/course instructor as she conducted class each week (Grossman et al., 2009). The professor had designed the course to provide the GTAs with the opportunity to gradually enter into teaching teacher candidates. I was asked to design one session of my choice, relevant to the course content and use the resources of the on-site location. I wanted to build on my earlier experiences of looking at student work (Seidel, 1998). I also had to determine the specifics of my lesson, especially how the lesson would enhance the specific knowledge, skills, and so forth, of our teacher candidates. For our students, this came as a pause—a time to stop, critically look at the students' work, and consider what it was, how it was being produced, what the work meant, and then move to who the student was, why the student was writing/sketching, how good was the work, and how we might help her further. Three years later, as I am now designing the details of this course as the instructor-of-record, this experience of scaffolding learning practices, of teaching to pause and wonder about students and their work, and of building relationships with mentor teachers comes as a valuable resource to me.

Another example of the opportunities afforded to me as a doctoral student working within the clinically intensive space of a PDS is found in my experience with a programmatic innovation implemented soon after my arrival as a doctoral student. In the fall, teacher candidates were offered the opportunity to join classroom teachers during pre-planning before the school year began, and also attend the first full week of school prior to the beginning of the university semester. Some teacher candidates chose to join the practicum later when the university semester officially began. During the semester, we had impressionistic conversations with teacher educators, mentor teachers, and our teacher candidates about how they felt about beginning their field-based practicum earlier or later. To gather more systematic feedback on this innovation, another graduate assistant and I were encouraged by the instructor for the on-site course to conduct a survey study and systematically seek comments of all teacher candidates about their experiences. We analyzed their responses, and that report was instrumental in the decision of other teacher education programs in our academic department to require teacher candidates to participate in pre-planning and the full first week of the school year. We learned that experiencing pre-planning and the first days of school helped our teacher candidates learn valuable lessons about building classroom community, arranging the material space, and building initial relationships with children and their families.

This support and emphasis on inquiring into a programmatic aspect was encouraging, and following this experience my colleague and I engaged in a full-fledged practitioner inquiry into our own development as novice teacher educators and supervisors. The practices of scaffolding graduate teaching assistants in our early childhood program helped me to view myself as an emerging teacher educator who was simultaneously a researcher.

From the survey study to the conceptualization of semester long practitioner inquiry, I have progressed as a PhD candidate to work on an international study of university-based initial teacher education. My experiences as a novice teacher educator have helped me conceptualize my dissertation. Through my experiences in this multifaceted setting I feel that I have become an insider. I know how courses are designed, the intricacies of working in a university–school partnership, the constraints and possibilities of placement practices, and I am vested in the interests of new educators. I am also practicing theorizing teacher education through my teaching, research, and coursework. These experiences make me confident about my future as a teacher educator, scholar, and researcher.

REFLECTIONS ON THE NARRATIVES

The narratives written by Kajal and Ashley paint a detailed picture of both the complexity inherent in clinically intensive settings and the opportunities this complexity provides for the development of expertise in teacher education. Ashley speaks of her "baptism by fire" when she was thrown into a multifaceted role with a new summer program while Kajal describes her position as a new international student suddenly thrust into a group of professionals with varying roles and backgrounds. The worlds they had entered were full of nuance and variation that called upon these beginning doctoral students to consider options and explore possibilities while they simultaneously accomplished tasks for real people in real time. The reassuringly slow pace of graduate classes at a university was notably absent from their experiences in these clinically intensive settings.

Both of these doctoral students engaged in a wider variety of activities than would have been possible in more traditional programs of teacher education. Ashley explains that her involvement in "logistical planning...negotiating between faculty members...communicating our mission to the community and maintaining communication with our affiliated school district" placed her at the center of practice and, she feels, prepared her for the varied roles and responsibilities of a teacher educator. Kajal's account of her experiences includes the initial design of a classroom experience for teacher candidates and the implementation of a small research project, both conducted within the context of the PDS. In addition, she highlights the ways in which these experiences paved the way for her current dissertation research and for her responsibility as the instructor-of-record for an on-site methods course.

In her narrative, Melissa examines the ways in which her identity as a teacher educator was influenced by her experiences as a doctoral student in a clinically intensive setting that situated doctoral studies, assistantships, and research in the heart of a school district–university partnership. She states that her experiences as a doctoral student in the PDS "fostered a strong belief that clinically intensive experiences are vital for pre-service teacher education." As a result, she sought out higher education positions that "focused on building and sustaining school-university partnerships."

A critical aspect of developing one's identity as a teacher educator is conducting research. According to Melissa, the research she conducted in a PDS middle school had a profound impact on her development as a teacher educator. She did not merely come up with a research topic and then seek approval to conduct the research. Instead, the research grew out of conversations, as part of an on-site doctoral course, that she had with school faculty about the school's needs, issues, and concerns. This inquiry approach to developing a research agenda led to a study that was "supported and valued by the school's faculty" and that addressed a genuine school need. Participating in doctoral coursework that was connected to the life of a real middle school helped Melissa realize that her inquiry work with schools "should capitalize on the assets of the site and school community members."

All three novice teacher educators found value in the collaborative nature of the PDS. Their engagement with PDS communities of practice as doctoral students taught them how to listen to and learn from school partners, as well as interrogate their own practice, support the learning of teacher candidates, and initiate meaningful research projects.

CONCLUSIONS

Our initial question was: How is the preparation of teacher educators as practitioners, scholars, and researchers facilitated, supported, challenged, or enhanced by work in a clinically intensive setting like a PDS? The answer we have found is that the complexity of clinically intensive settings affords future teacher educators the opportunity to develop and thrive. We used complexity theory as a lens with which to view narratives describing the experiences of veteran and novice teacher educators and, thus, were able to see the power and potential of clinically intensive settings. The narratives all describe a multifaceted context with many different interactions and processes at play. In addition, the narratives highlighted relationships, variety, and authenticity, characteristics that are consistent with the perspective of complexity theory (Cochran-Smith, Ell, Ludlow, Grudnoff, et al., 2014). For example, Melissa explicitly described the ways in which participation in the work of the PDS supported her ability to understand and develop "trust and meaningful relationships within...partnerships." Complexity theory also recognizes the variety of people and places that create educational settings and the varied nature of the teaching and learning process. This vision is evident in all four narratives: Kathy described the value of teacher candidates learning about teaching and learning beyond the four walls of a classroom, Melissa and Kajal explored the ways teacher candidates learn from experienced practicing teachers in planned and informal ways, and Ashley drew a picture of the community of practice within which she developed her identity as a teacher educator. In each case, the writer was attuned to the specifics of a learning situation and the multiple factors that created it. Finally, the narratives written by Ashley and Kathy make note of the authentic nature of clinically intensive teacher preparation and point out the fact that connections between theory and practice can be made in "real time."

Although there are many logistical and dynamic challenges to preparing teacher candidates in clinically intensive settings, the challenges are fundamental and, in fact, form the building blocks with which we, as veteran teacher educators, scaffold the growth of our doctoral students and novice teacher educators. In essence, the challenges *are* the support. Without experiencing real problems in real time our doctoral students would not be prepared for their future work as teacher educators. In contrast, when we immerse our doctoral students in clinically intensive settings, we model an appreciation for the complexity of the daily work of classroom teachers and, more importantly, we create situations in which they, like all engaged learners, gain new understanding through action. Thus, the rich variety inherent in clinically intensive spaces enables veteran teacher educators to offer highly mentored and supported learning opportunities for doctoral students.

Despite the clear advantages of preparing future teacher educators within the framework of a clinically intensive setting, there are those who would caution that time spent "in the field" may detract from the ability of doctoral students to engage in thoughtful and rigorous research. We would argue that the opposite is, in fact, true. It is clear to us that participation in school-based settings provides our doctoral students with access to a more fertile and relevant research context.

There are both theoretical and practical reasons for the value and import of research conducted within practice-based spaces. From the vantage point of theory, research that emanates directly from problems of practice has the potential to disrupt the troubling binary between scholarship and teacher preparation. We have suggested that the very real complexities and challenges of practice-based preparation are not impediments to the growth and learning of doctoral students, but rather form the foundation for a sophisticated understanding of the processes of learning to teach. Similarly, the artificially constructed binary between practice and research is problematic (Dinkelman, 2011) because as Cochran-Smith and Lytle (2009) have pointed out "in all educational settings, practice, which is deeply contextual, relational and interdisciplinary, is also and always theoretical and interpretive" (p. 134). As a result, research and practice are, in reality, dependent upon one another (Zeichner, 1999).

Further, the reification of the theory/practice binary fosters the belief that one must choose to act or to think. Nonetheless, it is clear from the scholarship on reflective practice (Cochran-Smith & Lytle, 2009; Darling-Hammond, 2006; Schon, 1983; Zeichner & Liston, 2014) that competent teaching practice, at all levels, requires thought and action, and that the assumption of a binary choice is counterproductive to quality in practice, research, and theory.

Although research and practice are inextricably intertwined, this may not always be evident to the casual or uninformed observer. Engaging in practical work may have the ironic effect of obscuring the very principles and values that form the foundation for that work. Because the day-to-day work of teaching is powerfully present, the theories, philosophies, and ideologies that undergird the choices involved in daily practice may fade into the background. These abstract concepts do not disappear, but to many it may appear as if they have.

Thus, the improvement of research in teacher education depends not on moving beyond the world of practice, but on viewing that practice world clearly and through multiple lenses. The clear vision of practice necessary for powerful research requires close attention to both big picture principles and many small important details. Research within a clinically intensive context has the potential to make explicit the conceptual bases of exemplary practice that are so often hidden beneath the complex web of practice.

The narratives shared by the authors of this chapter present clear and practical examples of the intertwined path from engaged practice to powerful research. Inquiry questions which emanated from the very real concerns of teachers, parents, administrators, doctoral students, and faculty members became the centerpiece of research projects for both Kajal and Melissa. Their efforts to clarify underlying principles of practice while contributing to that practice were facilitated by the trusting relationships which developed over time among the extended community of practice. Efforts to disentangle research from practice in these stories of growth and insight will prove futile, if not harmful, to the ultimate goal of productive learning for all.

We have concluded that preparing teacher educators in a PDS or other clinically intensive settings enables them to learn to support teacher candidates, engage in meaningful scholarship and, through their stance as educators and inquirers, reject the notion that they must choose to be one or the other. We have found that preparing teacher educators within clinically intensive settings has, through effort and intention, made it possible to avoid the trap posed by viewing research and practice as opposing activities. Instead, by accepting and admiring the complex interactions among all aspects of the work, we and our doctoral students have witnessed a dynamic synergy that, like the pattern of a quilt, has emerged to enrich our lives and our work.

Discussion Questions

1. As noted in the chapter, Goethe said, "Knowing is not enough, we must apply. Willing is not enough, we must do" (Institute of Medicine, 2010). How can you take the experiences described in the four narratives shared in this chapter and apply them to your own context?

2. As researchers and practitioners, we use theory to frame and ground our work, noting "complexity is not only unavoidable, but intellectually sustaining and ultimately useful." How do the narratives exemplify complexity theory? In what ways, if any, do the narratives seem inconsistent with this theoretical perspective? What connections can you make between complexity theory and your own practice?

3. Melissa, Ashley, and Kajal share the impact of working in a PDS on the development of their respective identities as teacher educators. How can university faculty leverage relationships within their communities to expand and deepen opportunities for the development of teacher educator identities for their doctoral students? What factors contributed to the development of your own identity as a teacher educator?

4. Despite the challenges, the authors of this chapter express a strong belief in the power of clinically intensive settings for teacher preparation. What challenges have you experienced in working in such settings? Do you share the authors' commitments? Why or why not?

REFERENCES

Andrews, G., & Thompson, K. F. (2016). Relationships and context matter: Tales from a middle school/university partnership. In P. Howell, J. Carpenter, & J. Jones (Eds.), *Clinical preparation at the middle level: Practices and possibilities* (pp. 5–34). Charlotte, NC: Information Age.

Andrews, G., Thompson, K. F., Naughton, C., & Waters, M. (2017). Genius hour inquiry initiative: Ongoing, innovative, reciprocal, professional learning for teacher and teacher candidates. *School-University Partnerships, 10*(4), 83–94.

Ball, D. L., & Forzani, F. M. (2009). The work of teaching and the challenge for teacher education. *Journal of Teacher Education, 60*(5), 497–511.

Bullough, R. V. (2005). Being and becoming a mentor: School-based teacher educators and teacher educator identity. *Teaching and Teacher Education, 21*(2), 143–155.

Caruso, J. J. (1998). What cooperating teacher case studies reveal about their phases of development as supervisors of student teachers. *European Journal of Teacher Education, 21*(1), 109–119.

Cochran-Smith, M. (2012). Composing a research life. *Action in Teacher Education, 34*(2), 99–110.

Cochran-Smith, M., Ell, F., Ludlow, L., Grudnoff, L., & Aitken, G. (2014). The challenge and promise of complexity theory for teacher education research. *Teachers College Record, 116*(5), 1–38.

Cochran-Smith, M., Ell, F., Grudnoff, L., Ludlow, L., Haigh, M., & Hill, M. (2014). When complexity theory meets critical realism: A platform for research on initial teacher education. *Teacher Education Quarterly, 41*(1), 105–122.

Cochran-Smith, M., & Lytle, S. L. (2009). *Inquiry as stance: Practitioner research for the next generation.* New York, NY: Teachers College Press.

Dana, N. F., & Yendol-Hoppey, D. (2014). *The reflective educator's guide to classroom research: Learning to teach and teaching to learn through practitioner inquiry* (3rd ed.). Thousand Oaks, CA: Corwin Press.

Darling-Hammond, L. (2005). *Professional development schools: Schools for developing a profession.* New York, NY: Teachers College Press.

Darling-Hammond, L. (2006). Constructing 21st-century teacher education. *Journal of Teacher Education, 57*(3), 300–314.

Dewey, J. (1938). *Experience and education.* New York, NY: Touchstone.

Dinkelman, T. (2011). Forming a teacher educator identity: Uncertain standards, practice and relationships. *Journal of Education for Teaching, 37*(3), 309–323.

Duckworth, E. R. (2006). *"The having of wonderful ideas" and other essays on teaching and learning.* New York, NY: Teachers College Press.

Grossman, P., Compton, C., Igra, D., Ronfeldt, M., Shahan, E., & Williamson, P. (2009). Teaching practice: A cross-professional perspective. *Teachers College Record, 111*(9), 2055–2100.

Hollins, E. (2011). Teacher preparation for quality teaching. *Journal of Teacher Education, 62*(4), 395–407.

Institute of Medicine. (2010). *Redesigning continuing education in the health professions.* Washington, DC: The National Academies Press.

Juliani, A. J. (2015). *Inquiry and innovation in the classroom: Using 20% time, genius hour, and PBL to drive student success.* New York, NY: Routledge.

Kennedy, M. (2016). Parsing the practice of teaching. *Journal of Teacher Education, 67*(1), 6–16.

Korth, B. B., Erickson, L., & Hall, K. M. (2009). Defining teacher educator through the eyes of classroom teachers. *Professional Educator, 33*(1), 16–27.

Lave, J., & Wenger, E. (1991). *Situated learning: Legitimate peripheral participation.* Cambridge, MA: Cambridge University Press.

Maiers, A. (2010). *The passion-driven classroom: A framework for teaching and learning.* New York, NY: Routledge.

Murray, J., & Male, T. (2005). Becoming a teacher educator: Evidence from the field. *Teaching and Teacher Education, 21*(1), 125–142.

National Association for Professional Development Schools. (2008). *What it means to be a professional development school.* Retrieved from NAPDS website: https://napds.org/wp-content/uploads/2014/10/Nine-Essentials.pdf

National Council for Accreditation of Teacher Education. (2010). *Transforming teacher education through clinical practice: A national strategy to prepare effective teachers*. Report of the Blue Ribbon Panel on Clinical Preparation and Partnerships for Improved Student Learning. Washington, DC: Author.

Rust, F. O., & Clift, R. T. (2015). Moving from recommendations to action in preparing professional educators. In E. R. Hollins, *Rethinking field experience in preservice teacher preparation: Meeting new challenges for accountability* (pp. 47–69). New York, NY: Routledge.

Seidel, S. (1998). Wondering to be done: The collaborative assessment conference. In D. Allen (Ed.), *Assessing student learning: From grading to understanding* (pp. 21–39). New York, NY: Teachers College Press.

Schon, D. A. (1983). *The reflective practitioner: How professionals think in action*. New York, NY: Basic Books.

Stairs, A. J. (2011). Preservice teacher learning in a PDS. In J. L. Nath, I. N. Guadarrama, & J. Ramsey (Eds.), *Investigating university–school partnerships* (pp. 95–118). Charlotte, NC: Information Age.

Zeichner, K. (1999). The new scholarship in teacher education. *Educational Researcher, 28*(9), 4–15.

Zeichner, K. M., & Liston, D. P. (2014). *Reflective teaching: An introduction* (2nd ed.). New York, NY: Routledge.

Zeichner, K., Payne, K. A., & Brayko, K. (2015). Democratizing teacher education. *Journal of Teacher Education, 66*(2), 122–135.

Zepeda, S. J. (2015). *Job-embedded professional development: Support, collaboration, and learning in schools*. New York, NY: Routledge.

CHAPTER 4

PREPARING THE TEACHER EDUCATOR

Negotiating the Tensions of Teacher Educator Preparation Within the Research Institution

Lara H. Hebert
University of Illinois at Urbana-Champaign

Lindsayanne (Annie) Insana
Tennessee Department of Education

Alexis L. Jones
Eastern Illinois University

Meghan A. Kessler
University of Illinois Springfield

Annie's story: I remember once, years ago when I was a new graduate student, I was making small talk with an acquaintance who asked me what I

Preparing the Next Generation of Teacher Educators for Clinical Practice, pages 73–92
Copyright © 2019 by Information Age Publishing
All rights of reproduction in any form reserved.

was studying in my program. I spent a few minutes discussing some of the classes I was taking and the articles I was reading until I noticed her eyes begin to glaze over. I stopped short and said, "I hope to teach teachers someday." She paused for a moment and then responded, "Hmm . . . I never really thought that teachers needed to be taught!"

This comment still resonates with Annie years later, and it rings true for the rest of the authors as well. Working in the field of teacher education, we often encounter those who view teacher education as a "self-evident activity" (Hollins, Luna, & Lopez, 2014, p. 118). To label teacher education as a self-evident activity assumes that the practice of teaching teachers can be done naturally, without careful study or intent. Essentially, this perspective is an extension of Lortie's (1975) description of the apprenticeship of observation which is a term used in teacher training to describe teachers who teach the way they have been taught. Teacher education as a self-evident activity supposes that preparing teachers of teachers is unnecessary or that someone who was a strong K–12 teacher will naturally be a strong teacher educator.

The literature is full of examples of how and why the practice of teaching teachers is difficult (Labaree, 2006; Lortie, 1975), and the field has dispelled many of the myths about the simplicity of teaching. However, it is time to turn that same kind of attention to the development of teacher educators. For those who know the field well, teacher education is anything but an obvious activity. It is a practice laden with assumptions that requires rigorous discussion, particularly when we shift focus from teaching teacher candidates to teaching teacher educators.

The field of teacher education is highly complex and requires a shift in thinking that is not only tolerant of, but thrives on multiple and often conflicting, models, theories, and paths toward successful preparation of teachers and teacher educators (Rust, 2017). This chapter offers a discussion of tensions, defined as tendencies that are held in conflict with one another, in an attempt to make sense of the complexity within the field (Dewey, 1895). The authors—each a relatively new teacher educator herself—contribute personal narratives that bring a relatability to each of the tensions. Each tension and narrative argues for reasons to push back against the idea that teacher educator practice is self-evident and illustrates the complexity of what it takes to be a teacher and what it takes to become a teacher educator. The chapter concludes with recommendations meant to inform future teacher educators as well as institutions that prepare teacher educators.

NARRATIVE AND SELF-STUDY

This chapter highlights the tensions that the four of us negotiated as we worked within a teacher education program housed in a research-focused university. In each section below, we used *narrative* to highlight the complexity of educating pre-service teachers and our own education as teacher educators. Clandinin (2013) described how narrative honors and illuminates the complex, contextual knowledge of teachers. Similarly, we have used narrative to sketch scenarios that highlight the tensions we encountered during and after our graduate programs.

We also reference examples of *self-study* as a way to consider the difficult questions arising from our experiences. Self-study has been used to examine undergraduate teacher preparation (Swartz, 2003) and teacher educator preparation (e.g., Allen, Park Rogers, & Borowski, 2016; Johnston-Parsons, Lee, & Thomas, 2007; Zollers, Albert, & Cochran-Smith, 2000). For this chapter we reflect on a number of ways we questioned, investigated, and addressed needs within our college classrooms.

AUTHOR POSITIONALITY

A chapter relying on narrative and self-study would be incomplete without addressing how our thoughts on these issues inform and are informed by our unique and overlapping experiences. For example, all four of us are graduates from the curriculum and instruction doctoral program at the University of Illinois at Urbana-Champaign. The University of Illinois is a land-grant university with a focus on research, teaching, and public engagement. Our experiences at the university were situated within a particular time and context. The university and its college of education had recently experienced significant reduction in funding due to a multi-year state budget impasse. Additionally, a number of faculty had retired and were not replaced. Some of these faculty had focused on teacher education as a primary research endeavor. The remaining, minimal resources (both financial and human) were spread thin among departments, including teacher education. Reduction in funding and faculty necessitated a heavier reliance on graduate teaching assistants. Our narratives are not intended to *call out* the shortcomings of any particular institution, rather they serve to illuminate what we see as necessary elements of an environment supportive of teacher educator preparation.

Two of us, Lara and Alexis, had doctoral timelines that did not overlap, but we were colleagues in more than one professional arena, prior to graduate school. All four of us worked at one time with new teachers as part of the Illinois New Teacher Collaborative, but were employed by that organization at different times. All four of us had years of teaching experience: Annie and Alexis taught at the elementary level, Lara at the middle level, and Meghan at the middle and secondary level. We all taught courses as teaching assistants during our doctoral programs. Annie and Alexis continued to teach courses at the university immediately following graduation, and Lara provided professional learning expertise for a national teachers' association before returning to teacher education at the university. At the time of this writing, we all self-identify as novice teacher educators, a voice often missing from the literature on teacher education. Our experiences are representative of one type of doctoral-granting institution, yet our research areas are all different, as are our areas of expertise. Just as we tell our student teachers that they bring all of themselves (perspectives, backgrounds, biases, etc.) into their K–12 classrooms, we bring ourselves into this chapter and the current body of research on teacher education.

THE TENSIONS

As the four of us discussed our work as teacher educators within the research institution, we grounded our narratives in the questions and situations that emerged as well as challenged us during and immediately following our doctoral programs. Informed by Holladay (2017), we describe these experiences as *tensions*:

> [Tension is] the energy generated by a system as it navigates and negotiates differences. As tension of difference builds over time, system conditions shift to relieve that tension, leading to system change. Some changes damage or stunt the system's growth or productivity. Other system changes can release positive, productive energy and propel the system into higher levels of functioning. (para. 3)

Holladay's discussion of *tension within a system* encouraged us to consider how discomfort or feeling conflicted can be a force for change.

As we considered the tensions at play in our own experiences, we found four areas in which we negotiated differences between our goals as teacher educators and the systems in place at the research institution. In the section, "Connecting Research and Teaching Within Teacher Education," we address the pull between studying teacher education programmatically and learning *how* to be a teacher educator. Here we wonder how much of teacher educator preparation should be focused on teacher educator learning (research) and how much should be about teacher candidate learning (teaching). In "Navigating Institutional Expectations of Expertise," we confront the difficulty of establishing our identities within contexts that value certain parts of the whole teacher educator more than others. When is it important to be a teacher education specialist as opposed to a content specialist? While the phrase, "Practicing What You Preach," is at times overused in well-meaning advice, it is particularly apropos to the field of teacher education, where we *preach* and *practice* with pre-service teachers who will do the same with their own students. Finally, we focused on "Learning With and From Others" in order to highlight the importance and difficulty of finding excellent mentors, peers, and partners with whom to collaborate. We consider how teacher educator program structures and contexts allow for relationship-building and the modeling of this partnership for future educators.

In the four sections below, we introduce each tension by using the literature of learning to teach, teacher education, and self-study for teacher educators. This is followed by a brief narrative, presented in italics to differentiate it from the rest of the text. Each narrative illustrates the tension as it played out in our personal realities. As described above, tensions offer opportunities for action, and with this in mind, we conclude each section with questions the tension raises for the field of teacher education and the preparation of teacher educators.

Connecting Research and Teaching Within Teacher Education

As teacher educators, we must help our candidates begin to comprehend the complexity of teaching. A key component of this process is helping candidates to understand why it is necessary "to be both learners of learning and learners of teaching at the same time" (Loughran, Korthagen, & Russell, 2008, p. 409). Teacher educators help candidates understand the inseparable nature of theory and practice, in a constant dance of one informing the other to best facilitate student learning. Considering this complexity in relation to teacher educator preparation, we find ourselves in a programmatic tension between the graduate programs where we study and research various aspects of teacher education, and the responsibilities embedded within the practice of teaching teachers in the role of teaching assistant.

Such programmatic responsibilities inform teacher educator identity development. At institutions that focus on high research production, a PhD student's programmatic responsibilities prioritize learning to be researchers first with research methods courses, research assistantships, writing, and other program benchmarks. These responsibilities often demand a great deal of graduate students, diminishing their capacity to engage in other developmental opportunities, such as mentoring teacher candidates and establishing relationships with K–12 partners (Intrator & Kunzman, 2009).

Furthermore, novice teacher educators are mentored and supervised by faculty who are themselves under pressure to produce research. As their mentors work to achieve a robust research agenda, the responsibility of teaching undergraduates often falls to graduate students. Therefore, graduate teaching assistants are essential partners for the teaching of undergraduate courses and supervising student teachers. This reliance has its benefits for graduate students, of course, as it is often a financial and professional necessity. However, the time consuming demands of teaching conflicts with the demands of a rigorous program of study. In this context, formation of a teacher educator identity can be neglected, as it is often concurrent with learning about the myriad expectations of academia (Loughran, 2011).

For teacher educators who are in the early stages of identity formation and transformation, muddled messages are communicated about what professional experiences are *best* and how to balance priorities. While told their research programs are key, they are also given a great deal of responsibility for teaching the college's teacher candidates. As Loughranet al. (2008) asserted, "learning about teaching involves continuously conflicting and competing demands" (p. 409). The same can be said for learning about teaching teachers. Just as their pre-service candidates are making the transition from student to teacher—attempting to balance their coursework, edTPA, and teaching responsibilities—graduate students are attempting to navigate the expectations and practices of academia.

In our doctoral programs, we simultaneously studied teacher education while also learning to teach future educators. While one practice was not necessarily better than another, they were sufficiently different to result in a pull or tension between them. Rather than viewing the two practices as an either–or dichotomy, we see these as two poles on a continuum of practice. We rarely sit at one extreme or the other. Even so, for all of the authors of this chapter, we found the focus of our program to be overwhelmingly and consistently weighted toward the study of teacher education side of this continuum with minimal programmatic focus on learning to be teacher educators.

Lara's story: During my first year as a doctoral candidate, I held great interest in how teachers grew into their use of educational technology in classrooms. This interest was informed by my previous 13 years as a sixth grade science, math, and English language arts teacher who viewed the use of authentic applications of new technologies in the classroom as a necessity for students heading into the 21st century. As a result, my course of study included classes such as, "Learning and Human Development Within Educational Technology" and "Computer Mediated Communication." My course projects focused on peer-reviewed literature on models for teaching educational technology to teacher candidates and initiatives using technology as a tool for teacher professional learning. At the same time, my advisor encouraged me to take a teaching assistantship for the elementary science methods course. Teaching this class was a way to bring in a small income, to maintain a tuition waiver, and to model what I saw as quality instruction. I took a syllabus with few hands-on opportunities to engage with technology and added lessons where students practiced using digital sensors and probes and designed webquests for use in their classrooms. As I look back on this first year as a graduate student, I realize that I never made a conscious connection between my studies of technology in teacher education with my experiences teaching technology in teacher education courses. One was my research and the other was my job. I wonder, what would it have taken for me to notice that this experience was important to my development as a teacher educator as well as being tied to my research interests?

A vast majority of faculty positions require combined expertise in research and teaching. Just as a teacher educator's role is to help candidates bridge the theory and practice divide, it is important to consider how teacher education doctoral programs help future faculty to make connections between their research on teacher education with the practice of being teacher educators. This tension leads us to wonder, "How might we better connect research and teaching within teacher education to help novice teacher educators navigate and integrate the two rather than be caught in the middle?"

Navigating Institutional Expectations of Expertise

An exploration of the history of teacher education indicates that our out-of-balance experiences with research and practice are not unique. Historically, universities provided the training of high school teachers and administrators, and they were the source for research of teaching and learning; while normal schools provided the teaching of large numbers of elementary teachers (Labaree, 2008). As normal schools grew into regional universities, teacher education began to be pitted against theory and research goals. As Labaree argued, universities chose "rigor over relevance" (p. 293). Research in and of itself, especially in education, brought limited funding to sustain the institution. Preparation of teachers provided a source for reliable income for the institution (Labaree, 2006). Lanier and Little made note of a "common knowledge that professors in the arts and sciences risk a loss of academic respect" when they exhibited an interest in educating teachers (as cited in Labaree, 2006, p. 34). This historical context is relevant to current trends in institutional expectations of expertise.

Loughran asserted that self-study is how we hold ourselves accountable as researchers and practitioners of teacher education, that "to genuinely be scholars of teaching, we need to be able to demonstrate that we learn through the challenges created by our own actions in our practice" (p. 17, in Samaras, 2011). Loughran et al. (2008) made the case for the following foundational principle for teacher education: "Learning about teaching is enhanced through (student) teacher research" (p. 411). As teacher educators and teacher education researchers, we agree that this principle might just as well apply to the preparation of teacher educators, but we find this concept at tension with the institutional context of a research university. Self-study is often treated as less valuable to the field than studying other forms of research, questioning whether it is truly more than a form of personal reflection (Loughran & Northfield, 1998, p. 8). Samaras (2011) described self-study as "critical collaborative inquiry, a systematic research process that can lead to knowledge production" (p. 10). Danielewicz (2001) argued that becoming a teacher means more than adopting a role. Instead, teachers are in the process of constructing identities, finding influence and inspiration in their unique contexts—"the process of teaching, at once so complicated and deep, involves the self" (p. 9). Similarly, new teacher educators are in the process of constructing identities as they learn the skills, knowledge, and dispositions relevant to teaching future teachers. This identity work is as complex as the work of teaching itself, and intersects significantly with institutional values and expectations.

Among the challenging elements of this identity development is the question of specialization. Not unlike the pressure our candidates experience in choosing their content area or grade level specializations, PhD students are expected to choose a research area very early in their programs. As novice researchers interested in the professional growth of teachers, we each struggled with this pressure. Some of us sensed that our research must be focused on a content area separate from teacher education. It seemed that teacher education as a research endeavor was not specific enough; that teacher education as a field should be self-evident. For others, research in teacher education was fully supported while the assumption of content area expertise for instructional purposes was self-evident. This tension became especially apparent during the job search. Pressured, in part, by financial necessity, our university and others sought to hire scholars who specialize in a particular content area (e.g., STEM, literacy), and the emphasis on teacher education was diminished.

Lara's story: In the final year of my graduate program, a colleague familiar with my interest in technology and professional learning called my attention to a job opening in the professional learning division at the National Council of Teachers of English (NCTE). As the search team provided details of the work, I found myself getting more and more excited by the position.

I remember thinking, "This is what professional learning should look like!" I took the professional development position, developing online and hybrid learning modules, writing and developing grants, collaborating across content area associations, and building relationships with educators across the country. What I didn't realize was how a position I took for purposes of applying my expertise in teacher professional learning would later be interpreted by future employers as a position of content area expertise.

After a few years, I realized that I wanted to return to teaching teachers. I reached out to my graduate school mentors for advice. I vividly remember sharing a dinner with one of my advisors. I told her my story and how I missed teaching. "I've been thinking a lot about this. I want to return to higher education, especially teaching teacher candidates. What would it take for me to get back there?"

As all good mentors do, my question was met with questions of her own. "Have you been publishing and presenting?"

"Yes."

"What are your research interests?"

"Integration of technology in classrooms and professional learning."

"What will you teach?"

Pause.

Uncertainty crept in. As I responded with, "Math or science methods, general elementary methods, middle school philosophy," I realized that I just spent 5 years at the national organization for English teachers. Even though I went there to practice my teacher education interests, others will only see the content area of the organization. My mentor responded with a similar reflection about the perception that comes from seeing NCTE on my curriculum vitae. While I like English language arts, my heart lies in teaching middle grades math and science.

We continued our conversation about the work necessary to make a shift back into academia. I am so thankful for the frankness of that conversation. But that sudden feeling of uncertainty I experienced at dinner that night left me wondering, "Why didn't I think of this before? Why is this the first time I'm hearing about this need to pick a content focus?" As I entered the teacher education job market, the assumption that I'm best suited for teaching English language arts coursework held true as anticipated.

We have each experienced this pressure to specialize in a particular content area. Job listings often focused on finding, for example, a science education researcher. The message from the job market implied that teacher education is not currently at the forefront of a profession tasked with preparing teachers. This is not to imply that content area specialization is self-evident or will take care of itself, but to argue that teacher education expertise deserves more significant placement in teacher education programs. Recognizing the importance of teacher education expertise would allow institutions to better support the identity development of novice teacher educators.

This tension leads us to wonder, "How then do teacher education doctoral programs better support the early career teacher educator's identity exploration and formation in a manner that recognizes the whole teacher educator—the teacher educator, the researcher of teacher education, the content specialist—within institutions that favor one over others?"

Practicing What You Preach

When we focus in on the practice of teaching teachers, we note the irony of college classrooms where instructors lead a lesson on the benefits of cooperative learning by showing a PowerPoint presentation. As teacher educators, we may even wince when reflecting on those courses that address student-led instruction, just after the agenda was established in class and all the readings designated for the semester. What practices do we describe as opposed to model? Do our students leave our classrooms feeling this disconnect between our words and demonstrated teaching techniques; or worse, do they enter their own classrooms doing what we do, rather than what we say? Darling-Hammond (1999) wrote:

> Uninspired teaching methods: for prospective teachers to learn active, hands-on and minds-on teaching, they must have experienced it for themselves. But traditional lecture and recitation still dominates in much of higher education, where faculty do not practice what they preach. (p. 612)

One arena where this conflict between modeling and assigning is at play is when we examine the nature of teaching—a complex and holistic profession—as opposed to a series of technical tasks. Possibly because of the demands of classroom teaching, student teachers come to our classrooms wanting to know *how to do something* in their classrooms (e.g., arrange their space to best suit their students' needs, differentiate, manage challenging students). This technical view of teaching leaves out quite a bit of what confounds teachers and teacher educators including their own difficult emotions in the classroom, the collaboration necessary for innovative practices, and the development of personal and professional theories of education. There is a tension between a practical view of teacher preparation (developing a toolkit of strategies) and a more holistic, humanist view of teacher development.

Alexis's story: In the final year of my doctoral program, feeling fairly confident about my instructional decisions and relationships with students, I was confronted with a student who confounded me and her other instructors. She did not struggle with the coursework but with time management and prioritizing her schedule. As a result, her assignments were excellent, but often late. She kept a brutal schedule, sleeping as few as 3 hours per night in order to get her work done. As a result, she occasionally fell asleep in class. I had so many questions about the best way to facilitate her success. Do I give her extensions and grade the quality of the work, or should her issues with time management affect her grade? How much should the decisions of her other instructors impact my actions? How can I respect who she is while still fulfilling the goals of my class?

Because of work with UIUC professors and readings by the aforementioned authors, I developed a strong belief that teaching is a unique and human task (Jones, 2017). Human beings are not widgets, nor do they respond the same ways to our content and methods. I felt, and conveyed to my preservice teachers, that teachers cannot provide responsive instruction without recognizing the humanness of students. I began to ask myself whether the ethic of care recommended and practiced in elementary classrooms had an equally valid place in the college classroom. How do we prepare future teachers, those who will be responsible for the well-being of hundreds of children, while also respecting and honoring their personhood? Because of these wonderings, I began a year-long self-study of the different types of noticing, questioning, worry, guilt, and relationships that exist in the college classroom between professor and student. In essence, how do I practice what I preach in my college classrooms? If I recommend that they be flexible, shouldn't I then be flexible?

Loughran (2006) suggested there are major weaknesses in the knowledge base of teacher educators. *Teaching student teachers* is distinct from *teaching student teachers about teaching.* The former involves a more technical approach, a focus on *how to,* while the latter requires an awareness of the field of teaching itself, including such topics as teacher identity, emotion, and activism. As teacher educators, it is important that we know our field of study and our practice so we can go beyond *technical-rational* or *tips and tricks* approaches to teaching about teaching. Teacher education programs can emphasize community and school connections, reconsidering what counts as expert knowledge in teacher preparation (Zeichner, Payne, & Brayko, 2015). Loughran et al. (2008) described this as "a shift in focus from the curriculum to the learner" (p. 410).

This tension leads us to wonder, what would teacher education programs look like if the *whole future teacher educator* became the focus of the doctoral program? More specifically, how might the system provide opportunities and resources that allow teacher educators to grow and develop their practices of teaching teachers to be better models of what we expect and recommend our candidates carry into their own classrooms?

Learning With and From Others

Part of the complexity in learning to be a teacher educator involves the ways student teachers, teachers, and teacher educators learn with and from others. As the four of us have reflected upon more than once, we felt fortunate to have been mentored by a few select individuals and to have found ourselves in a community of practice with our peers. Within this community, we share a common understanding that in order to be effective teacher educators, we must never lose perspective of the realities of the classroom. Often we hear from candidates that professors are too far removed from the classroom to understand the daily challenges and demands.

When we put the learner at the center of all we do, we must acknowledge that teacher candidates are our learners, and a key component of their learning involves field classrooms. Therefore, to leave local school partners out of our community of practice would be problematic. High-quality teacher preparation requires deep partnerships between districts and universities. These partnerships should prioritize a shared understanding of *what* new teachers need to learn and develop a common language and approach that explicitly connects *how* teachers learn in teacher education (Toon & Jensen, 2017). Creating and maintaining these partnerships is difficult (Allen, Butler-Mader, & Smith, 2010; Toon & Jensen, 2017). For example, teacher education programs depend upon schools in order to provide pre-service students with their required field experiences. Additionally, faculty at research universities depend upon schools for research purposes. This relationship of dependence often creates an uneasy atmosphere between K–12 schools and universities.

Teacher education programs *need* schools, but also risk something in being associated (Labaree, 2008). In our experiences, schools may, at times, establish practices that are not recommended by individuals in higher education, and even when unspoken, this creates tension between K–12 schools and universities. Featherstone (2007) explained:

> Staffed with graduate students, temporary and part-time faculty and with few resources to develop field placements, U.S. teacher certification programs are the Cinderellas of the American university. Ideas and money are rarely spent on coordinating what is learned on campus with what goes on in schools. (p. 210)

From the university perspective, how can they place pre-service teachers in schools that are initiating practices they would not recommend in their content classes? From a school's perspective, why should they accept pre-service teachers when their classroom practices will be criticized by professors? Teacher educators find themselves in the middle of this tension; hoping to negotiate the best solution for the K–12 student, pre-service teacher, and teacher educator-researcher.

Another way to imagine this relationship might be to consider schools and universities *engaging with* one another. Zeichner (2010) recommended creating a hybrid space, where there existed a less hierarchical way of conceptualizing the education of pre-service teachers. However, that would involve reconsidering the university's deficit view of schools toward a belief that higher education can learn from and with their K–12 partners.

Annie's story: Early on in my doctoral preparation, I had the opportunity to participate in a two-year, college-wide teacher education redesign, which focused on determining the overall content and experiences for a progressive curriculum across each of our programs. I worked as a graduate assistant for an interim teacher education director who led the charge. The first few months of the redesign showed great promise of real change. Faculty and staff from various departments across the college collaborated with local school partners to create a vision statement for the college and to determine how to achieve this vision for distinctive and distinguishable graduates. Initial conversations were optimistic and fruitful.

Shortly before the first year of the redesign came to a close, the Illinois State Board of Education published new Professional Teaching Standards. Quickly, the vibe of the redesign turned from innovation to compliance. The state requirements necessitated alignment to the new standards, which unintentionally abated the creative programmatic ideas generated from the collaborative work groups. Eventually, many members of the redesign became frustrated with the slow pace of change and the tediousness of scheduling, and the collaborative work groups eventually shrank to a just few members of the college. As a result, the relationships that already existed between the college and local schools continued on in the same manner as before (i.e., placing candidates with mentor teachers for clinical experiences; individual research projects conducted by a faculty member with K–12 classrooms). Few mutually beneficial partnerships that would significantly improve the preparation of the candidates were built.

Without conscious efforts to partner with one another and collaboratively identify strengths and needs, candidate engagement with the local schools becomes a matter of luck. Loughran et al. (2008) made this case for institutional collaboration, but extended this learning partnership to include the student teachers as well:

> While school-university cooperation is often seen as the broad goal, it is easy to overlook the teacher candidate who is passing through...Ironically, if we were to view the temporarily present teacher candidate as the one with the most to gain from closer cooperation, that goal might be much more readily achieved. (p. 414)

When the student teacher becomes the central focus of the partnership, universities and schools must accept the challenge of learning from the student teacher how to strengthen the field experiences. When the student teacher reports incoherent messages between instructor and mentor, then collaborative partners work together to clarify the discrepancies together. But at what point, then, does the teacher educator learn to build partnerships such as these?

Learning with and from others supports concerted efforts to align classroom practices and coursework. In addition, the experiences of the authors of this chapter call into question the formal, systemic supports that scaffold and coach us toward becoming effective teacher educators. Through various stages of our doctoral studies, each of us was fortunate to work with the same advisor, a professor renowned in the field of teacher education, who was passionate about engaging her students in every facet of the profession—research, scholarly writing, teaching, supervision of candidates. She embraced each of her students (and many that were not her students), and created a culture of learning through highly reflective practice. We were often reminded of our fortune when we would hear the quiet inquiries from other graduate students asking, "How did you get her as your advisor?" This situation is not unlike the conversations we hear among our teacher candidates when they discuss their mentor teachers. "Oh you have Ms. Baker? You're going to *love* her," gushes one candidate to another, while another candidate looks dejected at the lack of support she received with another mentor teacher the semester prior.

Our fortunate relationships were not part of an official mentoring program and may not have been with our doctoral advisors, but were relationships that simply happened.

Meghan's story: It's fair to say that I started my path to PhD with a bit of naiveté. Having acquired my previous degrees at a small liberal arts college and a cohorted, practitioner's MA program, I was completely unfamiliar with the paths of graduate students at large, Research One universities. I applied to the program uncertain I had what it took to be admitted, and was thrilled to find that I could swap teaching for tuition.

By a series of coincidences, I was one of very few graduate teaching assistants who was able to co-teach with my supervisor and mentor. Even more fortunately, my mentor was just as well-versed in pre-service teacher field experiences and student teaching as he was in classroom instructional methods. Until recently, I hadn't considered the degree to which he put this knowledge to use for my benefit. My time with him functioned as a kind of teacher educator apprenticeship. During our semester of co-teaching, I gradually assumed leadership within the classroom, starting with small group instruction and moving to planning full lessons for the students. My mentor and I worked together on syllabus revisions, plans for class, and feedback on assignments. I learned a great deal about pacing, assessing, and mentoring pre-service teachers.

This apprenticeship-style learning was advantageous to me in two significant ways. First, it gave me the time and space to learn about my new institutional context, the pre-service teachers I would be teaching, and the progression of their preparation program. Without a semester of gradually assuming responsibility, I wonder how overwhelmed I may have been by all of these new contexts. By the end of that first semester, I was feeling confident enough to take on the next course in the social studies pre-service sequence on my own. And now, at the end of my own program, I have been able to teach each social studies teaching methods course in the secondary social studies sequence. That experience provided me with a basic understanding of the full continuum of pre-service teacher development.

The second major advantage to co-teaching with my mentor that semester was the chance it afforded me to develop a true appreciation for teacher education. I'm somewhat embarrassed to say that, in my first few months of PhD studies, I did not even realize that "teacher education" was a scholarly field. Over and over I would comment to others about the "fascinating" progress of my pre-service teachers. Supporting their learning and growth into thoughtful, critical, inquisitive new teachers was (and is) truly thrilling to me; it continues to drive my professional passions. If I hadn't been lucky enough to happen upon that early relationship with my mentor, I know this learning would have been significantly delayed, if not missed entirely.

There are no assurances for future doctoral students, that those interested in teacher education, will also find these relationships, unless there is a program to support these efforts. This is further complicated by the fact that, by the nature of doctoral work, those teaching assistants who work with future teachers, will do so for a few years and then graduate. Without a cohesive support network to develop their teacher education practices, these doctoral students will likely not identify as teacher educators (Zeichner, 2010). This tension leads us to wonder, "How might teacher education doctoral students have access to induction support and high quality mentoring that emphasize collaboration with schools as well as learning with and from others?"

SUMMARY AND CONCLUSION: A CALL TO ACTION

The four tensions presented resulted from our shared questions, concerns, and quandaries as we navigated issues in our graduate programs and post-doctoral work. We found that learning to be a teacher educator, a common goal for the four of us, was difficult when the pre-service educator program at times focused on content and logistical aspects of teaching. This in turn led us to question our own developing identities as researchers of teacher education as opposed to content specialists. Given our teaching backgrounds, we found it problematic to encounter ways of teaching and responding to our undergraduates that may not have been recommendations for the students they would eventually be teaching. Finally, we attempted to negotiate our needs and our undergraduates' needs for effective partnerships as opposed to relying on the luck of being given an excellent mentor.

As we worked through the development of this chapter, we found that our stories of learning to teach teachers gave voice to layers of complexity, challenging the notion of teacher education as a self-evident practice. While the issues discussed above are not new to those who already study teacher education, it is our hope that our personal experiences with these tensions can help readers tease apart the complexity of learning to be a teacher educator and lead to action in responses to the questions offered by each of the four tensions. Dewey (1895) discussed the power of illuminating tensions, or potentially conflicting tendencies, to help us better understand complexity.

We see evidence of small changes occurring within our stories above. These individual changes came in the form of revised syllabi, of self-initiated practitioner research, of seeking out mentors and peer communities, and even writing a book chapter to give voice to early career teacher educators experiencing similar tensions as our own. For us, these actions emerged from the issues we were experiencing at the time, but you can also see a need for more coherence among our individual shifts in practice. It's for this reason that we lay out a set of recommendations for a more systemic, coherent, and holistic experience of preparing teacher educators.

Just as a teacher educator's role is to help candidates bridge the theory and practice divide, teacher educators need to make connections between their research on teacher education with the practice of being a teacher educator. First, leaders of the institutions must make teacher education a serious responsibility (Zeichner, 2006). Make "how to be a teacher educator" an intentional part of what we do in graduate programs, and encourage a culture of inquiry that acknowledges and rewards scholarship that is about, informed by, and accomplished through teaching (Boyer, 1990). This becomes a space for not only defining our research interests and expertise, but where we reflect upon the relevance of our research in relationship to our role as a teacher of teachers. Bain (2004) called this the "learning university" that concerns itself with both research and teaching, and how learning in one informs the other.

Van Manen (2015) discussed how college classrooms are only the beginning of a teacher's professional development. New teachers may not know *how* to respond to students who say, "No, I'm not going to do this work." Teacher education, then, should spend more time highlighting the connections between recommended practices and personal and professional theories such that new teachers may begin to understand the philosophical grounding for their teaching actions and the confusions that arise when working with students. We contend that the same should be true for the preparation of teacher educators. PhD candidates should develop a deep knowledge of our teacher candidates' abilities and development trajectories, including understanding and negotiating the assumptions regarding adult learners such as young college students and second-career educators.

This development must occur in collaboration across institutions and multiple partnerships. With teacher candidates, we ask what kind of quality control can be assumed from a preparation program that relies on only one primary relationship between a mentor teacher and teacher candidate? Instead of a reliance on one primary *relationship* to determine an individual teacher's success in a program, teacher educators must consider the mutually beneficial *partnerships* they need to build with schools. This implies a need for teacher educator preparation to include opportunities to build and navigate partnerships with classroom teachers and schools. In addition, it calls into question the programmatic dependence on the singular doctoral advisor. A future teacher educator would benefit from multiple mentors to support the development of an identity encompassing both research and the teaching of teachers.

Lastly, in order for doctoral candidates to be simultaneously mentored in research and in teacher educator practice, teacher education institutions should recruit and reward teacher educator researchers who take an inquiry stance in their professional practice. What we do well as university folks is holistic preparation of teachers (as opposed to technist approaches), making space for theory, research, and practice to coexist and inform (Zeichner, 2011). We owe the same to the preparation of teacher educators.

As referenced in the introduction, learning to teach teachers is complex, and no one solution is going to be the singular right solution (Rust, 2017). Differing contexts will require different approaches. For us, we intend to harness the energy of the tensions as they present themselves in our home institution. At the time of this writing, we are developing a series of supports that put our doctoral candidates in the field of teacher education at the core of our program by increasing the support systems available. We designed an orientation for new teaching assistants focused on interactive classroom strategies, and we facilitated a peer-to-peer learning community for teaching assistants interested in discussing the problems of practice experienced when teaching teachers (Dana & Yendol-Hoppey, 2014). It is our hope that in the not too distant future, new faculty and partnering schools will also participate in designing for stronger supports for novice teachers and teacher educators at our institution. When tensions of difference juxtapose the status quo against possibility, then the energy generated by this tension has potential to breed creativity and innovation, if we are aware of the differences that can make a difference. By holding a mirror to our practices of preparing teacher educators, we identify those opportunities for change. With courage and conviction, we take action.

Discussion Questions

1. What intentional structures can be incorporated into a doctoral program or induction program to assist novice teacher educators in noticing and acting on intersections between the study of teacher education and the practice of teaching teachers?
2. How might the voice of novice teacher educators play a more prominent role in identifying and navigating institutional challenges to ensure a teacher education environment that is *teacher centered* and at all levels of engagement (e.g., pre-service, inservice, teacher educator)?
3. In what ways are we practicing what we preach to support the learning of our novice teachers *and* teacher educators?
4. What relationships and resources are already present in our teacher educator preparation contexts? How might we better leverage these assets to ensure a supportive environment for novice teacher educators?
5. Considering your institution's preparation of teacher educators, what tensions exist and how might these tensions be balanced to strengthen both teacher *and* teacher educator learning?

REFERENCES

Allen, J., Park Rogers, M., & Borowski, R. (2016). "I am out of my comfort zone": Self-study of the struggle of adapting to the professional identity of a teacher educator. *Studying Teacher Education: A Journal of Self-study of Teacher Education, 12*(3), 320–332.

Allen, J. M., Butler-Mader, C., & Smith, R. A. (2010). A fundamental partnership: The experiences of practising teachers as lecturers in a pre-service teacher education programme. *Teachers and Teaching: Theory and Practice, 16*(5), 615–632.

Bain, K. (2004). *What the best college teacher do.* Cambridge, MA: Harvard University Press.

Boyer, E. (1990). *Scholarship reconsidered: Priorities of the professoriate.* Princeton, NJ: Carnegie Foundation for the Advancement of Teaching.

Clandinin, D. J. (2013). *Engaging in narrative inquiry.* Walnut Creek, CA: Left Coast Press.

Dana, N. F., & Yendol-Hoppey, D. (2014). *The reflective educator's guide to classroom research: Learning to teach and teaching to learn through practitioner inquiry.* Thousand Oaks, CA: Corwin Press.

Danielewicz, J. (2001). Teaching selves. *Identity, pedagogy, and teacher education.* Albany: State University of New York Press.

Darling-Hammond, L. (1999). The case for university-based teacher education. In M. Cochran-Smith, S. Feiman-Nemser, D. J. McIntyre, & K. E. Demers, (Eds.), *Handbook of research on teacher education: Enduring questions in changing contexts* (pp. 333–346). London, England: Routledge.

Dewey, J. (1895). The theory of emotion. *Psychological Review, 2*(1), 13–32.

Featherstone, J. (2007). Values and the big university education school. In D. Carroll, H. Featherstone, J. Featherstone, S. Feiman-Nemser, & D. Roosevelt (Eds.), *Transforming teacher education: Reflections from the field* (pp. 203–220). Cambridge, MA: Harvard Education Press.

Holladay, R. (September, 2017). *The tension in tension: Leveraging potential in complex adaptive systems.* Circle Pines, MN: Human Systems Dynamics Institute. Retrieved from http://www.hsdinstitute.org/resources/The_Tension_in_Tension.html

Hollins, E. R., Luna, C., & Lopez, S. (2014). Learning to teach teachers. *Teaching Education, 25*(1), 99–124.

Intrator, S. M., & Kunzman, R. (2009). Grounded: Practicing what we preach. *Journal of Teacher Education, 60*(5), 512–519.

Johnston-Parsons, M., Lee, Y. A., & Thomas, M. (2007). Student of colour as cultural consultants: A self-study of race and social justice issues in a teacher education programme. *Studying Teacher Education: A Journal of Self-study of Teacher Education, 3*(1), 67–84.

Jones, A. (2017). *Relational knowing and responsive instruction* (Doctoral dissertation). University of Illinois, Champaign-Urbana. Available at https://www.ideals.illinois.edu/handle/2142/97680

Labaree, D. F. (2006). *The trouble with ed schools.* Yale University Press.

Labaree, D. F. (2008). An uneasy relationship: The history of teacher education in the university. In M. Cochran-Smith, S. Feiman Nemser, & J. McIntyre, John (Eds.), *Handbook of research on teacher education: Enduring issues in changing contexts* (3rd ed.; pp. 290–306). Washington, DC: Association of Teacher Educators.

Lortie, D. (1975). *Schoolteacher: A sociological study.* London, England: University of Chicago Press.

Loughran, J. (2006). *Developing a pedagogy of teacher education.* New York, NY: Routledge.

Loughran, J. (2011). On becoming a teacher educator. *Journal of Education for Teaching, 37*(3), 279–291, https://doi.org/10.1080/02607476.2011.588016

Loughran, J., Korthagen, F., & Russell, T. (2008). Teacher education that makes a difference. *Action in Teacher Education, 29*(5/6), 405–421.

Loughran, J., & Northfield, J. R. (1998). A framework for the development of self-study practice. In M. L. Hamilton (Ed.), *Reconceptualizing teaching practice: Developing competence through self-study* (pp. 7–17). Bristol, PA: Taylor & Francis.

Rust, F. (2017). Making teacher education matter. *Teachers and Teaching: Theory and Practice, 23*(4), 383–386.

Samaras, A. P. (2011). *Self-study teacher research.* Thousand Oaks, CA: SAGE.

Swartz, E. (2003). Teaching White preservice teachers: Pedagogy for change. *Urban Education, 38*(3), 255–278.

Toon, D., & Jensen, B. (2017). *Teaching our teachers a better way: Developing partnerships to improve teacher preparation.* Melbourne, Australia: Learning First.

van Manen, M. (2015). *Pedagogical tact: Knowing what to do when you don't know what to do.* New York, NY: Taylor & Francis.

Zeichner, K. (2006). Reflections of a university-based teacher educator on the future of college- and university-based teacher education. *Journal of Teacher Education, 57*(3), 326–340. https://doi.org/10.1177/0022487105285893

Zeichner, K. (2010). Rethinking the connections between campus courses and field experiences in college- and university-based teacher education. *Journal of Teacher Education, 61,* 89–99. https://doi.org/10.1177/0022487109347671

Zeichner, K. (2011). Assessing state and federal policies to evaluate the quality of teacher preparation programs. In P. Earley, D. Imig, & N. Michelli (Eds.), *Teacher education policy in the United States: Issues and tensions in an era of evolving expectations* (pp. 75–105). New York, NY: Routledge.

Zeichner, K., Payne, K., & Brayko, K. (2015). Democratizing teacher education. *Journal of Teacher Education, 66*(2), 122–135.

Zollers, N. J., Albert, L. R., & Cochran-Smith, M. (2000). In pursuit of social justice: Collaborative research and practice in teacher education. *Action in Teacher Education, 22*(2), 1–14.

CHAPTER 5

THE CHANGING ROLE OF UNIVERSITY-BASED TEACHER EDUCATORS

Lessons Learned in a Clinical Elementary Teacher Preparation Program

Ann C. McCoy
University of Central Missouri

Nicole M. Nickens
University of Central Missouri

The National Council for the Accreditation of Teacher Education (NCATE) Report of the Blue Ribbon Panel on Clinical Preparation and Partnerships for Improved Student Learning (2010) demanded teacher education "must move to programs that are fully grounded in clinical practice and interwoven with academic content and professional courses" and "must work in close partnership with school districts to redesign teacher preparation to better serve prospective teachers and the students they teach" (NCATE,

Preparing the Next Generation of Teacher Educators for Clinical Practice, pages 93–111
Copyright © 2019 by Information Age Publishing
All rights of reproduction in any form reserved.

2010, p. ii). Taking this edict to heart, faculty in our university decided to revise the elementary and early childhood education programs and create heavily clinical programs.

In revising our programs, we anticipated we would see changes in the knowledge, skills, and dispositions of our teacher candidates and we certainly have. However, we did not expect the role of our university-based teacher educators (UBTEs) to change as significantly as what has occurred. Nor did we anticipate the need to adjust our hiring practices and orientation of new faculty members, or the need to consider how the work of clinical educators impacts faculty evaluation processes.

In this chapter, we share information about the process we use to revise our program and the resulting structure of our new program. We describe how the roles of the UBTEs in our program have changed and how our program continues to evolve based on these changing roles. We share what we have learned regarding how the knowledge, skills, and dispositions needed by UBTEs working in a clinical program have changed from those needed previously. Finally, we share how the implementation of a clinical model has resulted in changes in the hiring of new faculty, new faculty orientation, and the need for changes in how clinical work is valued in the context of promotion and tenure. We conclude with a brief discussion of implications for those institutions with doctoral programs in teacher education.

OUR STORY: TRANSITIONING TO A CLINICALLY BASED TEACHER EDUCATION PROGRAM

Our Starting Point: Recognizing the Need for Change

Prior to the release of the Blue Ribbon Report on Clinical Education, our elementary and early childhood education programs incorporated a Professional Development School (PDS) experience. The structure was two traditional classes blocked together on two mornings per week (Tuesdays/Thursdays); class was held on campus on Tuesdays and the candidates completed practicum hours on Thursday mornings during the same block of time. This was the first opportunity for our candidates to see ongoing modeling by the classroom teacher, observe and participate in classroom management, and experience teaching whole-group lessons (generally in literacy). While this model prepared our candidates adequately, the program still offered very limited classroom experience prior to student teaching. We realized the need to provide additional classroom experience in order to truly prepare teacher candidates for their own classrooms. We envisioned a program in which candidates "spend extensive time in the field throughout the entire program, examining and applying the concepts and strategies they are simultaneously learning about in their courses" (Darling-Hammond, 2010, p. 40).

During the planning phase for the revision of our elementary and early childhood education teacher preparation programs, themes emerged through faculty discussions that evolved into commonly held beliefs that would guide the design of our revised program. We felt strongly that

- teachers need to understand the developmental needs of the learner which underlie all instructional decisions,
- the theory and principles that have always been the underpinnings of teacher education are most meaningful when candidates can learn and apply them in close temporal proximity and within an authentic context, and
- the essential ability of developing relationships with students could be practiced and mastered through significant time spent in the classroom and through the modeling of relationships built with faculty mentors.

Our Redesigned Program: A New Clinical Model

The themes identified during the planning phase of our program redesign efforts provided the foundation for the revision of our programs to include greatly expanded clinical experiences for our teacher candidates. In an effort to enact these themes, our program structure utilizes a series of clinical blocks, a developmental approach, careful organization of courses and practica, consistent partner school districts, and UBTEs working in the field with our candidates.

Series of Clinical Blocks

The primary goal behind developing a more clinical program was obviously to provide more time for teacher candidates to spend in classrooms learning to interact with, teach, and assess students as well as learning principles of classroom management prior to the student teaching semester. Our existing program provided field time in lieu of class time for only 3 hours per week the semester prior to student teaching. Prior to that semester, our teacher candidates experienced only classroom observation, not classroom teaching. Traditional college course scheduling was a big obstacle to this goal, as every college student has a different schedule, and few have full school days or even hours to spend time in a public school classroom. Thus, the decision was made to create blocks of courses with scheduled practicum time attached, similar to a lab being attached to a science course. Figure 5.1 provides a diagram of the structure of our program.

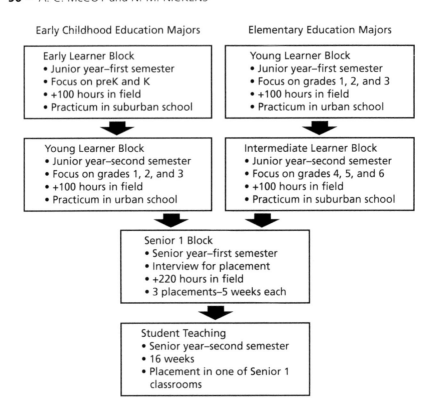

Figure 5.1 Program block structure.

Three blocks of courses were developed for junior year requirements. Blocks are scheduled from 8:30 a.m. to 3:00 p.m. two days each week so during a 16 week semester, 32 full days are completely blocked off and students cannot schedule other classes during those days. Half of these days are devoted to covering the content of the required major courses in the block while the other half are designated as field days with students spending the entire school day in their classroom placements. Teacher candidates gain more than 100 hours of experience working with children and 2 hours of university credit each semester during their junior year.

Senior year begins with the final semester of coursework for our elementary and early childhood education students. In the first senior semester, 13 credit hours of senior level courses are blocked together into one full class day each week. Our candidates also spend two days each week in their public school placements and are placed in three different grade levels for 5 weeks each. During this semester, our candidates begin truly assuming the work of the teacher as they plan and implement whole group instruction and assessment, attend professional development, participate in data teams, and participate in meetings with parents as appropriate. The second senior semester is a 16-week full-time student teaching experience completed in one of the three classrooms in which the candidate was placed in the previous semester. Our university has adopted a co-teaching model for all student teaching.

Developmental Approach

As stated in the description of philosophy, we believe teachers need to understand the developmental needs of the learner which underlie all instructional decisions. Development of the learner is the theme around which the blocks were structured.

Our clinical program serves early childhood education majors who will be certified to teach birth through Grade 3, and elementary education majors who will be certified to teach Grades 1–6. Each candidate completes two junior-level blocks with coursework and practicum aligned with the age groups they will be certified to teach. Early childhood education majors first complete the early learner block which focuses on pre-kindergarten and kindergarten followed by the young learner block which focuses on Grades 1–3. Elementary education candidates begin junior-level requirements with the young learner (Grades 1–3) and then second semester they progress to the intermediate learner block which focuses on fourth, fifth, and sixth grade elementary classrooms.

Organization of Courses and Practica

The curriculum for the blocked courses was carefully constructed by faculty around common themes of assessment, instructional technology, classroom management, differentiated learning, response to intervention, and accommodations and modifications for learners with exceptionalities. Courses were specifically designed to teach principles and theory underlying curriculum, instruction, and assessment while using specific applications from the schools in which candidates complete practica to bridge the gap from theory into practice. Courses are heavy with application and synthesis of content and skills. Teacher candidates develop lessons and units, create assessments, administer assessments, scrutinize and analyze data collected from children, practice lessons on each other, and use various methods and strategies to teach different content areas. Consideration of the developmental needs of the learners is of primary importance in each block.

In the practicum setting, the junior blocks require teacher candidates to work with a small group of children, the "focus groups," chosen by the school-based teacher educator (SBTE). Our teacher candidates are assigned to elementary classroom in pairs so that stronger candidates may provide additional coaching and "another voice in the areas in which the partner needs to make changes" (Dee, 2012, p. 160). Candidates work with the same focus group all semester to teach lessons and assess student learning. The focus group format allows the candidate to learn to interact and communicate effectively, study the developmental needs of each child, recognize developmentally appropriate milestones and capabilities, observe social interaction of different age groups, and step carefully into beginning to learn classroom management skills. Extensive work with small groups of students prepares candidates well to teach whole group lessons during the senior year semesters.

Partner Schools

Our clinical program is designed to ensure that candidates have extensive field placements in at least two demographically different school settings. Our teacher candidates come primarily from rural and suburban areas, and many teacher candidates express the desire to return to their home district to teach after graduation. However, a goal of our clinical program is to expose candidates to settings that are very different from the schools they attended and thereby encourage them to consider teaching in a district that has more difficulty recruiting highly qualified teachers.

Careful planning ensures our candidates have practicum placements in a variety of settings. We utilize area rural schools for classroom placements in the field experience that is part of the foundations block teacher candidates complete prior to acceptance into the elementary and early childhood education programs. The practica for our early and intermediate learner junior level blocks are based in suburban districts while our young learner block practicum (completed by all of our teacher candidates) is based in urban districts.

University-Based Teacher Educators' Role

At the junior level, the same UBTEs who teach the coursework also fulfill the clinical educator role of supervising teacher candidates in the field. Each UBTE is assigned a specific group of teacher candidates and is responsible for coaching and mentoring, assessing professional dispositions, and evaluating these teacher candidates in the practicum. The UBTE provides feedback on the planning, content, and delivery of lessons; interactions with the children; and classroom management skills. He or she also fosters the ability of the teacher candidate to effectively reflect upon his/her lesson, performance, and impact on student learning.

During Senior I, the scaffolded design of the program allows for more autonomy of the teacher candidates, who are ready for this autonomy since they begin the senior year with over 200 hours total classroom teaching across two different types of classrooms and two different age groups. UBTEs who teach in the senior block of courses also supervise the clinical component but unlike at the junior level, the UBTEs do not accompany candidates into the field every single field day. Instead, supervision is scheduled every other week or every third week with flexibility for faculty to supervise more intensively candidates who need more support.

Through the development, piloting, full implementation, and growth of our clinical program, we have learned that to have a high-quality clinical education program, high-quality university clinical teacher educators must be part of the infrastructure. Effective university clinical teacher educators have a fundamentally different job than faculty members in more campus-based or online teacher education programs.

Many professors in campus-based teacher education programs have classes on two or three days each week. They focus primarily on teaching, scholarship, and service to the university and to the profession of education; prepping and grading for classes, corresponding with and meeting with students, answering endless emails, doing committee work and participating in scholarly endeavors. They work very hard. As the launch of our clinical model neared realization, our faculty had a realization of their own: This work was going to be even harder. On top of all of the existing faculty obligations, our clinical program requires faculty members to keep one foot on campus, teaching college courses to college students and one foot in the public schools, supervising teacher candidates' growth across 2 years. A new type of program that is significantly different requires a new type of faculty member and we learned that not all UBTEs could make the transition. Nor did all of them want to make this transition.

Our Clinical Model: A Work in Progress

We firmly believe our clinical program has significantly and positively impacted our candidates' readiness for their own classrooms and data we have collected supports this. As noted earlier, the implementation of this program has also brought about changes in the work of our UBTEs. While we celebrate the success of our program and the teacher educators working within it, we acknowledge the need to consider and address ongoing issues with direct implications for the work of our teacher educators.

The NCATE Report of the Blue Ribbon Panel on Clinical Preparation and Partnerships for Improved Student Learning (2010) and the report of the American Association of Colleges for Teacher Education's (AACTE) Clinical Practice Commission (2017) both speak of the importance of partnerships. AACTE's Partnership Proclamation states, "Effective clinical partnerships allow for mutually beneficial outcomes and are gateways to developing reflective practice while simultaneously renewing teaching and learning in K–12 classrooms" (AACTE, 2017, p. 3). Standards of the Council for the Accreditation of Educator Preparation (CAEP) include an explicit focus on clinical partnerships and clinical practice. Standard 2 specifically addresses clinical partnerships calling for mutually beneficial outcomes, the co-construction of experiences and the co-selection of clinical educators (CAEP, 2013).We have established relationships with a number of partner schools districts and our teacher candidates have benefitted from these relationships; however, we have not fully achieved the vision of clinical partnerships described by NCATE, AACTE, and CAEP. As we redesigned our program, we did not fully involve school-based teacher educators and, in retrospect, doing so would have been an important first step in forming true partnerships with districts. Even now, the bulk of the planning and organizing involved in our clinical program is completed by our UBTEs. We realize that in order to establish true partnerships, we must relinquish some control of our program in favor of increased collaborative work with our partners. This will result in additional changes in the work of our UBTEs and some further shifts in beliefs and practices.

Yendol-Hoppey and Franco (2014) identified six pedagogical routines for clinical practice that include inquiry, focused observation, mentoring and coaching, co-teaching, reflection, and integrate coursework and fieldwork. Elements of each of these are present in our work but using the routines as a frame for working with our partner districts will strengthen our partnerships. A focus on developing these routines with our district partners will impact the work of our UBTEs. For example, currently our UBTEs work together to design and refine the mentoring and coaching that occurs in practicum placements. While mentoring and coaching certainly is provided by both the UBTEs and the SBTE, we have not formalized the process. As a program, collaboratively with our SBTEs to craft observation tools and establish expectations will directly involve our teacher educators. In addition, while we collect data regarding our program and candidates from our district partners (SBTEs and administrators) and use this data to guide program changes, we have not actively involved our partners in helping us utilize reflection to guide our practice. Engaging in shared reflection with our partners will require our UBTEs to demonstrate to an even greater extent the collaborative skills required for work in our clinical program.

The changing role of UBTEs is key to each of the aspects of our ongoing work described above. The knowledge, skills, and dispositions of UBTEs are important aspects of the role they plan in our evolving model. Next, we share what we have learned about the knowledge, skills, and dispositions of faculty members serving as UBTEs.

KNOWLEDGE, SKILLS, AND DISPOSITIONS
OF UNIVERSITY-BASED TEACHER EDUCATORS

Like other teacher education programs, our program considers the knowledge, skills, and dispositions of prospective teachers in program evaluation and planning. As we implemented our clinical program, we learned we must also consider the knowledge, skills, and dispositions needed by our UBTEs working in the clinical program. Consider these scenarios, representative of situations encountered by UBTEs in our program, that provide a glimpse of the knowledge and skills needed by UBTEs working in clinical programs.

- Emily is a second semester junior teacher candidate working in a third grade classroom. In Emily's first junior semester, Mrs. C., her UBTE, noted that Emily struggled with forming relationships with her students and that she seemed distant and disinterested in them. Mrs. C. hoped to see improvement during the second junior semester when Emily moved to a new classroom and a different grade level. However, Emily has continued to struggle with connecting with her students and seems to lack commitment to teaching.
- Mark, a junior level teacher candidate, is preparing a mathematics lesson on two-digit addition for his small group of second graders. He visits with his SBTE about the lesson and mentions using base-ten blocks to introduce the concept. His SBTE discourages this and suggests Mark rethink his strategy. During an earlier methods class, the use of base-ten blocks was strongly encouraged by Mark's professor, and UBTE, Dr. B., and Mark would like to include the blocks in his lesson. He asks Dr. B. for advice about how to proceed and how to approach his SBTE.
- Junior level teacher candidate, Maddy, taught a lesson that involved the use of a children's book. Although her SBTE quickly glanced at the book prior to the lesson, she did not read it thoroughly. In the middle of the book, the SBTE stops Maddy and redirects the children to a different activity. She tells Maddy the book is not appropriate for second graders and that the principal must be notified immediately. The SBTE and principal summon Maddy's UBTE suggesting Maddy be removed from the classroom.

As these three scenarios illustrate, UBTEs working in clinical models experience situations very different from those experienced by faculty working in more campus-based programs. In these examples, the UBTE is required to determine when to confront a TC about dispositional concerns, to carefully navigate the relationship between a TC and his SBTE, and to advocate for a TC while honoring an existing partnership with a school district. Situations such as these provide evidence that the changing role of UBTEs requires a new set of knowledge, skills, and dispositions. Below we share what we have learned about how the implementation of our clinical model has led to changes in the necessary knowledge, skills, and dispositions of our UBTEs.

Knowledge of University-Based Teacher Educators

UBTEs working in clinical programs must possess the same knowledge of their discipline as those in more campus-based teacher preparation programs. All elementary teacher educators must have knowledge of child growth and development, elementary content, standards, curriculum, learning theories, developmentally appropriate practices, and assessment. However, UBTEs in clinical programs must possess additional knowledge not necessarily needed in traditional settings.

UBTEs working in our program must have knowledge of the context in which they are working. Our program includes practicum placements in rural, urban, and suburban schools in a variety of school districts. This means our faculty must understand the complexities and challenges that exist in each of these settings and they must be able to help teacher candidates successfully navigate these as well. We have learned that our program is strengthened by having teacher educators with varied background experiences as part of our program. Since the implementation of our clinical program, we have had the opportunity to hire new teacher educators to join our faculty. As part of the hiring process, we have actively looked for teacher educators with knowledge of and experience in rural or urban schools to provide expertise in teaching in these settings.

In addition, UBTEs working in clinical programs must have knowledge of the connection between theory and practice and an understanding of how to help teacher candidates make these connections. Burns, Jacobs, and Yendol-Hoppey (2016) indicate the relationship between theory and practice is complex and has long proved challenging to prospective teachers. They add that when teacher educators are not able to connect theory and practice effectively, teacher candidates may actually ignore the knowledge gained in coursework and instead follow the practices observed in their practicum placements. UBTEs in our program, who teach university-based courses as well as providing supervision in practicum placements, must be equipped with the knowledge required to help teacher candidates analyze the "conflict between the curriculum in the teacher education program world and the curriculum in the field" (Burns, Jacobs, & Yendol-Hoppey, 2016, p. 419).

Skills of University-Based Teacher Educators

Two very essential skills related to the function of teaching faculty as clinical faculty have emerged as we have implemented our clinical program. First, the coaching and mentoring provided individually and for the group by the university clinical faculty is of paramount importance in the professional growth of each teacher candidate. Second, the ability to develop positive relationships with each teacher candidate is essential and the relationships developed is a powerful influence on the teacher candidate's attitudes about and confidence in teaching.

These two skills mark an important difference between UBTEs in traditional teacher preparation program and those in programs following a clinical model. UBTEs in clinical teacher education programs must not only be effective instructors, they must also be skilled in coaching and mentoring. According to Payor (2016), emerging and current models of clinical education fall short because they operate on the assumption that anyone who has been an effective classroom teacher is able to simply "do" the behaviors desired of a clinical educator. We have learned that not all effective instructors are also effective mentors and coaches as the skills involved in teaching are not identical to those required in mentoring. In addition, while developing relationships with students is important for all instructors, this need is magnified for coaches and mentors for whom developing a trusting relationship with teacher candidates is essential for the candidates to grow as educators. Further, as Bullock (2012) states, "The relationship between a teacher educator and a teacher candidate can send a powerful message to candidates about the importance of developing relationships with their students" (p. 153).

An additional skill required of clinical UBTEs is the ability to form, nurture, and maintain a triad relationship among the teacher candidate, district SBTE, and the UBTEs (Burns, Jacobs, & Yendol-Hoppey, 2016). The district SBTE and the UBTEs must work collegially, collaboratively, and respectfully to provide teacher candidates experiences that allow them to grow as educators. We believe that UBTEs play a primary role in the development of this important relationship. A study of the activities and characteristics of teacher candidates, SBTEs, and university supervisors found university supervisors who are viewed as effective have good communication skills, are available to student teachers, provide feedback to teacher candidates, mediate conflicts as needed, and serve as mentors for teacher candidates (Koerner, Rust, & Baumgartner, 2002). These characteristics and practices may help the UBTEs successfully foster and maintain the triad relationship (Burns et al., 2016). At times, the UBTE must skillfully and carefully navigate conversations when differences between what is learned in university coursework and practices observed in the practicum classroom exist. Our UBTEs are expected to demonstrate these skills and behaviors as they work with SBTEs and teacher candidates.

Finally, UBTEs in clinical programs must be skilled in helping teacher candidates deal with the stress that accompanies learning to teach in a clinical setting (Burns et al., 2016). We have observed "block shock" in many of our teacher candidates completing their first junior level clinical block. The need to be both a student while on campus and a teacher while in the practicum placement is challenging for our novice teachers. In their first block experience, our candidates begin learning that "teaching is complex work that looks deceptively simple" (Grossman, Hammerness, & McDonald, 2009) and this can increase the stress they experience. Most of our candidates are fully committed to teaching and to making a difference through their teaching; however, the realization that teaching is such hard work has, at times, caused some candidates to question their choice of education as their profession. Our UBTEs must be skilled in helping teacher candidates work through the stress they experience and the questions that arise. At times, they must initiate hard conversations that help students realize they may fit better in another profession.

Dispositions of University-Based Teacher Educators

NCATE (2007) and now CAEP (2013) both have ambiguously defined dispositions as "professional attitude, value, and beliefs demonstrated through both verbal and nonverbal behaviors..." Many teacher education programs base their definition of professional dispositions on the Interstate Teacher Assessment and Support Consortium (2011) framework, to include such "critical dispositions" as "the teacher is a thoughtful and responsive listener and observer," and "the teacher values planning as a collegial activity that takes into consideration the input of learners, colleagues, families, and the larger community." As mentioned earlier, some UBTEs are not successful in transitioning to a clinical model and, in some cases, this has been due to their dispositions and beliefs. UBTEs who are successful in our clinical program firmly believe that preparing future teachers occurs best through strong partnerships between school districts and universities. They must respect and appreciate the expertise of the classroom teachers and they must welcome the opportunity to continue to grow professionally by working alongside the elementary teachers and children. Our UBTEs must actively welcome collaboration with the elementary teachers serving as SBTEs for our teacher candidates and seek to understand the practices of the schools in which our candidates are placed (Zeichner, 2010).

Our clinical program requires UBTEs to collaborate extensively with other teacher UBTEs in the program. Because of our block structure in which our faculty both teach university based courses and supervise field placements, the UBTEs in each block must work together to create aligned learning experiences, to coordinate dates for major assignments to support candidates, and to establish common expectations for performance in the practicum placements. Some of our faculty, who are outstanding teachers, simply are not comfortable with the level of collaboration required for our clinical program to be successful. We have learned that collaboration does not come easily or naturally to our entire faculty and this is complicated by the fact that some faculty may perceive the university values individual efforts more highly than collaborative work (Gardiner & Salmon, 2014).

Finally, UBTEs, especially those working in a clinical model, must demonstrate an ongoing commitment to learning about teaching. Ritter (2009) suggests a key difference in the work of a classroom teacher and a teacher educator is that teacher educators must be willing to engage in "sustained inquiry into practice," to "problematize the act of teaching" (p. 59), and to engage in critical reflection as a model for teacher candidates. Allowing and encouraging scrutiny of one's teaching practices is not comfortable for all UBTEs.

IMPLICATIONS AND CONCLUSIONS

Implications for Our Practice

The changing role of the UBTEs in our clinical model have led to the need for these educators to possess new knowledge, skills, and dispositions. As we moved away from a campus-based approach to teacher education to a clinical, not all of our faculty easily made the transition. As we reflected on the changing role of our UBTEs and our observations of the response of our faculty to a clinical model, we realized the need to make changes in the hiring and orientation of new faculty.

Changes in Hiring Practices at Our Institution

As our program has grown and faculty have left our university for a variety of reasons, we have had the opportunity to bring new faculty into our clinical model. Our new model has resulted in the need to think about the characteristics desired in teacher educators, the orientation provided for new teacher educators, and how to best support them in their new roles.

Our university is typical in that faculty are expected to demonstrate excellence in teaching, scholarship, and service. In the past, search committees for new faculty have considered candidates' records in each of these areas. Rubrics used to assess the applications and resumes of potential faculty members included equal weights for evidence of quality teaching, scholarship, and service. On-campus interview days usually included a presentation of the candidate's research and in-depth questions about research agendas.

While these three traditional areas for faculty are still valued in our program, for faculty seeking to join our clinical program the weight placed on these three areas has shifted. When assessing potential faculty's applications and resumes, we actively look for evidence of collaboration and an ability to partner with school districts. Interviews have shifted from detailed discussions about research agendas to discussions of the candidate's experience working with school districts and mentoring teacher candidates. We are somewhat wary of faculty candidates for whom traditional research seems to be of primary importance. Payor (2016) comments that "in both medical education and teacher education, research demands more of faculty members' attention than teaching. There is of course great irony in that two professions where teaching is— or ought to be—central, it is not highly respected work" (p. 29). In our experience, some teacher educators coming to us with research-heavy backgrounds tend to struggle adjusting to the demands of working as teacher educators in our clinical program, and their prioritization of teaching versus research may not be a good "fit" with a clinical program.

Many elementary UBTEs have experience teaching in elementary schools and this provides a foundation for their work with prospective teachers; however, the reality is that not all UBTEs have this experience. Some UBTEs begin teaching at the university level immediately after graduate school while others come to us after working in research settings. Gardiner and Salmon (2014) indicate university faculty with limited K–12 experience are often disciplinary experts with minimal contextual understanding. We have learned our program works well with a mix of practitioners who come to the university with a wealth of elementary teaching experience and tenure track faculty with a strong background in research. This mix of practitioners and researchers has provided our program with the varied perspectives and skill sets to ensure our candidates have a high-quality experience that prepares them well for their own classrooms.

Orientation of New Faculty at Our Institution

When we first implemented our clinical program, we underestimated the changes that would need to occur for UBTEs. We naively assumed that because the majority of our teacher educators have elementary teaching experience, the transition to supervising in a clinical setting would be easy for them. In fact, Murray and Male (2005) suggest it may take 3 years for UBTEs to establish an identity and the process to do so is complex. While elementary teaching has a great deal in common with teacher education, the two differ significantly and the knowledge and skills used in one setting will not simply transfer to the other setting (Dinkelman, Margolis, & Sikkenga, 2006; Ritter, 2009). The need for careful orientation of new teacher educators followed by ongoing professional development became quickly apparent.

Each new faculty member teaching in our clinical program is assigned another clinical UBTE as a mentor. The mentor is responsible for helping the new faculty member with understanding the structure of our program, expectations for clinical faculty, paperwork for observation and evaluation, and time management. The UBTEs for each block meet several times during the summer and include new faculty members in these meetings. During these summer meetings, the faculty work together to analyze data from the previous year, align curriculum, plan assignments and assessments, and organize field placements. These summer meetings as well as planned meetings throughout the academic year have helped to develop a "culture of collaboration" (Waddell & Vartuli, 2015). We have purposely assigned the same group of UBTEs to a particular block for several consecutive semesters. This allows the group to develop a level of comfort with course material, to develop strong working relationships, and to make informed decisions about needed change in the block courses and practicum.

Needed Changes in Promotion and Tenure Guidelines at Our Institution

Finally, we have work to do regarding how clinical teaching and supervision is valued and reflected in faculty evaluation and tenure/promotion. Our program has certainly made changes in how faculty are hired and evaluated, but this is not the case in our university as a whole. We have struggled with how to include clinical supervision as part of our university tenure and promotion guidelines that continue to very traditional in terms of what is considered appropriate service and research. This has resulted in stress to our UBTEs in the tenure and promotion process as their daily work is not viewed in the same way as that of traditional faculty. Providing the level of support and mentoring required by our program means reduced time to work on traditional scholarly activity. Part of our future efforts will be to make the case for the vision of NCATE, "Higher education must develop and implement alternative reward structures that enhance and legitimize the role of clinical faculty and create dual assignments for faculty with an ongoing role as teachers and mentors in schools" (NCATE, 2010, p. iii).

Implications for Preparing the Next Generation of Teacher Educators

As noted above, implementation of our clinical model has resulted in changes in our hiring practices for new faculty. As we interview faculty candidates, we look for a different type of knowledge than in the past, a different set of skills, and a disposition that acknowledges the importance of partnering with schools. The changes we have made have implications for those institutions with doctoral programs in teacher education.

First, just as we now look for a different faculty candidate than in the past, institutions may also consider making changes in the candidates they accept into programs. Cochran-Smith and Lytle (1999) defined different conceptions of teacher learning: knowledge-*for*-practice, knowledge-*in*-practice, and knowledge-*of*-practice. Knowledge-for-practice refers to knowledge typically gained in teacher education coursework about education history and foundations, content, theories of learning and human development, pedagogy, assessment, school law, and other information about the teaching profession. Knowledge-in-practice includes understandings and knowledge acquired through classroom teaching experience and observation of others. Knowledge-of-practice refers to engagement in teacher education research. While strong content knowledge (knowledge-for-practice) and research skills (knowledge-of-practice) will continue to be a great importance to doctoral candidates, institutions may also need to consider the understanding these candidates have of the preK–12 school context (knowledge-in-practice). Previous classroom teaching experience may prove to be of great value to those pursuing doctoral programs who may be hired to work as UBTEs in clinical programs upon degree completion. Such experience may enhance doctoral candidates' understanding of the need for partnering with school districts in preparing effective educators and of the vital role SBTEs play.

Skills in coaching and mentoring TCs and in working with SBTEs could become important aspects of a doctoral program for teacher educators. According to Mott (1992), the coaching of teaching skills is based on the assumptions that a teacher has basic skills and wishes to refine and enhance those skills. UBTEs need to be comfortable and effective in observing TCs as they work with preK–12 students, then reflecting with them to identify strategies that improve the proficiency of TCs. Additionally, effective UBTEs must be trained in cognitive coaching, which requires knowing how to analyze the teaching/learning experience, facilitate reflection in TCs, and how to suggest improved and innovative teaching practices. UBTEs are encouraged to draw from their own significant classroom experiences and apply their own personal, practical knowledge in making suggestions to TCs.

Again, the implications of effective coaching and cognitive coaching are that UBTEs must have more classroom experience to draw from in addition to an advanced degree. As we learned, assuming these are natural skills is simply incorrect and for doctoral candidates with little experience in schools, work to develop these skills is of primary importance. These skills could be developed through coursework and through extended work with undergraduate TCs in the institution.

Finally, institutions with doctoral programs have the resources and opportunity to contribute to the research base around the changing role of UBTEs in clinical models. As universities work to prepare the next generation of teacher educators to work in clinical models, the need for guidance from research is necessary. A strong focus on this area of research will support the efforts of all teacher education programs.

CONCLUSION

When we made the decision to transition to a clinical model for elementary teacher preparation, we did so with excitement fully expecting greatly improved outcomes for our teacher candidates. The resulting changes in the role of our UBTEs were not as expected but have served to impact our program positively. The daily work of our UBTEs has changed and the knowledge, skills, and dispositions needed by these clinical educators have led to revisions in our hiring practices. We actively search for faculty with experience working collaboratively with K–12 schools in varied settings and we purposefully hire both practitioners and tenure track faculty for our clinical program. We have realized the need for careful orientation of new faculty and ongoing professional development and support.

Bullock (2012) writes of the problem of enactment and likens his own journey as a new teacher educator to that of a pre-service teaching learning to teach. Although he possessed informal and intuitive knowledge of learning to teach from his own experience and formal knowledge of learning to teach from his doctoral program, using this knowledge in his work with pre-service teachers was challenging. In reality, translating theory into practice is complex regardless of the context and participants.

In many ways, our implementation of a clinical model parallels the problem of enactment experienced by novice teachers and new teacher educators. A growing body of research provides knowledge of what works in clinical programs and of the characteristics and roles of UBTEs in such programs. As we learn more, both formally and informally, about the work of UBTEs in clinical programs, we are tasked with using this knowledge to enact revised practices that support our candidates on their journeys to their own classrooms.

Discussion Questions

1. A minimum of 3 years of classroom teaching experience is a common requirement for a tenure-track position in a teacher education program. When searching for faculty members, is additional classroom experience (beyond a 3-year minimum) of lesser, greater, or similar value to a terminal degree? Can extensive classroom experience combined with a Master's degree be considered as valuable as a terminal degree coupled with less classroom experience?
2. What personal characteristics would be most beneficial in a faculty candidate for an intensive clinical program? How have the desired characteristics changed as programs have introduced more clinical experiences?

3. We realize not all teacher educators make the transition to a clinical model easily; this may be an issue of philosophy. What measures can be taken to aid in this transition? Are there faculty who simply cannot make the transition and should not be required to do so?

4. Our clinical faculty seem to utilize two approaches to teaching and supervising/coaching in the field: those who want our teacher candidates to learn to think like teachers and those who explicitly teach "how to" teach to our candidates. We realize the need for some of both approaches. How can these approaches be balanced in a clinical model?

5. In clinical models, faculty members have a responsibility to identify candidates who do not seem to fit the education profession and then to hold hard conversations with those candidates. Do clinical faculty members need training in identifying those candidates and when those conversation should be held? How might training in planning and holding hard conversations (including "counseling out") look?

6. How should the ability of clinical faculty to coach and mentor candidates in the field be weighed against their classroom teaching ability in faculty evaluation?

7. What can UBTEs do to ensure that partnerships between school districts and universities are mutually beneficial?

REFERENCES

American Association of Colleges of Teacher Education. (2017). *A pivot toward clinical practice, its lexicon, and renewing the profession of teaching.* [White Paper, Executive Summary]. Retrieved from http://www.nysed.gov/common/nysed/files/cpceexecutivesummary-accessible.pdf

Bullock, S. M. (2012). Creating a space for the development of professional knowledge: A self-study of supervising teacher candidates during practicum placements. *Studying Teacher Education, 8*(2), 143–156.

Burns, R. W., Jacobs, J., & Yendol-Hoppey, D. (2016). The changing nature of the role of the university supervisor and function of preservice teacher supervision in an era of clinically-rich practice. *Action in Teacher Education, 38*(4), 410–425. http://doi.org/10.1080/01626620.2016.1226203

Cochran-Smith, M., & Lytle, S. (1999). Relationships of knowledge and practice: Teacher learning in communities. In G. Griffin (Ed.), *Review of research in education* (Vol. 24, pp. 249–305). Washington, DC: American Educational Research Association.

Council for the Accreditation of Educator Preparation. (2013). Council for the Accreditation of Educator Preparation Report to the Public, the States, the Policymakers, and the Education Profession. Retrieved from http://caepnet.files.wordpress.com/2013/05/annualreport_final.pdf

Darling-Hammond, L. (2010). Teacher education and the American future. *Journal of Teacher Education. 61*(1–2), 35–47.

Dee, A. L. (2012). Collaborative clinical practice: An alternative field experience. *Issues in Teacher Education, 21*(2), 147–163.

Dinkelman, T., Margolis, J., & Sikkenga, K. (2006). From teacher to teacher educator: Experience, expectations, and expatriation. *Studying Teacher Education, 2*, 5–23.

Gardiner, W., & Salmon, D. (2014). Faculty research residencies: A response to the problem of enactment. *Professional Educator, 38*(1). Retrieved from https://wp.auburn.edu/educate/archives/

Grossman, P., Hammerness, K., & McDonald, M. (2009). Redefining teaching, reimagining teacher education. *Teachers and Teaching, Theory and Practice, 15*(2) 273–289. https://doi.org/10.1080/13540600902875340

Interstate Teacher Assessment and Support Consortium. (2011). *InTASC model core teaching standards: A resource for state dialogue.* Washington, DC: Council of Chief State School Officers.

Koerner, M., Rust, F. O., & Baumgartner, F. (2002). Exploring roles in student teaching placements. *Teacher Education Quarterly, 29*(2), 35–58.

Mott, M. (1992). Cognitive coaching for nurse educators. *Journal of Nursing Education, 31*(4), 188–190.

Murray, J., & Male, T. (2005). Becoming a teacher educator: Evidence from the field. *Teaching and Teacher Education. 21*(2), 125–142.

National Council for Accreditation of Teacher Education, Report of the Blue Ribbon Panel on Clinical Preparation and Partnerships for Improved Student Learning. (2010). *Transforming teacher education through clinical practice: A national strategy to prepare effective teachers.* Retrieved from https://files.eric.ed.gov/fulltext/ED512807.pdf

Payor, T. (2016). Perspective from two professions: Two professionals making meaning of the clinical educator role. University of South Florida, ProQuest Dissertations Publishing. (10107981)

Ritter, J. K. (2009). Developing a vision of teacher education: How my classroom teacher understandings evolved in the university environment. *Studying Teacher Education, 5*(1), 45–60.

Waddell, J., & Vartuli, S. (2015). Moving from traditional teacher education to a field-based urban teacher education program: One program's story of reform. *Professional Educator, 39*(2). Retrieved from https://wp.auburn.edu/educate/archives/

Yendol-Hoppey, D., & Franco, Y. (2014). In search of signature pedagogy for PDS teacher education: A review of articles published in "School-University Partnerships." *School–University Partnerships, 7*(1), 17–34.

Zeichner, K. (2010). Rethinking connections between campus courses and field experiences in college and university based teacher education. *Journal of Teacher Education, 61*(1–2), 89–99.

CHAPTER 6

"HOW DID I GET TO WHERE I AM?"

Turning Points in the Personal and Professional Lives of Literacy Teacher Educators[1]

Pooja Dharamshi
Simon Fraser University

Clare Kosnik
University of Toronto

Lydia Menna
University of Alberta

Storying . . . defines humanity . . . in one way or another we tell ourselves and each other stories about life
—Chambers, 1985, p. 3–4)

Preparing the Next Generation of Teacher Educators for Clinical Practice, pages 113–135
Copyright © 2019 by Information Age Publishing

113

The research *Literacy Teacher Educators: Their Backgrounds, Visions, and Practices* which includes 28 literacy/English teacher educators (LTEs) in four countries (Canada, United States, England, and Australia) is studying in-depth their backgrounds, pedagogies, and practices. The specific questions that guided this aspect of the study were:

- What do LTEs identify as turning points in their personal and professional lives?
- Is there a connection between LTEs' turning points and how they enact clinically intensive practices?

Identifying the turning points and how they influenced their pedagogies may help the field of teacher education, in particular how to incorporate rich field experiences into teacher education in a meaningful way. Focusing on the lives of teacher educators, this chapter begins with a general discussion of research on teacher educators then moves to the importance of story followed by the findings and discussion.

TEACHER EDUCATORS

Effectively preparing teacher candidates for 21st century classrooms presents a number of challenges for teacher educators. One of the challenges that is most persistent is the disconnect between university-based courses and school-based components of teacher education programs (Darling-Hammond, 2006; White 2016, 2018; Zeichner, 2010). In response, the National Council for Accreditation of Teacher Education's (NCATE) report *Clinical Preparation in Teacher Education* (NCATE, 2010) clearly states:

> To prepare effective teachers for 21st century classrooms, teacher education must shift away from a norm, which emphasizes academic preparation and course work loosely linked to school-based experiences. Rather, it must move to programs that are fully grounded in clinical practice and interwoven with academic content and professional courses.

Scholars of teacher education are calling for "interplay between academic, practitioner, and community expertise" (Zeichner, 2010, p. 90) to develop effective clinically intensive practices. This connection would expand upon learning opportunities for teacher candidates and in turn better prepare them for working in contemporary classrooms with a diverse student body (p. 91). Clinically intensive practices, however, are often difficult to accomplish because they require bringing together academic and practitioner knowledge in meaningful and nonhierarchical ways. Some examples of how these practices have been integrated into teacher education include:

- bringing K–12 educators and their knowledge into campus courses and practice teaching placements;
- incorporating representations of teachers' practices in campus courses (e.g., K–12 teachers' research integrated into the teacher education curriculum);
- incorporating knowledge from communities into pre-service teacher education (Zeichner, 2010, p. 93); and
- building strong connections between the preparation of teachers and schools through professional development schools or "hybrid institutions" (NCATE, 2010, p. 8).

Understanding the work of teacher educators, those who prepare future teachers, has been an emerging field of study. There has been growing attention in research looking at the transition from classroom teacher to teacher educator (Dinkelman, Margolis, & Sikkenga, 2006; McKeon & Harrison, 2012; Murray & Male, 2005; Williams, Ritter, & Bullock, 2012) and their knowledge, practices, and pedagogies (Goodwin & Kosnik, 2013; Korthagen, Kessels, Koster, Langerwarf, & Wubbels, 2001; Loughran, 2011, 2014); however, what remains missing from the literature is how teacher educators are being prepared for clinically intensive teacher preparation.

Understanding the Power of Stories

Lortie (1975) argues teacher candidates are not blank slates, they come to their teacher education program with beliefs, values, and views. Moving them beyond their own experiences and beliefs requires skillful and intentional work. To help make explicit how their own experiences have shaped them, some teacher educators have teacher candidates complete an autobiography and some often in a specific area such as literacy (Williamson, 2013). Similarly, LTEs come to teacher education with beliefs, values, and views which shape their pedagogy. Edwards (2009) notes "story is also important in terms of our literate identities, defining where we come from, who we are in the present and what we hope for the future as well as assisting to sort and understand experience" (p. 51). Fevre (2011) argues narrative can be an important part of a pedagogy for teacher education:

> Kierkegaard claims life is lived forwards but understood backwards (cited in Peter, 2009). In retelling and interpreting stories from one's own past, and examining stories from the past of one's peers, these preservice teachers have had opportunities to create understandings out of their experiences that could affect their future actions... (p. 786)

Although not specific to teacher educators, the research on narrative as pedagogy in teacher education is important for understanding teacher educator development and so highly relevant to this study. By listening to teacher educators' stories, patterns may emerge. Educators can use narrative work to "assist in critiquing the larger stories in which they have been positioned, to re-story their own lives and relationships and to author a more complete self and world story" (Fevre, 2011, p. 780).

Huber, Li, Murphy, Nelson, and Young (2014) remind us "[t]eachers and teacher educators compose their lives in the midst of the complexity of relationships and situations not only in school landscapes, but in the midst of relationships and situations across multiple contexts" (p. 184). Consequently, it is a challenge to inquire into the ongoing and complex experiences that inform who they are and who they are becoming (Huber et al., 2014, p. 184). Dewey was one of the first researchers to recognize teachers as "moved by their own intelligences and ideas" (Dewey, 1908/1981, p. 16). He recognized that past–present–future are all part of an individual.

This leads to the question: What stories do the teacher educators tell? Zeichner (2005) was one of the first to describe his journey of becoming a teacher educator. He argues "that those who work in teacher education programs need to think consciously about their role as teacher educators and engage in the same sort of self-study and critique of their practice as they ask their students to do in their elementary and secondary school classrooms" (p. 123). In Cochran-Smith's (2012) chronicle of her journey as a researcher she notes "one of the most important lessons I learned as an emerging scholar was that I needed to figure out how to position myself and where to locate myself in terms of research on teaching and teacher education" (p. 101). Reflecting and interpreting our stories helps to create understandings which could inform practices and pedagogies as a teacher educator and researcher.

Although the research on teacher educators has increased, the European Commission notes they are still an under-researched group and an under-supported group (2013). Serious consideration should be given to teacher educators individually and collectively.

METHODOLOGY

Initially, invitations to participate in the study were sent to 15 LTEs. This led to "snowball sampling" whereby some LTEs who had accepted the invitation then suggested a colleague who might be relevant for the study. Punch (2014) describes snowball sampling as "identifying cases of interest from people who know people who know what cases are information rich" (p. 163). Suggested individuals were invited to the study after reviewing faculty profiles on their university websites to ensure they were teaching literacy courses. To make the sample consistent only those who had a doctorate were invited. Efforts were made to ensure a range of experience (e.g., elementary/primary and secondary teaching), and a gender representation comparable to that in the profession as a whole. Six declined the invitation to participate for a variety of reasons (e.g., assuming a new administrative position and therefore not teaching literacy/English methods courses). None declined because of lack of interest. All 28 participants were interviewed three times over the period April 2012 to August 2014. Each semi-structured interview took approximately 60–90 minutes. The same questions were asked of all participants, but probe questions were posed and additional comments were welcomed. Most of the questions were open-ended in that they sought more than a yes/no responses or simple factual answers. Interviews were done either face-to-face or on Skype and were audio-recorded and transcribed.

The first interview had five parts: background experiences, qualities (in their view) of an effective literacy educator, identity (e.g., their academic community), turning points in their career (personal and professional), and research activities. The second interview had four parts: framework and goals for their literacy course(s), pedagogies used and reasons for using them, assignments and readings, and how and why their views and practices have changed over the years. The third interview focused on use of digital technology and future plans. Sample interview questions are provided in Table 6.1.

TABLE 6.1 **Sample Interview Question**		
Interview	**Focus**	**Sample Questions**
1	Background experiences, qualities of an effective literacy educator, identity, turning points in their career, and research activities	• What jobs/positions did you have prior to joining the university? • How did you acquire skills for teaching in higher education? • Do you have a community of scholars in your university? • What qualities do you feel that you bring to your work as a literacy teacher educator? • Do you think it is important for teacher educators to be doing research? If yes, why?
2	Framework and goals for their literacy course(s), pedagogies used and reasons for using them, assignments and readings, change in views and practices	• Which literacy theorists resonate with you? • Tell me about your teaching style. • What do you find most challenging about teaching literacy courses? • How has your practice as a literacy teacher educator changed? Why have they changed?
3	Use of digital technology and future plans	• What place should digital technology have in a teacher education program? • Looking ahead, what research would you like to do?

Much of the methodology was qualitative as defined by Merriam (2009) and Punch (2014). Qualitative inquiry is justified as it provides depth of understanding and enables exploration of questions that do not on the whole lend themselves to quantitative inquiry (Guyton & McIntyre, 1990; Merriam, 2009). It opens the way to gaining entirely unexpected ideas and information from participants in addition to finding out their opinions on simple preset matters. A modified grounded theory approach was used, not beginning with a fixed theory but generating theory inductively from the data using a set of techniques and procedures for collection and analysis (Punch, 2014).

For data analysis, qualitative software NVivo 9 was used. The first level of analysis, "open coding" (Strauss & Corbin, 2000), was used to examine properties of the data (Creswell & Miller, 2000) by identifying salient words and phrases, relating to the research questions and any other categories or themes, which were emerging. The interview transcripts were read several times line-by-line and important words and phrases were coded. To initially generate open codes, the clearest transcripts were analyzed; they were "richly descriptive" (Merriam, 1998, p. 7) and had few disruptions (e.g., phrases transcribed as "XXX" because transcriber could not hear what was being said). During the open coding process, transcripts were first coded by hand. Then, all transcribed interviews were imported into NVivo 9 software for analysis "to allow rigorous interrogation of the data" (Crowley, Harre, & Tagg, 2002).

Approximately 35 nodes (themes) that related to development as teacher educators were analyzed. There were a number of relevant nodes beyond the "turning points" node that were relevant. For example, some relevant nodes included: early life experiences, family and cultural context, work as a classroom teacher, doctoral studies, university community, identity as an academic, qualities of teacher educators, efforts for self-improvement, and political context. By analyzing these nodes a number of common categories/themes/nodes were identified. The next step was axial coding which led to four sub-nodes (themes/categories) being created: influence of childhood/family, influence of their own classroom teaching, influence of their doctoral studies, and influence in their current work as teacher educators. For almost all of the participants there were key turning points in these four periods of their lives. As the analysis progressed, key findings were identified and refined—adding some and deleting or merging others—through "constant comparison" of the interview transcripts. Through axial coding connections were identified across the nodes. Queries were run to determine connections among these four experiences and their pedagogy of literacy teacher education. Selective coding led to a key finding that experiences, beginning in childhood, influenced the current practices and beliefs of LTEs.

FINDINGS

To provide an overall picture of the 28 LTEs, their background, experiences, and common turning points are represented in Table 6.2, Table 6.3, and Table 6.4.

Most LTEs had a fair amount of experience as classroom teachers in K–12 settings. As a result, they had a level of comfort teaching in schools and had developed views of what pre-service and in-service teachers need.

Several LTEs conducted their doctoral research in classroom settings. This experience strengthened their familiarity with and commitment to clinically intensive teacher education. The experiences they gained while conducting research in schools (including their own classrooms) helped them develop deeper connections between theory and practices, a key aim of clinically intensive teacher education.

In the second interview, participants were asked to draw a timeline of their turning points. All but one began in early childhood. Through analysis, four distinct periods emerged: in early childhood, during classroom teaching, during doctoral studies, and as teacher educators. See Table 6.4 of key turning points identified by the LTEs.

TABLE 6.2 Experience as a Classroom Teacher	
Number of Years as a Classroom Teacher (Overall Sample of 28 LTEs)	
0 years	1
1–5 years	2
6–10 years	13
11–20 years	6
20+ years	6

TABLE 6.3 Research Topics of 28 LTEs	
PhD Research (Overall Sample of 28 LTEs)	
Research conducted in K–12 schools	18
Research conducted in own classrooms	14
Examples of research topics	• "Newstime" as a practice in Grade 2 classroom • Use of poetry in a fifth grade classroom • On-line activities of Grade 8 students • First grade children learning to read • Student dialogue in high-school English classes • Ethnography of writing practices in first grade classroom

TABLE 6.4 Turning Points of Overall Sample of 28 LTEs

Turning Points of LTEs (Overall Sample of 28 LTEs)	Number
As Classroom Teachers	
Involved in teacher inquiry groups	6
Had a mentor who encouraged him/her to do a PhD	11
Involved in a professional development project with teachers	20
Involved in a research project (research conducted in his/her classroom)	14
Had a leadership position in school district	17
Had a pivotal experience while a teacher (e.g., discrimination against children)	12
As Doctoral Students	
Taught in teacher education	13
Was part of a research team that conducted research in schools	10
As Faculty Members	
Has a project in a local school/community center	21
Involves teacher candidates in community-based/tutoring project	11

As noted above, several LTEs had pivotal experiences while they were classroom teachers, which shaped their views of what new teachers need to know and do. As a result, these turning points often influenced the focus of their work as teacher educators, in particular making stronger connections between the academic program and practice teaching. For example, Sara identified teaching in rural communities as a turning point in her career. The community in which she taught was deeply divided along racial lines. She noted the complexities of teaching in this context, "although I had grown up in lots of rural regional communities, I really didn't think I was quite prepared for the work of a teacher in a rural regional context...I didn't know how to fight against a community where I was already being socialized as the new White teacher." As a teacher educator, she focused on preparing teacher candidates for working in rural communities by creating opportunities for them to disrupt biases and get to know the community in which they would be teaching. She also provided learning opportunities that encouraged them to view pupils in rural communities as "knowledgeable" and as "curricular resources." Like Sara, there was often a direct link between LTEs early experiences and their practices and pedagogies as teacher educators.

Not all of the participants were as committed to clinically intensive practices. Twenty-one were currently conducting research in a local school/community center while 11 involved teacher candidates in community-based/tutoring project. For all, these projects were their own initiative.

TABLE 6.5 Examples of Clinically-Intensive Practices
Examples of Clinically Intensive Practices
Organizing a tutoring program in a local school
Conducting their classes in a local school
Involving teacher candidates in the community (e.g., church-based group of new immigrants)
Involving teacher candidates in their professional work (e.g., writing support group for struggling adolescent writers)
Visiting a youth center for incarcerated adolescents
Including teacher candidates in their research projects
Studying local community where teacher candidates are doing their practice teaching
Connecting with local business to support the community (e.g., local book store)
Co-teaching their courses with a practicing teacher
Interviewing secondary school students who feel marginalized
Supporting teacher candidates' efforts to raise funds for a community-initiative (e.g., wildlife preservation project)

In-Depth Examples: The Practices of Hope, Giovanni, and Martha Ann

To better understand the rationale for clinically intensive practices and provide more in-depth examples, the practices of three LTEs, Hope, Giovanni, and Martha Ann, are presented. Their turning points are described at four significant times in their lives: early life, classroom teaching, doctoral studies, and as a teacher educator showing how these experiences led to them including clinically intensive practices in their literacy course.

Hope

Hope has been a faculty member for five years at a tier one research-intensive university in the Northwest United States.

Early life experiences. When constructing her timeline Hope described her early life as posing a number of challenges. She struggled with learning to read, "If you look at my report cards from first and second grade, the teacher is sort of imploring somebody to please read with me at home, which didn't really happen." After completing secondary school, she chose to attend a community college rather than university. In her college years as a result of her family circumstances, she explains:

> I had to [care] for two half-sisters who were much younger...And then I continued, after college, to take care of them and I was really their primary

> caregiver. I was kind of the anchor there. And so I started doing things for and with them that I thought would nurture them.

After two and a half years at the community college where she did fairly well, she realized that she had "an intellectual side." This was a pivotal moment because it led to her transferring to a university.

While completing her bachelor of arts degree in literature she continued to be heavily involved in the life of her half-sisters. She enrolled them in Girl Guides, volunteered in their schools, and took them to their dance classes which was a turning point for her, "I think through those experiences of being in school, and particularly through being a Girl Scout leader, I realized that I really enjoyed working with kids, younger ones in particular, and giving them opportunities for leadership and empowerment." After completing her BA, she decided to become a teacher and completed a teacher credential program. Her master of education thesis was an action research project studying her own teaching.

Classroom teaching.   Hope was a classroom teacher for seven and a half years teaching kindergarten and second grade. She quickly moved into a leadership role because she became a literacy coach after teaching for only two and a half years. Although she had been a struggling reader, literacy was her passion. The professional development offered by her school district and her involvement in a national writing project were key turning points because they opened up the possibility for her to become a literacy coach and to see herself in a leadership position. She worked with teachers on their literacy programs and this involvement with both children and adults was a turning point for her because she enjoyed the latter yet realized she had much still to learn. She enrolled in a doctoral program to further her studies, which was a key turning point.

Doctoral studies.   When considering a doctoral program, Hope applied to one of the top universities in the world and was accepted. During her doctoral studies she had opportunities to teach literacy methods courses to elementary teacher candidates. Teaching methods courses was a turning point because it reinforced her enjoyment of working with adults. Her doctoral research was a study of

> writing instruction preparation in two elementary teacher preparation programs... I looked both at the methods courses and the placement classrooms. And I looked for anything, any other places where they might have had learning about writing instruction. It turns out there wasn't any.

Observing a lack of effective preparation for teacher candidates, Hope saw the need for more explicit connections between academic courses and practice teaching placements which strengthened her commitment to clinically intensive practice especially regarding the teaching of writing.

As a teacher educator.   Hope secured a tenure stream position in a top-tier university. In her pedagogy, she drew on her work as a classroom teacher because she could offer specific examples of teaching. For example, when her teacher candidates designed lesson plans, she gave them "the nitty gritty feedback" based on her experiences of "having been a teacher and [knowing] how a lesson's going to roll out or how kids are going to respond." Hope's teaching style at the university was consistent with who she was as an individual: Drawing on her team approach informed by her work as a Girl Guide Leader and as a literacy coach, she involved classroom teachers and teaching assistants heavily in the delivery of her courses. She continues to do so because they have current, relevant teaching experience. This team approach represents the type of clinical preparation in teacher education that NCATE (2010) advocates is necessary to link university faculty, clinical faculty (in P–12 classrooms), and pre-service teachers.

Hope described the goals for her literacy courses as: deepening student teachers' understanding of practice, approximation of practice, learning to write lesson plans, reflection, and deconstruction of knowledge. Her teaching style was very consistent with who she is as an individual and how she lives her life: extensive use of small group work, plentiful time for discussion with little time devoted to lecture, co-constructing community with her student teachers, being responsive and modelling responsiveness, being transparent about pedagogical challenges she faces, being honest and showing her vulnerability, and knowing how to listen. One of her major assignments required teacher candidates to create a video to show their conceptual and pedagogical knowledge in content areas. Making the video was often done in the school where they were doing their practice teaching, which helped to bridge theory and practice. Her goals and teaching style were consistent with how she learned (to be a teacher, coach, and literacy teacher educator) and who she was as individual (emphasis on the interpersonal).

Hope's research agenda was a continuation of her doctoral work and examines writing programs in schools. This work, which is tied directly to her doctoral research and her work as a classroom teacher, provides her with an ongoing and authentic connection to schools. She felt "all of that experience, really helped me because I'm in schools, I work, my research agenda right now is around professional development with fourth and fifth grade teachers in writing." In addition to her research, she offered summer institutes for teachers (on the teaching of writing) and invited teacher candidates to attend. Having teachers and teacher candidates in the same professional development session is another example of Hope's clinically intensive pedagogies. Effectively teaching writing through bridging academic courses and practical experiences is a theme of Hope's work from her time as a classroom teacher, the focus of her doctorate, and now as the cornerstone of her work in academia.

Giovanni

Giovanni is an associate professor and chair of the Department of Reading, Writing, and Literacy at a large research-intensive university in the Northeast region of the United States.

Early life experiences. Giovanni is a second-generation born American from a mixed-race family. His mother and father's family immigrated from Europe and Southeast Asia, respectively. Giovanni's family history shaped his research interests, as well as his views on literacy teaching and learning. Growing up in an "immigrant household," Giovanni recalled his parents placing emphasis on education; attaining high levels of education were highly valued and encouraged. Giovanni attributed these values to his father's immigrant experiences. His father, a first-generation immigrant from South East Asia, grew up in a "tough, working-class, [and] poor neighborhoods" in the United States. As a young adult, Giovanni's father experienced segregation; he was subject to the Jim Crow laws[2] in the South. These experiences of marginalization influenced Giovanni's father a great deal, and in turn Giovanni's upbringing, "I was raised [being told] education is something no one can take away from you...someone can persecute you based on all sorts of arbitrary characteristics, but they can never take [education] away." After completing his BA, he applied for the alternative certification-teaching program, Teach for America (TFA).

Classroom teaching. Giovanni was a classroom teacher for 10 years teaching a range of students (primary, middle, and senior) in a variety of contexts, in and outside of the United States. Giovanni's stance on teaching, learning, and teacher education was informed by his diverse teaching experiences in various contexts and levels. As a member of TFA, Giovanni taught in under-resourced areas where he was endlessly "confronting issues of inequality and social injustices." As a novice classroom teacher, Giovanni taught the first grade where he had to administer standardized tests for the first time. He identified this experience as a turning point because his class, which included many ELL and immigrant students, was expected to participate in annual standardized testing. Giovanni witnessed the inequities his students faced as non-native English speakers. He recalled, "I had children who had never been to school before who were forced to fill out bubble exams and in a language that wasn't their native language." Although Giovanni created a "loving and supportive environment," he felt it was not enough to make his students feel safe. Remembering the tremendous pressure they were under from the standardized test, he viewed what they endured as a form of "symbolic violence." Giovanni made every attempt to live in the community in which he taught and conducted his research so he could "get to know the families" and build "good relationships with parents." Giovanni's classroom teaching experiences informed his current practice as an LTE. For instance, in his practice, he brokered difficult conversations with student teachers that aim for developing an "awareness about the ways in which the system [can be] inequitable in many ways." In turn, he wanted student teachers to see their role as advocates for their students. He has facilitated this emerging identity through involving teacher candidates in the community, as well as including them in his community-based research projects.

Doctoral studies.   After several years in the classroom, Giovanni was admitted to a doctoral program in the Department of Reading, Writing and Literacy at an American university. His doctoral research studied his own fifth grade classroom and focused on the narratives of immigrant and migrant students, as well as studying and his own practice; "I was theorizing my own classroom practice," he recalled. Giovanni's research topic and context were personal to him because they were closely linked to his own familial heritage: "It was a back to roots things. California was where my grandfather had been a migrant laborer. So I went there to explore the history." By conducting his doctoral research in his own classroom, Giovanni was able to make connections between theory and practice. Beyond completing his doctoral studies, he saw the value of teachers and teacher candidates adopting a critical perspective on teaching. To achieve this he believes in having clinically intensive work embedded in his teacher education courses both in his goals and pedagogy, which often means extending his course beyond the classroom walls. In many ways, Giovanni's current research was a continuation of his doctoral work. He continued his research as a community and school based researcher with students and community members who face social injustices and inequities.

During his graduate studies Giovanni identified an assignment, which specifically influenced him. He had to interview someone from a different background, and so he interviewed his grandfather who was a migrant worker in the 1920s. Giovanni recalled this assignment to be a "powerful experience" because it revealed to him his own "family literacies." The assignment was the first time he was invited and encouraged to explore his history. He commented, "There was a buried history...that I'd never had the opportunity to inquire and to explore through my formal education." Giovanni truly valued family and community literacy practices; his research examined the out-of-school literacy practices through "community-based action research."

As a teacher educator.   Giovanni's experience as a classroom teacher shaped the goals for his teacher education courses. He aimed for the democratization of knowledge; he "invited" multiple perspectives into his courses by using multicultural texts and resources. He explained, "My own narratives and memories as a teacher are very much a resource of my teaching and pedagogy" and in turn he invited students to share their own narratives and memories. To better understand the multiple narratives of those in the local community Giovanni delivered much of his in a Catholic church that had a school attached to it. He had secured a grant, which encouraged community engagement through a focus on asset-based community development. By engaging with community members in a place where they were regarded as knowledgeable and successful, the teacher candidates in Giovanni's class were able to experience firsthand expansive literacy practices taking place outside of traditional sites of literacy learning, and an authentic enactment of clinically intensive practice. Many of his teacher candidates became highly committed to the immigrant community and volunteered far beyond what was required. By building strong connections between the preparation of teachers and local communities he conceptualized teacher education as a "hybrid" space (NCATE, 2010, p. 8).

Giovanni wanted his teacher candidates to "see themselves as advocates," as well as assume an "activist stance in their work." To achieve this, Giovanni had his teacher candidates engage in readings and assignments which uncover "the power of the children's own literacy practices, their narratives, their own testimonials." Giovanni placed social justice at the core of his teaching and research, and aimed for his teacher candidates to view "teaching as an intellectual enterprise," and to see "students as intellectuals." As an LTE, Giovanni drew on the experiences of his immigrant students to discuss issues of language and power with his teacher candidates. In his practice, he brokered difficult conversations with teacher candidates that aimed for developing an "awareness about the ways in which the system [can be] inequitable in many ways."

Martha Ann

Martha Ann is a full professor with 28 years of experience as a faculty member at a Canadian university.

Early life experiences.   Martha Ann described herself as an avid reader who carved out time every day to read for pleasure. As she reflected on early literacy experiences she traced her love of reading and appreciation for storytelling back to family members, "My great aunt lived with my family and she was a wonderful storyteller. Having her in our lives impacted every single one of us." As a child, listening to her great aunt weave colorful tales featuring "imaginary creatures, kings and queens of Ireland, leprechauns and fairies" exposed Martha Ann to the power of storytelling. Family literacy practices also inspired her appreciation for diverse text formats. Her father "was a great reader of comic books" who shared this passion with his children.

When Martha Ann started school, learning to read and write were skills she acquired quite easily. She did well in school and decided to further her education. Neither of her parents were afforded the opportunity to pursue higher education. She noted, "My father finished Grade 8. My mother finished Grade 6 and went on to secretarial school." At a young age, Martha Ann decided to become a teacher. She described "starting university was a huge turning point in life." After completing Grade 11 she enrolled in "s teacher's college and completed a two-year degree." She started her career as a classroom teacher at the age of 19. She noted, "I was very young, that's why when I finished my undergraduate [training] I went back to [university] for my master's degree." She completed a master's degree, at a prestigious Canadian university, with a focus on the diagnosis and treatment of reading disabilities. Her graduate training informed her practice as a classroom teacher. As Martha Ann progressed in her career her passion for literacy, especially family literacy, became a central component of her work.

Classroom teacher. Martha Ann was a classroom teacher for 16 years teaching in both the primary and middle school divisions and working with special needs students in the secondary division. In the later stages of her teaching career she took on leadership positions that provided the opportunity to work directly with classroom teachers. She spent 2 years as a literacy consultant providing workshops for classroom teachers. The experience of working with teachers to "collaboratively inquire" into how particular instructional strategies informed their literacy program planning represented a key turning point, and provided her with experiences of working with adult learners. This experience helped her acquire strategies for working with adults and shaped her view of the importance of teacher candidates continually studying practice. Although she did not use the term clinically intensive practices, this was in essence what she believed was essential for both teachers and teacher candidates.

Doctoral studies. Martha Ann had not initially planned on pursuing doctoral studies. The inspiration to pursue a PhD was rather unexpected. While completing a master's degree she enrolled in a summer course with a young instructor who "was doing all these creative things" in the course and "was so thrilled with the things he had done" throughout his doctoral studies. He was just embarking on an academic career and would enthusiastically "talk about the PhD" process. She fondly referenced this encounter as "the seed that planted [doctoral studies] in my mind." Some years later, as a divorced, single mother with two children, she enrolled in a doctoral program and "forged a new career" path. She completed her doctorate at a university in the Midwestern United States, with two areas of specialization, curriculum studies and language education. Pursuing doctoral studies was a key turning point in her life. Her doctoral research focused on "teacher change processes" which entailed "interviewing fifty classroom teachers to find out what changes they had made in their language arts programs." Given the focus of her doctoral research, in which she worked closely with classroom teachers, Martha Ann saw the importance of unpacking teaching practices with teachers (and later with teacher candidates).

As a teacher educator.   Martha Ann's extensive experience in the classroom was the foundation for her practice as a teacher educator in a number of ways. As an LTE, she shared her rich and varied experiences with teacher candidates to "spark empathy and understanding of why [as teachers] we have to address the needs of every student in our classroom." She noted, "I had lots of teaching experience and consulting experience when I came to Far North University," and "I had an incredible amount of credibility with the young people who were coming into" the teacher education program. The teacher candidates appreciated her deep understanding of the complexities of literacy pedagogy, which she acquired through years of working with both pupils and classroom teachers. Martha Ann's life experience also gave her "credibility" with mature students who had returned to university to pursue a career change. Her experience as a single mother raising two children, while pursuing an academic career, allowed Martha Ann to connect with mature students on a different level. She explained that for the "older women who had gotten divorced and were coming back to university, it was helpful for them to know that I too was divorced, got my PhD when I was divorced, and was able to forge a career for myself." She noted, "I'm approachable, I try to understand the circumstances they're living through."

Martha Ann's commitment to family literacy played itself out in an interesting manner. Given that she teaches in a northern community in Canada, she invited indigenous elders into her class to tell their stories (as her great aunt did with her), which incorporated knowledge from communities into pre-service teacher education (Zeichner, 2010, p. 93). She had an assignment focused specifically on Canadian children's literature which brought to light stories of children not typically represented in literature (e.g., indigenous children in residential schools) which in turn exposed teacher candidates to different kinds of communities and stories.

Martha Ann's current program of research investigated how collaborative inquiry groups facilitated teachers' use of Canadian children's literature to explore social justice issues. This research allowed her to maintain connections with classroom teachers and gain insight into how they structure and enact their literacy programs. She noted, "I have learned so much with the Canadian literature picture book study about the values the teachers have, the way they think about social justice, how they go about developing units. I share those things in turn with my student teachers" in my literacy courses. Indeed the research project has in many ways informed the goals she has defined for her literacy courses. As an LTE Martha Ann endeavored to help student teachers develop a sense of self-efficacy and the initiative to continue learning, empowered them to make a difference and understand how to effectively use children's literature to inquire across the curriculum. She attempted to scaffold these principles through her instruction and assignments. For example, one of her assignments required student teachers to create a multimodal response to a Canadian picture book focused on a social justice issue. She hoped assignments such as this would help student teachers to take "ownership for looking up resources and doing research, as this is part of developing their teacher identities." To prepare for this assignment, Martha Ann invited the teachers who were part of her inquiry groups to participate in her academic courses as well as make arrangements for the teacher candidates to visit classrooms especially when teachers were doing novels/books about underrepresented voices. This was a way to bring K–12 educators and their knowledge into campus courses and practice teaching placements.

DISCUSSION

Across the 28 LTEs in the study, clinically intensive practice took a variety of forms and levels of commitment. In some cases there was interest but institutional barriers prohibited their efforts. Revising teacher education programs to be more clinically intensive seems valuable; however, there is a danger it could simply be layered onto a program. It should not simply be conceptualized as "more time in schools" but needs to be intertwined thoughtfully into the entire program. And for teacher educators, clinically intensive practice will "look" different because of who they are and what they bring to the program.

The three case studies demonstrated how these LTEs carefully wove clinical experiences into all aspects of their courses. The experiences (turning points) served as a form of preparation for Hope, Giovanni, and Martha Ann's work as teacher educators. Their deeply held beliefs about particular issues were rooted in their lives, continued as a priority while classroom teachers, explored in their doctoral research, and continued to be central to their research. Therefore, they could talk with first-hand experience, passion, and knowledge about the importance of having teacher candidates involved in specific clinically intensive projects. It was not simply tacked onto a course but was the foundation and/or essential dimension to the course.

Providing more time in schools or communities is not sufficient; teacher candidates and teachers need to debrief during and after the experiences to help them make sense of the experience because there is a risk of biases being reinforced. And it needs to be carefully incorporated in the program/courses. The LTEs in this study provided teacher candidates with opportunities to engage with many members of the learning community, including children, teachers, fellow candidates, community members, and university faculty. These experiences were carefully incorporated and tied to the LTEs goals and assignments for their course. Hope, for example, believed more explicit connections were needed between theory and practice, particularly around teaching of writing. Drawing on her past experiences she developed opportunities for teacher candidates to co-construct knowledge with practicing teachers in the Summer Institute she facilitated. By having teacher candidates and teachers work together, she modeled the importance of being involved in the larger learning community. Teacher candidates were able to examine their views through a culminating assignment which asked them to create a video to show their conceptual and pedagogical knowledge in content areas. Giovanni, who invited multiple perspectives into his course and invited teacher candidates to participate in community-based projects used a discussion based approach to "broker difficult conversations" around issues such as literacy, equity, and race. Narrative was an integral component to his pedagogy and so he often invited his teacher candidates to share their own narratives and created opportunities for them to understand narratives from the community in which they would be serving (i.e., involvement in community-based research projects). Finally, Martha Ann, who focused on teacher candidates developing a socially just stance towards literacy teaching, regularly had community stakeholders such as indigenous elders and practicing teachers come into her course to share their knowledge. Her teacher candidates would also frequently visit teachers' classrooms when they were facilitating books and novels featuring underrepresented voices. This model of knowledge integration from multiple sources helped teacher candidates grapple with issues related to structuring and enacting literacy programs in iterative ways so they could arrive at their own informed and nuanced understandings over the course of the term. This learning was represented through assignments such as the multimodal response to a Canadian picture book which focused on a social justice issue. The teacher candidates in Hope, Giovanni, and Martha Ann's courses were offered rich experiences which aimed to broaden their horizons, improve their teaching skills, and develop dispositions to see each child as an individual. Does it matter that the teacher candidates in the three case studies were provided different opportunities? We suspect not because the efforts made by teacher educators to embrace clinically intensive practices came from their life experiences and were deliberately and thoughtfully designed to provide powerful learning opportunities to their teacher candidates.

The LTEs' pedagogy was consistent with examples of clinically intensive practices noted in the Introduction. The LTEs interwove academic and practitioner knowledge in meaningful and non-hierarchical ways; incorporated representations of teachers' practices in their courses, as well as including K–12 educators and local community members into their teacher education courses (Zeichner, 2010). Hope was able to accomplish this by linking the work of university faculty, clinical faculty, and preservice teachers. By drawing on multiple voices to inform her literacy education courses, Hope modeled integrating academic and practitioner knowledge in non-hierarchical ways. Clinically intensive practices such as these demonstrated to teacher candidates the many ways in which schools and communities contribute to the learning of pupils. By including teacher candidates in community-based research projects and engaging candidates in community literacy spaces (local churches), Giovanni conceptualized his course as a "hybrid" classroom and enacted a pedagogy which aimed to "democratize knowledge." Similarly, Martha Ann incorporated representations of teachers' practices in her campus courses (Zeichner, 2010) by integrating teachers' inquiry research into her teacher education curriculum. Individually they established and maintained relationships with classroom teachers and community members. Because of their previous experiences, they were comfortable involving teachers in their classes, visiting teacher candidates in schools, and starting teacher inquiry groups. Although this work was demanding and time-consuming they felt it was essential to being a teacher educator.

For teacher educators, what clinically intensive practice "looked" like was different because of who they are and what they bring to the program. It was their deliberate and thoughtful efforts, however, to enact clinically intensive practices informed by their life experiences that served as powerful learning opportunities for their teacher candidates. The LTEs in this study drew on their own experiences to develop clinically intensive practices and connect theory and practice. Commitment to developing authentic and meaningful clinically intensive practices requires ongoing efforts of reflection and action and should be a process which begins when doctoral students are preparing to become teacher educators. To prepare doctoral students to recognize, value, and integrate clinically intensive practices, teacher educators need to create opportunities for them to make connections with local schools and communities. These opportunities could include collaborative research in local schools and communities, seeking community mentors, co-constructing curriculum, and team-teaching. This approach to teacher educator preparation could serve to sustain opportunities for growth and begin to bridge the gap between university-based courses and school-based components of teacher education programs (Darling-Hammond, 2006; White 2016, 2018; Zeichner, 2010).

Further, teacher education programs can work with doctoral students and new teacher educators to "re-story their own lives and relationships" (Fevre, 2011, p. 780) through the use of stories as related to early life experiences, classroom teaching practices and literacy teacher education. While each will bring their own lived experiences, interests, and strengths to their work, anchoring teacher educator preparation in reflection and authentic engagement with schools and communities will demonstrate to teacher educators authentic enactments of and commitment to clinically intensive practices.

Making explicit what clinically intensive practice entails and providing detailed examples will hopefully help teacher educators to revise their courses so that they are not simply university-based lectures/activities. Moving beyond the campus to create hybrid "classrooms" can help both teacher candidates and the community grow beyond themselves. In order for LTEs to learn with and from one another they need opportunities to collaborate within and across institutions and share practices of clinically intensive preparation. This will allow for a meaningful exchange of perspectives, while broadening the experiences from which they construct their literacy education curriculum.

CONCLUSION

The three case studies showed the relevance of early childhood experiences, classroom teaching, and doctoral work in shaping pedagogy of LTEs. In other words, *you teach who you are*. The LTEs' lived experiences shaped them as individuals, which influenced their personal visions and priorities for literacy teacher education, and led them to develop courses that were clinically intensive. Hearing their stories revealed how they are shaped by both their context and experiences.

Simply mandating more clinical-intensive practices is shortsighted and bound to fail; rather, these practices need to be intertwined thoughtfully into the entire program. For most teacher educators providing rich field experiences for their teacher candidates is tied to their personal/professional experiences. The mini case studies described in this chapter offer some insight into the complex, intentional, and highly individualized work of LTEs, as well as point to implications of how teacher educators are prepared. Teacher educators require institutional encouragement and support to engage with classroom practitioners and community experts in order to co-construct clinically intensive pedagogies. A first step, however, is having teacher educators tell their stories because their experiences have a tremendous influence on their pedagogy and can be integrated in genuine ways into their courses.

Discussion Questions

1. As teachers/teacher educators how have you used your "stories" to inform your practice and identity as an educator?

2. What are the pros and cons of focusing on clinically intensive practices in literacy teacher education?
3. Based on the information presented in this chapter, what are some collaborative and immediate actions that you can take to meet the needs of teacher candidates and local communities?

NOTES

1. We wish to thank the Social Sciences and Humanities Research Council of Canada for their generous support of this research.
2. Racial segregation laws enacted by Southern U.S. states between 1890–1965.

REFERENCES

Chambers, A. (1985). *Booktalk: Occasional writing on literature and children.* London, England: The Bodley Head.

Cochran-Smith, M. (2012). Composing a research life. *Action in Teacher Education, 34*, 99–110.

Creswell, J., & Miller, D. (2000). Determining validity in qualitative inquiry. *Theory into Practice, 39*(3), 124–130.

Crowley, C., Harre, R., & Tagg, C. (2002). Qualitative research and computing: Methodological issues and practices in using QSR NVivo and NUD*IST. *International Journal of Social Research Methodology, 5*(3), 193–197.

Darling-Hammond, L. (2006). *Powerful teacher education.* San Francisco, CA: Jossey-Bass.

Dewey, J. (1981). The practical character of reality. In J. McDermot (Ed.), *The philosophy of John Dewey.* Chicago, IL: University of Chicago Press. (Originally published in 1908)

Dinkelman, T., Margolis, J., & Sikkenga, K. (2006). From teacher to teacher educator: Experiences, expectations, and expatriation. *Studying Teacher Education, 2*(1), 5–23.

Edwards, D. (2009). Tracing literacy journeys: The use of the literacy autobiography in preservice teacher education. *Australian Journal of Teacher Education, 43*(4), 51–61.

European Commission. (2013). *Supporting teacher educators for better learning outcomes.* Brussels, Belgium: European Commission.

Fevre, D. (2011). Creating and facilitating a teacher education curriculum using preservice teachers' autobiographical stories. *Teaching and Teacher Education, 27*(4), 779–787.

Goodwin, L. A., & Kosnik, C. (2013). Quality teacher educators = quality teachers?: Conceptualizing essential domains of knowledge for those who teach teachers. *Teacher Development: An International Journal of Teachers' Professional Development, 17*(3), 334–346.

Guyton, E., & McIntyre, J. (1990). Student teaching and school experiences. In W. R. Houston (Ed.), *Handbook of research on teacher education* (pp. 514–534). New York, NY: Macmillan.

Huber, J., Li, Y., Murphy, S., Nelson, C., & Young, M. (2014). Shifting stories to live by: Teacher education as a curriculum of narrative inquiry identity explorations. *Reflective Practice, 15*(2), 176–189.

Korthagen, F. A. J., Kessels, J., Koster, B., Langerwarf, B., & Wubbels, T. (2001). *Linking theory and practice: The pedagogy of realistic teacher education.* Mahwah, NJ: Erlbaum.

Lortie, D. (1975). *Schoolteacher: A sociological study.* Chicago, IL: University of Chicago Press.

Loughran, J. (2011). On becoming a teacher educator. *Journal of Education for Teaching, 37*(3), 271–291.

Loughran, J. (2014). Professionally developing as a teacher educator. *Journal of Teacher Education, 65*(4), 271–283.

McKeon, F., & Harrison, J. (2012). Developing pedagogical practice and professional identities of beginning teacher educators. *Professional Development in Education, 36*(1–2), 5–44.

Merriam, S. B. (1998). *Qualitative research and case study applications in education,* (2nd ed.). San Francisco, CA: Jossey-Bass.

Merriam, S. (2009). *Qualitative research: A guide to design and implementation.* San Francisco, CA: Jossey-Bass.

Murray, J., & Male, T. (2005). Becoming a teacher educator: Evidence from the field. *Teaching and Teacher Education, 21,* 125–142.

National Council for Accreditation of Teacher Education. (2010). *Transforming teacher education through clinical practice: A national strategy to prepare effective teachers.* Washington DC: New Planet Studios.

Peter, M. (2009). Drama; narrative pedagogy and socially challenged children. *British Journal of Special Education, 36*(1), 9–17.

Punch, K. (2014). *Introduction to social research: Quantitative and qualitative approaches.* London, England: SAGE.

Strauss, A., & Corbin, J. (2000). *Basics of qualitative research: Grounded theory procedures and techniques for developing grounded theory.* Newbury Park, CA: SAGE.

Williams, J., Ritter, J., & Bullock, S. (2012). Understanding the complexity of becoming a teacher educator: Experience, belonging, and practice within a professional learning community. *Studying Teacher Education, 8*(3), 245–260.

Williamson, P. (2013). Engaging literacy practices through inquiry and enactment in teacher education. In C. Kosnik, J. Rowsell, P. Williamson, R. Simon, & C. Beck (Eds.), *Literacy teacher educators: Preparing student teachers for a changing world* (pp. 135–148). Rotterdam, The Netherlands: Sense.

White, S. (2016). Teacher education research and education policymakers: An Australian perspective. *Journal of Education for Teaching, 42*(2), 252–264.

White, S. (2018). An insider look at the implications of 'partnership' policy for teacher educators' professional learning: An Australian perspective. In J. Murray, A. Swennen, & C. Kosnik (Eds.), *International research, policy and practice in teacher education: Insider perspectives* (pp. 31–45). Dordrecht, The Netherlands: Springer.

Zeichner, K. (2005). Becoming a teacher educator: A personal perspective. *Teaching and Teacher Education, 21*, 117–124.

Zeichner, K. (2010). Rethinking the connections between campus courses and field experiences in college and university-based teacher education. *Journal of Teacher Education, 89*(11), 89–99.

PART II

THE PREPARATION OF SCHOOL-BASED
TEACHER EDUCATORS

The importance of developing the next generation of school-based teacher educators cannot be ignored. School-based teacher educators are those teachers who work side-by-side university-based teacher educators as they support teacher candidates who are learning to teach. Today, with the increasing importance of the clinical component in teacher education, the nature of the partnership between schools and higher education institutions is changing. As a result, experienced teachers are assuming a shared responsibility for teacher education while remaining in their school as classroom teachers. This new role asks those who work in schools to strengthen their ability to support teacher candidate development and partner with university-based teacher educators to offer coherently designed preparation programs that provide strong theory to practice links. This expectation occurs while these same teachers are simultaneously teaching PK–12 students.

One context where school-based teacher educators are typically found is the professional development school (PDS). As PDSs began emerging, Darling-Hammond (1994) described professional development schools as contexts where teacher candidate, mentor teacher, and university faculty learning becomes: (a) experimental; (b) grounded in teacher questions; (c) collaborative; (d) connected to and derived from teachers' work with their students; and (e) sustained, intensive, and connected to other aspects of school change. The complexity of these goals requires school-based partners with a specialized skill set and orientation to their work.

Preparing the Next Generation of Teacher Educators for Clinical Practice, pages 137–140
Copyright © 2019 by Information Age Publishing
137

To further clarify the work that would become a part of school-based teacher education, NAPDS (2008) identified nine essentials:

1. A comprehensive mission that is broader in its outreach and scope than the mission of any partner and that furthers the education profession and its responsibility to advance equity within schools and, by potential extension, the broader community.
2. A school–university culture committed to the preparation of future educators that embraces their active engagement in the school community.
3. Ongoing and reciprocal professional development for all participants guided by need.
4. A shared commitment to innovative and reflective practice by all participants.
5. Engagement in and public sharing of the results of deliberate investigations of practice by respective participants.
6. An articulation agreement developed by the respective participants delineating the roles and responsibilities of all involved.
7. A structure that allows all participants a forum for ongoing governance, reflection, and collaboration.
8. Work by college/university faculty and P–12 faculty in formal roles across institutional settings.
9. Dedicated and shared resources and formal rewards and recognition structures.

The school-based teacher educators will need to become full partners in order to enact these nine essentials while simultaneously strengthening the education of future teachers.

Today, with the call for more intense, high quality clinically intensive teacher education, the role of the school-based teacher educator is becoming more complex (Zeichner & Bier, 2015). Research indicates that the school-based teacher educator, sometimes referred to as a mentor, greatly influences how the novice teaches and how the novice thinks about teaching (Clarke & Jarvis-Selinger, 2005). While mentors have not been traditionally viewed as teacher educators, mentors are now being recognized as important collaborators and school-based teacher educators (Feiman-Nemser, 1998) and it is becoming increasingly clear that their roles are complex. Given the shifting importance of the clinical component of teacher education, recognizing the growing importance of highly skilled mentors is essential (Feiman-Nemser & Parker, 1993; Nolan & Parks, 2011; Parker-Katz & Bay, 2007; Yendol-Hoppey & Dana, 2007).

Part II of the book presents two chapters on the development of school-based teacher educators. In Chapter 7, "From Teacher Candidate to

Teacher Educator: What It Means to 'Grow Up' in a Professional Development School Partnership," Sara Helfrich, Sara Hartman, and Larina Sisson begin our exploration about the work of school-based teacher educators. In this chapter the authors offer a case study that focuses on the path of two practicing teachers as they progress from teacher candidate to school-based teacher educator. Their experiences in a clinically based professional development school (PDS) program, as undergraduate and graduate students, shed light on the role of a teacher preparation program in preparing school-based teacher educators. The findings highlight the importance of PDS structures and the benefits a clinically based model provides in becoming a teacher educator, as well as challenges related to developing an identity as a school-based teacher educator. This chapter is meaningful for stakeholders who are involved in creating and sustaining strong clinically based teacher preparation programs.

In Chapter 8, Courtney Lynch digs deeply into what and how school-based teacher educators learn through the collaborative teaching of a methods course. She examines the collaborative planning of a team of school- and university-based teacher educators who co-taught an elementary mathematics methods course in a Grades K–4 PDS. She explores how the PDS spans the boundaries between the school and university creating a third space for hybrid teacher educators. The team of four hybrid teacher educators formed a methods planning community of practice (MPCoP). Lynch found that the MPCoP, operating without a guiding protocol, spent the majority of its time determining the instructional details for methods course experiences. She concludes by describing opportunities for learning while engaging in each of the co-planning activities. The chapter provides insight to the learning of both school and university-based teacher educators working in the shared space of hybrid teacher educators.

In both of these chapters, the PDS is the context for supporting the development of school-based teacher educators and engaging these educators in the core work of educating future teachers. Together, these two chapters provide insight into the complex knowledge, skills, and dispositions needed to develop as school-based teacher educators. Although these two chapters offer exemplars for discussion, much more attention needs to be given to school-based teacher education as an area of future scholarship.

REFERENCES

Clarke, A., & Jarvis-Selinger, S. (2005). What the teaching perspectives of cooperating teachers tell us about their advisory practices. *Teaching and Teacher Education, 21*(1), 65–78.

Darling-Hammond, L. (1994). Developing professional development schools: Early lessons, challenge, and promise. In L. Darling-Hammond (Ed.), *Professional development schools: Schools for developing a profession* (pp. 1–27). New York, NY: Teachers College Press.

Feiman-Nemser, S. (1998). Teachers as teacher educators. *European Journal of Teacher Education, 21*(1) 63–74.

Feiman-Nemser, S., & Parker, M. B. (1993). Mentoring in context: A comparison of two U.S. programs for beginning teachers. *International Journal of Educational Research, 19*(8), 699–718.

National Association for Professional Development Schools. (2008). *What it means to be a professional development school.* Retrieved from http://napds.org/9%20 Essentials/statement.pdf

Nolan, J., & Parks, K. (2011, March). *Mentors as teacher educators: Unpacking mentor knowledge of skilled, veteran mentors in the PDS context.* Presented at the Annual Meeting of the National Association of Professional Development Schools, New Orleans.

Parker-Katz, M., & Bay, M. (2007). Conceptualizing mentor knowledge: Learning from the insiders. *Teaching and Teacher Education, 24*(5), 1259–1269.

Yendol-Hoppey, D., & Dana, N. (2007). *The reflective educator's guide to mentoring strengthening practice through knowledge, story, and metaphor.* Thousand Oaks, CA: Corwin Press.

Zeichner, K., & Bier, M. (2015, March). Opportunities and pitfalls in the turn toward clinical experience in U.S. teacher education. In E. Hollins (Ed.), *Rethinking field experiences in pre-service teacher preparation: Meeting new challenges for accountability* (pp. 20–46). New York, NY: Routledge.

CHAPTER 7

FROM TEACHER CANDIDATE TO TEACHER EDUCATOR

What It Means to "Grow Up" in a Professional Development School Partnership

Sara R. Helfrich
Ohio University

Sara L. Hartman
Ohio University

Larina I. M. Sisson
Ohio University

The work of the school-based teacher educator is becoming increasingly important as teacher education programs become more clinically based. Clinically based teacher education refers to a program in which

> clinical practice is central [and] coursework is designed and sequenced to support candidates' developing knowledge and skill. Candidates are observed

Preparing the Next Generation of Teacher Educators for Clinical Practice, pages 141–163
Copyright © 2019 by Information Age Publishing
All rights of reproduction in any form reserved.

through authentic practice in diverse learning environments. Coursework complements and aligns with field experiences that grow in complexity and sophistication over time and enable candidates to develop the skills necessary to teach all learners. (AACTE, 2018, p. 14)

As teacher candidates spend considerable time working with students in classrooms, the role the school-based teacher educator plays in preparing high-quality teachers becomes increasingly important (Burns, Yendol-Hoppey, & Jacobs, 2015; National Association for Professional Development Schools, 2008; National Council for Accreditation of the Teacher Education [NCATE], 2010). Without the expertise and guidance that school-based teacher educators provide in the field, the essential connection between theory and practice is often limited. In many cases, teacher candidates are left to independently find and negotiate the space to practice the skills and strategies they learn in the university classroom from university-based teacher educators. School-based teacher educators provide teacher candidates the essential support needed to successfully link the theory, research, and practice.

Preparing school-based teacher educators to engage in clinical coaching, a mentoring activity, with the teacher candidates who work in their classrooms may be approached in a multitude of ways. This chapter focuses on how one clinically based teacher preparation program located in the Midwestern United States simultaneously prepares future school-based teacher educators, also referred to as mentor teachers, as they work with teacher candidates within the professional development school.

Within our university's teacher preparation program, early childhood teacher candidates are prepared through the clinically based professional development school (PDS) model. Over the past several years, within the early childhood program, we have observed some early childhood candidates transition from the role of teacher candidates being mentored by school-based teacher educators to *becoming* school-based teacher educators responsible for the clinical coaching of teacher candidates. Our clinical model of teacher education, aided by the close-knit PDS community in which we are located, provides the unique opportunity for our graduates to be mentored not only to become strong classroom teachers, but also to one day become school-based teacher educators themselves.

In this chapter, we draw on the voices of former teacher candidates to share the elements of our early childhood teacher education and master's fellowship programs, which they credit in helping to prepare them to become the next generation of school-based teacher educators. This study identifies the importance of a strong connection between theory and practice, relationships with others, co-teaching, and reflective practice as key themes that inform their development as school-based teacher educators. The participants also identify challenges they face in becoming an effective teacher educator.

LITERATURE REVIEW

The National Council for the Accreditation of Teacher Education (2010), in their *Blue Ribbon Panel Report,* states that "prospective teachers must be prepared to become expert practitioners who know how to use the knowledge of their profession to advance student learning and how to build their professional knowledge through practice" (p. 2). Clinically based teacher education programs that exist within a PDS model do just this. Founded on the Nine Essentials of effective collaborative practices, PDSs create a climate where teacher candidates are immersed in sustained school experiences, welcomed to a school building as active participants in children's education, and offered opportunities to learn alongside staff who are committed to working as equal partners with university-based teacher educators to prepare teacher candidates (NAPDS, 2008).

Critical to the successful development of teacher candidates are preparatory programs that include extended and carefully designed clinical teaching opportunities supported closely by school and university-based teacher educators (Darling-Hammond, 1997; NCATE, 2010). The value of clinically based preparation programs has been noted throughout the research (see Grossman, 2010; Hollins, 2011). Yendol-Hoppey and Franco (2014) identified six core practices of clinically based teacher education programs including focused observation, coaching, co-teaching, direct dialogue, inquiry, and reflection on teaching. Through participation in these practices within the context of the PDS, teacher candidates' professional and pedagogical knowledge is deepened, "resulting in a seamless transition between university and school based contexts" (Henry, Hyde, & Keifer Kennedy, 2017, p. 130).

Paramount to the success of teacher candidates are the mentor teachers with whom they work (Anderson, 2009; Graham, 2006; Killian & Wilkins, 2009; Whitney, Golez, Nagel, & Nieto, 2002). One way mentor teachers can help teacher candidates improve their skills is through co-teaching. Regardless of the style or type of instruction, co-teaching involves two or more adults working together to instruct students (Cook & Friend, 1995). When teacher candidates are able to co-teach with knowledgeable, experienced mentor teachers, they "become an integral part of preparation for and delivery of instruction, as well as partners in assessment and data-driven planning" (Tschida, Smith, & Fogarty, 2015, p. 13). Engaging in co-teaching allows teacher candidates to further their own practice by working closely with an expert model.

Reflection is an important aspect of teacher preparation, and "institutions count on their cooperating teachers to be conduits for reflective practice and to provide learning environments that support it" (Kalchman, 2015, p. 4). From school-based teacher educators and mentor teachers, teacher candidates receive consistent, constructive feedback that enables them to reflect and grow as teachers (Kalchman, 2015). This feedback allows them to engage in an analysis of all aspects of their teaching, with a focus on students and their learning (Davis, 2006; Dewey, 1933).

The clinical coaching provided by school-based teacher educators informs teacher candidates' learning and beliefs about teaching (Uibo, Salo, Ugaste, & Rasku-Puttonen, 2017), which follows them throughout their development and work as teachers when they enter their own classrooms. Jaspers, Meijer, Prins, and Wubbels (2014) assert that the role of school-based teacher educators is to model what it means to be a teacher by way of their own teaching and provide an example to teacher candidates for implementing teaching practices that support student learning. Within a PDS model, the development of students is not limited only to P–12 students. Teacher candidates also learn from school-based educators what it means to work with other adults as colleagues and to gain insight into the work they might one day do as future school-based educators themselves. Therefore, the school-based teacher educator's role as mentor is critically important to the development of teacher candidates (Henning, Gut, & Beam, 2015) as well as the next generation of school-based teacher educators.

Finally, research emphasizes the importance of the relationship cultivated between school- and university-based teacher educators so that collegial collaboration (Bullough, 2005) and a community of inquiry supporting growth (Darling, 2001) is established. This community of inquiry is a place where both school- and university-based stakeholders are equal partners in teacher candidate development. As indicated, clinically based teacher education involves support by multiple teacher educators, involves a unique set of pedagogical practices, relies on co-teaching to develop instructional practice, provides opportunities for guided reflection, uses clinical coaching to shape beliefs about learning, and models the importance of relationships in shaping professional learning. Throughout the remainder of this chapter, we take a closer look at the PDS experiences that shaped the development of two former teacher candidates into the school-based teacher educators they are today.

DESCRIPTION OF CLINICAL EXPERIENCES

Our clinical experiences are enriched by two key structures. These include the design of the undergraduate early childhood program and the uniquely configured graduate teaching fellowship. These structures often result in the opportunity for our graduates to come full circle from learning to teach to becoming school-based teacher educators in a PDS school.

Undergraduate Early Childhood Program

The early childhood program at the university utilizes a well-developed PDS model to create clinically based experiences for its early childhood teacher candidates (see Figure 7.1). The early childhood program prepares teacher candidates to work with children birth to Age 8 and provides licensure for Age 3 to Grade 3. As part of the PDS structure, clinical experiences are guided by the Center for Clinical Practice in Education, which is staffed by a full-time director and part-time administrative support. Special care is given to the NAPDS Nine Essentials (2008) and the role of these essential traits in facilitating strong PDS partnerships with an emphasis on sustained experiences, reciprocal partnerships, and embedded theoretical curriculum.

Beginning in the sophomore year, teacher candidates spend one semester in the Rural-Urban Collaborative. This field placement provides our candidates with 40 hours of classroom experience in an urban school setting. As this university is situated in a rural area of the state, and all other field placements will be made within the region, the Rural-Urban Collaborative provides candidates with a more diverse teaching experience. In the second semester of the sophomore year, early childhood candidates experience the *preschool block*. In this clinical experience, candidates spend 42 hours in a birth to Age 5 setting, typically in the university's early childhood lab school, the Child Development Center. During the junior year, candidates spend an entire year in a K–3 PDS school, spending one semester in a Kindergarten or first-grade classroom and the second semester in a second- or third-grade classroom. Teacher candidates are in their PDS school every Tuesday and Thursday from 8:00 a.m.–4:00 p.m., and complete over 500 sustained field hours before the year is over. During the junior year primary experience, coursework is held on Mondays and Wednesdays so that candidates have sustained experiences in K–3 classrooms. During the

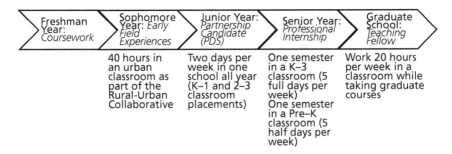

Figure 7.1 Undergraduate partnership program for early childhood education majors, leading to the optional graduate teaching fellowship program.

senior year, early childhood candidates also complete two semesters of professional internship, one semester in a birth to Age 5 setting and a second semester in a primary K–3 setting. The professional internships result in approximately 900 hours of clinical field experiences in both preschool and primary classrooms.

Foundational structures of clinical model implementation at the university include a teacher liaison (school-based partner) and faculty coordinator (university-based partner) during the junior year. The teacher liaison and faculty coordinator engage in clinical coaching, a term established by the American Association of Colleges for Teacher Education's (AACTE) Clinical Practice Commission (2018) and defined as the mentoring and supervision that university- and school-based teacher educators do to help prepare teacher candidates. They also co-teach a weekly two-hour seminar that is school-located and places heavy emphasis on critical reflection and examining the connection between theory and practice. Clinical educators also conduct seminars with candidates who are engaged in their professional internships. In both the sophomore and junior year, candidates are grouped in cohorts that share a common set of instructors. This allows for a high degree of collaboration between instructors and for faculty to be integrally involved and visible within clinical placement sites. Throughout the program, there is a strong emphasis on utilizing a co-teaching model in clinical experiences and on the value of reflective practices.

In all years of the program, school- and university-based partners work together to make programmatic changes and improvements. School-based partners are an integral part of clinical practice committees at the college, attend collaborative meetings throughout each semester, and deliver professional development workshops each semester for early childhood candidates. In this way, the program strives to develop equitable and sustainable PDS partnerships that eschew traditional roles where universities are the sole decision makers and possessors of knowledge.

Graduate Teaching Fellowship

At the graduate level, the university offers a unique experience for those wishing to further their education and receive funding to pursue a master's degree (see Figure 7.1). Prospective graduate students can apply to the college's teaching fellows program. If accepted, the candidate will receive free tuition and a monthly stipend in exchange for working 20 hours per week in a P–12 classroom (determined by licensure area) and taking classes to earn a graduate degree (e.g., curriculum and instruction, reading education, or special education). Around 20 teaching fellows are hired each year, and they are assigned to classrooms in the PDS schools in which the undergraduate teacher candidates complete their junior year field placements. They often work closely with many of the teachers in the school, especially those teaching at the same grade level and those serving as mentors to the undergraduate teacher candidates. While the majority of teaching fellows have recently completed their undergraduate program at the university, the program is open to all that are interested. For the purposes of this study, we worked with individuals that completed the undergraduate early childhood education program and also served as teaching fellows (see Figure 7.1).

Coming Full Circle: Recent Graduates Teaching in a PDS School

Graduates of our teacher education program go on to obtain classroom teaching positions across the state and beyond, but several each year choose to stay within the region. This allows them the potential for a unique opportunity. Specifically, if they work within one of the university's PDS sites, they will not only serve as a teacher to K–3 students, they will also serve as a *teacher educator* for our teacher candidates completing their junior year placements. They may take on this role as early as their first year, if the principal agrees, and work with up to four teacher candidates per year (two per semester), depending on how the university places teacher candidates across school sites. Figure 7.2 illustrates this process.

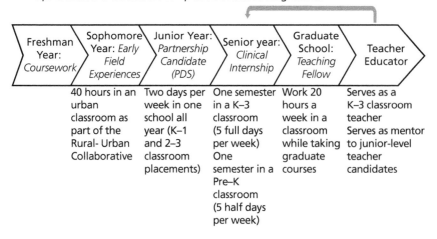

Figure 7.2 Undergraduate and graduate teaching fellow program model including the progression to teacher educator.

METHODOLOGY

This qualitative study utilizes a case study design to investigate the role a teacher preparation program played in the development of two school-based teacher educators. Case study research is beneficial as it provides depth in data collection and the ability of the researcher to tell a story that gives life to the participants' experiences (Stake, 1995). The research was guided by the following research question: How does a teacher preparation program help to prepare school-based teacher educators?

Setting

The research was conducted in two schools where our early childhood teacher candidates (birth through Grade 3) completed clinically based experiences via a PDS model. The first school, Hill Elementary, is a rural school located about 20 minutes from main campus. Class sizes are typically low, around 15–18 children per classroom. Although a partnership at Hill Elementary existed for many years, the year of data collection was the first time in 4 years that teacher candidates were placed in the school. The second school, Cedar Valley Elementary, is 1.5 miles from main campus and is home to a longstanding early childhood partnership. Both schools educate children Grades K–6 and have an average of 12 teacher candidates placed in K–3 classrooms each semester. Within our PDS model, mentor teachers, a school-based teacher liaison, and a university-based faculty coordinator work collaboratively to prepare teacher candidates. As such, all fulfill roles as teacher educators at each of the research site PDS schools.

Participants

Both participants are graduates of the university's teacher preparation program, where they earned degrees in early childhood education with licensure for Age 3 to Grade 3. Both also participated in the university's teaching fellowship program, where they both received a master's degree in reading education. During the study, both participants were school-based teacher educators within PDS partnership schools in the teacher preparation program. Ms. Elizabeth Wanta is a second-year teacher at Hill Elementary, where she teaches third grade. A first-year full-time teacher, Ms. Audrey Oliver teaches third grade at Cedar Valley Elementary.

Immediately upon completing their graduate programs, both accepted their first full-time classroom teaching positions within the university's PDS network. Ms. Wanta is now in her second year teaching third grade, while

TABLE 7.1   Educational Background and Teaching Experience of Study Participants

Education and Teaching	Ms. Wanta	Ms. Oliver
Undergraduate major	Early childhood education	Early childhood education
Junior PDS experience	Kindergarten; third grade	First grade; second grade
Senior primary clinical internship	Third grade	Kindergarten
Graduate major	Reading education	Reading education
Teaching fellow position	First grade	Kindergarten
Current position	Third grade	Third grade
Number of years as a full-time teacher	2	1
Number of years as a teacher educator[a]	3	2

[a] Number of years as a teacher educator includes the number of years as a full-time teacher and teaching fellow.

Ms. Oliver is in her first year. Neither Ms. Wanta nor Ms. Oliver have any additional teaching experience outside of those experiences provided as part of their undergraduate and graduate programs. It is important to note that while Ms. Wanta completed her PDS experience and clinical internship and worked as a teaching fellow at three different schools, as is typical of candidates in these programs, Ms. Oliver completed her clinical internship and teaching fellowship at the same school and was then hired to work at that school as a full-time teacher. The participants' teaching and mentoring experiences are summarized in Table 7.1.

Data Collection and Analysis

Data was collected via formal interviews, written responses, document review, and detailed field notes. Formal interviews were conducted with each participant at their schools and lasted approximately 45 minutes to one hour. In response to five prompts, each participant completed detailed written responses. Researchers also collected documents related to the participants' clinical coaching of teacher candidates. These included midterm and final evaluations of the teacher candidates' lesson plans and classroom instruction. Finally, detailed field notes were kept about interactions with each participant during and after interviews.

Consistent with qualitative data analysis techniques, data was coded to allow for broad themes to emerge (Creswell, 1998; Patton, 2015). Examples of broad themes include facilitating factors and challenges. From the broad themes, multiple instances allowed narrower codes to be identified, including the application of theory to practice, the importance of relation-ships, and a programmatic emphasis on co-teaching and reflective practices. Direct interpretation and the development of naturalistic generalizations were also components of the data analysis piece. Finally, trustworthiness was established using researcher triangulation. While the second author com-pleted the initial coding of data, in order to ensure a high degree of inter-rater reliability, the first author reviewed the data for consistency. Finding discrepancies in individual analyst coding was discussed until full agree-ment was achieved.

FINDINGS

Analysis of the data reveals several important findings that influenced the development of the teacher educators described in this case study. Key themes that facilitated the participants' development as teacher educa-tors are a programmatic emphasis on highlighting theory to practice prin-ciples, the development of positive relationships, recognizing co-teaching as a foundational model, and the value of embracing reflective practices. Participants also identified challenges associated with becoming a teacher educator, including recognizing the considerable time commitment to en-gage effectively in the work of a school-based teacher educator and devel-oping a professional identity as a teacher educator. Importantly, the case study findings clearly reveal that experiencing the clinical model of teacher preparation via undergraduate and graduate programs was significant in preparing the participants to become teacher educators themselves, as will be illustrated in the following sections.

Building Understanding of Theory to Practice

The importance of embedded coursework and its role in creating a strong connection between theory and practice emerged as a key finding. In effective teacher preparation programs, theory and practice should go hand-in-hand with neither viewed as more important than the other (Zeich-ner, 2018). Theory is made more relevant when teacher candidates are able to see how particular ideas are applied in a classroom setting (Henry, Hyde, & Keifer Kennedy, 2017). As part of the clinical model in which Ms. Wanta and Ms. Oliver were teacher candidates, coursework goes hand-in-hand with clinical fieldwork. Topics covered and assignments given in university courses are closely aligned with what teacher candidates will see and do in their clinical field placements. For example, many of the schools with which the university partners for the PDS utilize a specific classroom management program. University-based educators frequently include elements of this program within the context of their content courses. Likewise, literacy activities described and used in university courses are chosen specifically because they demonstrate best practices and are also used in the K–3 classrooms in which teacher candidates are placed.

There is constant communication between the university-based teacher educators teaching courses each semester in order to ensure that there is appropriate overlap of content among different courses in an effort to reinforce learning. One example of this is the use of read alouds across all courses: The theory behind it would be discussed and initial practice of it would occur in the reading methods course, then the assignment would be repeated across other methods courses (e.g., math, social studies, science) to tie together literacy and content learning, and finally, teacher candidates would deliver read alouds in their K–3 classrooms.

The participants felt that the embedded and integrated nature of their teacher preparation coursework was helpful in preparing them to be teacher educators. Throughout their undergraduate and graduate programs, the coursework was embedded within the participants' clinical field placements, creating a bridge to their methods courses. Ms. Oliver further reflected on her experiences with literacy and math in her K–3 classrooms and university coursework stating:

> [In] a few of our other [reading] classes we did like running records and studied students. I think that was really helpful because now I do running records and I go back to when I did a running record in college because that's what we learned to do. I feel like math was a really great course for me . . . I see math in a different way [as a teacher now compared to when I was taught math,] and I think that was helpful to kind of learn it, as well as seeing it in the classroom, because it's kind of uncomfortable for us. And, then we realize the kids are kind of okay with it, and it kind of makes sense. So, I feel like a lot of my classes just gave me a lot of different guidelines and lessons to try in the classroom, and it has given me the confidence to go ahead and try.

Similarly, reflecting on her coursework, Ms. Wanta states, "[My undergraduate courses] were really important classes to me. I mean . . . they were really important for me, when I was applying what I had learned all those four years in the actual classroom. Especially even those first 3 years when I went to my partnership." She also spoke about work in a reading methods course where she did a lot of work she found to be meaningful because she was able to immediately see it—and teach it—in the K–3 classrooms. Speaking of graduate coursework during her teaching fellowship, Ms. Wanta says, "The coursework during the fellowship was also essential to me in becoming a teacher educator, because it gave me more depth of knowledge in a content area that is so crucial to me as an early childhood educator." Seeing the natural connections between the theory presented within coursework and the application within classrooms made the content more meaningful and relevant. In both of these examples, understanding how to make theory to practice connections as they support teacher learning is something that is applicable to them in their role as school-based teacher educators.

Role of Relationships

Another key theme in the findings is the major role that relationships had on the participants' development as school-based teacher educators. Although both participants recognize the value of the content presented in their university-based methods courses, they are quick to identify the significant role that building positive relationships had on their growth and development as teacher educators. They cite their work with university- and school-based teacher educators as essential components of their teacher preparation experiences and credit these relationships for their success in their current positions. Ms. Oliver notes that, over time, she became much more aware of the close connections between university-based and school-based teacher educators within the clinical model. She stated:

> It started as a junior when we had meetings discussing the partnership experience. Then my senior year and fellowship year [graduate program] the importance of relationship continued to be reinforced. Many professors were visiting us in the [K–3] classroom and [they] had strong relationships with our mentor teachers as well as a strong understanding for the expectations in the classroom.

Sustained and engaged contact with children and mentors is a hallmark of the clinical model of teacher preparation (Henry, Hyde, & Keifer Kennedy, 2017; NCATE, 2010), and trust is a key ingredient needed for building and sustaining a positive mentoring relationship. The participants in this study spent approximately 1,500 hours in clinical placement sites during their undergraduate program. This contrasts sharply to field placement requirements in traditional undergraduate teacher preparation programs, which consist of an average of 650 over the totality of the program (U.S. Department of Education, 2016). Trust between a mentor teacher and teacher candidate may take time to develop, and may be better facilitated through sustained contact between the mentor and teacher candidate (Stanulis & Russell, 2000).

Findings reveal that the participants value the time that their sustained clinically based experiences gave them to develop trust with their mentor teachers. In their junior year, time within a K–3 classroom is approximately 500 hours. Of this time, Ms. Wanta says, "We were there 2 days a week, all day for an entire year. It was a lot of experience and a lot of practice doing this job." Teacher candidates also spend approximately 900 hours completing their clinical internships (student teaching) over the course of a full academic year. During a teaching fellowship, 20 hours a week are spent working directly with children while also taking full-time graduate classes. Ms. Wanta explained:

> During my teacher prep program, I had multiple opportunities to be around young children and students (in the age band that I was going to school to teach). In my opinion, the best and really the only way that you can learn how to be a teacher is to get in the classroom and gain the experience. That is exactly what my teacher prep program provided me.

This sustained time allowed the participants to develop the trust needed to have open relationships with their mentor teachers. Illustrating this, Ms. Oliver explained:

> I think my mentor and I had a pretty good relationship that we were able to talk through different things and see other teaching styles that went well with what I was trying to learn about teaching and teaching a whole child.

The participants strongly believe the number of hours spent with children and mentor teachers helps them when working with the teacher candidates placed in their classrooms.

Both candidates believe the relationships they developed through clinical coaching made a significant impact on their work as teacher educators today. The value of clinical coaching (e.g., mentoring and/or supervision) as part of teacher preparation programs is unquestioned in the research literature (Henning et al., 2015; Henry et al., 2017). Repeatedly, the participants spoke of the importance of the relationships they developed with their mentor teachers and the value of those relationships as models for what they are doing in their classrooms as teacher educators today. Ms. Wanta explained how one of her best mentor teachers supported her learning:

> She modeled how to be a mentor (e.g., with partnership students) to other teachers and students, and now that I have my own students and teachers to mentor, I use her model as a place to start.

Their relationships with mentor teachers also illustrate the importance of keeping student learning at the center of all their work with teacher candidates. Ms. Oliver speaks of this as she reflects on an experience with one of her mentor teachers, "They all have a different teaching style, but it was all centered around our students. I was able to pick up on those different parts of their teaching and then now apply it to my own." The value of relationships with mentor teachers and its impact on the participants as teacher educators was important in the findings of this study.

PDS clinical structures that promote collaborative relationships between stakeholders create meaningful experiences for teacher candidates (Henry et al., 2017; NAPDS, 2008; NCATE, 2010). Other valuable relationships for learning included the teacher liaisons and faculty coordinators. Findings reveal that boundary spanners, or university- and/or school-based faculty who spend considerable time in both settings (AACTE, 2018), developed relationships that the participants found particularly impactful. Starting in the sophomore year and continuing through the teaching fellowship, teacher candidates work with school-based teacher liaisons and university-based faculty coordinators. Working together, instructors in these roles collaborate to create a meaningful and integrated experience for teacher candidates. Liaisons and coordinators partner to determine which classrooms are a good fit for teacher candidates, collaborate with mentor teachers when issues arise, and work with methods teachers to integrate course content with clinical field experiences in a meaningful way.

To effectively meet teacher candidates' needs in these roles, developing positive relationships with them is essential. The findings reflect the participants' strong feelings about the relationships formed with their teacher liaisons and faculty coordinators. Ms. Oliver explained, "As an undergraduate I [felt] my liaisons were able to pair me with teachers that would best help me grow as a teacher." The importance of these roles in modeling effective practices for teacher educators should not be underestimated. Throughout their preparation program, faculty in these positions designed and led school-located seminars that helped teacher candidates reflect on their work. Strong and positive relationships with their liaisons and faculty coordinators allowed conversations to be rich and deep. About this, Ms. Wanta indicated, "The seminars after our partnership days. The conversations that we would have...all of that was just so important to me." The clinical structures provided by boundary spanners such as teacher liaisons and faculty coordinators allowed close relationships to develop that facilitated positive growth and development in both participants.

Co-Teaching as a Foundational Practice

The value of co-teaching as part of the clinical model of teacher preparation is well established (Bacharach, Heck, & Dahlberg, 2012; Badiali & Titus, 2010; Thomas, 2014; Yendol-Hoppey & Franco, 2014). Badiali and Titus (2010) suggest that co-teaching can take one of six forms: mentor modeling, one teach-one guide, station teaching, parallel teaching, alternative teaching, and synchronous teaming. While the needs of the students should always be at the forefront of any instructional decisions that are made, it is also important to consider the strengths of the teachers when choosing the type of co-teaching model to utilize.

With this in mind, an emphasis on co-teaching—most commonly mentor modeling, one teach-one guide, and station teaching—is an essential component of the clinical model of teacher preparation at our university. Consequently, both participants experienced a co-teaching model early as part of their undergraduate preparation program. The co-teaching model that underpins the early childhood PDS program allowed the participants to feel like a partner in the education of the classroom's children. The model provided a safe environment for them to observe their mentor teachers and to independently, yet with support, practice their own teaching. Of this supportive co-teaching structure, Ms. Wanta shared:

> I had a lot of experience being in charge of a classroom and planning. I thank my mentor for giving me that opportunity, even though it was kind of a little scary. But still, I had a lot of time to really find my voice, and become more confident, being in charge of and managing a whole classroom of students.

Since the participants and their mentor teachers engaged so often in co-teaching, the participants felt comfortable having others in the room watching their interactions with children. This encouraged them to try new practices in a risk-free environment. Of this dynamic, Ms. Oliver says:

> I think it just makes it easier for you to not worry about other people being in the room and observing you and talking to your teacher. I think it just helps you become more confident in what you're doing and learning from other mentors' constructive criticism and not taking offense to it. They're telling you this because they want to help you.

The co-teaching model was accomplished through scaffolded opportunities that facilitated the gaining of new teaching experiences in small steps. Although the findings reveal that the undergraduate program provided numerous valuable scaffolded experiences, both participants believe that their graduate teaching fellowship was a very important part of their preparation as school-based teacher educators. Ms. Wanta explains:

> The fellowship position was such an integral step that helped scaffold me to become a full-time teacher educator and mentor teacher. After I had graduated with all of the experience and knowledge my undergraduate teacher prep program provided me, I applied all of it to my first class of students. However, I was still working closely with a mentor every step of the way.

Having been trained in a co-teaching model, the teacher educators report continuing to emphasize co-teaching with the teacher candidates in their own classrooms. This represents an important benefit of preparing teacher educators via their own teacher preparation programs.

Value of Embracing Reflective Practice

Reflective practices should be a critical component of teacher preparation programs, a practice that hopefully follows its graduates into their own classrooms (NCATE, 2010; Yendol-Hoppey & Franco, 2014). Both participants identified an emphasis on reflective practices as essential to helping them become effective teacher educators. Within the context of undergraduate coursework, Ms. Wanta recalled learning new instructional skills as being something that "we talked about it [in the university classroom], and we planned it and then we actually did it in [the K–3] class. Then, we talked about it again." The ability to engage in reflection on how a specific task went greatly impacted her understanding and skill related to the teaching of it.

Within the K–3 classrooms, reflection was ongoing. Ms. Oliver remembers her first mentor teacher helping to build her confidence by encouraging her to reflect on lessons and consider not what went wrong, but what she could do to make it better for the next time. The participants reflect that during their junior year, a weekly 2-hour seminar was dedicated to reflection, a time that also existed during their clinical internships. Altogether, this time spent reflecting had a lasting impact on these teacher educators' learning and development.

Now as teacher educators, they continue to recognize the value of encouraging reflective practices. Nearly 2 years removed from her graduate coursework, Ms. Wanta explains the value of critical reflection, "The reflection piece, I think is kind of really the driving force and what makes you who you are as a teacher." Speaking of the programmatic structure of her teacher preparation program and the time dedicated to reflection, she states, "I just know that, that's how [teaching] works because that's what I had modeled for me in every experience that I had during this program." As a result of the emphasis on reflective practices during their own preparation programs, both teacher educators work to develop this quality in the teacher candidates who are placed in their classrooms.

Perception of Challenges

Although the study participants learned to mentor while learning to teach in a professional development school context, they also identified time and identity as challenges that they continue to face in their work. Despite becoming teacher educators via the clinical PDS model, the participants were surprised at the amount of time being an effective teacher educator requires. Both participants reflected that finding time to collaborate with the teacher candidates and the other faculty and teachers who work with them can present a challenge. Despite this, they feel that a time commitment to these relationships is essential and worth pursuing. Ms. Wanta explains this by saying, "Being a mentor requires some extra time and effort that is not included in your everyday teacher planning. Luckily, I had a place to start because of prior relationships with my mentors, so over time this has been, and will get, easier." Of prior relationships, Ms. Wanta discusses all the time she spent being mentored by her teaching fellow co-teacher, and that she uses these experiences to guide her mentoring of candidates. She lists practices that she still uses today, including, "daily meetings, emails, text messages, and weekly planning meetings." Although these practices require a time commitment, she believes they are valuable.

In addition to these time demands, the participants also noted their developing identity as a teacher educator a challenge. Considerable research has been done to examine the development of teacher identity, and research about the development of teacher identity is considered to be an important mechanism for understanding how to best support both teacher candidates and practicing teachers (Beijaard, Meijer, & Verloop, 2004; Volkman & Anderson, 1998). Despite their considerable experience with both university- and school-based teacher educators, findings reveal that developing an identity as a school-based teacher educator is a work in progress. The participants sometimes needed to be redirected to answer questions from the point of view as a teacher educator, and Ms. Oliver reflected on this directly saying:

> During my fellowship, I had the opportunity to be a mentor teacher. At first, I felt nervous about this, and I was unsure if I was going to be able to be the best mentor for the partnership students. But as the semester went on, I was able to notice how I was able to connect with them because I was recently in their position. After having experiences with the partnership students for two semesters during my fellowship, I was then able to transfer a lot of this learning to my partnership student this past semester.

Ms. Wanta also explains that she continues to grow in her role as a teacher educator by exploring her place as a collaborator with university- and school-based partners. She revealed her reluctance to approach university- and school-based teacher educators about concerns as an undergraduate, but goes on to express her increased confidence in that role today. She describes how, as a teaching fellow, she became more empowered to use her voice to ask questions and seek clarification, and how in her role as a teacher educator she continues this on behalf of the teacher candidates she mentors. Of this, she says:

> As a fellow... I was in more of a position to take action. I realized how simple it was to contact the university partners and clear up any misunderstandings or create more of an open line of communication. As a professional teacher, I feel the same. In fact, I mentioned to the liaison at Hill Elementary just the other day if there was a way to bring the university partners and classroom teachers together for more open lines of communication.

No matter their challenges in viewing themselves as school-based teacher educators, the participants both felt that their recent graduation from their teacher preparation programs allowed them to better mentor the teacher candidates in their classrooms.

DISCUSSION AND IMPLICATIONS

The findings illustrate several themes that allowed the participants to become school-based teacher educators via their teacher preparation programs. Today, as teacher educators, the participants incorporate co-teaching into their work with teacher candidates and believe that their educator preparation programs prepared them well to engage in co-teaching with the teacher candidates in their classrooms. Additionally, having seen and benefited themselves from the natural connections between theory and practice presented within the clinically based PDS model, teacher educators see value in supporting these practices with the teacher candidates with whom they work. These are practices that they want to continue and see as beneficial to the children and teacher candidates in their classrooms. As such, teacher preparation programs should be aware that a programmatic focus on co-teaching within a program that closely ties theory to practice may influence a teacher educator's work years later. Finally, the findings reinforce the importance of developing positive relationships in teacher preparation programs. Due to the amount of sustained time in classrooms and built-in support structures, clinically based teacher preparation programs may be especially conducive to developing strong relationships that positively impact teacher candidates' development.

Despite acknowledging that viewing themselves as teacher educators is a big change in professional identity, these school-based teacher educators have ideas about how to improve the experiences of teacher candidates in their classrooms. Based on the significance that reflection played in her development, Ms. Wanta recommends an increase in the amount and type of feedback given to teacher candidates. Now that she is a teacher educator herself, she works hard to provide thorough and conscientious feedback to the teacher candidates who work in her classroom—feedback that encourages reflection.

Document analysis of midterm and final evaluations reveals that both participants give thoughtful feedback to the teacher candidates who are placed in their rooms. Both believe in giving frequent feedback and often meet with teacher candidates both during and after school to plan and provide opportunities for ongoing reflection. The participants spend a minimum of one hour per week planning and giving feedback to the candidates, although that time is often closer to one and a half to two hours. The connecting of their preparation experiences to their current roles is significant and shows the value of becoming a teacher via a PDS model of clinical teacher preparation.

The most important implication of this research is that we—all teacher educators—must be aware that when we work with teacher candidates, not only are we preparing future teachers, we are also preparing future teacher educators. An understanding of this phenomenon as part of teacher preparation programs is an essential component of educating teacher candidates. Simply put, our graduates are likely to work with teacher candidates one day in their own classrooms, and it is critical that they are prepared for this role by having the knowledge and skills needed to work with teacher candidates as mentors.

As the findings presented in this chapter suggest, this preparation begins during their undergraduate preparation programs. Colleges of education must be prepared to discuss the value of topics such as co-teaching, clinical coaching, and critical reflection. They must make sure that teacher candidates understand the importance of engaging in these practices as teacher candidates, not just as future teachers. Emphasis on these foundational components of becoming a teacher educator must continue through graduate coursework and implemented as essential pieces of clinically based graduate school experiences. Throughout the teacher preparation process and beyond, this will benefit teacher candidates in their work as classroom teachers and as a colleague to other teachers, while also helping them to realize their role as a future teacher educator and the important work that goes into this task. By focusing on this early on, teacher candidates can begin to form their identity as teacher educators and consider the role they will play in the development of future teacher candidates. In this way, teacher preparation programs may not just prepare future teachers but also teacher educators with the skills and knowledge to contribute in many ways to the profession and to the education of children.

As this study reflects experiences of two participants, a larger study could be planned in the future to examine the experiences of additional participants. Despite this, case study research provides rich detail and is valuable in many ways. Additionally, the researchers are faculty members in the

Department of Teacher Education where the research was conducted, and, as such, researcher bias is likely to exist. Conversely, the researchers' understanding of the clinical structures of the program may have added intricacy and depth to the study's analysis and implications.

CONCLUSION

School-based teacher educators play an invaluable role in the development of teacher candidates. Without the strong clinical coaching these individuals provide, teacher candidates would miss out on the opportunity to practice and develop their skills in a P–12 classroom. As teacher educators, it is our job to prepare teacher candidates to become school-based teacher educators themselves one day. Colleges of education must recognize that the work of developing teacher educators should begin in undergraduate years and continue throughout graduate school and beyond. We must work to shape them into strong teachers for all the students with whom they will one day work, and to realize the impact they can have on future teacher candidates. As Ms. Oliver concluded her first semester in her own classroom working as a teacher educator:

> As the semester has ended I have noticed how much the partnership candidate has grown. I notice how excited [she is] when a lesson goes well and I notice [her] reflecting when the lesson does not go as well. It is very fulfilling to give the [teacher candidates] an experience of what an everyday classroom is like and how it is not perfect every day.

The work of teacher educators, in the words of one, is fulfilling. We must ensure that the experiences and opportunities we provide teacher candidates have an eye toward the work they will one day do with others as teacher educators themselves. As indicated in this case study, "Growing up" in a PDS partnership can facilitate the development of a teacher candidate to one day become a teacher educator.

Discussion Questions

1. What steps does your teacher education program take toward preparing future school-based teacher educators (mentor teachers)? How might you incorporate some of the work presented in this chapter in your own efforts?
2. How might the structure of your teacher education program lend itself to a similar process of school-based teacher educator development? Which elements of your program may enhance the process?

Which elements may make it more difficult, and what steps can be taken to mitigate these potential issues?

3. The teacher education program discussed in this chapter is situated in a rural area at a mid-size university. How might a differently sized or located university positively or negatively impact the success of a similar program?

4. Mentoring is a critical component of the work of school-based teacher educators. In the program discussed in this chapter, candidates have the opportunity to engage in mentoring of other, less experienced peers as both undergraduate and graduate students. How does your teacher education program engage candidates in mentoring in preparation for work they may do as future school-based teacher educators?

REFERENCES

American Association of Colleges for Teacher Education Clinical Practice Commission. (2018). *A pivot toward clinical practice, its lexicon, and the renewal of educator preparation.* Washington, DC: Author. Retrieved from https://aacte .org/professional-development-and-events/clinical-practice-commission -press-conference

Anderson, D. (2009). The impact of cooperating teachers on the teaching perspectives of student teachers. *The International Journal of Learning, 16*(1), 119–133.

Bacharach, N., Heck, T. W., & Dahlberg, K. (2012). Changing the face of student teaching through co-teaching. *Action in Teacher Education, 32,* 3–14.

Badiali, B., & Titus, N. E. (2010). Co-teaching: Enhancing student learning through mentor-intern partnerships. *School-University Partnerships, 4,* 74–80.

Beijaard, D., Meijer, P. C., & Verloop, N. (2004). Reconsidering research on teachers' professional identity. *Teaching and Teacher Education, 20*(2), 107–128.

Bullough Jr., R. V. (2005). Being and becoming a mentor: School-based teacher educators and teacher educator identity. *Teaching and Teacher Education, 21(2)* 143–155.

Burns, R. W., Yendol-Hoppey, D., & Jacobs, J. (2015). High-quality teaching requires collaboration: How partnerships can create a true continuum of professional learning for educators. *The Educational Forum, 79*(1), 53–67. https://doi.org/ 10.1080/00131725.2014.971990

Cook, L., & Friend. M. (1995). Co-Teaching: Guidelines for creating effective practices. *Focus on Exceptional Children, 28*(3), 1–16.

Creswell, J. W. (1998). *Qualitative inquiry and research design: Choosing among five traditions.* London, England: SAGE.

Darling, L. F. (2001). When conceptions collide: Constructing a community of inquiry for teacher education in British Columbia. *Journal of Education for Teaching, 27*(1), 7–21.

Darling-Hammond, L. (1997). *Doing what matters most: Investing in quality teaching. National Commission on Teaching & America's Future.* Kutztown, PA: Kutztown Distribution Center.

Davis, E. A. (2006). Characterizing productive reflection among preservice elementary teachers: Seeing what matters. *Teaching and Teacher Education, 22*(3), 281–301.

Dewey, J. (1933). *How we think: A restatement of the relation of reflective thinking to the educative process.* Boston, MA: DC Heath and Company.

Graham, B. (2006). Conditions for successful field experiences: Perceptions of cooperating teachers. *Teaching and Teacher Education, 22*(8), 1118–1129.

Grossman, P. (2010). *Learning to practice: The design of clinical experience in teacher preparation.* Policy Brief, May 2010. American Association of Colleges for Teacher Education and National Education Association: Washington, DC. Retrieved from http://citeseerx.ist.psu.edu/viewdoc/summary?doi=10.1.1.178.4088

Henning, J. E., Gut, D., & Beam, P. (2015). Designing and implementing a clinical coaching program to support clinically-based teacher education. *The Teacher Educator, 50*(2), 145–162.

Henry, L. A., Hyde, L., & Keifer Kennedy, M. (2017). Teacher inquiry and clinical partnerships help transform teacher preparation. *School-University Partnerships, 10*(4), 127, 136.

Hollins, E. (2011). Teacher preparation for quality teaching. *Journal of Teacher Education, 62*(4), 395–407.

Jaspers, W. M., Meijer, P. C., Prins, F., & Wubbels, T. (2014). Mentor teachers: Their perceived possibilities and challenges as mentor and teacher. *Teaching and Teacher Education, 44*, 106–116.

Kalchman, M. (2015). Focusing on reflective practice: Reconsidering field experiences for urban teacher preparation. *Perspectives on Urban Education, 12*(1), 3–17.

Killian, J. E., & Wilkins, E. A. (2009). Characteristics of highly effective cooperating teachers: A study of their backgrounds and preparation. *Action in Teacher Education, 30*(4), 67–83.

National Association for Professional Development Schools. (2008, April). *What it means to be a professional development school.* A statement by the Executive Council and Board of Directors of the National Association for Professional Development Schools. Retrieved from http://napds.org/9%20Essentials/statement.pdf

National Council for the Accreditation of Teacher Education. (2010). *Transforming teacher education through clinical practice: A national strategy to prepare effective teachers. A report of the Blue Ribbon Panel on Clinical Preparation and Partnership for Improved Student Learning.* Washington, DC: Author.

Patton, M. Q. (2015). *Qualitative research and evaluation methods* (3rd ed.). London, England: SAGE.

Stake, R. E. (1995). *The art of case study research.* London, England: SAGE.

Stanulis, R. N., & Russell, D. (2000). "Jumping in": Trust and communication in mentoring student teachers. *Teaching and Teacher Education, 16*(1), 65–80.

Thomas, J. D. (2014). Co-teaching: Enhancing the student teaching experience. *Kappa Delta Pi Record, 50*, 76–80.

Tschida, C. M., Smith, J. J., & Fogarty, E. A. (2015). "It just works better!": Introducing the 2:1 model of co-teaching in teacher preparation. *Rural Educator, 36*(2), 11–26.

Uibu, K., Salo, A., Ugaste, A., & Rasku-Puttonen, H. (2017). Beliefs about teaching held by student teachers and school-based teacher educators. *Teaching and Teacher Education, 63*, 396–404.

U. S. Department of Education. (2016). *Preparing and credentialing the nation's teachers: The secretary's 10th report on teacher quality, Office of Postsecondary Education.* Washington, DC: AUthor

Volkmann, M. J., & Anderson, M. A. (1998). Creating professional identity: Dilemmas and metaphors of a first-year chemistry teacher. *Science Education, 82,* 293–310.

Whitney, L., Golez, F., Nagel, G., & Nieto, C. (2002). Listening to voices of practicing teachers to examine the effectiveness of a teacher education program. *Action in Teacher Education, 23*(4), 69–76.

Yendol-Hoppey, D., & Franco, Y. (2014). In search of signature pedagogy for PDS teacher education: A review of articles published in School-University Partnerships. *School-University Partnerships, 7*(1), 17–34.

Zeichner, K. M. (2018). *The struggle for the soul of teacher education.* New York, NY: Routledge.

CHAPTER 8

TEACHER EDUCATOR COLLABORATIVE PLANNING AND OPPORTUNITIES FOR LEARNING IN A PROFESSIONAL DEVELOPMENT SCHOOL

Courtney Lynch
The Pennsylvania State University

Whereas academic expertise has typically been privileged over practitioner expertise in teacher education, Zeichner (2010) calls for *third spaces* to bring together both types of expertise. Zeichner describes third spaces in teacher education as "hybrid spaces in preservice teacher education programs that bring together school and university-based teacher educators and practitioner and academic knowledge in new ways to enhance the learning of prospective teachers" (p. 92). Third spaces have been identified as a transformative environment for learning (Gutiérrez, 2008; Gutiérrez, Baquedano-López, & Tejeda, 1999).

Preparing the Next Generation of Teacher Educators for Clinical Practice, pages 165–191
Copyright © 2019 by Information Age Publishing
165

The notion of third spaces supports a dialectical rather than a dichotomous relationship between practitioner and academic expertise (Zeichner, 2010). Gorodetsky and Barak (2008) described this dialectical relationship in their analysis of an "edge community," a third space comprised of preservice teachers, inservice teachers, and university faculty members. They write, "It was accepted that each participant has the potential for constructive contribution to the collaborative learning process, whether it stems from experience, theoretical knowledge, common sense or genuine novice questions that probe the obvious" (p. 1911). Third spaces create the potential to value the expertise of each participating member regardless of background; the differences in expertise are meant to complement one another. By their very nature, third spaces demand that participants cope with power differentials and multiple, sometimes conflicting roles in their teacher education work (Gutiérrez, 2008; Martin, Snow, & Franklin Torrez, 2011; Williams, 2014; Yendol-Silva & Dana, 2004).

In response to the disconnect between universities and schools as sites for teacher preparation programs, and with a commitment to improving teacher education, the Holmes Group (1990) called for the creation of an investment in professional development schools (PDSs). PDS partnerships offer a unique model for the inclusion of both academic and practitioner knowledge in teacher education. In many PDSs, methods course instructors include both university teacher educators and inservice or retired teachers co-planning and co-teaching (Burns, Yendol-Hoppy, & Jacobs, 2015). PDSs offer a unique model for this inclusion of horizontal expertise to occur as methods courses can and have included a university teacher educator and an inservice or retired teacher co-planning and co-teaching the methods courses (Burns et al., 2015). As the field of teacher education moves towards increased roles for hybrid teacher educators who span the boundary between schools and universities (Zeichner, 2010), the work of teacher educators becomes increasingly complex (e.g., Martin et al., 2011; Williams, 2014; Wood & Turner, 2015).

COMMUNITIES OF PRACTICE IN THIRD SPACES

Wenger-Trayner and Wenger-Trayner (2015) succinctly describe *communities of practice* (CoP) as "groups of people who share a concern or a passion for something they do and learn how to do it better as they interact regularly" ("What are Communities of Practice?" section, para. 2). The dimensions of practice of a community of practice include: (a) mutual engagement, (b) joint enterprise, and (c) a shared repertoire (Wenger, 1998). To have mutual engagement, members must be engaged in practice; it is not enough to be a group of people who share a characteristic. As Wenger points out, "Whatever it takes to make mutual engagement possible is an essential component of any practice" (p. 17). The joint enterprise of a CoP "is not just a stated goal, but creates among participants relations of mutual accountability that become an integral part of the practice" (p. 19). Along with the mutual engagement and joint enterprise, a community of practice develops a shared repertoire through its work.

Hybrid teacher educators working in third spaces come to their roles with varied experiences, even within the field of education, and belong to multiple CoP. These teacher educators may have membership in CoP, such as those belonging to the university or the schools. Wenger-Trayner and Wenger-Trayner (2015) contend "that the 'body of knowledge' of a profession is best understood as a 'landscape of practice' consisting of a complex system of CoP and the boundaries between them" (p. 13). Inservice teachers offer *horizontal expertise*; they bring valued and relevant expertise to a collaborative activity (Zeichner, Payne, & Brayko, 2015). Anagnostopoulos, Smith, and Basmadjian (2007) introduce the construct of horizontal expertise as emerging from

> boundary crossings as professionals from different domains enrich and expand their practices through working together to reorganize relations and coordinate their work... it emphasizes the commitment and capacity to move between activity contexts and to engage in the exchange and mixing of domain-specific expertise. (p. 139)

Zeichner et al. (2015) concisely describe horizontal expertise as "the unique knowledge and understanding that each professional brought to the collective activity" (p. 125). The authors contend that considering expertise in this manner, "treats the knowledge [of each professional] as equally valuable, relevant, and important" (p. 125). Zeichner et al. also noted, "In the examples that best denote horizontal expertise, classroom teachers are active participants in the planning, instruction, and evaluation activities related to a [methods] course, thereby creating more authentic, acceptable, and accessible possibilities for inclusion of teachers' expertise" (p. 127). While third spaces create opportunities for horizontal expertise and boundary crossing between schools and universities, they also open the doors to widen the landscape of practice and increase the complexity of understanding the expertise of teacher educators.

Fenton-O'Creevy, Brigham, Jones, and Smith (2015) highlighted a challenge in the work of CoP, "Not all participants in communities of practice understand their journeys as leading to full participation; some are just visiting" (p. 44). Levels of participation in a community of practice are influenced by the imagined trajectory of the individual. Fenton O'Creevy and colleagues suggest that students may assume the identity of a *tourist* and "engage superficially in the academic practices but with no commitment to an academic identity and no engagement with the meaning of these practices" (p. 46). Conversely, those on a *sojourner* trajectory "are actively engaged in integrating their understanding of academic and workplace practices, and in reconciling their different experiences of themselves in these different domains" (p. 46). Supporting preservice teachers (PSTs) as they transition to inservice teaching, or inservice teachers to teacher educators, requires appropriate support. Otherwise participants are more likely to maintain a tourist identity, perceiving a disconnect between communities of practice.

Specifically, Dinkelman, Margolis, and Sikkenga (2006) contend, "Even if one becomes a teacher educator at the moment one begins working as a teacher educator, one's professional identity as a teacher educator is constructed over time" (p. 6). These researchers found that classroom teachers who became teacher educators during a doctoral program struggled to make sense of the differences between school and university settings and to reconcile the lack of connection between doctoral coursework and their teaching. Murray and Male (2005) similarly found that inservice teachers turned teacher educators required two to three years to develop a professional identity change from teacher to teacher educator. They were experts of their teaching practice only to find themselves novices in the field of teacher education where they experienced challenges in relinquishing their identities as inservice teachers. Given various paths to becoming a teacher educator, including the aforementioned discussion of inservice teachers, those in this profession may find themselves identifying with different professional communities depending on their expertise (Berry & Van Driel, 2012). These studies and others (e.g., Berry, 2008; Loughran, 2014) underscore the challenges to becoming a teacher educator that are directly linked to navigating the differences between CoP relating to the university and the schools.

COLLABORATIVE PLANNING IN A THIRD SPACE AS A BOUNDARY ENCOUNTER

The work of teacher educators in third spaces results in boundary crossings as they navigate the landscape of practice wherein they must navigate memberships in multiple communities of practice. Many professionals experience challenges when they cross boundaries and enter unfamiliar territory (Suchman, 1994). We can consider some teacher educators in a third space to be *boundary spanners* or *boundary brokers* (Sztajn, Wilson, Edgington, & Myers, 2014; Wenger, 1998). Boundary spanners or brokers have the complex job of navigating different perspectives while maintaining legitimacy with both sides of the boundary to move cooperative work forward (Wenger, 1998). Martin et al. (2011) acted as boundary spanners in their work developing a third space in a school–university partnership. They cultivated relationships with various stakeholders in the partnership, including preservice teachers, mentor teachers, and principals. Brokering the boundaries between school and university, the teacher educators discovered tensions, such as issues of power among hybrid teacher educators and mentor teachers, as they navigated complex relationships.

Collaborative Planning

Collaborative planning (co-planning) is an example of a *boundary encounter* in education. Boundary encounters occur when two or more individuals with differing membership in CoP interact (Wenger, 1998). To conceptualize co-planning, I draw on practical approaches for co-teaching. When more than one teacher or teacher educator teach together, they are said to be *co-teaching*. Villa, Thousand, and Nevin (2008) describe four forms of co-teaching in which teachers assume different roles and responsibilities. In supportive co-teaching, "one teacher is assigned primary responsibility for designing and delivering a lesson, and the other member(s) of the team provides support to some or all of the students in the class" (p. 34). The parallel co-teaching approach describes teachers instructing different groups of students at the same time in the classroom where the teachers may or may not be teaching the same content; this approach includes station teaching. Complementary co-teaching involves a one lead teacher who has the primary responsibility for designing a lesson or presenting new content while the other teacher(s) do something to enhance the instruction. In this approach, one teacher is considered the expert. The fourth approach is team-teaching in which "two or more people do what the traditional teacher used to do" (p. 64). There is a shared responsibility for planning, teaching, and assessing.

Drawing on the four conceptions of co-teaching described above, I propose the following categories on a continuum of co-planning (Figure 8.1): *unilateral co-planning*, *parallel co-planning*, and *team co-planning*. Table 8.1 summarizes the three categories.

Unilateral co-planning consists of one teacher educator assuming primary responsibility for designing part of a class session. In parallel co-planning,

Unilateral   Parallel   Team
Co-planning   Co-planning   Co-planning

Figure 8.1 Continuum of co-planning.

TABLE 8.1 Roles and Responsibilities for Co-Planning	
Approach to Co-Planning	**Roles and Responsibilities**
Unilateral co-planning	• One teacher educator has primary responsibility for designing (part of) a lesson
Parallel co-planning	• Teacher educators independently plan for the same lesson • Together teacher educators decide which plan to use or merge the plans
Team co-planning	• Shared responsibility for planning • Obvious equity and parity in the planning process

teacher educators independently plan for the same lesson and then decide together to choose one plan or another or to merge the plans together. Team co-planning describes teacher educators fully developing the plan together. The continuum of co-planning (see Figure 8.1) allows for other forms of co-planning to exist. For example, we might consider unilateral-parallel co-planning, in which two teacher educators independently plan separate sections for the same episode, to fall between unilateral and parallel co-planning.

Most existing research about co-planning assumes a team co-planning approach. This research has documented the benefits of co-planning among teachers (e.g., Goodchild, Fuglestad, & Jaworski, 2013; Lewis, Perry, & Hurd, 2009; Watson & De Geest, 2014). Co-planning can lead to an awareness of practice that keeps students at the center of the learning (Bleiler, 2015; Fernandez, 2010; Lewis et al., 2009; Van Zoest & Bohl, 2002). Co-planning creates the environment for teachers to discuss and broaden their pedagogical content knowledge because they may be asked to make their own knowledge and understanding knowable to others (e.g., Goodchild et al., 2013; Roth McDuffie & Mather, 2009). Co-planning also deprivatizes practice, allowing teachers to develop a collective attitude and sense of ownership towards the collaboratively planned lesson(s). The deprivatization of planning removes the sole ownership of the planned lesson from one individual teacher and places the ownership on the group thereby removing the personal attachment teachers can have towards their work (Boylan, 2010).

While we have some examples of teachers co-planning, we have few examples in the literature of teacher educators co-planning (Nevin, Thousand, & Villa, 2009). Studies have examined collaboration among university- and school-based teacher educators (e.g., inservice teachers) with the intention of supporting preservice teachers in their methods coursework (Bleiler, 2015; Wood & Turner, 2015). University teacher educators were able to leverage the contributions of school-based teacher educators by providing structure from academic expertise, however, this effectively increased the complexity of the teacher educators' work (Wood & Turner, 2015). While these studies extend our understandings of that work, there are few studies that focus on the details of teachers' co-planning. Many reports that include co-planning do so as part of other activities, such as lesson study or professional learning communities, and therefore, lack details about the work of the teachers (e.g., Fernandez, 2010; Wake, Swan, & Foster, 2016). Further, we lack studies about the co-planning of teacher educators, and specifically lack studies about hybrid teacher educators in third spaces such as a PDS where theory and practice comes together. Given the increased movement towards spanning the boundaries between school and university settings, it is likely for the next generation of teacher educators to engage in co-planning and co-teaching as a significant part of their job responsibilities. Understanding the co-planning of the hybrid teacher educators in third spaces provides insights to the work and learning of current teacher educators and informs how we prepare the next generation of teacher educators to fill this role.

CO-PLANNING IN A PROFESSIONAL
DEVELOPMENT SCHOOL

Hybrid teacher educators can come from a variety of backgrounds. In the case of a professional development school (PDS) at a large mid-Atlantic university, there is a long-standing PDS partnership between the university and the elementary schools of the local school district. Preservice teachers from the university who are accepted into the PDS program complete a yearlong internship within the local school district as they concurrently finish their bachelor's degree and PreK-4 certification requirements over two semesters. The extended field experience that PDS interns complete is one unique aspect of the teacher education setting of this study; another is the composition of instructional teams for methods courses.

As part of their fall semester coursework, the preservice teachers (interns) complete an elementary mathematics methods course that is co-taught by a university teacher educator and one, or more, other *Professional Development Associates* (PDAs) in a local elementary school classroom. Both the university- and school-based teacher educators who work in the PDS are known as PDAs. Professional development associates include university faculty members (both tenure track and non-tenure track), graduate students, retired teachers, and reassigned teachers. Reassigned teachers are a special category of PDAs who are released for 1–3 years from K–5 classroom responsibilities to work full time in the PDS. Most, but not all PDAs are also responsible for supervising interns in their grades K–4 classroom internship sites.

To understand the work of hybrid teacher educators in this collaborative third space in the PDS, I examined the collaborative planning of a team of four school- and university-based teacher educators who co-taught an elementary mathematics methods course in a PDS in Fall 2015. I refer to this team as the Methods Planning Community of Practice (MPCoP). Over the course of the semester, as part of a larger curriculum, the MPCoP co-planned methods course experiences to prepare beginning teachers to select and adapt mathematical tasks. I focused my study on this area of the elementary mathematics methods course curriculum because selecting and adapting mathematical tasks has become a prevalent and important component of preservice mathematics teacher education (e.g., Drake, Land, & Tyminski, 2014; Lloyd & Pitts Bannister, 2011), is an area with an existing robust body of literature related to teaching and professional development (e.g., Arbaugh & Brown, 2005; Stein & Smith, 1998; Stein, Smith, Henningsen, & Silver, 2009; Watson & Mason, 2007), and seems to hold the potential to allow for contributions from both school- and university-based teacher educators.

In the rest of the chapter, I focus on exploring the general co-planning activities of this MPCoP comprised of hybrid teacher educators and the opportunities for learning that they experienced as they engaged in these activities to develop course experiences to prepare beginning teachers to select and adapt mathematical tasks. The activities of co-planning provide a unique opportunity to prepare a next generation of teacher educators as they engage in the work alongside one another, can support and learn from each other, and can discover how their unique knowledge and experiences connect to the work they are doing together.

METHODOLOGY

The interpretive research genre and ethnographic traditions informed the design of this study (Borko, Liston, & Whitcomb, 2007; Borko, Whitcomb, & Byrnes, 2008; Spradley, 1979; Wolcott 1994). This study focused specifically on the collaborative planning of a team of teacher educators with diverse backgrounds as they designed experiences for preservice teachers in one focus area (selecting and adapting mathematical tasks) of an elementary mathematics methods course. I sought to explore and describe the team's co-planning activities and to communicate the types of varied expertise that the team members drew upon in those co-planning activities. In keeping with the interpretive research genre, I represented participant voice through recordings of the co-planning sessions, conducting interviews, and curating written artifacts using qualitative data collection and analysis methods (Borko et al., 2008).

Participants

The four participants of this study compose a team of hybrid teacher educators, which is a community of practice (Wenger, 1998). These hybrid teacher educators had varied backgrounds and experiences that led them to their work within the PDS:

1. Ainsley, a second-year doctoral student with 10 years of elementary school teaching experience in her first year co-teaching the methods course;
2. Colleen, a reassigned elementary teacher from the school district in her 27th year of teaching with 5 years of experience co-teaching the methods course who would be returning to her classroom full time the year following the study;
3. Olivia, a tenured faculty member in mathematics education in her fourth year of co-teaching the methods course in the PDS, with over 20 years of experience as a mathematics teacher educator; and
4. Sara, the PDS coordinator and a retired teacher from the school district who graduated with her PhD from the university the year prior to this study in her fourth year of co-teaching the methods course in the PDS.

Using the construct of communities of practice, each individual participant maintains memberships in multiple CoP, including the MPCoP. When the MPCoP comes together, it is operating in a boundary-spanning third space between the university and the school.

My Role as Researcher

Prior to the study, I had professional relationships with the participants. I had graduate courses with both Sara and Ainsley. I completed a class project with Ainsley in 2014 for which we co-taught 2 days in the PDS elementary mathematics methods course led by Olivia, Sara, and Colleen. I interacted with Sara and Colleen in other PDS activities such as Jumpstart (2012, 2015), a video analysis workshop (2014), and math manipulative seminars (2014, 2015). I participated in university retreats for the elementary education program with Olivia. I also took graduate courses with Olivia and worked on several research projects with her, which included presenting at conferences.

Consistent with the interpretive research genre and ethnographic research methods (Borko et al., 2008; Patton, 2002; Spradley, 1979), I spent significant time within the research setting. I attended each of the team's collaborative planning meetings throughout the semester. During the co-planning sessions, I took field notes and audio recorded the meetings. I established my role within the meetings as an observer and not a participant. Though not part of the data collected for this study because it was outside of the scope of my research questions, I attended two methods course class meetings (October 6, 2015 and November 17, 2015) to better understand the context for the team's co-teaching. The team gave me access to all of their collaborative planning files, which were stored and edited electronically.

Data Collection and Analysis

Data sources for this study consisted of audio recordings of three of the team's co-planning sessions (labeled sequentially as Co-Planning A, B, and C), during which I took field notes as an observer, individual background interviews, 16 semi-structured interviews (four with each team member), two semi-structured group interviews, and the team's planning documents. Artifacts from interviews also became part of the data corpus.

Initially, I focused on identifying the co-planning activities through a domain analysis (Spradley, 1979). Once I determined the activities, I went through the transcripts for each co-planning meeting and coded for the types of activities. I wrote analytic memo descriptions (Groenewald, 2008) of each type of activity and described an example from a co-planning meeting. Then I listed any other examples of that activity that I found in the transcripts of the co-planning meetings. As I worked through the transcripts I refined the language of the categories to better capture the group's work. As a final step, I reviewed the transcripts for the interviews looking for descriptions of the group's work to confirm or disconfirm the results of my domain analysis.

Then, I developed timelines to provide the time progression, or "timeline of the story" (Chatman, 1980) of the co-planning activities. The timelines (Figure 8.2) illustrate the flow of activities, and relative time spent on individual activities, for each of the three co-planning meetings. To create the timelines, I simultaneously listened to the recordings of each planning meeting while I read through the corresponding transcript that had been coded for the co-planning activities from the domain analysis. I noted the start and end time of each co-planning activity as I progressed through the recordings as well as who initiated each activity (see Table 8.2).

TABLE 8.2 CPA Initiation by Team Member			
	EG	GB	DD	Total
Olivia	12	5	6	23
Sara	4	1	4	9
Colleen	1	0	3	4
Ainsley	1	0	1	2
Total	18	6	14	38

Codes: Establishing goals (EG); General brainstorming (GB); Determining instructional details (DD)

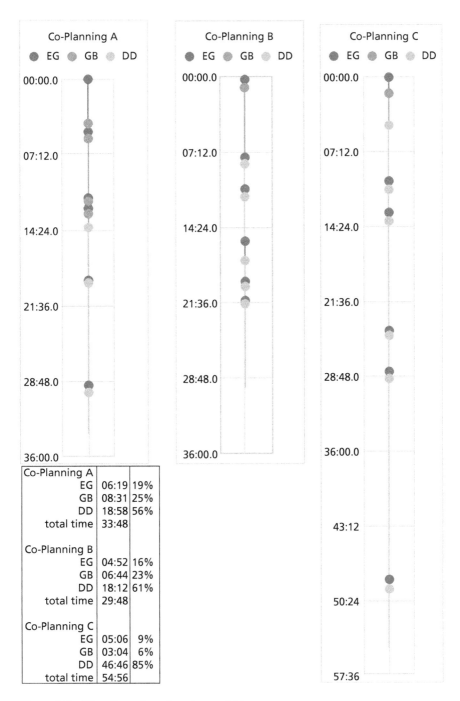

Figure 8.2 Timeline of co-planning activities.

CO-PLANNING ACTIVITIES

Throughout their co-planning meetings, the MPCoP engaged in three general co-planning activities: (a) establishing goals, (b) general brainstorming, and (c) determining instructional details. *Establishing goals* (EG) involved stating or inquiring about the purpose of the co-planning meeting. *General brainstorming* (GB) involved the suggestion of ideas for a methods course experience. *Determining instructional details* (DD) involved sorting out the details of the methods course experience taken up by the group within the co-planning meeting. These general co-planning activities of the MPCoP make up the joint enterprise and shared repertoire that define the community of practice. Table 8.3 provides a concise summary of each of the three different co-planning activities (CPAs) and the occurrences of the activity within the team co-planning meetings.

TABLE 8.3 Occurrences of Co-Planning Activities	
Co-Planning Activity	**Occurrences**
Establishing Goals (EG)	• Following up a visit from an instructional coach • Purpose of task activity • Responding to interns not engaging with the Mathematical Tasks Framework • Final opportunity to address tasks with interns • Responding to interns struggling with adapting tasks • Wanting to give interns more practice with classifying tasks • How to give interns a chance to connect and reflect on tasks in relation to all four domains of course curriculum • Responding to interns' confusion about only using high-level tasks
General Brainstorming (GB)	• Using tasks from the district textbook • Classifying tasks based on concepts • Comparing tasks from the district textbook to other tasks • Classifying tasks instead of adapting • Building on material the team already has • Using Kindergarten Tasks from previous year • Connecting math talk and math tasks by asking interns to analyze tasks and generate discussion questions • Gallery Walk with questions about when to use high- and low-level tasks for interns to reflect upon
Determining Instructional Details (DD)	• Using tasks from within the district textbook lesson • Selecting and sorting tasks from district textbook • Instructions for task sorting • Tasks to use for sorting • How to enact task sorting and discussion • Time constraints • Generating reflective questions for Chart Talk activity • How interns will engage with the reflective questions • How will interns take home a record of the Chart Talk • Potential responses to reflective questions

The timelines in Figure 8.2 represent how the CPAs progressed over time within the meetings. As evidenced by conversations in the co-planning meetings, and supported by interviews, the team arrived at the co-planning meetings with ideas about the methods course experiences. Sara explained in an interview, "We do some planning prior to [the co-planning meetings]. We have [shared files and folders] that we often come to a [co-]planning meeting with ideas ready to discuss. We don't necessarily start from scratch when we get physically together" (Background Interview, September 30, 2015). Olivia supports the comments made by Sara in her interview, "Our planning involves sort of constantly revisiting things that we've done in the past and thinking about what happened and what we want to do this time and talking about why and talking through all the details" (Background Interview, September 21, 2015). The MPCoP worked together in co-planning to develop course experiences to prepare the interns to select and adapt mathematical tasks. In the following sections, I describe each CPA with an example and identify opportunities for learning within each activity.

Establishing Goals

The team typically engaged in the activity of establishing goals as an initial step of co-planning. This CPA included verbally stating a purpose or goal for the co-planning. For example, in the third co-planning meeting, Olivia expressed her desire to develop a culminating, reflective course experience for the interns:

Ainsley: Olivia, you have for that week of the 17th and 18th—when their assignments are due—[in the planning document] you have time allotted for them to share about A3 [Mathematical Discourse Project] and/or A4 [Mathematical Tasks Project].
Olivia: Right.
Ainsley: So, what were you thinking?
Olivia: I was thinking we would come here and plan that together ... I was wondering if there was some creative way to give [interns] a chance to share things about A3 and A4 that maybe weren't written in the assignments. (Co-planning C, November 5, 2015)

A3: Mathematical Discourse Project, which attended to a different part of the course curriculum, required the interns to prepare and conduct mathematical discussions with small groups of students in their K–4 classrooms. A4: Mathematical Tasks Project was the culminating course assessment for learning to select and adapt mathematical tasks. Interns were required to select and adapt two mathematical tasks from their classroom textbooks. In this instance of EG, Ainsley asked Olivia to tell her thoughts to the team about notes Olivia had made in the planning document to offer an opportunity in class for interns to share about their projects. Olivia established the goal to create a methods course experience that would allow the interns to share about the two projects. This established goal set the focus for the team's subsequent co-planning during that meeting.

At times, team members referred back to a goal during other CPAs— general brainstorming and determining instructional details, both of which are described below. In the first co-planning meeting after Olivia voiced an established goal to create a methods course experience to follow a visit from the district instructional coaches, the team promptly started to look at the mathematical tasks within the district textbook lesson that would be the focus of the coaches' visit. Olivia restated the established goal to move forward with the planning process, "My thought was this week, in this little tiny half hour that we have after the lesson, we could do something with... these tasks from this lesson" (Co-planning A, October 1, 2015). In another instance, Olivia asked the team "What's our purpose here? What are we trying to do?" (Co-planning B, October 15, 2015). Ainsley commented on this remark in an interview, "[Olivia] knows there has to be a purpose to the activities that we do and that we need to know exactly what we want the interns to do so that we can make sure the activity gets them to that goal" (Interview #2, October 22, 2015). Olivia confirmed in her interview, "I'm big picture. What are we doing? Why are we doing this? Let's make sure with our purpose... did what we decide match?" (Interview #2, October 20, 2015).

As the team worked, they stated new goals as their plans developed and they made decisions moving toward a final instructional plan. For example, as stated above, in Co-Planning C, the team initially wanted to develop a methods course experience that would connect the interns' Mathematical Discourse Project and the Mathematical Tasks Project. Throughout the planning meeting, the goal was refined to create an opportunity for the interns to make connections across and reflect upon all parts of the course curriculum.

Discussions during this CPA included the goals of the course as well as the individual course experience they were planning. Engaging in this CPA may have offered the teacher educators the opportunity to learn more about the course curriculum. The four domains that comprised the course curriculum for this course were: (a) doing and learning meaningful mathematics, (b) selecting and adapting mathematical tasks, (c) planning and facilitating mathematical discourse, and (d) understanding and honoring children's mathematical thinking. Olivia, the university faculty member, developed the framework for the methods course curriculum and the initial planning ideas for co-planning meeting. This activity, which comprised less than 20% of each co-planning session (see Figure 8.2), was important for communicating the focus of the meeting and to guide the teacher educators in their work, especially since not all teacher educators contributed to the development of the goals.

The activity of establishing goals created an opportunity for the teacher educators to learn more about the goals for the course, including the implementation of the course framework. Understanding the goals of the course helped to focus the team on what they were planning. Not all teacher educators were involved in the development of the course framework, a scenario hybrid teacher educators may encounter in their work. By engaging in this activity, they were able to deepen their understanding of the course framework and it gave the teacher educators the opportunity to learn about the broader goals for the course. For example, Olivia asked the team "What's our purpose here? What are we trying to do?" (Co-planning B, October 15, 2015). Ainsley commented on this remark in an interview, "[Olivia] knows there has to be a purpose to the activities that we do and that we need to know exactly what we want the interns to do so that we can make sure the activity gets them to that goal" (Interview #2, October 22, 2015). Ainsley, and others, may have learned from Olivia's participation to reflect on the alignment of planned course experiences to the goals for the course.

General Brainstorming

After the team established a goal, they typically engaged in GB. During this activity, the team shared ideas to respond to the established goal. Olivia acknowledged this brainstorming when describing the team co-planning in an interview, "Our planning involves constantly revisiting things we've done in the past and thinking about what happened" (Background Interview, September 21, 2015). General brainstorming included opportunities for the team to share ideas about how to respond to the specific needs of the interns. Ainsley commented in an interview, "We just kind of throw out ideas...just think through what's best for the preservice teachers to learn" (Background Interview, September 23, 2015).

The team shared ideas with one another until agreement among some or all of the teacher educators was reached. Ainsley described the team's collaborative work:

> I think we do a good job at giving input when we feel like we have something
> to say. I feel like we're all really good at listening to each other's ideas and
> really piggybacking off of each other's ideas. And it seems like most of the

time we're okay if we choose to table something for another time for further discussion. (Background Interview, September 23, 2015)

General brainstorming ended when the team moved forward with an idea and shifted to the CPA DD.

For example, in Co-Planning C, Olivia noted that the interns were questioning when to use high- and low-level tasks. She said, "One of the things that has come up a little bit this week is . . . are we saying that you guys should always teach with high-level tasks—that's what all the tasks you use in the classroom should be?" The team then brainstormed ways to respond to this issue. Colleen first suggested asking the interns to look at tasks and generate questions a teacher could ask students, "As a way of forcing the issue of when you have really low-level tasks you ask really low-level questions." Olivia listened to Colleen and asked, "Does this match what you're saying?" She described that interns had been asking in class if high-level tasks are the only type of task they should use in the classroom. She wondered aloud if interns could do a gallery walk, an activity where the interns rotated in small groups around the room answering questions and reflecting on the responses of others written on hanging posters. Interns could ponder questions such as "When are low-level tasks appropriate?" Colleen responded, "I love that." In this example of GB, it is possible that Colleen drew on her experience as a classroom teacher to suggest asking the interns to consider tasks from a teacher's perspective. Olivia suggested a course experience that would both match the established goals and honor Colleen's thoughts, and confirmed with Colleen that her ideas were accurately understood.

In this activity, the teacher educators may have had the opportunity to learn about how to respond to the established goals for the co-planning meeting. It was an opportunity for the team to share ideas with one another, learn about what they are thinking in terms of meeting the goals, and to eventually see where the ideas end up. While examining a chunk of transcript from the second co-planning session, Colleen reflected on the team's discussion:

> I feel like a lot of this [discussion] is on the effective teaching and experience as teacher educators—trying to figure out what we want to do that's going to help [the interns] further their thinking about high- and low-level tasks and then how do we get them to do that in a way that will help them. (Interview #2, November 2, 2015)

Colleen was referring a part of the co-planning session in which the team engaged in GB. She highlights the opportunity for learning as they engaged in this activity. The team was working towards helping the interns better understand high- and low-level tasks. By doing so, they suggested ideas to attend to this goal, creating the opportunity for the teacher educators to learn what others were thinking and what was taken up as appropriate to address the established goal. As Ainsley described above discussing the team's collaborative work, not all ideas were taken up. For example, in the third co-planning meeting, Olivia suggests having the interns pass around notebooks and responding to one reflective question in each notebook. Initially this seems to be a good way to share ideas, however, the team realizes that the interns would leave class with a notebook filled with responses to one question rather than all of the questions that were posed and this idea not taken up to move into DD.

Determining Instructional Details

The team spent more than 50% of its time in each meeting determining the instructional details of the methods course experiences for the interns in the methods course. After a general idea had been agreed upon, either explicitly or implicitly, the team discussed how the activity would play out in the classroom. In an interview, Sara acknowledged this focus on logistics during co-planning when she mentioned questions they thought about, "What is this going to look like when we actually do it? And is it going to take too long? Are [the interns] not going to understand the directions?" (Interview #2, October 21, 2015). Olivia also described the work during co-planning, "We try to work out the nitty-gritty details. How are we going to do it?" (Interview #2, October 20, 2015). During these discussions of determining the instructional details, the team worked out how to respond to the established goal. This created an opportunity for learning about what methods course experiences would look like to attend to specific goals as well as created a space to discuss instructional details such as which teaching strategies would be used, how to engage the interns, how much time would be devoted to the methods course experience, where it fell within the class period, and what instructions the interns would receive for it. Determining instructional details also gave team members a chance to draw on prior experiences in both teacher education and elementary school settings.

At times during the co-planning meetings the team engaged with potential methods course experiences as they worked through the instructional details, specifically when selecting tasks for the interns to examine during class and classifying the tasks according to the levels of cognitive demand within the mathematical tasks framework (MTF). The MTF and the associated task analysis guide (Stein & Smith, 1998) provide characteristics for identifying tasks according to lower-levels of cognitive demand (*memorization* and *procedures without connections*) and higher-levels of cognitive demand (*procedures with connections* and *doing mathematics*). The team engaged in the sorting as a means to both select the tasks for use by the interns in class and to come to a consensus as instructors about how to classify the tasks. This provided an opportunity for the teacher educators to further their understanding about sorting tasks according to the level of cognitive demand. For example, in Co-Planning A, one of the tasks from the district textbook that the MPCoP considered using with the interns asked second-grade students to partition a square to make a 4×4 area model and then shade regions to show halves in two different ways. The team discussed their thoughts about the level of cognitive demand of this task:

> **Olivia:** So there's that one [Given an open array: Measure in inches. Draw rows and columns. Write the number of small squares.] and then there's the one we were just talking about with the halves. They're very similar in terms of the level of cognitive demand.
>
> **Sara:** Well, showing it two ways bumps it up [from lower to higher level of cognitive demand] a little bit.
>
> **Olivia:** Does it?
>
> **Colleen:** Not when you're being told you have to do it this way.
>
> **Sara:** What do you mean?
>
> **Olivia:** Are you saying it bumps it up to another category?
>
> **Sara:** Well, within a category maybe, yeah. Shade to show halves two different ways.

Olivia then invited Ainsley to share her thoughts about the level of cognitive demand of the task. Ainsley hesitated with her response and expressed uncertainty when she said, "I don't know if that makes it...high-level." Sara conceded that this task might be categorized as procedures without connections, a low-level task. Olivia asserted that it is a low-level task. In this instance, the team discussed a common misconception among their interns that a task requiring two different solutions was the determining characteristic of a high-level task, which it appears some of the team members also held. Colleen, the district teacher who would be returning to the classroom, reflected on her work with sorting tasks:

> I've learned a lot about the math task framework but that's something that I feel like I need to keep working on.... I plan on photocopying that table [levels of cognitive demand], laminating it, and sticking it in my planning book and on my desk. (Interview #4, December 9, 2015)

Engaging in task sorting and the discussions surrounding the application of the MTF led to opportunities for learning among the teacher educators.

PARTICIPATION IN THE MPCOP

The MPCoP worked through the three co-planning activities (CPAs) to arrive at final plans for the methods course experiences to prepare the interns to select and adapt mathematical tasks. In each co-planning meeting, the MPCoP began with the activity of EG, and then moved to GB. From GB, the group either moved on to DD or returned to the original goal. The group moved back and forth between DD and EG before finalizing their plans. As discussed above, each activity held opportunities for learning for the teacher educators. All four team members actively participated in the co-planning, though there was variation in how they participated within the MPCoP.

Both Sara and Olivia held more permanent roles within the MPCoP with their respective roles as PDS coordinator and tenured faculty member, whereas Colleen and Ainsley were in transitory positions. In the year following the study, Colleen would be leaving the team to return to her classroom after three years of service in the PDS. Ainsley, a graduate student, held different roles for her assistantship, which varied year-to-year, offering a lack of permanency. Compared to Sara and Olivia, Colleen and Ainsley were "just visiting" (Fenton-O'Creevey, Brigham, Jones, & Smith, 2015) the MPCoP, which may account at least in part for differences in participation among the team members. Table 8.2 depicts the number of times each team member initiated one of the CPAs in the three co-planning meetings. Even though not all team members initiated each type of CPA, they each contributed to the co-planning meetings overall.

In addition to their trajectory out of the MPCoP, fewer occurrences of initiation by Colleen and Ainsley may also be accounted for by their perception of their respective roles within the co-planning activities. Colleen, a returning member of the team, explained, "I'm doing better this year of suggesting things or I continue to ask questions, because that's partially how I operate, and I feel more like we are creating a lot of the ideas together" (Background Interview, October 7, 2015). Ainsley, the newest team member, described her role in the co-planning meetings: "I feel like I'm just kind of listening to [the other teacher educators] talk about what they did in the past and how they could tweak it to now . . . I just try to put in any input that I can" (Background Interview, September 23, 2015). It seems that Colleen and Ainsley were comfortable with listening to others, asking questions, or offering suggestions when they could, rather than taking the lead in initiating planning.

Olivia initiated the CPAs more than the other three team members combined. Sara follows Olivia in her initiation of the CPAs with a total of nine times throughout the three meetings. When asked to describe her role in the co-planning meetings, Sara responded:

> My role is probably to keep the conversation going . . . I'm typically the person that might take what one person says and what another person says and then make that statement like, "It sounds like we're trying to go here." And sometimes, it moves the planning forward. (Background Interview, September 30, 2015)

Sara saw her role as one that synthesized the contributions of team members to progress in getting plans made.

The team engaged in the CPA EG 18 times over the three co-planning meetings. Of those 18 times, 12 of them were initiated by Olivia. She self-identified in an interview as focusing on the purpose of the co-planning, "I'm big picture: What are we doing? Why are we doing this? Let's make sure what we decide matches with our purpose" (Interview #2, October 20, 2015). Olivia explained in her initial interview:

> I spend a lot of time on planning for the class. I feel very responsible for making sure the class gets planned . . . I don't feel like I'm the leader of the team, but I sometimes feel like I do a lot of the planning . . . I feel like part of my role in the planning is to try to make sure that all of us have a role in it even when that means that I have to invite people to participate in the planning (Background Interview, September 21, 2015).

Olivia wanted to share decision-making out of respect for what others could contribute:

> I'm influenced by [my] lack of elementary school teaching experience in the sense that I really want people on the team who have that to bring that to the planning. Because I think that's where this co-planning and co-teaching makes a better class than if I was just doing this by myself . . . I think other members bring a lot of experience with their own use of math textbooks and curriculum materials . . . and children from their classrooms and how those children engaged with tasks and textbooks. (Background Interview, September 21, 2015)

Olivia's position and participation within the MPCoP appears to be that of a *boundary broker* (Wenger, 1998). As indicated above, she wanted to invite other team members to participate in the activities of co-planning because she valued their diverse expertise. The other members of the team had significantly more elementary teaching experience than Olivia and she valued that experience in their work together. The work of a boundary broker is complex as the position requires knowledge of the landscapes of practice of each team member within the MPCoP and a legitimacy to be able to navigate the boundaries between them.

The other three team members seem to support Olivia's position as a boundary broker when they describe her work in the MPCoP. Ainsley articulated:

> I would have to say that Olivia takes on a majority of the planning for the course and we meet bi-weekly to…discuss the plans for a class and we each give our feedback and input into whatever Olivia has come up with and Sara seems to put in a lot of input, too, before…our planning meetings. And we just kind of throw out ideas, just think through what's best for the preservice teachers to learn. (Background Interview, September 23, 2015)

Colleen offered a similar perception of Olivia's role when she reflected:

> [Olivia] definitely had a roadmap in mind for this semester's class and not that she decided everything on her own but she would say "I'm thinking we should do this" and as a group of people, we tend to all say, "Oh, okay, well let's try that." (Interview #4, December 9, 2015)

Finally, when examining a transcript from Co-Planning A, Sara pointed to a suggestion from Olivia and explained, "Olivia obviously had an idea here [looking at a piece of transcript from Co-Planning A]. She wanted to make sure that she was checking in with us and trying to get some ideas" (Interview #1, October 7, 2015). These descriptions, along with Olivia's own understanding of her role in the MPCoP seem to indicate that she was acting as a boundary broker.

DISCUSSION AND IMPLICATIONS

Co-planning is a tool that can be used prepare the next generation of teacher educators. It gives a role for novice and experienced teacher educators to work in the same space while offering meaningful contributions. In the present study, it created opportunities for learning for the hybrid teacher educators and helped to strengthen their collective work. By engaging in co-planning, the teacher educators were able to learn not only about the act of co-planning but also more deeply understand the course framework and the content (e.g., the MTF) to be delivered to the interns. They were also able to learn from one another as they had diverse backgrounds that they brought to the co-planning. Olivia lacked elementary teaching experience, yet each of the other three team members had more than 10 years' experience in that area. Olivia, on the other hand, had a deep understanding of the course framework and the MTF as well as more than 20 years of teacher educator experience. Co-planning offered a third space for these hybrid teacher educators to work on closing the gap between schools and universities, as Zeichner (2010) calls for.

Contrary to collaborative planning within lesson study (e.g., Lampert et al., 2013; Suh & Seshaiyer, 2015), the MPCoP did not have an imposed protocol to guide its collaborative planning. For this reason, it was necessary to investigate the particular activities of this team. Whereas all three of the general CPAs (EG, GB, and DD) appeared to be essential components of the MPCoP's planning process, the MPCoP spent the majority of its time on the co-planning activity *determining instructional details.*

Given that the MPCoP co-taught the methods, all members of the MPCoP were responsible for knowing and being able to enact the plans for the methods course experiences that were developed during the co-planning meetings. The MPCoP deprivatized the work of the teacher educators and removed sole ownership of the planned course experiences from one individual TE and placed the ownership on the group thereby removing the personal attachment educators can have towards their work (Boylan, 2010). Collaboration of this kind supports a collective attitude during the planning process and gives educators an incentive to be invested in the final product (Sims & Walsh, 2009). Perhaps due to the nature of team teaching, the MPCoP spent considerable time on determining the instructional details as each individual would be held responsible for the methods course experience.

It is possible that the MPCoP's lesser time spent on the other two co-planning activities (*establishing goals* and *general brainstorming*) may have related to the teacher educators' memberships in other communities of practice. As relatively novice teacher educators, it is possible that Ainsley, Colleen, and Sara had less experience in teacher education CoP, and therefore, might not have had as many ideas for contributions to EG and GB activities as did Olivia. The opportunities for their contributions to these activities may have been limited by the type of co-planning the team engaged in. The first two co-planning meetings can be characterized as *unilateral co-planning*; Olivia wrote plans for the class session in the shared planning document prior to the co-planning meeting. Ainsley, Colleen, and Sara may have defaulted to Olivia for her academic expertise given that the course is for university credit and she represented the university in setting the course curriculum.

In order to invite more team members to initiate co-planning activities, rather than one individual consistently leading, it may be useful to use a guiding protocol in preparation for co-planning sessions (see Figure 8.3) and as a tool while engaging in the activities.

Perhaps Ainsley and Colleen would have initiated more often had they engaged in such a protocol. The protocol could serve as an individual record for the meetings and create further opportunities for learning and reflection as the semester and co-planning progresses. Especially given that teacher

---

Research-Informed Co-Planning Protocol

1. What are the specific goals for this co-planning session?

2. What initial ideas do I have about meeting these goals?

3. What are the details of the course experience we developed?

4. What ideas did we table today that we might use in the future? What might our goals be for the next meeting?

Figure 8.3   Research informed co-planning protocol.

educators may enter the position with much training (Berry, 2008; Dinkelman et al., 2006) and be engaging in new professional responsibilities (Labaree, 2003), this may also serve as a tangible entry point for novice hybrid teacher educators, such as Ainsley, to engage in the co-planning process.

CONCLUSION

The boundary-spanning work of hybrid teacher educators is complex and warrants attention. Hybrid teacher educators may undergo a shift in their professional roles which could require a change in their focus and priorities, just as teachers turned researchers experience (Labaree, 2003). Co-planning with other experienced teacher educators creates opportunities to learn not only about the co-planning process but also what may be contributed to the new role. Experienced teacher educators may learn new ideas from novice teacher educators as they offer fresh perspectives and unique experiences to the table. Bringing together hybrid teacher educators who have had different professional priorities prior to their joint work may allow methods courses to be a blend of theory and practice with input from both sides of the school and university divide. Co-planning can be used as a tool to prepare the next generation of teacher educators for the work they will be doing by potentially providing a supportive environment for teacher educator learning.

While I identified three general CPAs for this specific team, they are likely to appear in the co-planning of other teams. Furthermore, other teams, or even this one, might have additional CPAs and patterns. Given the complex work of hybrid teacher educators (Martin et al., 2011; Williams, 2014), future research should examine the activities of other communities of practice composed of hybrid teacher educators. It may also be worthwhile to examine the differences between the organic co-planning activities of this group with those of CoP that use a guiding protocol.

In this chapter, I identified and illustrated the general co-planning activities of a team of hybrid teacher educators working in a PDS and their opportunities for learning while engaging in these activities. Documenting the team's collaboration provides insight into their work, identifies how hybrid teacher educators may learn from engaging in co-planning, and opens up the possibility of comparing collaborations in the future. It offers an example of the collaborative work occurring within a PDS and raises questions for future work about how hybrid teacher educators can navigate diverse communities of practice within the collaborative work of a PDS.

Discussion Questions

1. In your current context, how might you use co-planning?
2. What are your areas of expertise that you bring to the table? In what areas do you wish you had more expertise?
3. What role do you think you play or would play in co-planning?
4. Can you identify any boundary brokers in your context? Who might they be? Why?

REFERENCES

Anagnostopoulos, D., Smith, E. R., & Basmadjian, K. G. (2007). Bridging the university-school divide: Horizontal expertise and the "two-worlds pitfall." *Journal of Teacher Education, 58*(2), 138–152.

Berry, A. (2008). *Tensions in teaching about teaching: Understanding practice as a teacher educator.* Dordrecht, The Netherlands: Springer.

Berry, A., & Van Driel, J. H. (2012). Teaching about teaching science: Aims, strategies, and backgrounds of science teacher educators. *Journal of Teacher Education, 64*(2), 117–128.

Bleiler, S. K. (2015). Increasing awareness of practice through interaction across communities: The lived experiences of a mathematician and mathematics teacher educator. *Journal of Mathematics Teacher Education, 18*(3), 231–252.

Borko, H., Liston, D., & Whitcomb, J. A. (2007). Genres of empirical research in teacher education. *Journal of Teacher Education, 58*(1), 3–11.

Borko, H., Whitcomb, J. A., & Byrnes, K. (2008). Genres of research in teacher education. In M. Cochran-Smith, S. Feiman-Nemser, D. J. McIntyre, & K. E. Demers (Eds.), *Handbook of research on teacher education: Enduring questions in changing contexts* (3rd ed., pp. 1017–1049). New York, NY: Routledge.

Boylan, M. (2010). "It's getting me thinking and I'm an old cynic": Exploring the relational dynamics of mathematics teacher change. *Journal of Mathematics Teacher Education, 13*(5), 383–395.

Burns, R. W., Yendol-Hoppey, D., & Jacobs, J. (2015). High-quality teaching requires collaboration: How partnerships can create a true continuum of professional learning for educators. *The Educational Forum, 79*(1), 53–67.

Chatman, S. (1980). What novels can do that films can't (and vice versa). *Critical Inquiry, 7*(1), 121–140.

Dinkelman, T., Margolis, J., & Sikkenga, K. (2006). From teacher to teacher educator: Experiences, expectations, and expatriation. *Studying Teacher Education, 2*(1), 5–23.

Fenton-O'Creevy, M., Brigham, L., Jones, S., & Smith, A. (2015). Students at the academic-workplace boundary: Tourists and sojourners in practice-based education. In E. Wenger-Trayner, M. Fenton-O'Creevy, S. Hutchinson, C. Kubiak, & B. Wenger-Trayner (Eds.), *Learning in landscapes of practice: Boundaries, identity, and knowledgeability in practice-based learning* (pp. 43–63). New York, NY: Routledge.

Fernandez, M. L. (2010). Investigating how and what prospective teachers learn through microteaching lesson study. *Teaching and Teacher Education, 26*(2), 351–362.

Goodchild, S., Fuglestad, A. B., & Jaworski, B. (2013). Critical alignment in inquiry-based practice in developing mathematics teaching. *Educational Studies in Mathematics, 84*, 393–412.

Gorodetsky, M., & Barak, J. (2008). The educational-cultural edge: A participative learning environment for co-emergence of personal and institutional growth. *Teaching and Teacher Education, 24*(7), 1907–1918.

Groenewald, T. (2008). Memos and memoing. In L. Given (Ed.), *The SAGE encyclopedia of qualitative research methods* (pp. 505–506). Thousand Oaks, CA: SAGE.

Gutiérrez, K. D. (2008). Developing a sociocritical literacy in the third space. *Reading Research Quarterly, 43*(2), 148–164.

Gutiérrez, K. D., Baquedano-López, P., & Tejeda, C. (1999). Rethinking diversity: Hybridity and hybrid language practices in the third space. *Mind, Culture, and Activity, 6*(4), 286–303.

Holmes Group. (1990). *Tomorrow's schools: Principles for the design of professional development schools.* East Lansing, MI: Author.

Labaree, D. F. (2003). The peculiar problems of preparing educational researchers. *Education Researcher, 32*(4), 13–22.

Lampert, M., Franke, M. L., Kazemi, E., Ghousseini, H., Turrou, A. C., Beasley, H., & Crowe, K. (2013). Keeping it complex: Using rehearsals to support novice teacher learning of ambitious teaching. *Journal of Teacher Education, 64*(3), 226–243.

Lewis, C. C., Perry, R. R., & Hurd, J. (2009). Improving mathematics instruction through lesson study: A theoretical model and North American case. *Journal of Mathematics Teacher Education, 12*(4), 285–304.

Loughran, J. (2014). Professionally developing as a teacher educator. *Journal of Teacher Education, 65,* 271–283.

Martin, S. D., Snow, J. L., & Franklin Torrez, C. A. (2011). Navigating the terrain of third space: Tensions with/in relationships in school-university partnerships. *Journal of Teacher Education, 62*(3), 299–311.

Murray, J., & Male, T. (2005). Becoming a teacher educator: Evidence from the field. *Teaching and Teacher Education, 21*(2), 125–142.

Nevin, A. I., Thousand, J. S., & Villa, R. A. (2009). Collaborative teaching for teacher educators—What does the research say? *Teaching and Teacher Education, 25*(4), 569–574.

Patton, M. Q. (2002). *Qualitative research and evaluation methods* (3rd ed.). Thousand Oaks, CA: SAGE.

Roth McDuffie, A., & Mather, M. (2009). Middle school mathematics teachers' use of curricular reasoning in a collaborative professional development project. In J. T. Remillard, B. A. Herbel-Eisenmann, & G. M. Lloyd (Eds.), *Mathematics teachers at work: Connecting curriculum materials and classroom instruction* (pp. 302–320). New York, NY: Routledge.

Sims, L., & Walsh, D. (2009). Lesson study with preservice teachers: Lessons from lessons. *Teaching and Teacher Education, 25*(5), 724–733.

Spradley, J. P. (1979). *The ethnographic interview.* Belmont, CA: Wadsworth, Cengage Learning.

Stein, M. K., & Smith, M. S. (1998). Selecting and creating mathematical tasks: From research to practice. *Mathematics Teaching in the Middle School, 3*(5), 344–350.

Suchman, L. (1994). Working relations of technology production and use. *Computer Supported Cooperative Work, 2,* 21–39.

Suh, J., & Seshaiyer, P. (2015). Examining teachers' understanding of the mathematical learning progression through vertical articulation during Lesson Study. *Journal of Mathematics Teacher Education, 18*(3), 207–229.

Sztajn, P., Wilson, P. H., Edgington, C., & Myers, M. (2014). Mathematics professional development as design for boundary encounters. *ZDM—International Journal on Mathematics Education, 46*(2), 201–212.

Van Zoest, L. R., & Bohl, J. V. (2002). The role of reform curricular materials in an internship: The case of Alice and Gregory. *Journal of Mathematics Teacher Education, 5*(3), 265–288.

Villa, R. A., Thousand, J. S., & Nevin, A. I. (2008). *A guide to co-teaching: Practical tips for facilitating student learning* (2nd ed.). Thousand Oaks, CA: Corwin Press and Council for Exceptional Children.

Wake, G., Swan, M., & Foster, C. (2016). Professional learning through the collaborative design of problem-solving lessons. *Journal of Mathematics Teacher Education, 19*(2), 1–18.

Watson, A., & De Geest, E. (2014). Department-initiated change. *Educational Studies in Mathematics, 87*(3), 351–368.

Wenger-Trayner, E., & Wenger-Trayner, B. (2015). *Communities of practice: A brief introduction.* Retrieved from http://wenger-trayner.com/introduction-to -communities-of-practice/

Wenger-Trayner, E., & Wenger-Trayner, B. (2015). Learning in a landscape of practice: A framework. In E. Wenger-Trayner, M. Fenton-O'Creevy, S. Hutchinson, C. Kubiak, & B. Wenger-Trayner (Eds.), *Learning in landscapes of practice: Boundaries, identity, and knowledgeability in practice-based learning* (pp. 13–30). New York, NY: Routledge.

Wenger, E. (1998). *Communities of practice: Learning, meaning, and identity.* Cambridge, England: Cambridge University Press.

Williams, J. (2014). Teacher educator professional learning in the third space: Implications for identity and practice. *Journal of Teacher Education, 65*(4), 315–326.

Wolcott, H. F. (1994). Adequate schools and inadequate education: The life history of a sneaky kid. In *Transforming qualitative data: description, analysis, and interpretation* (pp. 61–102). Thousand Oaks, California: SAGE.

Wood, M. B., & Turner, E. E. (2015). Bringing the teacher into teacher preparation: Learning from mentor teachers in joint methods activities. *Journal of Mathematics Teacher Education, 18*(1), 27–51.

Yendol-Silva, D., & Dana, N. F. (2004). Encountering new spaces: Teachers developing voice within a professional development school. *Journal of Teacher Education, 55*(2), 128–140.

Zeichner, K. (2010). Rethinking the connections between campus courses and field experiences in college- and university-based teacher education. *Journal of Teacher Education, 61*(1–2), 89–99.

Zeichner, K., Payne, K. A., & Brayko, K. (2015). Democratizing teacher education. *Journal of Teacher Education, 66*(2), 122–135.

PART III

INQUIRY AS A MECHANISM
FOR TEACHER EDUCATOR PREPARATION

In Parts I and II of this book, the focus was on the *who* in teacher education as we explored the preparation and work of two distinct types of teacher educators—those who receive their paychecks from a university (referred to as *university-based* teacher educators), and those who receive their paychecks from a K–12 school setting (referred to as a *school-based* teacher educators). In this third and final section, we turn our gaze from the *who* to the *how*, as we consider one mechanism for teacher educator preparation—the systematic and intentional study of one's own professional practice as a teacher educator.

The process of studying one's own professional practice can take many forms that are referenced by different names that include "teacher research, action research, self-study, the scholarship of teaching and learning, and the use of teaching as a context for research" (Cochran-Smith & Lytle, 2009, p. 39–40). The term "inquiry" has been used as both an umbrella label to encompass all aforementioned forms of practitioners' engagement in researching practice (Cochran-Smith & Lytle, 2009), as well as the expression most commonly used in K–12 schools to describe one form of job-embedded professional development where teachers study the acts of teaching and learning as they unfold in their own classrooms on a daily basis (Yendol-Hoppey & Dana, 2010; Nichols & Cormack, 2017). In this section, we use the school-based common-term inquiry to reflect the language most often used with teacher candidates in teacher education programs across the nation that embed the study of one's own practice into the initial

Preparing the Next Generation of Teacher Educators for Clinical Practice, pages 193–197
Copyright © 2019 by Information Age Publishing
193

preparation of teachers (Delane, Hooser, Richner, Wolkenhauer, Colvin, & Dana, 2017) as well as the term self-study, as this expression is "used almost exclusively to refer to inquiries at the higher education level by academics involved in the practice of teacher education, broadly construed" (Cochran-Smith & Lytle, 2009, p. 40).

Regardless of the language used, the process of studying one's own professional practice becomes an important ingredient in the preparation of the next generation of teacher educators for the same reason it is commonly woven into the fabric of initial teacher preparation programs. Teaching, whether it is being done in a K–12 school setting where children are learning subject matter, or it is being done in a university setting where adults are learning how to teach, is an inherently complex endeavor. Leading scholar of the practitioner inquiry movement and prolific teacher education researcher Marilyn Cochran-Smith has discussed the complex nature of teaching for years, describing the evolution of her thinking about teaching's complexity in 2013 as follows:

> A decade ago, I realized that, oddly enough, a book about writing—Anne Lamott's (1994) *Bird by Bird: Some Instructions on Writing and Life*—could be helpful in imagining and drawing attention to other ways of thinking about the nature of the work of teaching (Cochran-Smith, 2003). I pointed out in an editorial that Lamott advised writers to avoid simple oppositions in their writing; she said, "I used to think that paired opposites were a given, that love was the opposite of hate, right the opposite of wrong. But now I think we sometimes buy into these concepts because it is so much easier to embrace absolutes than to suffer reality. [Now] I don't think anything is the opposite of love. Reality is unforgivingly complex" (p. 104). It seemed to me that Lamott's writing advice and her ideas about the nature of reality could be instructive to our thinking about the nature of teaching if we really wanted to understand it and if we wanted to engage in research that had any chance of helping to improve it. So editing Lamott's phrase somewhat, I emphasized that *teaching* was unforgivingly complex, not simply good or bad, right or wrong, working or failing. Although absolutes and dichotomies like these were (and are) popular in headlines and campaign slogans, they're limited in their usefulness. They don't raise any questions about what it means to be engaged in the process of becoming an educated person in a democratic but also global society or whose knowledge and values are of most worth or what counts as evidence of the effectiveness of teaching and learning. They ignore all the nuances of "good" (or "bad") teaching of real students collected in actual classrooms at particular times and places and in fluid social, cultural, and political contexts within a long history of inequities in opportunities and outcomes. (Cochran-Smith, 2013, p. x)

Because educating students is such a complex endeavor (whether "students" refers to K–12 children or to adults in teacher education programs across the nation), it is natural and normal for many issues, tensions, problems, and dilemmas to arise as we work to prepare the next generation of teachers. Rather than sweeping these issues, tensions, problems, and dilemmas under the carpet and pretending they don't exist, studying one's own practice as a teacher educator creates a space to embrace all of the rich complexity inherent in the work of teaching, and to gain important insights that will help us improve our work as teacher educators. Embracing complexity and gaining important insights through inquiry is demonstrated in the three chapters that appear in this section.

First, in Chapter 9, Jennifer Jacobs and Elizabeth Currin specifically address the role inquiry can play in doctoral education in their chapter entitled, "Making the Case for Practitioner Inquiry in Doctoral Student Education: Supporting the Development of Future Teacher Educators," by reviewing and analyzing four different studies focused on this topic that were conducted across the two universities where they work. This chapter offers a summary of each individual study as well as looks across them to derive two lessons learned about engagement in inquiry focused on one's own emerging teacher education practice during doctoral education. We learn that doctoral student engagement in inquiry can lead to individual and programmatic improvement in teacher education coursework and supervision, as well as introduce doctoral students to some of the enduring tensions they will encounter throughout their careers in teacher education. These authors purposefully use the broader construct of practitioner inquiry in their work with doctoral students rather than the more specific construct of self-study in order to reflect the framework being used with teacher candidates at the institutions where the doctoral students across the four studies were learning to be teacher educators. Hence, one valuable contribution of this chapter is the overview provided of the practitioner inquiry movement in general and the ways doctoral student education can be situated within it. This description paves the way for the second chapter in this section, focused specifically on self-study.

In Chapter 10, straightforwardly titled "Self-Study and Preparing the Next Generation of Teacher Educators," Brandon Butler explores the history and underpinnings of self-study in teacher education, teaching the reader about this very particular brand of practitioner inquiry that is conducted in higher education contexts by teacher education academics. This chapter beautifully follows the Jacobs and Currin chapter as Butler describes his experiences with self-study beginning during his own doctoral education and the ways self-study helped launch and shape his career in higher education once he graduated and began work as a teacher education professor. This chapter also provides insights into the ways self-study can inform the particular practice of clinical supervision undertaken by many teacher educators as a part of their work. Butler both explains and illustrates the process of self-study by reflecting on his own experiences learning about, doing, and leading the self-study of his own doctoral students. Explaining and illustrating self-study in teacher education naturally leads to the final chapter in this section, the complete write-up of a self-study by teacher educators at Boise State University.

Chapter 11, entitled "Facing Practice as Teacher Educators: A Self-Study of Program Graduates," details the self-study of Jennifer Snow, Cheryle Dismuke, Julianne Wenner, and Serena Hicks as they systematically reflect on their experience studying their program graduates in their early years of teaching. Through this study, these teacher educators illuminate just how complex it is to be a teacher educator in the age of accountability where teacher education programs must provide evidence of their graduates' impact on pre-K–12 student learning for accreditation purposes. Studying their graduates in their early years of teaching led these teacher educators to "eat humble pie," scale their expectations to focus on the development of "well-started" teachers, and become more deliberate about integrating various aspects of their teacher education program. The process of self-study also led to these teacher educators questioning beliefs such as the value of their teacher candidates completing their major clinical experience all in the same school setting. Taken collectively, the findings of this self-study indicate that when teacher educators engage with one another in the same ways they hope the teacher candidates they are preparing to enter the profession will do both within their program and after graduation, parallels develop between teacher educator stance of lifelong professional learning and their graduates' professional stance. Through self-study, the authors of this chapter became more explicit about modeling stance for their teacher candidates.

In sum, the three chapters in this section celebrate the complex nature of both teaching and teacher education by showing the reader the ways naming, framing, and studying problems of practice as a teacher educator does not eradicate problems but leads to new (and hopefully better) problems to study as teacher educators live out the multiple tensions that are inherent in their work beginning during doctoral education and throughout the entirety of their careers. Hence, teacher educator preparation is not about enacting a plan to develop a "finished product," but instead, perhaps the field needs to focus on developing a "well-started" teacher educator (borrowing language from the self-study completed at Boise State). The chapters in this section all point to engagement in practitioner inquiry and self-study to be of critical importance to the "well-started" teacher educator. Important questions this section raises for a community of scholars focused on preparing the next generation of teacher educators include how best to embed the study of one's own professional practice within teacher educator preparation while simultaneously preparing future teacher educators for university contexts that may not embrace self-study. The next generation of teacher educators must develop the skills to work within the system as they change the system. This section reveals the role inquiry can play in this endeavor.

REFERENCES

Cochran-Smith, M. (2013). *Forward.* In N. Dana (Ed.), *Digging deeper into action research* (pp. ix–xii.) Thousand Oaks, CA: Corwin Press.

Cochran-Smith, M. (2003). The unforgiving complexity of teaching: Avoiding simplicity in the age of accountability. *Journal of Teacher Education, 54*(1), 3–5.

Cochran-Smith, M., & Lytle, S. L. (2009). *Inquiry as stance: Practitioner research for the next generation.* New York, NY: Teachers College Press.

Delane, D. C., Hooser, A., Richner, M., Wolkenhauer, R., Colvin, S. M., & Dana, N. F. (2017). Practitioner inquiry as the anchor of clinical practice throughout the teacher education program. In R. Flessner & D. R. Lecklider (Eds.), *The power of clinical preparation in teacher education* (pp. 69–86). Lanham, MD: Rowman & Littlefield Education.

Lamott, A. (1994). *Bird by bird: Some instructions on writing and life.* New York, NY: Anchor Books.

Nichols, S., & Cormack, P. (2017). *Impactful practitioner inquiry: The ripple effect on classrooms, schools, and teacher professionalism.* New York, NY: Teachers College Press.

Yendol-Hoppey, D., & Dana, N. F. (2010). *Powerful professional development: Building expertise within the four walls of your school.* Thousand Oaks, CA: Corwin Press.

CHAPTER 9

MAKING THE CASE FOR PRACTITIONER INQUIRY IN DOCTORAL STUDENT EDUCATION

Supporting the Development of Future Teacher Educators

Jennifer Jacobs
University of South Florida

Elizabeth Currin
University of Florida

The teacher education community has called for centering teacher preparation on high quality clinical experiences (Darling-Hammond, 2009; National Council of Accreditation of Teacher Education, 2010). This means that teacher education programs can no longer be designed as clinically accompanied where the field and the university coursework are separated (Dennis et al., 2017). Teacher educators must now weave together academic

Preparing the Next Generation of Teacher Educators for Clinical Practice, pages 199–226
Copyright © 2019 by Information Age Publishing

content, professional courses, and clinical experiences. To accomplish this, teacher education programs would benefit by rethinking the preparation and support provided to doctoral students who will one day be responsible for preparing teacher candidates. Actualizing clinically rich teacher education requires a greater emphasis on the development of future teacher educators who are prepared to navigate many practical, conceptual, and structural challenges (Burns, Jacobs, & Yendol-Hoppey, 2016). These new teacher educators will be responsible for developing high quality coursework (Ball & Forzani, 2009), planning integrated field experiences (National Association for Professional Development Schools, 2008; NCATE, 2001), preparing teacher candidates to meet diverse students' needs (Cochran-Smith, Barnatt, Friedman, & Pine, 2009; Howard & Aleman, 2008; Villegas & Lucas, 2002), and cultivating in teacher candidates an inquiry orientation towards teaching and learning (Cochran-Smith & Lytle, 2009). Today's calls for teacher education reform necessitate future teacher educators who understand the need for innovation; are invested in the work of clinically rich teacher education; and possess the knowledge, skills, and abilities to develop new roles and practices.

Unfortunately, little empirical evidence demonstrates how teacher education doctoral programs are retooling the way they prepare teacher educators to facilitate, engage in, and lead this important reform work. Compounding this void, academics from all disciplines are susceptible to attrition stemming from isolation and lack of structure (Baker & Pifer, 2011), fragmented or conflicting roles (Colbeck, 1998; Dunn-Haley & Zanzucchi, 2012; Fain, 1987), and general frustration due to a host of contextual factors (Gardner, 2008a). Doctoral students, who are transitioning "from being consumers of knowledge, such as they have experienced within the classroom, to creators of knowledge through their original research" (Gardner, 2008b, p. 328), may feel these pains most acutely.

In response to these challenges, the purpose of this chapter is to describe how practitioner inquiry, or the systematic study of one's practice, when infused within doctoral preparation can serve as a signature pedagogy to develop future teacher educators who are capable of actualizing teacher education reform. During the last few decades, inquiry has enjoyed heightened attention as a process that contributes to pre-service and in-service teacher learning (Cochran-Smith & Lytle, 2009; Dana & Yendol-Hoppey, 2014; Grossman, 2005; Hall, 2009; Mockler & Groundwater-Smith, 2015; Newman & Mowbray, 2012; Price & Valli, 2005). This chapter serves as a conceptual revisiting of existing research by analyzing four studies from two different contexts to examine how practitioner inquiry can support the development of future teacher educators within the current context of teacher preparation reform.

CONCEPTUAL FRAMEWORK

To situate this conceptual review of four existing studies, we draw on several bodies of literature, including the role of teacher educators, doctoral education, and practitioner inquiry.

Role of Teacher Educators

Preparing the next generation of teacher educators requires recognizing the complexity of their future responsibilities. Cochran-Smith (2012) described the multifaceted and intensive work of teacher educators as including:

> Curriculum development; program evaluation; recruitment and admission of students; participation in professional and state-level accreditation reviews; establishment and maintenance of fieldwork sites; supervision of fieldwork experiences for teacher candidates in school and community settings; supervising and mentoring student teachers; providing professional development for experienced teachers; teaching courses with fieldwork components; collaborating with school-and community-based educators; providing career advice about teaching and other roles in schools; working in professional development or partnership schools; and developing, administering, and evaluating professional assessments (or assessment systems) for teacher candidates. (p. 100)

These expectations are further complicated when teacher educators arrive at research institutions and face more pressure to publish than to contribute to program development and high quality teaching (Beaumont, 1998; Colbeck, 1998; Murray & Male, 2005). Balancing quality teacher education and a productive research agenda can be an elusive goal.

Like other academics, teacher educators thus experience role conflict, which is especially prevalent among new, untenured faculty, particularly women. Mindful of these high-risk populations, Lease (1999) explains how "faculty who are experiencing more stress than they can cope with are likely to withdraw from student–professor interactions, be less accessible to students, and be less involved in the departmental decision making and committee work" (p. 287), rendering teacher educators largely incapable of enacting necessary reform. Role conflict and the stress it brings have detrimental, even career-ending effects (Klenke-Hamel & Mathieu, 1990), but "an active and problem-oriented approach," marked by critical thinking and creativity, can prevent these outcomes (Hornung, Lampert, & Glaser, 2016, p. 502). Colbeck (1998) also reminds us of the socially constructed nature of role expectations. Context is key.

Nearly two decades ago, Tom (1997) argued that teacher education reform would require teacher educators to make identity shifts as faculty expanded, renegotiated, and redefined their roles in teacher education. More recently, Dinkelman (2011) described the ideal teacher educator as fluid, always developing, shaped by a broad range of sociocultural power relationships, relational, and strongly influenced by any number of relevant contexts. These identities are both claimed by teacher educators and given to them through the institutional roles that frame their profession. Ultimately, the way teacher educators learn to perceive their learning and understand their contextualized roles influences their choices and actions (Watson, 2009). We thus turn to literature on doctoral education to consider how those perceptions come to be.

Doctoral Education

Like teacher educators and even the teacher candidates in their charge, doctoral students also experience role conflict, owing to the tension of simultaneously being students and professionals (McAlpine & Amundsen, 2009; Munby, Lock, & Smith, 2001; Weidman & Stein, 2003). Jazvac-Martek (2009) describes education doctoral students as precariously oscillating between disparate identities. In extreme cases, this leads to procrastination and even attrition (Gardner, 2008a; Senécal, Julien, & Guay, 2003), yet scholars warn there is no sure-fire way to avoid such outcomes, in part because the doctoral student experience is neither linear nor monolithic (Acker & Haque, 2015; Gardner, 2010; Gopaul, 2011; Portnoi, Lima Chlopecki, & Peregrina-Kretz, 2015). McAlpine and Norton (2006) stress the need for a holistic view of the interconnected contexts bearing down on graduate students.

Heeding this advice may mean looking beyond the traditional advisor–advisee dyad to recognize the necessarily collaborative nature of doctoral student socialization (Baker & Pifer, 2011; Dunn-Haley & Zanzucchi, 2012; Gardner, 2008b; Weidman & Stein, 2003). Indeed, Watts (2010) endorses team supervision in PhD programs because mentor–mentee relationships can sometimes be fraught. Other scholars have pointed to the invaluable impact of peers and the often-overlooked agency of doctoral students themselves (Jazvac-Martek, 2009). Portnoi et al. (2015) maintain "intentionally recognizing doctoral student agency holds promise for improving the socialization experiences of doctoral students, and therefore has implications for both emerging scholars and the faculty who work with them" (p. 13). We agree, and we see practitioner inquiry as the ideal vehicle for achieving that aim within a teacher education context.

Given the expanding roles associated with being a teacher educator, Zeichner (2006) argued that the next generation of teacher educators would need to receive greater and different attention, challenging research universities "to take the preparation of teacher educators more seriously" (p. 335). In addition, the European Commission's Report (2013), "Supporting Teacher Educators for Better Learning Outcomes," espouses a commitment to preparing as well as sustaining teacher educators. Noting glaring inconsistencies among teacher education doctoral programs, Goodwin et al. (2014) stressed "the need to engage teacher-educators-to-be in systematic opportunities to develop pedagogical practices" (p. 292). Likewise, Balaban (2016) insists that PhD students be "given a voice" regarding the policies that shape their doctoral experiences (p. 91), and Gardner (2010) similarly recommends inviting doctoral students to engage in routine evaluation of graduate school guidelines and policies. Again, we see inquiry as well suited for all of these tasks.

Practitioner Inquiry

Rooted in the work of John Dewey (1933), practitioner inquiry is the systematic and intentional study of a teacher's own practice. For decades, teacher candidates around the world have used the process to explore their new profession (Cochran-Smith et al., 2009; Grossman, 2005; Price & Valli, 2005; Rinke & Stebick, 2013; Zellermayer & Tabak, 2006), and practicing teachers have turned to inquiry for professional development (Ermeling, 2010; Hall, 2009; Levin & Rock, 2003; Mockler & Groundwater-Smith, 2015; Newman & Mowbray, 2012; Zeichner, 2003).

Practitioner inquiry integrates multiple conceptions of knowledge as articulated by Cochran-Smith and Lytle (1999). Knowledge *for* practice is the formal knowledge base for teaching developed by outside experts within research publications, university coursework, trainings, and so forth. Knowledge *in* practice recognizes the importance of practical knowledge and its role in improving teaching practice. Teachers engage in knowledge construction within their classroom context in authentic, experiential ways. Knowledge *of* practice develops when "teachers treat the knowledge and theory produced by others as generative material for interrogation and interpretation" (Cochran-Smith & Lytle, 1999, p. 250). When educators engage in practitioner inquiry, they have the opportunity to generate knowledge *of* practice as they work together to analyze, critique, and understand practices and beliefs.

Inquiry promotes deeper reflection about teacher identity, as teachers move from observers and consumers of research to see "teacher-as-researcher" as part of who they are (Hall, 2009; Levin & Rock, 2003; Newman

& Mowbray, 2012; Rock & Levin, 2002). No longer disconnected and in opposition to classroom practice, research becomes an empowering process that promotes teachers' autonomy as change agents (Hall, 2009; Newman & Mowbray, 2012; Zellermayer & Tabak, 2006). Opportunities for deep and powerful knowledge construction can occur within collaborative inquiry communities where teachers inquire alongside one another (Cochran-Smith & Lytle, 1999; Levin & Rock, 2003; Newman & Mowbray, 2012; Tillema & van der Westhuizen, 2006; Zellermayer & Tabak, 2006). Dialogue within these communities provides opportunities for teachers to "actively and critically engage with new and different ways of thinking and try new approaches" (Newman & Mowbray, 2012, p. 462).

Whether undertaken alone or within a community, practitioner inquiry can be a powerful, transformative process for teachers. Scholars point to inquiry's ability to shift teacher beliefs about instruction (Hagevik, Aydeniz, & Rowell, 2012; Levin & Rock, 2003; Rock & Levin, 2002), deepen teacher understanding of curriculum (Levin & Rock, 2003), increase teachers' knowledge and understanding of students (Butler & Schnellert, 2012; Dresser, 2007; Levin & Rock, 2003; Rinke & Stebick, 2013; Rock & Levin, 2002; Wallace, 2013), promote growth and change in teaching practice (Dresser, 2007; Ermeling, 2010; Levin & Rock, 2003; Newman & Mowbray, 2012; Rock & Levin, 2002), and improve data literacy (Athanases, Wahleithner, & Bennett, 2012). Inquiry also fosters attention to social justice and diversity issues (Athanases et al., 2012; Hyland & Noffke, 2005; Martin, 2005) as it empowers teachers, too (Bonner, 2006; Esposito & Smith, 2006; Merino & Holmes, 2006; Newman & Mowbray, 2012). In combination, these findings illustrate the power that practitioner inquiry offers educators interested in innovation that strengthens teacher and student learning.

To date, research has focused primarily on the influence of practitioner inquiry on both pre-service and in-service teacher learning, with few studies exploring the use of inquiry within teacher educator preparation. Notable exceptions to this trend, two self-studies describing doctoral seminars that supported emerging teacher educators by developing a collaborative community, building an understanding of the teacher education research base, cultivating expertise as teacher education researchers, influencing identity formation, and promoting changes in teacher education practice (Dinkelman, 2011; Kosnik et al., 2011). Acknowledging both the formal and informal socialization of doctoral students (Portnoi et al., 2015), these studies suggest inquiry is a powerful tool for supporting the development of future teacher educators in diverse and ever-changing contexts.

Given Gopaul's (2011) recommendation that reflection be incorporated in doctoral student socialization, teacher educator preparation should cultivate an inquiry stance, "a worldview and a habit of mind—a way of knowing and being in the world of educational practice that carries across educational contexts and various points in one's professional career" (Cochran-Smith & Lytle, 2009, p. vii). Cochran-Smith (2004) suggests, "the course of [a teacher educator's] professional career is substantially enriched when inquiry is regarded as a stance on the overall enterprise of teacher education and when teacher educators inquire collaboratively about assumptions and values, professional knowledge and practice, and the contexts of schools as well as higher education, and their own as well as their students' learning" (p. 7). This career-long stance towards learning can be initiated during doctoral education by offering students opportunities to "link [...] present actions to past experiences and future intentions" (McAlpine & Amundsen, 2009, p. 112). Looking across four studies, we explore this possibility.

We were purposeful in our decision to describe this work using the term *practitioner inquiry*. While the terms *action research* and *self-study* are also used in relation to studying one's practice, we chose to use *practitioner inquiry* as it aligned with the framework doctoral students used with teacher candidates in both contexts' teacher education programs.

RESEARCH REVISITED

This chapter reviews four previously reported studies conducted within two different contexts, an approach that allowed us to strengthen our understanding of the phenomenon and generate new insights. Our process included both analytical and interpretive moves designed to systematically, comprehensively, and transparently ascertain the role practitioner inquiry played in the development of the teacher educators featured in these studies. We maintained fidelity to the original studies while looking for thematic patterns across the set, striving, like McAlpine and Amundsen (2009), "to shed light upon often invisible aspects of doctoral studies and to use what we learn to interrogate our own current pedagogical policies and practices" (p. 124). By revisiting four studies conducted across two different contexts and focused on the same phenomenon, we hope to show how the infusion of practitioner inquiry can prepare doctoral students to become the next generation of teacher educators. Jennifer (first author and teacher educator) was involved in all four studies, while Elizabeth (co-author and doctoral student) provided an outsider perspective during data analysis and writing.

All four studies took place across two research-one university contexts. In total, these four studies involved the experiences of 26 doctoral students and three faculty members. All doctoral students were enrolled in programs that prepared them to be teacher educators and emphasized coursework in curriculum, teaching, and teacher education.

Context 1

At one university, inquiry was purposefully built into two courses taken by doctoral students as they began teaching undergraduate coursework and supervising clinical experiences. The first semester focused on learning about the process of practitioner inquiry and becoming familiar with the literature on teacher education. During the second semester, students continued to explore the teacher education literature and delved deeper into the field of supervision. Both courses allowed opportunities for nine beginning doctoral students to explore the literature, study their practice, and come together within a community to share problems of practice and receive support. In addition to the first-year doctoral students, seven doctoral students who completed these two doctoral courses during the previous year voluntarily created an informal collaborative group called the "Inquiry Team" (I-Team). These doctoral students met once a month for a full year and supported each other's continued engagement in inquiry.

Context 2

After seeing a group of students and their professors from Context 1 present at a conference, a group of doctoral students from Context 2 wished to use that work as a model at their own institution, forming a voluntary colloquium for those interested in engaging in inquiry. Their goal was also to study their own practice as teacher educators. Ten doctoral students met every other week for 2 hours, advised by a faculty member. The colloquia series was designed to explore literature on practitioner inquiry and collaboratively examine the doctoral students' own instruction and/or supervision in Context 2's teacher preparation program.

The Studies

The studies revisited here all focus on practitioner inquiry and teacher educator doctoral preparation. These four studies were selected because they all included formal write-ups (i.e., conference papers, papers for courses, etc.) and were written during a one-year period of time in either Context 1 or 2. Table 9.1 provides an overview of the four studies.

As noted in Table 9.1, the researchers across the four independent studies varied in positionality. In the first three studies, novice as well as advanced doctoral students served as the researchers. In the fourth study, three faculty members studied doctoral students as a means to better understand practitioner inquiry and doctoral preparation. Positionality

TABLE 9.1   Practitioner Inquiry and Teacher Educator Doctoral Preparation Studies

Study	Authors	Method	Participants	Research Question	Data	Findings
1	(Study 1 includes all of the individual doctoral student inquiries described in Table 9.2.)					
2	Smith et al. (2013)	Self-Study	7 doctoral students from Context 1	What insights do prospective teacher educators gain from engaging in practitioner research within the context of a supervised teaching course designed to scaffold their professional development as future teacher educators and teacher researchers?	Artifacts, field notes, reflections, individual study write-ups	1. Inquiry prompted transferability, multi-modal experiences, self-study/collaboration, and insight referred to as a "meta-awareness" into instructional practice. 2. Inquiry focus on student growth led to transformation of instructional practice, greater feelings of accountability, and programmatic modeling of inquiry stance.
3	Arndt et al. (2013)	Self-Study	5 doctoral students across both contexts	What do doctoral students learn as a result of engaging in inquiry into supervision?	Individual study write-ups, reflections	1. Inquiry created space for exploring new supervision tools (e.g., questioning, PLCs, lesson study). 2. Inquiry strengthened theory to practice connections. 3. Inquiry helped supervisors better understand differentiation. 4. Inquiry created shifts in perceptions and definitions of practice, and surfaced supervisors' needs.
4	Jacobs, Yendol-Hoppey, & Dana (2015)	Case Study	16 doctoral students across both contexts, 2 facility members from Context 1, 1 faculty member from Context 2	What do doctoral students learn about being a teacher educator as a result of engaging in inquiry?	Interviews	1. Doctoral students gained appreciation of inquiry as a tool for continuous instructional improvement, student centeredness, and innovative pedagogy; and supported teacher candidate understanding and value of inquiry. 2. Doctoral students learned to participate in program innovation, created influential dialogue, broadened their understandings of educational research, and uncovered key tensions.

influences knowledge construction and representation in qualitative research (Merriam et al., 2001). By analyzing findings from a multitude of voices, we can better capture, from different positions, the role inquiry played in supporting doctoral students' development as teacher educators. The studies progressed from the position of "I learned" to "we learned" to "they learned," encapsulating the internal and external nature of doctoral socialization (Jazvak-Martek, 2009), as students transition through iterative phases of support and self-direction (Gardner, 2010). The findings from the individual inquiry reports and papers served as a type of audit trail or a "residue of records stemming from inquiry" (Lincoln & Guba, 1985, p. 319) that allowed us access to the results of the four studies.

Study 1

Study 1 was comprised of 26 doctoral student inquiries targeting the overarching question, "How can I improve my practice as a teacher educator?" The positionality of the researchers in Study 1 focused on what "I learned" about my practice and my development as a teacher educator. An overview of each inquiry from Study 1 is presented in Table 9.2.

TABLE 9.2   Summary of Study 1 Doctoral Student Inquiries

Student(s)	Inquiry Topic(s)	Inquiry Question(s)
Jenna	Multimodal literacies reading disabilities	How do I facilitate teacher candidates' developing conceptualizations of literacy through a multimodal, participatory learning environment?
Lori	Instructional practice arts-integrated instruction	How can time-lapse photography be used to document teaching practices? How can time-lapse photography inform teaching practices over prolonged periods of time? In what ways can creativity and arts integration pedagogy be incorporated in pre-service teacher preparation?
Monique	Teacher Candidates "transference" arts-integrated instruction	How does my literacy course content transfer to teacher candidate instruction delivery?
Mallory	Multimodal learning defining "literacy" teacher candidate self-efficacy	What is the influence of multimodal literacy instruction for teacher candidates with reading disabilities?
Susan	Reading assessment teacher self-efficacy	How do my instructional practices in the classroom help my elementary education students increase their self-efficacy as reading teachers specifically focused on reading assessment, delivery, and analysis?
Piper	Multilingual awareness, multicultural awareness, technology integration	How does my multilingual and multicultural awareness influence my teaching as I interact with my students?
Yolanda	Teacher candidate inquiry, teacher education pedagogy	In what ways do I facilitate the development of teacher candidates' conceptualization of a teacher's roles beyond instruction?

(continued)

TABLE 9.2 Summary of Study 1 Doctoral Student Inquiries (cont.)		
Student(s)	Inquiry Topic(s)	Inquiry Question(s)
Kerrie	Classroom management	In what ways can I facilitate the development of classroom management strategies by making theory to practice connections between the classroom management course and the field experience?
Valerie & Mallory	Developing concepts of culture supervision	In what ways can I facilitate critical reflection of culture within my teacher candidates throughout the seminar component and coaching sessions during the field experience? What experiences do I face when trying to promote critical reflection into culture within a Level 2 field experience?
Ann	Lesson study field experience	What happens when lesson study is incorporated into the clinical field experience of pre-interns at a PDS?
Darlene	Protocols seminar field experience	How might the use of National School Reform Faculty (NSRF) Consultancy Protocol impact teacher candidates' thinking about their dilemmas in practice?
Cindy	Student engagement teacher candidates university coursework	How can I promote the engagement of teacher candidates and subsequent learning within an elementary emergent literacy methods course?
Rachel	Theory in practice literacy	How can I facilitate the transfer of theory to practice as it relates to effective literacy instruction? What specific pedagogies in my supervision and instruction facilitate the transfer of theory to practice? What challenges do I face in the dual roles?
Jackie & Rachel	Reflections field experience	In what ways can we facilitate teacher candidates' understandings about teaching through assignments and coaching, in the field, and through reflective practices? In what ways did student reflections on assignments impact our own thoughts and follow-up activities?
Nancy	Knowledge relationships diversity	In what ways can I help interns "dig deeper" into their knowledge of how students they teach: develop stronger relationships with their students, enhance their understanding of the concept of diversity, and apply this knowledge towards becoming a better teacher educator?
Matt	Journaling teacher candidates	How can I help teacher candidates conceptualize and utilize journaling as a mechanism to make sense of their experiences learning to teach during the pre-internship semester?
Jackie	Developmentally appropriate practice field experience	In what ways can I support EC teacher candidates in unpacking instances of DAP within a Kindergarten field placement?
Kerry & Valerie	Peer coaching teacher candidates	How can we coach teacher candidates to successfully engage in peer coaching?
Mallory	Diversity teacher candidates supervision seminar	What strategies can I use to support teacher candidate learning in the area of cultural diversity through my field supervision seminar?
Cindy	Teacher inquiry coaching teacher candidates	How can I support the learning of teacher candidates in the area of practitioner inquiry through my field supervision?

Within each of the contexts, the doctoral students asked a research question connected to their teaching/supervision, collected data about their question, analyzed the data, and developed claims/themes based on this evidence. Their data collection methods included teacher candidate reflections, teacher candidate work, observational data, surveys given to teacher candidates, focus groups with teacher candidates, and a researcher's journal/blog. In addition to generating themes, the doctoral students reflected on their findings to identify how what they learned would inform future teaching. Findings from this study can be found in Table 9.2.

Study 2

The second study was comprised of the seven doctoral students who made up the I-Team in Context 1. Two research questions framed this self-study: "What insights do prospective teacher educators gain from engaging in practitioner inquiry within the context of a Supervised Teaching Course designed to scaffold their professional development as future teacher educators and teacher researchers?" and "How does prospective teacher educator engagement in practitioner inquiry enhance teacher candidate coursework and program implementation?" The researchers used artifacts and documents from their individual inquiries (all data collected, papers written, and posters presented), their online community dialogue, and written reflections as the data for their study. These seven doctoral students collaboratively engaged in independent data analysis without the support of instructors. The positionality of the researchers in Study 2 focused on what "we learned" as a collaborative group of teacher education doctoral students through practitioner inquiry. Findings for this study can be found in Table 9.1.

Study 3

The third study was comprised of five doctoral student researchers across Context 1 and Context 2 focused specifically on the question, "How does inquiry prepare the next generation of teacher candidate supervisors?" The researchers engaged in an exploratory study of ten of the individual practitioner inquiries from Study 1. These inquiries specifically focused on questions related to teacher candidate supervision. Data collected to address the research question included the doctoral students' inquiry papers and narrative reflections written by each doctoral student participant. The study looked across the narratives to share collective lessons learned about the role engagement in inquiry plays in the preparation of the next generation of supervisors. Findings for this study can be found in Table 9.1.

Study 4

Two faculty members from Context 1 and one faculty member from Context 2 conducted the fourth study. The research question guiding the study was, "What do doctoral students learn about being a teacher educator as a result of engaging in practitioner inquiry?" Interviews served as the primary mechanism to capture the experiences of doctoral students across both contexts (Kvale, 2008). The positionality of the researchers in Study 4 focused on what "they learned" as they studied the perspectives of the doctoral students (Jacobs, Yendol-Hoppey, & Dana, 2015). Findings for this study can be found in Table 9.1.

PROCEDURE

The question guiding us while revisiting the four studies above was, "How does the infusion of practitioner inquiry within doctoral preparation support the development of the next generation of teacher educators?" We compiled the written findings from the four previously described studies (Table 9.1), including a description of each finding as well as the actual data quoted or described. We then used an open-coding approach (Patton, 2002) to name and describe the individual findings. We did not want to lose the nuances that made up each finding by just engaging in an overall analysis. For Study 1, this meant looking across all the write-ups for the individual inquiries to examine not only the focus of the questions they asked, but also what the doctoral students learned through the process. Next we connected individual codes across the studies. This moved us into a more holistic analysis across the findings. Using thematic analysis (Boyatzis, 1998), we collaboratively took an inductive data-driven approach by discussing recurring patterns and emerging themes common across all four studies. These themes included: programmatic change, teacher educator pedagogy, and supporting teacher candidate inquiry.

Based on this analysis, two overarching findings emerged. We present them in this chapter as lessons learned to explain how practitioner inquiry supported the development of the future teacher educators featured in the four studies. These lessons, presented in the next section of this chapter, represent a holistic look across all the studies.

LESSONS LEARNED

Lesson 1: Doctoral Student Engagement in Inquiry Led to Enhanced Coursework and/or Supervision Work Both Individually and Programmatically

Across the four studies we saw findings related to how doctoral students enhanced their coursework and supervision through inquiry. These innovations did not just make an impact on individual practice, but strengthened doctoral students' knowledge and skills to be able to participate in overall program enhancement and innovation. Specifically, inquiry supported the doctoral students' teaching and supervision practices by: (a) promoting a student-centered and innovative approach, (b) building their capacity to support teacher candidates with inquiry, and (c) promoting participation in program innovation.

Promoted a Student-Centered, Innovative Approach to Teacher Education

Engaging in inquiry prompted both new and more experienced doctoral students to focus on teacher candidate learning, subsequently allowing them to become more student-centered in their approach to teaching and supervising. Doctoral students described the move from a focus on self to an increased focus on the teacher candidates. In addition, inquiry prompted doctoral students to take risks in their teaching by trying out innovative practices that would better meet the needs of students as a natural part of the inquiry process.

Inquiry promoted looking beyond self to collecting systematic data about the teacher candidates during methods instruction and supervision. Becoming student-centered meant moving away from just implementing a syllabus. Instead, inquiry facilitated reflection on instructional practices that involved being responsive throughout the semester and adjusting the course based on systematic data collection about teacher candidate learning and needs. Doctoral students talked about how they could use this data to differentiate their instruction based on teacher candidate needs.

One example, drawn from an interview in Study 4, exhibited how a doctoral student used practitioner inquiry to help teacher candidates develop a critical lens toward education through enhanced dialogue. As a secondary social studies teacher, she had been encouraged to lecture within her courses, so she did not feel comfortable acting as a facilitator of class discussions, despite identifying them as a necessary component of teacher education. As a result, her inquiry focused on learning how to facilitate what she called "critical conversations." Using student surveys and exit tickets, this doctoral student moved from using predetermined lectures as the focus of her teaching to basing instruction on student responses and needs. Inquiry helped to accelerate doctoral student movement from a focus on themselves to a focus on their students.

Not only did engaging in inquiry promote student-centered practices, but the process also facilitated doctoral students' development of innovative teaching practices beyond the traditional course assignments. One example, drawn from an individual practitioner inquiry in Study 1, illustrated changes to a journal assignment. This doctoral student's inquiry explored ways to enhance teacher candidates' ownership of journal entries by making the assignment more meaningful and authentic. He explained how the nature of the assignment shifted as a result of his inquiry from a "meaningless end of the week empty reflection" to "something they would look forward to doing, something they could interpret in their own ways and make useful for them." Journaling stopped being a check-off task for teacher candidates to becoming a meaningful, authentic professional expectation.

In another example, drawn from Study 3, a doctoral student described how she felt the current university observation tool did not align well with her inquiry regarding the promotion of culturally responsive teaching through field supervision. Therefore, she transformed her traditional observational practices and created new tools as a part of her inquiry. She explained,

> In order to better explore the teacher candidates' teaching practices and examine how they are using culturally responsive teaching I found myself using supplemental tools in my coaching. I noticed the university's official coaching tool was not sufficient enough to provide my teacher candidates enough insight into their lessons. As a result, I often collected data through field notes or diagrams on a specific aspect of my teacher candidates' lessons. For example, if my teacher candidates were concerned with student engagement during the lesson, I would make a diagram showing student engagement at different intervals in the lesson. This tool provided a talking point for student engagement, which led into a discussion of culturally responsive teaching. The university coaching tool alone would not yield enough information to elicit these types of discussions.

Collectively, the doctoral students no longer envisioned their role as passively following the syllabus, but became empowered to make changes and adjustments for their students. Inquiry thus helped to create a context of questioning, experimentation, and innovation.

Built Doctoral Student Capacity to Support Teacher Candidates With Inquiry

Many of the doctoral students had little experience with inquiry as PK–12 teachers; thus, expecting them to support teacher candidates' engagement in inquiry, a signature pedagogy within both contexts' teacher education programs, was potentially problematic. Engaging in inquiry as teachers or supervisors helped build doctoral students' capacity to support teacher candidate inquiry. Consistently across all of the studies, doctoral students shared that going through the inquiry process helped them provide more meaningful support to their teacher candidates as they facilitated teacher candidate inquiry. For example, one doctoral student shared in Study 2,

> [Engaging in inquiry] has helped me figure out how to teach them to go through the process, because I mean as a doc student first starting inquiry I really didn't know what I was doing, and it was difficult and I had to navigate and figure out what was happening . . . So I try to think about what would have helped me when I was first going through it and what did help me and we try to scaffold our teaching based on that.

The doctoral students believed this understanding could only come through engaging in inquiry themselves.

In addition to learning about the power of inquiry by engaging in their own inquiry, the doctoral students also shared the power of modeling the inquiry process for their teacher candidates. They used the data they collected to transparently and intentionally model the process, and serving as an inquiry role model was a common theme in the doctoral students' reflections. They found that being explicit about their study of their own teaching helped model inquiry as a valued and meaningful process. Collectively, the studies spoke about inquiry as a powerful tool that promoted a student-centered pedagogy, innovative practices, and modeling for teacher candidates. Doctoral students began to view inquiry as a regular part of their work as teacher educators.

Promoted Participation in Program Innovation

In addition to using inquiry to improve their own teaching and supervision, the doctoral students identified inquiry as a tool that helped them participate in innovation within their respective teacher education programs. Each of the studies pointed to the belief that through inquiry, doctoral students influenced the undergraduate teacher education program and also who they were becoming as teacher educators. Sharing inquiry with others served as a vehicle for creating important program dialogue, strengthening program strands even beyond the infusion of inquiry. For example, many doctoral students identified the impact they had on one another in the area of technology. By sharing inquiry efforts that studied technology integration, they began to influence each other to try new technologies in their teaching. Collaboratively they began to offer program enhancement. Doctoral students also spoke of how their inquiries created programmatic attention to equity and social justice. These studies included investigations of coursework and fieldwork with the goal of enhancing understanding of diverse populations and developing culturally relevant instruction. One doctoral student shared in Study 4, "We're now weaving equity work throughout the cohort program. We've been working to figure out across the program what topics we want to cover in their seminar, coursework, fieldwork . . . and how we are going to do it systematically. So I think that's changed the program."

In addition to creating programmatic change, doctoral student engagement in inquiry also stimulated important conversations within programs through inquiry dialogue, sharing new tools, and providing opportunities to learn from one another. Doctoral students also shared their findings with other program instructors and new doctoral students. In addition to informal dialogue, inquiry findings were shared during professional development opportunities. These examples suggest that doctoral student inquiry shows promise as a catalyst for building relationships and creating conversation within and about programs.

Lesson 2: Engaging in Inquiry Increased Doctoral Students' Familiarity With Tensions They Will Face as Future University Teacher Educators

Two key elements that comprise this lesson included (a) doctoral students' expanded understanding of the role of teacher educators, and (b) doctoral students' unearthed tensions related to how research is positioned in the academy.

Expanded Doctoral Student Understanding of the Role of Teacher Educator

In Study 1, the doctoral students learned the inquiry process while positioned as learners. Their inquiries were typically related to the question, "What did I learn?" During this phase, the doctoral students identified that engaging in inquiry positioned them to focus their attention on their own practice. Doctoral students identified their role as teacher educators as delivering high quality and innovative methods of instruction and supervision. In addition, given that the majority of the students in the first study were new to scholarly research, inquiry provided them the space to become familiar with the research process in general. They noted how inquiry provided them a foundation for thinking about their role in relation to research. Doctoral students noted how the process offered them support as they designed and executed the various phases of question formation, data collection, data analysis, and findings generation. Based on their prior conceptions about research, the movement to focus on "I" required them to shift their understanding of the role a researcher could play as they saw the integration between teaching and research.

Although a number of the doctoral students shared their findings with teacher candidates as they engaged in their own inquiry during Study 1, the value of making their inquiry insights transparent to their students did not fully emerge until they engaged in the collective self-study work described in Studies 2 and 3. These two studies suggested that the doctoral students' positioning moved away from the focus on "I" that guided their initial studies toward the "we" in terms of "what we learned." They found that inquiry helped them understand how to better support undergraduates in the process of teacher inquiry, which they named as a key pillar of their context's undergraduate programs. Additionally, the inquiry work led the doctoral students to notice the role they were playing in program improvement, as they were both better able to support this program pillar and felt empowered to share data that demonstrated the power of this pedagogy with colleagues and faculty. The doctoral students described how engaging in multiple inquiries supported their move from focusing on simply understanding the inquiry process and helping teacher candidates to seeing how engaging in inquiry was key to their program. Their participation led to program cohesion and improvement. Evidence drawn from the findings of Studies 2 and 3 indicated that these future teacher educators began to see their role as empowered reform agents.

Unearthed Tensions Related to How Research Is Positioned in the Academy

The fourth study offered a new set of insights into the doctoral students' experiences with inquiry that were not present in the findings of the first three studies but were alluded to in the doctoral students' reflections. Findings suggested that prospective teacher educators began to broaden their understanding of research while simultaneously uncovering tensions related to the value of various forms of educational research within the academy. For example, many of these doctoral students entered their studies with preconceived notions of what constitutes educational research, and for most students in this study, engagement in practitioner inquiry was not part of the educational research picture they had previously understood. One doctoral student said:

> It's really broadened what I think of educational research. When I first became a doctoral student I just thought of educational research as being very disconnected from practice. I know that's terrible to say, isn't it? I thought of having a group of students in an elementary classroom and running stats, numbers on them . . . I think engaging into inquiry into my own practice allowed me to understand how deeply we need to go into what's actually happening—we can't just have kids take a survey and think we're going to understand it all; we're going to have to really observe, journal, . . . and put (all kinds of educational research) together to really understand what's happening.

Even for the few students who had experience with practitioner inquiry as K–12 classroom teachers, their understandings of what constituted educational research in the academy marginalized inquiry and self-study methodologies.

As doctoral students engaged in practitioner inquiry across both contexts, the prior conceptions they held regarding what constitutes educational research began to be called into question, their knowledge of the various types and approaches to educational research expanded, and they came to value inquiry as a viable and informative type of educational research. Data indicated that engagement in practitioner inquiry was becoming an integral part of their practice as teacher educators and teacher education scholars. As the doctoral students' conceptualization of educational research broadened, they became active inquirers into their own practice as instructors and supervisors within their teacher education program. In addition, they became more vocal about the value of practitioner inquiry when talking about research with faculty. During these discussions, doctoral students experienced cognitive dissonance when faculty questioned their newfound and broadened notions of educational research. Across the studies, doctoral students articulated a growing tension with the belief held amongst some faculty in their departments that practitioner inquiry is not worthwhile or meaningful research. In Study 4, one doctoral student shared, "Not that anybody comes right out and says it, but you know you heard that so and so said, that kind of thing, that (practitioner inquiry) is not real research, that it's not real. It's fine for you to do in your free time but it shouldn't get in the way of your coursework and your real research."

The tensions the doctoral students experienced led them to question their futures in relationship to engagement in inquiry as teacher educators as they struggled to reconcile the negative messages they received from others with their positive lived experience of engaging in and teaching the process to the teacher candidates with whom they worked. These research tensions remained unresolved for many of the doctoral students. They wondered, "If practitioner inquiry is transformative for teacher education coursework and programs, then why wasn't it recognized as a valued form of scholarship in their field?" Fortunately, inquiry welcomes such questions, offering a means for future teacher educators and the faculty working with them to name and navigate these and other tensions in an ever-changing teacher education context.

DISCUSSION

The lessons we learned by looking across these four studies demonstrate how engaging in the process of practitioner inquiry enhanced doctoral students' development and supported their preparation as teacher educators in a context of reform. While the positionality of the researchers differed across the four studies, common themes emerged about the role of practitioner inquiry within doctoral preparation. Through inquiry, doctoral students strengthened their teacher education pedagogy related to both course delivery and supervision, built understanding about and opportunities to contribute to high quality program delivery and innovation, and expanded their role as teacher educators, while at the same time surfacing tensions related to educational research. Looking across four studies underscored the movement from "I learned" to "we learned" to "they learned," modeling a process for preparing future teacher educators. These experiences served as a foundation to doctoral student development both individually and collectively as stewards of the discipline of teacher education (Golde, 2006; Lawson, 2016).

Opportunity to Reflect Upon Role and Confront Role Conflict

As Baumann (1996) has acknowledged, "discontinuities associated with researching while teaching are not only inevitable but also productive" (p. 32). The experiences of the doctoral students reveal how inquiry's infusion in doctoral education supplied emerging teacher educators with the capacity to unearth as well as navigate role conflict. Identities often come into question as many of these new doctoral students were making the transition from PK–12 classroom teacher to higher education teacher (Jazvac-Martek, 2009; McAlpine & Amundsen, 2009; Munby et al., 2001). This can often be a stressful time when doctoral students have to navigate what teaching means in this new context. Inquiry gave these doctoral students the space to develop and reflectively grow as teacher educators (Goodwin et al., 2014). Not only could this development support their ability to engage in reform within future positions upon graduation, but it served to benefit the undergraduate teacher candidates who were able to experience the fruits of their labor within coursework and supervision.

Inquiry required doctoral students to ask questions to help position themselves as learners from the start of their development as teacher educators. A variety of facilitators supported this work. First, doctoral students had the opportunity to develop practitioner inquiry skills as they inquired into their practice as teacher educators. This "I"-centered positionality enhanced their understanding of their role. Other facilitators included the collaborative learning spaces created by learning together ("we learned"), engaging in inquiry as a part of these formal and informal communities. As Baumann (1996) explains, "by struggling with ways to integrate inquiry into their work, teacher researchers come to know themselves better as teachers and persons" (p. 35). Through inquiry, the role conflict and ambiguity that other academics face can become fodder for professional learning, actualizing Lease's (1999) prescription for coping with professional stressors by viewing them as "meaningful, changeable, and of value for future growth" (p. 288). Practitioner researchers see their problems of practice as opportunities for improvement.

An initial, but not inconsequential, barrier was the doctoral students' inchoate understanding of research as well as the messages about what "counts" as research given to doctoral students, both implicitly and explicitly, by those in the academy. By engaging in inquiry, doctoral students also had the opportunity to begin to wrestle with the relationship between research and teaching in their role as teacher educators (Colbeck, 1998; Murray & Male, 2005). They began to question some of the socialization that was already beginning to occur as they received pushback from other faculty about the process of studying one's practice. These doctoral students began to see the interconnections that could occur between research and teaching as well as learn about the process of research from early on in their programs.

Opportunity to Innovate and Collaborate for Reform

In order to answer calls for reform in teacher education (NCATE, 2010), we will need to prepare teacher educators who can work to closely couple clinical experiences and methods coursework (Zeichner, 2006). Teacher educators will need to innovate as they find new ways to foster relationships between schools and universities, requiring increasingly complex knowledge and skills. Revisiting these four studies demonstrated how inquiry promoted an experimental stance within the role of teacher, through which doctoral students felt they had "permission" to try out innovative, student-centered practices as a natural part of the inquiry process. Across the studies we saw examples of how the doctoral students broke down barriers and began to innovate in their pedagogical approaches and design of assignments. In addition, they learned how to work collaboratively with fellow doctoral students and faculty as colleagues moving forward with reform. As one doctoral student shared, a group of doctoral students was able to support a strand of social justice as a focus within the undergraduate program based on their collective efforts with inquiry. Engaging in inquiry promoted doctoral student agency to have a voice in programmatic innovation efforts (Jazvac-Martek, 2009; Portnoi et al., 2015).

If involving doctoral students in this type of inquiry work facilitates teacher education reform, as these collective findings suggest, teacher education programs need to elevate this work as an important and recognized feature for faculty and doctoral students alike. Given the Council for the Accreditation of Educator Preparation's (CAEP, 2017) endorsement of enhanced self-study, attention to this type of work could be a viable tool for improving teacher education as well as preparing for accreditation. Likely challenges include the low status given to practitioner inquiry and the complexity associated with involving various teacher educators (graduate assistants, faculty, clinical faculty, adjuncts, and PK–12 educators) in this important work.

In our look across these four studies, noticeably absent are the insights of faculty members who facilitated the doctoral student work as well as those faculty members who watched from the outside. Many who were not involved with the initiative appeared to the doctoral students as less than supportive, but their own perspectives are missing. Likewise, we lack the voices of the teacher candidates who witnessed their instructors engaging in inquiry. The only insights related to the impact on teacher candidate learning must be garnered from the doctoral student reflections in Study 1 and the analysis provided in the three subsequent studies.

Future scholarship should investigate how teacher education programs comprised of faculty who both consider and do not consider themselves teacher educators understand the importance of practitioner inquiry. Do colleges of education share a common vocabulary and have the necessary buy-in to create authentic space for this shared work to unfold when facing the demands of the more traditional research community? In some cases, developing the role of doctoral student as teacher educator may create conflict or tension among faculty. Additionally, the perceived low status of teacher education work within research institutions may influence doctoral student development, and the belief that "at best, research and teaching are very loosely coupled" is likely to persist for some time (Marsh & Hattie, 2002, p. 606). Moreover, future studies could examine how practitioner inquiry is used across a wider number of contexts and institutions.

While a great deal of research is still needed, this chapter provides a conceptual impetus for discussion among teacher educators about the future of the teacher educator role and the importance of nurturing the next generation of teacher educators. These new teacher educators will face the challenge of enacting reforms, ideally continuing discussions begun by scholars such as Borko, Liston, and Whitcomb (2007) regarding what constitutes research in teacher education. Such efforts will generate knowledge about complex interrelationships between teacher educator research and teacher educator practice that are critical to the future of the profession. Implications garnered in this chapter suggest inquiry can be a powerful tool for courses, supervision, and program reform.

Discussion Questions

1. In this chapter, the authors followed McAlpine and Amundsen's (2009) advice "to shed light upon often invisible aspects of doctoral studies and to use what we learn to interrogate our own current

pedagogical policies and practices" (p. 124). How might this chapter prompt you to do the same? What are the "invisible aspects" of your own program that are worth examining?

2. The authors of Chapter 8 argue that practitioner inquiry offers a means for future teacher educators and the faculty working with them to name and navigate the tensions in their work, ultimately suggesting that inquiry can turn role conflict and ambiguity into opportunities for professional learning. In what ways have you seen doctoral students struggle along their journeys to becoming teacher educators? How might practitioner inquiry support you and your doctoral students in embracing the problems of practice they face?

3. As you consider your unique context, where might practitioner inquiry fit into the existing structures and practices? As a part of the curriculum, as in Context 1? As an add-on experience, as in Context 2? Or as an entirely new configuration? How might an infusion of practitioner inquiry prompt innovation in your teacher education program?

REFERENCES

Acker, S., & Haque, E. (2015). The struggle to make sense of doctoral study. *Higher Education Research & Development, 34*(2), 229–241.

Arndt, K., Casciola, V., Mallory, M., Pennington, S., Powell, R., Ward, J.,... Dana, N. F. (2013, October). *Preparing the next generation of supervisors and professors of instructional supervision: An inquiry approach.* Paper presented at the annual meeting of The Council of Professors of Instructional Supervision, State College, PA.

Athanases, S. Z., Wahleithner, J. M., & Bennett, L. H. (2012). Learning to attend to culturally and linguistically diverse learners through teacher inquiry in teacher education. *Teachers College Record, 114*, 1–50.

Baker, V. L., & Pifer, M. J. (2011). The role of relationships in the transition from doctoral student to independent scholar. *Studies in Continuing Education, 33*(1), 5–17.

Balaban, C. (2016). From steward to leader: A decade of shifting roles for the PhD student. *Learning and Teaching, 9*(1), 90–100.

Ball, D. L., & Forzani, F. (2009). The work of teaching and the challenge for teacher education. *Journal of Teacher Education, 60*(5), 497–511.

Baumann, J. F. (1996). Conflict or compatibility in classroom inquiry? One teacher's struggle to balance teaching and research. *Educational Researcher, 25*(7), 29–36.

Beaumont, J. J. (1998). Administrator and researcher: Conflicting dual roles in directing a school-university partnership. *Urban Education, 32*(5), 645–660.

Bonner, P. J. (2006). Transformation of teacher attitude and approach to math instruction through collaborative action research. *Teacher Education Quarterly, 33,* 27–44.

Borko, H., Liston, D., & Whitcomb, J. A. (2007). Genres of empirical research in teacher education. *Journal of Teacher Education, 58*(3), 3–11.

Boyatzis, R. E. (1998). *Transforming qualitative information: Thematic analysis and code development.* Thousand Oaks, CA: SAGE.

Burns, R. W., Jacobs, J., & Yendol-Hoppey, D. (2016). The changing nature of the role of the university supervisor and function of preservice teacher supervision in an era of clinically-rich practice. *Action in Teacher Education, 38*(4), 410–425.

Butler, D. L., & Schnellert, L. (2012). Collaborative inquiry in teacher professional development. *Teaching and Teacher Education, 28,* 1206–1220.

Cochran-Smith, M. (2004). *Walking the road: Race, diversity, and social justice in teacher education.* New York, NY: Teachers College Press.

Cochran-Smith, M. (2012). A tale of two teachers: Learning to teach over time. *The Record, 48,* 108–122.

Cochran-Smith, M., Barnatt, J., Friedman, A., & Pine, G. (2009). Inquiry on inquiry: Practitioner research and student learning. *Action in Teacher Education, 31*(2), 17–32.

Cochran-Smith, M., & Lytle, S. (1999). Relationships of knowledge and practice: Teacher learning in communities. *Review of Research in Education, 24,* 249–305.

Cochran-Smith, M., & Lytle, S. L. (2009). *Inquiry as stance: Practitioner research for the next generation.* New York, NY: Teachers College Press.

Colbeck, C. L. (1998). Merging in a seamless blend: How faculty integrate teaching and research. *The Journal of Higher Education, 69*(6), 647–671.

Council for the Accreditation of Educator Preparation. (2017). *CAEP handbook: Guidance on self-study reports for accreditation at the advanced level.* Retrieved from http://caepnet.org/~/media/Files/caep/accreditation-resources/handbook -guidance-self-study-reports-adv.pdf?la=en

Dana, N. F., & Yendol-Hoppey, D. (2014). *The reflective educator's guide to classroom research: Learning to teach and teaching to learn through practitioner inquiry* (3rd ed.). Thousand Oaks, CA: Corwin Press.

Darling-Hammond, L. (2009, February). Teacher education and the American future. Charles W. Hunt Lecture. Presented at the annual meeting of the American Association of Colleges for Teacher Education, Chicago.

Dennis, D. V., Burns, R. W., Tricarico, K., van Ingen, S., Jacobs, J., & Davis, J. (2017). Problematizing Clinical Education: What is our future? In R. Flessner & D. Lecklider (Eds.), *The power of clinical preparation in teacher education* (pp. 1–20). New York, NY: Rowan & Littlefeld.

Dewey, J. (1933). *How we think: A restatement of the relation of reflective thinking to the educational process.* Lexington, MA: Heath and Company.

Dinkelman, T. (2011). Forming a teacher educator identity: Uncertain standards, practice, and relationships. *Journal of Education for Teaching: International Research and Pedagogy, 37*(3), 309–323.

Dresser, R. (2007). The effects of teacher inquiry in the bilingual language arts classroom. *Teacher Education Quarterly, 34*(3), 53–66.

Dunn-Haley, K., & Zanzucchi, A. (2012). Complicity or multiplicity? Defining boundaries for graduate teaching assistant success. *New Directions for Teaching and Learning, 2012*(131), 71–83.

Ermeling, B. A. (2010). Tracing the effects of teacher inquiry on classroom practice. *Teaching and Teacher Education, 26*, 377–388.

Esposito, J., & Smith, S. (2006). From reluctant teacher to empowered teacher researcher. *Teacher Education Quarterly, 33*(3), 45–60.

European Commission. (2013). *Supporting teacher educators for better learning outcomes.* Brussels, Belgium: Author.

European Commission. (2014). *Initial teacher education in Europe: An overview of policy issues.* Brussels, Belgium: Author.

Fain, J. A. (1987). Perceived role conflict, role ambiguity, and job satisfaction among nurse educators. *The Journal of Nursing Education, 26*(6), 233–238.

Gardner, S. K. (2008a). Fitting the mold of graduate school: A qualitative study of socialization in doctoral education. *Innovative Higher Education, 33*(2), 125–138.

Gardner, S. K. (2008b). "What's too much and what's too little?": The process of becoming an independent researcher in doctoral education. *The Journal of Higher Education, 79*(3), 326–350.

Gardner, S. K. (2010). Contrasting the socialization experiences of doctoral students in high- and low-completing departments: A qualitative analysis of disciplinary contexts at one institution. *The Journal of Higher Education, 81*(1), 61–81.

Golde, C. M. (2006). Preparing stewards of the discipline. In C. Golde, G. Walker, & Associates (Eds.), *Envisioning the future of doctoral education: Preparing stewards of the discipline* (pp. 3–20). San Francisco, CA: Jossey-Bass.

Goodwin, A. L., Smith, L., Souto-Manning, M., Cheruvu, R., Tan, M. Y., Reed, R., & Taveras, L. (2014). What should teacher educators know and be able to do? Perspectives from practicing teacher educators. *Journal of Teacher Education, 65*(4), 284–302.

Gopaul, B. (2011). Distinction in doctoral education: Using Bourdieu's tools to assess the socialization of doctoral students. *Equity & Excellence in Education, 44*(1), 10–21.

Grossman, P. (2005). Research on pedagogical approaches in teacher education. In M. Cochran-Smith & K. M. Zeichner (Eds.), *Studying teacher education: The report of the AERA panel on research and teacher education* (pp. 425–476). Mahwah, NJ: Erlbaum.

Hagevik, R., Aydeniz, M., & Rowell, C. G. (2012). Using action research in middle level teacher education to evaluate and deepen reflective practice. *Teaching and Teacher Education, 28*, 675–684.

Hall, E. (2009). Engaging in and engaging with research: Teacher inquiry and development. *Teachers and Teaching: Theory and Practice, 15*(6), 669–681.

Hornung, S., Lampert, B., & Glaser, J. (2016). Dealing with organizational double binds: Three-way interactive effects of role stressors and coping on worker exhaustion. *Psychological Reports, 118*(2), 487–509.

Howard, T. C., & Aleman, G. A. (2008). Teacher capacity for diverse learners: What do teachers need to know? In. M. Cochran-Smith, S. Feiman-Nemser, D. J. McIntyre, & K. E. Demers. (Eds.), *Handbook of Research on Teacher Education* (3rd ed.; pp. 157–176). New York, NY: Routledge.

Hyland, N. E., & Noffke, S. E. (2005). Understanding diversity through social and community inquiry: An action research study. *Journal of Teacher Education, 56*(4), 367–381.

Jacobs, J., Yendol-Hoppey, D., & Dana, N. F. (2015). Preparing the next generation of teacher educators: The role of practitioner inquiry. *Action in Teacher Education, 37*(4), 373–396.

Jazvac-Martek, M. (2009). Oscillating role identities: The academic experiences of education doctoral students. *Innovations in Education and Teaching International, 46*(3), 253–264.

Klenke-Hamel, K. E., & Mathieu, J. E. (1990). Role strains, tension, and job satisfaction influences on employees' propensity to leave: A multi-sample replication and extension. *Human Relations, 43*, 791–807.

Kosnik, C., Cleovoulou, Y., Fletcher, T., Harris, T., McGlynn-Stewart, M., & Beck, C. (2011). Becoming teacher educators: An innovative approach to teacher education preparation. *Journal of Education for Teaching, 37*(3), 351–363.

Kvale, S. (2008). *Doing interviews.* Thousand Oaks, CA: SAGE.

Lawson, H. A. (2016). Stewarding the discipline with cross-boundary leadership. *Quest, 68*(2), 91–115.

Lease, S. H. (1999). Occupational role stressors, coping, support, and hardiness as predictors of strain in academic faculty: An emphasis on new and female faculty. *Research in Higher Education, 40*(3), 285–307.

Levin, B. B., & Rock, T. C. (2003). The effects of collaborative action research on preservice and experienced teacher partners in professional development schools. *Journal of Teacher Education, 54*(2), 135–149.

Lincoln, Y., & Guba, E. (1985). *Naturalistic inquiry.* Beverly Hills, CA: SAGE.

Marsh, H. W., & Hattie, J. (2002). The relation between research productivity and teaching effectiveness: Complementary, antagonistic, or independent constructs? *The Journal of Higher Education, 73*(5), 603–641.

Martin, R. J. (2005). An American dilemma: Using action research to frame social class as an issue of social justice in teacher education courses. *Teacher Education Quarterly, 32*(2), 5–22.

McAlpine, L., & Amundsen, C. (2009). Identity and agency: Pleasures and collegiality among the challenges of the doctoral journey. *Studies in Continuing Education, 31*(2), 109–125.

McAlpine, L., & Norton, J. (2006). Reframing our approach to doctoral programs: An integrative framework for action and research. *Higher Education Research & Development, 25*(1), 3–17.

Merino, B. J., & Holmes, P. (2006). Student teacher inquiry as an "entry point" for advocacy. *Teacher Education Quarterly, 33*(3), 79–96.

Merriam, S. B., Johnson-Bailey, J., Lee, M.-Y., Kee, Y., Ntseane, G., & Muhamad, M. (2001). Power and positionality: Negotiating insider/outsider status within and across cultures. *International Journal of Lifelong Education, 20*(5), 405–416.

Mockler, N., & Groundwater-Smith, S. (2015). Seeking for the unwelcome truths: Beyond celebration in inquiry-based teacher professional learning. *Teachers and Teaching: Theory and Practice, 21*(5), 603–614.

Munby, H., Lock, C., & Smith, L. (2001). Students or professionals: Identity conflicts in experience-based teacher education. *McGill Journal of Education, 36*(2), 115–130.

Murray, J., & Male, T. (2005). Becoming a teacher educator: Evidence from the field. *Teaching and Teacher Education, 21,* 125–142.

National Association of Professional Development Schools. (2008). *What it means to be a professional development school.* Retrieved from http://www.napds .org/9%20Essentials/statement.pdf

National Council for the Accreditation of Teacher Education. (2001). *Standards for professional development schools.* Washington, DC: Author.

National Council for the Accreditation of Teacher Education (2010). *Transforming teacher education through clinical practice: A national strategy to prepare effective teachers.* Retrieved from http://www.highered.nysed.gov/pdf/NCATECR.pdf

Newman, L, & Mowbray, S. (2012). "We were expected to be equal": Teachers and academics sharing professional learning through practitioner inquiry. *Teachers and Teaching: Theory and Practice, 18*(4), 455–468.

Patton, M. Q. (2002). *Qualitative research and evaluation methods.* Thousand Oaks, CA: SAGE.

Portnoi, L. M., Lima Chlopecki, A. A., & Peregrina-Kretz, D. (2015). Expanding the doctoral student socialization framework: The central role of student agency. *The Journal of Faculty Development, 29*(3), 5–16.

Price, J. N., & Valli, L. (2005). Preservice teachers becoming agents of change: Pedagogical implications for action research. *Journal of Teacher Education, 56*(1), 57–72.

Rinke, C. R., & Stebick, D. M. (2013). "Not just learning about it but actually doing it": The evolution of a teacher inquiry culture. *Action in Teacher Education, 35,* 72–84.

Rock, T. C., & Levin, B. R. (2002). Collaborative action research projects: Enhancing preservice teacher development in professional development schools. *Teacher Education Quarterly, 29,* 7–21.

Senécal, C., Julien, E., & Guay, F. (2003). Role conflict and academic procrastination: A self-determination perspective. *European Journal of Social Psychology, 33*(1), 135–145.

Smith, P., Franco, Y., Krause, M., Hagge, J., Persohn, L., Bransombe, M., & Bennett, M. (2013, April). *Scaffolding the next generation of doctoral students' engagement in clinically rich and inquiry driven teacher education coursework: Doctoral student insights.* Paper presented at the annual meeting of the American Educational Research Association, San Francisco, CA.

Tillema, H., & van der Westhuizen, G. J. (2006). Knowledge construction in collaborative enquiry among teachers. *Teachers and Teaching: Theory and Practice, 12*(1), 51–67.

Tom, A. R. (1997). *Redesigning teacher education.* Albany: State University of New York Press.

Villegas, A. M., & Lucas, T. (2002). Preparing culturally responsive teachers: Rethinking the curriculum. *Journal of Teacher Education, 53*(1), 20–32.

Wallace, C. S. (2013). Promoting shifts in preservice science teachers' thinking through teaching and action research in informal science settings. *Journal of Science Teacher Education, 24*, 811–832.

Watson, C. (2009). Narratives of practice and the construction of identity in teaching. *Teachers and Teaching, 12*(5), 509–526.

Watts, J. H. (2010). Team supervision of the doctorate: Managing roles, relationships and contradictions. *Teaching in Higher Education, 15*(3), 335–339.

Weidman, J. C., & Stein, E. L. (2003). Socialization of doctoral students to academic norms. *Research in Higher Education, 44*(6), 641–656.

Zeichner, K. (2003). Teacher research as professional development for P–12 educators in the US. *Educational Action Research, 11*(2), 301–306.

Zeichner, K. (2006). Reflections of a university-based teacher educator on the future of college-and university-based teacher education. *Journal of Teacher Education, 57*(3), 326–340.

Zellermayer, M., & Tabak, E. (2006). Knowledge construction in a teachers' community of enquiry: A possible road map. *Teachers and Teaching: Theory and Practice, 12*(1), 33–49.

CHAPTER 10

SELF-STUDY AND PREPARING THE NEXT GENERATION OF TEACHER EDUCATORS

Brandon M. Butler
Old Dominion University

Self-study research has been a fixture in my scholarship and teaching practice since I was a new doctoral student. When I struggled with my identity as a doctoral student, I relied on self-study to make sense of how and why my identity developed in the way it did. When questions arose about my role as a university supervisor and course instructor, I turned to self-study, and self-study has continued to serve me as a method to critically reflect upon and improve my practice as I now prepare the next generation of teacher educators. Yet, when one thinks about the relative newness of self-study research and small numbers of teacher educators who conduct self-study, it is highly likely that few doctoral students are prepared in programs where teacher research methods like self-study are taught as viable alternatives, or at the very least companions, to traditional research methods.

Although the research on self-study and novice teacher educator development remains in its infancy, there is enough evidence present that

Preparing the Next Generation of Teacher Educators for Clinical Practice, pages 227–247
Copyright © 2019 by Information Age Publishing
227

strongly suggests the positive impact that self-study learning spaces have upon new teacher educator practice and identity development (e.g., Butler et al., 2014; Foot, Crowe, Tollafield, & Allan, 2014), pedagogical practice related to course instruction and clinical practice (e.g., Butler & Diacopoulos, 2016; Cuenca, 2010; Logan & Butler, 2013), and the transition into academia (e.g., Bullock & Ritter, 2011; Dinkelman et al., 2012). In this chapter, my intention is to highlight self-study research as a powerful inquiry tool that can forge the next generation of teacher educators into critically minded, reflective, collaborative, and pedagogically focused scholars and educators. To accomplish this, I first share the history of self-study and its theoretical underpinnings (LaBoskey, 2004; Loughran, 2004; Samaras, 2011), followed by a review of literature related to self-study and teacher educator preparation, and conclude with a consideration of self-study scholarship associated with a specific type of teacher educator activity, clinical practice supervision. Given the personally situated nature of self-study research, interspersed throughout this chapter is my story as a novice and now experienced teacher educator invested in clinical practice work and teacher educator development.

THE HISTORY AND THEORETICAL UNDERPINNINGS OF SELF-STUDY IN TEACHER EDUCATION

The self-study of teacher education practices (S-STEP) has its roots in practitioner inquiry, specifically teacher inquiry, reflective practice and action research. However, self-study differs from action research and other forms of practitioner inquiry in that self-study focuses on an understanding of self and change in practice (Samaras, 2011). Self-study had its start in a Division K symposium at the 1992 annual meeting of the American Educational Research Association (Loughran, 2004). The following year saw the formation of the S-STEP Special Interest Group at AERA and it quickly grew into one of the largest SIGs at AERA and remains so to this day. The first International Conference of Self-Study of Teacher Education Practices was held in 1996, and continues to be held biennially in East Sussex, England. 2004 saw the publication of *The International Handbook of Self-Study of Teaching and Teacher Education Practices,* followed in 2005 by the publication of *Studying Teacher Education,* a peer-reviewed journal devoted to self-study scholarship. What is evident through this progression is the increasing presence of self-study in teacher education scholarship.

Over the years, I have interacted with many university faculty and doctoral students who assume that "self-study" is an individual endeavor and nothing more than simple reflection. For instance, one senior faculty member at my institution long questioned the validity, worth and empirical grounding of self-study until she attended a self-study session at a conference. After the session, she noted with surprise the scholarly rigor in which the research was conducted. Although she still did not fully understand self-study or see herself using the approach, she acknowledged the methodology's place alongside other qualitative methods. Even with Zeichner's (1999) argument that self-study would be one of the single greatest developments in teacher education scholarship, nearly 20 years later self-study is still viewed by many as an "emerging" methodology, maligned by some, and unknown by others. Perhaps this is due to misunderstandings about the nature of self-study research, as I noted occurred at my institution. Therefore, it his helpful to discuss the theoretical and methodological foundations of self-study (LaBoskey, 2004; Samaras, 2011) in order to properly frame the scholarship on teacher educator learning and to assist you, the reader, in developing a working understanding of self-study methods that would allow you to strengthen your work as a teacher educator. The most commonly cited theoretical understanding of self-study research design is that presented by LaBoskey (2004), who discusses five underpinnings that ground self-study work. I explain LaBoskey's five underpinnings in the remainder of this section.

Number One: Self-Study as Self-Initiated and Self-Focused Inquiry

Self-study researchers acknowledge the postmodern concept that "self" cannot be separated from the research, seen most evidently through the influence that personal and institutional contexts, interactions with students and colleagues, and personal biography have upon the outcomes of self-study research. Self-study is about you—either the individual or collective "you." But what it is not is research into the teaching and learning of others. Even after presenting the theoretical and methodological orientations of self-study to colleagues and students, I have witnessed many who immediately attempt to design a self-study project that focuses solely on student learning. That is not self-study. Yet, the desire to focus on others is understandable given the long-standing epistemological notions of research held by many in teacher education, as well as an innate discomfort in what my doctoral students have called an "airing of dirty laundry" (Butler et al., 2014). Who wants to share personal fears and uncertainties with others when you can simply isolate yourself or investigate others' fears and uncertainties about teaching? That way, you can maintain a comfortable illusion about a certainty of practice and expertise that is not actually present among many teacher educators (Murray & Male, 2005).

Number Two: Self-Study as Improvement-Aimed Scholarship

Samaras (2011) notes that self-study consists of personally situated inquiry driven by questions informed by specific contexts. Self-study researchers engage in investigations of self that are of interest to them and emerge from problems of practice experienced in their educational contexts. As such, self-study research seeks to improve teacher educator learning and understanding related to the specific problems identified (LaBoskey, 2004). Although self-study focuses on the self, the new self-study scholar should be careful to avoid the perception of narcissism. Too often someone new to self-study is prone to sharing a set of positive personal experiences while shying away from the struggles they experienced during study. There is a need to ensure the work is not simply laudatory and holds limited impact for the work of others. There must be honesty and an ability to expose the flaws in practice so that improvement can be found.

One of the doctoral students in Butler et al. (2014) provides an example of this initial struggle to open oneself to critique and improve practice. A few weeks into the course, this student shared that she had been ambivalent about the autobiography assignment I asked them to write at the start, noting, "I think it is likely that most people approached it more honestly than I did, as I am not sure how much of what I wrote was honest and how much was sarcasm" (p. 263). The student entered the course looking to share little beyond the surface and could have kept silent about her personal struggle with the assignment. But in learning and coming to value self-study research, this doctoral student came to see the necessity in showing vulnerability, which afforded her opportunities to improve her understanding of self and practice throughout the course.

Number Three: Self-Study as Interactive Inquiry

Self-study researchers are encouraged to collaborate with others. In contrast with notions that self-study is individual in nature, Samaras (2011) highlights the importance of collaborative inquiry in self-study as "learning, thinking and knowing arises through collaboration and appropriate feedback of others" (p. 10). LaBoskey (1998) notes the interactive nature of self-study in which "researchers are not just interacting around an external data set; the interactions are the data set, or at least a part of it" (p. 151). Collaboration in self-study affords opportunities for teacher educators to more critically interrogate problems of practice through the lens of trusted others. As LaBoskey (2004) states, "garnering multiple perspectives on our professional practice settings helps to challenge our assumptions and biases, reveal our inconsistencies, expand our potential interpretations, and triangulate our findings" (p. 849). That is not to say that self-study cannot be solo authored—I have conducted a few self-studies about my personal growth and practice. However, even within an individually authored self-study, there is the presence of interactions with colleagues and students that took place during the study, or ideally, validation of research findings through a sharing of initial findings with and receipt of feedback from trusted colleagues and others in educational settings.

A personal example may help here. When I first taught my pedagogy of teacher education course (Butler et al., 2014), the resulting study was truly representative of collaborative inquiry with six authors who collected and collectively analyzed data and wrote the results together. However, I also conducted a parallel self-study into my individual teaching of the doctoral course (Butler, 2014). Because I was the sole author of the study, I wanted to ensure trustworthiness in the findings I had identified and did so by seeking feedback from doctoral students enrolled in the course as to the accuracy of the findings and story I sought to share.

Number Four: Self-Study as Multiple, Primarily Qualitative Research

Self-study is comprised of formalized investigations into one's practice using well-established research traditions, draws largely from qualitative methods (LaBoskey, 2004), and seeks to impact the practices and understanding of others beyond the individual contexts of the original authors. Samaras (2011) adds that "self-study is a transparent and systematic research process requiring an open, honest, and clear description of the spiral of questioning, framing, revisiting of data, and reframing of a researcher's interpretations" (p. 11). Early self-study scholarship from the 1990s often lacked the empirical grounding noted by LaBoskey (2004) and Samaras (2011) as essential to self-study research. Much of this work was written in a format best described as reflective narratives with brief descriptions of methods and grounding literature. Understandably, there were critics among qualitative researchers about the empirical strength and validity of this work in the early years.

Although during the 2000s we saw a strengthening in the methodological quality of self-study scholarship (Loughran, 2004), there still remains no "one true way" or "template for a self-study method" (p. 17). As such, self-study researchers draw from a range of largely qualitative methods such as case study, narrative inquiry, autoethnography, and other research methods but use their associated data collection and analysis procedures in an inward-looking manner (Hamilton, Smith, & Worthington, 2008).

Data collection includes dialogic communities, in person or digital; auto-biographical writing; arts-based inquiry; active learning experiences such as course meetings and learning activities; and structured forms of reflec-tive inquiry like student teaching observation meetings (LaBoskey, 2004). An example may help here to make sense of the potential mixed uses for qualitative data. For instance, a group of doctoral students and I studied their identity development in a doctoral seminar on teacher education us-ing self-study (Butler et al., 2014). But if we had not been interested in our collective learning, we could have used the same data collection techniques (e.g., transcripts of course meetings, copies of student work, digital posts, and autobiographical writing) and data analysis measures (open coding) to publish a case study of their identity development. Whether research is self-study is not defined solely by the forms of data collection and analysis. Rather, it is the focus of the study that determines whether it is a self-study.

Number Five: Self-Study as Exemplar-Based Validation

Finally, self-study research is focused on knowledge generation, person-ally and publicly (Samaras, 2011), marked by validity through trustworthi-ness (LaBoskey, 2004). In a recent self-study, a group of doctoral students and I explored their learning of self-study in a doctoral seminar focused on a pedagogy of teacher education (Gregory, Diacopoulos, Branyon, & Butler, 2017). Having taken a range of qualitative research courses that focused on "traditional" methods such as case study research, self-study was absent from their research coursework. It took some time for them to overcome questions of self-study validity due to the quantitative and interpretive no-tions of generalizability highlighted in the research courses. However, they soon "came to appreciate that the answer [to validity] would come from the teachers and teacher educators who read and found value in our work. These readers would see their fears, anxieties, and struggles and likewise em-brace self-study" (p. 265). These students came to recognize that self-study could assist them in overcoming their fears, anxieties, and struggles but that in doing so they became obligated to make that knowledge public in hopes that others with similar experiences might learn from their research.

Self-study scholarship is meant to "contribute to the accumulation of pedagogical, content, and issue-based knowledge and serves to build vali-dation across related work" (Samaras, 2011, p. 11). Sharing your self-study outcomes reflects the "moral/ethical/political values and ideals" at the heart of self-study scholarship (LaBoskey, 2004, p. 834). For the doctoral students in our study (Gregory et al., 2017), participation in the seminar resulted in a scholarly identity in which personal and public learning and sharing of identity and practice became a central facet of their work as teacher educators. But saying scholarly identity developed through participation in the seminar is simply not enough. To ensure validity and trustworthiness (LaBoskey, 2004), we have to sufficiently describe the context of the course, and participant background while sharing fully the forms of data collection and analysis. As LaBoskey (2004) argues, "We must make visible our data, our methods for transforming the data into findings, and the linkages between data, findings, and interpretations" (p. 853).

SELF-STUDY AND TEACHER EDUCATOR PREPARATION

Teacher education is a complex practice. As teacher educators, it is our difficult task to educate future teachers who have a minimum of 12 years, hands-on experience with teaching before they arrive in our teacher education programs (Lortie, 2002). This "apprenticeship of observation" generates beliefs and dispositions toward teaching that are tough to overcome. The challenge for teacher educators is to assist teacher candidates in deeper interrogations of the purpose and practices of teaching *while* challenging those long-held beliefs and dispositions. This is a complicated task given that those beliefs and dispositions are often reinforced in clinical experiences even as teacher educators attempt to model visions for teaching that counter what teacher candidates see in classrooms and from their personal experiences as students in K–12 settings. Given this complexity, it is surprising that all too often the act and learning of teacher education is viewed as a "self-evident activity" (Zeichner, 2005).

Historically, and contemporaneously still, many doctoral programs have failed to implement in doctoral student training the very practices that teacher education faculty so regularly highlight in teacher preparation programs—modeling, reflection, and collaborative learning. Many doctoral students were and still are expected to teach and supervise teacher candidates with little modeling, reflection, and collaborative learning to support their development as teacher educators (Conklin, 2015; Goodwin et al., 2014; Zeichner, 2005). Often, teacher educator preparation follows the "sink or swim" model long critiqued in teacher candidate preparation.

As such, the shift from teacher to teacher educator is often an individualized experience in which doctoral students and new faculty are rarely or ineffectually mentored. They are often assigned courses and supervision with little understanding as to how teacher education is a unique practice separate from classroom teaching, or of the specific pedagogies associated with teacher education (Dinkelman, Margolis, & Sikkenga, 2006a, 2006b; Labaree, 2004; Loughran, 2006). Rarely are doctoral students asked to develop or participate in communities of practice and to use those spaces as places to overcome their fears about their identity, status, and any notions of inferiority. As a result, doctoral students regularly question whether they can succeed in their programs (Murray & Male, 2005), and, in my experience, look at their peers with some degree of awe even as those same peers experience their own feelings of inadequacy. More so, doctoral programs rarely teach and model self-study methods to doctoral students even though the process stands as a method through which those very students might make sense of and overcome their fears and uncertainties as they study their own problems of practice.

Williams, Ritter, and Bullock (2012) suggest that teacher educator identity development is informed by three contexts: "personal and professional biography; institutional contexts and the nature of community; and the ongoing development of a personal pedagogy of teacher education" (p. 256). Although doctoral programs cannot control the personal and professional biographies of doctoral students, they do have a say in the institutional contexts and professional learning that occurs in their programs. Recent research points to the positive influence formal spaces and collaborative learning communities framed through self-study can have on the development of novice teacher educators (e.g., Butler et al., 2014; Dinkelman et al., 2012; Foot et al., 2014; Kosnik et al., 2011). These spaces can be broken down into three categories: (a) formal spaces, or required and elective doctoral courses that follow the traditional course structure found in university settings; (b) semiformal spaces, which are somewhat structured and often longitudinal seminars that fall outside the traditional course structure and timeframe; and (c) informal spaces, or collaborative learning and research communities that exist outside the formal course structures found in higher education settings.

There is little research on the formal and semiformal spaces where teacher educator development occurs (Butler et al., 2014; Conklin, 2015). What does exist is largely based in self-study research, with Conklin's (2015) conceptual framework for teaching a pedagogy of teacher education something of an outlier in this literature base. However, the relative absence of research on the topic does not mean there are no courses on teacher education pedagogy—it is likely not being written about. As I noted, the scholarship of these formal and semiformal spaces is largely self-study in nature and predominately written in a collaborative manner between course instructor and students enrolled in the course. The scholarship on informal spaces are written principally by doctoral students and focused largely on supervisory practices, which I cover in the next section. However, there is some research on informal spaces that focus on methods course instruction, identity development, and the transition into teacher education, all of which I address toward the conclusion of this section. The literature in this section is not meant to be exhaustive, rather it paints a picture of the benefits of participation in the three spaces.

Formal Spaces of Teacher Educator Learning

Samaras et al. (2007) wrote of their experiences teaching and learning in a self-study research course. They found that from the student perspective, participation in the course helped in the co-construction of knowledge, provided peer support, assisted in assignment design, and created opportunities to engage in sustained reflection around self-study's application to personal and professional settings. Of interest in their course experience was the creation of reflective portfolios by instructor and students, which documented their personal and professional growth throughout the course. Such activities encourage doctoral students to engage in sustained reflection while forcing the instructor to model best teacher education practices for doctoral students.

Foot et al. (2014) share their experiences learning and applying self-study research in a multi-disciplinary doctoral seminar in curriculum and instruction. They share arguments like those already shared regarding the centrality of self-study to doctoral work, noting that, "Encouraging doctoral students to undertake self-study research to examine their work as doctoral practitioners and their ongoing identity transitions is one way to guide students through the challenges of doctoral study" (p. 103). From their investigations of self, Foot et al. (2014) found that participation in the doctoral course helped them "sustain multiple identities at once, such as practitioner, student, and emerging scholar" (p. 110). They also highlighted the sense of community that developed in the course, the time and space to engage in self-reflection, and the ability to overcome perceived personal inadequacies.

Butler et al. (2014) noted similar findings in their self-study of teaching and learning a doctoral course focused on pedagogy of teacher education. Although the course was more intently focused on learning specific pedagogies of teacher education (Loughran, 2006) and self-study research methods, we independently highlighted many of the same findings as Foot et al. (2014). Participation in the course afforded space to develop a sense of community that provided both emotional support and opportunities for learning. The course also provided space for doctoral students to develop a more complex identity as teacher educator-researchers while generating a critical self-awareness absent before enrollment in the course. The second cohort of students I taught used their application of self-study research to understand their learning and living of self-study methods (Gregory et al., 2017). In the pedagogy of teacher education course, I ask doctoral students to use the course itself as a research space. Their conversations, assignments, and personal interests dictate the direction of data collection and analysis. Like many who are new to self-study, Gregory et al. (2017) questioned their ability to engage in self-study, sharing skepticism about this "new" research method. However, sustained enactment of self-study and its close association with teacher educator practices and identity development facilitated doctoral student understanding, learning, and appreciation of collaborative forms of inquiry. Doctoral students also saw the need to trust one's peers, develop willingness to question and alter practice, and a desire to share their learning in professional settings.

Semiformal Spaces of Teacher Educator Learning

Following the enactment of a teacher education course, Kosnik et al. (2011) created an "informal group for doctoral students who wanted to continue the discussion that was started in the [teacher education] course" (p. 353). This semiformal space, which they called *Becoming Teacher Educators*, afforded doctoral students continued opportunities to more completely examine teacher education research and practices. Although not an official course of record, the space quickly turned into monthly meetings across 3 years in which a number of activities occurred, including reading research on teacher educator development and practice, observing teacher educators, hosting guest speakers, reviewing outside teacher education programs, discussing the academic job search, and examining curriculum and pedagogy. Each year, participants conducted self-study research of their experiences in the space. Participants noted several positive outcomes from their involvement in the *Becoming Teacher Educator* seminars. They noted that they developed a deeper knowledge of teacher education, developed the skills of teacher education researchers, developed identities as teacher educators, and grew in their practice as teacher educators. Doctoral students found that their participation in the seminar helped them develop a non-competitive atmosphere in which they assisted one another through the dissertation experience, job search, and questions related to teacher education practice.

Dinkelman, at the University of Georgia, developed a similar semiformal seminar in which full-time doctoral students in the social studies program were required to enroll (Dinkelman, 2011; Dinkelman et al., 2012). The bi-weekly seminar resembled Kosnik et al.'s (2011) space in that the content of the seminar was wide-ranging and co-constructed by professor and doctoral students. Participation in the seminar provided doctoral students with opportunities to examine teacher education and social studies education research and to make informed decisions about pedagogical decision-making. I collaborated with Dinkelman and five other recent doctoral graduates to explore the influence of the seminar on our scholarly and teacher educator development, noting that our collective experience, "present[s] a case for Seminar-like experiences for the challenges they offered teacher educators, novice and more experienced, to think more deeply about their pedagogies, the relationships of their practice to other program participants, and the assumptions we make about effective teacher education" (Dinkelman et al., 2012, pp. 184–185). From a scholarly perspective, we found that the seminar revealed disciplinary problems worthy of investigations, prompted research, provided a collaborative community of like-minded individuals, and reflected a climate of people who "cared" about disciplinary teacher education. Likewise, the seminar influenced our teacher educator development and helped us learn a language of teacher education, value collaborative inquiry, generate a broader understanding of teacher education, create purpose for our practice, and see the need to enact similar spaces elsewhere.

Although participation in formal and semiformal spaces can positively influence emerging teacher educator identity and practices, there do exist complications in enacting such spaces. Dinkelman et al. (2006b) argued, "Perhaps the most important element of the university context in helping the beginning teacher educator negotiate a move from the classroom concerns the quality, nature, and organization of time" (p. 130). With often opposing expectations placed upon faculty and doctoral students—coursework, teaching and supervision, and dissertation work for doctoral students; teaching, research, and service expectations for faculty—there is often limited space available within doctoral programs to enact these courses. University faculty may not have the availability in their schedule to teach a course on teacher education, even if they might see teacher education and self-study as areas of expertise. Faculty lines are often tied up with teaching in disciplinary education programs or more specific professional studies needs (e.g., classroom management, assessment). For example, the two sections of Pedagogy of Teacher Education I have taught to date have been summer special topics courses because they did not take away from my instructional responsibilities during the academic year. Over time, my administration and peers have seen the importance of such a class, its need to be taught during the academic year and its inclusion as an official course in our catalog, but my teaching schedule has yet to afford me that opportunity. From a student perspective, there are many required courses they must take and perhaps limited opportunities to take electives of interest to them. As such, there must be "buy-in" from administration, faculty, and doctoral students for formal and semiformal spaces to exist.

Informal Spaces of Teacher Educator Learning

Formal and semiformal teacher education and self-study spaces are highly beneficial to doctoral student learning, as evidenced by the research shared to this point, but perhaps more opportunities exist in the enactment of informal spaces for doctoral student and new faculty learning through self-study. Doctoral students or faculty teams can enter into collaborative research partnerships or communities of practice without concern for teaching load, service responsibilities, course enrollments, or required course assignments. Instead, the informal spaces can truly reflect the participants' interests, questions, problems of practice, and available schedule. Perhaps this is why the informal learning spaces are more prominent in the self-study literature on teacher educator development.

Bullock (2007) and Ritter (2007) individually explored their transition from classroom teacher to teacher educator, with both mentioning the significance of institutional context and mentorship in their professional development and personal interests in self-study. For Bullock (2007), that influence was Tom Russell, a founder of the self-study research movement, who was his doctoral adviser and with whom Bullock co-taught and engaged in research collaborations. Ritter (2007, 2009, 2011) was influenced by his participation in the informal seminar space and collaboration with faculty and other doctoral students at UGA (e.g., Dinkelman et al., 2012), and was advised by Todd Dinkelman, an early self-study scholar (e.g., Dinkelman, 2003). Both Bullock and Ritter found self-study assistive in their early transition phases in overcoming the fears, feelings of exhaustion, and cognitive dissonance that emerge when one moves into teacher education. They also found benefit in collaborating with others in their exploration of novice teacher educator development as they sought to understand the influence of personal and professional biography on identity and practice. Ritter (2009) saw the semiformal seminar space as an avenue through which he might gain support and encouragement, engage in communal inquiry, rethink assumptions, and provide increased connections to teacher education.

Although they came from different disciplinary contexts, Bullock and Christou (2009) claimed that "collaborative self-study helped us to find the courage to challenge and disrupt our own prevailing assumptions concerning the roles of theory and practice in teacher education" (p. 86). Through collaborative self-study, they were able to identify the shared challenges of transitioning from classroom teacher to teacher educator, with their supportive relationship providing the space necessary to question and disrupt the prevailing notions of doctoral education; that is, that doctoral students can easily transfer their classroom teaching to teacher education settings. These pages are full of examples of how this disruption occurs, but each is marked by a recognition that teacher education is more than a "self-evident activity" (Zeichner, 2005). Classroom experience does not equal ability or expertise in teacher education, and self-study and teacher educator learning spaces help counter this notion. Bullock later collaborated with Ritter to investigate their transition from doctoral student to university faculty (Bullock & Ritter, 2011). They found that their collaboration helped them come to terms with their shifts in identity, roles within their respective institutions, and questions of pedagogical prowess. Without the collaboration, which assisted them in better understanding those challenges, they would have navigated their first years as tenure-track faculty with little support for their advancement or insight into perceived areas of weaknesses.

Informal spaces of self-study collaboration also provide benefits to doctoral students beyond identity development and adapting to the transition into academia. Much of the research on informal spaces is framed through critical friendship, which Costa and Kallick (1993) define as the ability to "ask provocative questions, provide data to be examined through another lens, and offer critique of a person's work as a friend" (p. 50). Like Ritter, I was advised by Todd Dinkelman and participated in the UGA semiformal seminar space as a doctoral student and subsequently used the space as a jumping off point to engage in my own self-study collaborations. For instance, a fellow doctoral student and I were new to teaching an elementary social studies methods course. As secondary educators, we were uncomfortable with teaching the course and though the seminar space was helpful in addressing larger questions of teacher educator practice, we felt the need for a more focused and sustained collaboration on the course (Logan & Butler, 2013). We used critical friendship to provide intellectual, pedagogical, and affective support for one another in our new teaching assignments, and that even in an institutional context where isolated teaching was the norm, our "experiences reinforced the importance we placed upon engaging in collaboration with others who do the work of teacher education" (p. 280). Murphy, McGlynn-Stewart, and Ghafouri (2014) used critical friendship to frame their enactment of a writing support group that assisted in the transition from doctoral student to faculty member. Though the writing group helped further development of identities as teacher educators, Murphy et al. (2014) also noted the impact of the informal space on their research and writing skills, emotional well-being, and preparation for scholarly careers.

The benefits of formal, semiformal, and informal spaces of teacher educator preparation are clearly visible in the preceding scholarship. Such spaces provide doctoral students with opportunities to fully develop their identities as new teacher educators, question prevailing opinions of teacher educator preparation, learn and enact effective pedagogies of teacher education, witness the benefits firsthand of collaborative and non-judgmental communities of practice, and engage in meaningful scholarship related to their development as teacher educators. Needless to say, each of the teacher educators highlighted in this section felt well-prepared for the rigors of academic life, and when confronted with difficulty were cognizant enough to rely on peers who were working through similar struggles. As my colleague and I noted at the end of our critical friendship article, "If we as teacher educators are committed to effective teacher education, we must provide formal and informal support for faculty and graduate students that encourages and supports their practice as teacher educators" (Logan & Butler, 2013, p. 281). There is sufficient evidence demonstrating the importance of such spaces, all we need is the commitment from teacher educators, novice and experienced, to enact them.

SELF-STUDY AND CLINICAL PRACTICE

There exists general agreement among teacher education researchers that the work of supervision, a particular activity performed by teacher educators, is often left to graduate students or adjunct faculty (e.g., Beck & Kosnik, 2002; Zeichner & Paige, 2008). Unfortunately, the appropriation of supervision to those with little power or status within teacher education programs means that the preparation for supervisory work is either lacking or absent. This concern is evident in some of the self-study scholarship authored by novice supervisors. Cuenca (2010), in particular, wrote of his lack of supervision training, instead relying solely upon his classroom experience as a lens through which to observe teacher candidates rather than using those candidates' visions for teaching, programmatic aims, and effective disciplinary pedagogies. Through self-study, Cuenca was able to uncover his unfamiliarity with his new position so that he might effectively challenge what he perceived as a deficient approach to teacher education. Such explorations helped him develop more specific supervision pedagogies informed by care and tact (Cuenca, 2011).

Other novice supervisors also began their practice with perspectives informed by prior experience. For example, Ritter (2007) entered teacher education with a similar outlook as Cuenca, noting how he had "internalize[d] banking models of education as the way schooling was supposed to be done" (p. 10). For Ritter, this perspective informed his initial experiences as a university supervisor: "I naturally assumed that I was supposed to be the expert over my student teachers and that it was my responsibility to deposit into their minds appropriate information about effective teaching" (p. 11). Trout (2008, 2010), who perceived her supervision of teacher candidates through Noddings' (2003) ethic of care, held a more informed perspective. However, even this view toward supervision was learned through Trout's personal interactions with Noddings and other experiences as a teacher candidate years prior.

Of note in these self-studies is the lack of directed training in what it meant to be a field-based teacher educator. At UGA, doctoral students in our program were required to supervise teacher candidates. Due to this expectation, and the lack of associated training or coursework on supervision, we often developed our own informal supervisor learning spaces or redirected the focus of our informal, biweekly seminar meetings for short periods of time. Ritter, Powell, and Hawley (2007) used collaborative self-study to create an open and honest space in which they could share their challenges related to supervision, consider improvements for the enactment of supervisory practice at a programmatic level, and uncovered deeper understandings of what it meant to be a supervisor of teacher candidates. Likewise, several colleagues and I enacted our own collaborative self-study space as doctoral students to better understand our practices as supervisors (Butler, Cuenca, & Elfer, 2012). Like Ritter et al. (2007), we noted a number of tensions related to our supervisory identities. While they questioned whether they served as teacher, mentor, supporter, evaluator, or coach (p. 13), we framed our shifting practice through three metaphors, supervisor as uncertain judge, referee, and counselor. With little education in what it meant to be a supervisor, both collaborative groups were tasked with generating our own identities and conceptual frames through which we enacted our supervisory practice.

This is not meant to infer a lack of attention paid to supervision institutionally. Rather, considerable time was spent on our supervisory experiences in the semiformal seminar space. However, with a relative large number of doctoral students sharing their teaching and supervisory practices, there were few opportunities to mine one person or small group's problems of practice in a sustained manner. One exception was our experience in revising the student teaching experience through the enactment of a third space that afforded us additional, biweekly meetings with teacher candidates during their required student teaching seminar (Cuenca, Schmeichel, Butler, Dinkelman, & Nichols, 2011). We found that this new space helped us develop deeper relationships with our teacher candidates, largely negating the hierarchical and evaluative relationships long associated with supervision. Additionally, we were able to refine the focus of our supervision because the conversations shifted from specific examples of our supervisory visits to larger questions, concerns, and teaching practices.

As someone who lamented the lack of formal or informal training in supervisory practice, I saw an opportunity to counter that narrative when my current institution recently chose to allow doctoral students to serve as supervisors (Butler & Diacopoulos, 2016). I invited the first doctoral student assigned to supervise teacher candidates to enter into a critical friendship with me so that he might learn supervision in a more formal setting. I created an independent study focused on social studies teacher education, with particular attention paid to supervision. We met biweekly for 3 hours to discuss readings and his supervisory practice, I often attended field visits with him, and we regularly journaled about the experience. The result was that the supervisor had a more informed learning experience that enabled him to largely bypass the challenges highlighted earlier in this section. Additionally, we found that our critical friendship aided me in critically questioning my prior experiences as a supervisor so that I might better serve him and future supervisors in an advisory capacity.

The self-study scholarship of supervision to date, although limited, largely paints a picture of supervision as a somewhat maligned practice in which doctoral students and new faculty are expected to learn supervisory practices on their own or apply their classroom experiences or limited understandings of teacher education to their supervision of teacher candidates. This is an unfortunate reality given that clinical experience is seen by teacher candidates as the most influential aspect of their training. Increasing emphasis has been placed upon clinical practice as a central tenet of teacher education (e.g., AACTE, 2018), yet there is great irony that such attention is paid to specific forms of clinical partnerships, programmatic structures and language while ignoring the preparation and continued training of those who are actively engaged in enacting clinical practice. Placing teacher education, and self-study, at the center of teacher educator preparation rather than its periphery might help alleviate the notion that teacher education is a "self-evident activity" (Zeichner, 2005). Self-study provides opportunities not often seen in doctoral education—opportunities to unpack personal and professional biography and their influence on novice teacher educator identity, to critically explore pedagogies of teacher education that directly impact the teaching of teacher candidates and practicing teachers, to create collaborative communities that facilitate teacher educator learning and emotional support systems, and to engage in scholarship that can improve personal identity and practice and professional teacher education contexts. Within the context of clinical practice, self-study can assist supervisors in overcoming the default position of viewing their practice through personal experience so that supervisors might more positively influence teacher candidate preparation through transformative, purposeful, and well-intentioned supervisory practices (Butler & Diacopoulos, 2016; Cuenca, 2010; Ritter, 2007).

CONCLUSIONS

My intent is that this chapter provides an overview of self-study research and its place in teacher educator and supervisor learning. Teacher education, generally, and clinical practice, more specifically, are complicated tasks, and made more so when teacher educators lack explicit training in the knowledge, skills, and dispositions needed to be an effective teacher educator. Self-study serves as a vehicle through which future generations of teacher educators can better understand and improve their practices, and hold to the belief that teacher education is at the core of their work. Even in the absence of formal teacher educator training, any teacher educator can apply self-study research to make more informed decisions about their pedagogical decision-making, to better understand the influence of personal and professional biography on their identity and practice, and to develop collaborative communities that provide both emotional support and learning opportunities.

If we are to transform the preparation and focus of teacher educator practice for clinically intensive program settings, faculty and doctoral students should look to self-study as a way to develop their abilities as critically minded, reflective, collaborative, and pedagogically focused scholars and educators. Each of these abilities should be seen as central to successful teacher education, in contrast to individualistic and sometimes competitive attempts at scholarship that occur in spaces marred by a lack of attention paid to quality teacher education.

In my experience, what it takes is one teacher educator with a passion for self-study and teacher education paired with a commitment to shift the dynamics of a small collaborative group, program, or department. All it takes is the willingness to be open and honest about what you see as problems of practice and the will to share those problems and learning with the world. To do so requires a doctoral education focused on the teaching and modeling of critically reflective practice and an awareness of the pedagogy of teacher education. I had the benefit of studying in a doctoral program with these particular foci, and surrounded by faculty and doctoral students who embraced teacher education and self-study. I have also been the sole self-study and teacher education scholar in a university setting where it took several years to develop small cohorts of faculty and doctoral students with an interest in the work. But for those who invest themselves in teacher education and self-study, they are perhaps laying the groundwork for the future of teacher education scholarship and practice.

Discussion Questions

1. What tensions, problems of practice, or questions related to your development as a teacher educator might you investigate through self-study? Why do they stand out to you as worthy of investigation? And, what do you hope to better understand or improve in your practice?

2. Using the five theoretical underpinnings of self-study highlighted in this chapter (self-study as self-initiated and self-focused inquiry, self-study as improvement-aimed scholarship, self-study as interactive inquiry, self-study as multiple primarily qualitative research,

self-study as exemplar-based validation), describe what self-study of your practice might look like methodologically.

3. What spaces for teacher educator learning exist within your institution, and how might you introduce, sustain, or alter such spaces?

4. What training and support have you received for clinical supervision? What questions or uncertainties remain about this area of teacher education? How might self-study help you better understand and improve your supervisory practice?

REFERENCES

American Association of Colleges for Teacher Education. (2018). *A pivot toward clinical practice, its lexicon, and the renewal of educator preparation.* Washington, DC: Author.

Beck, C., & Kosnik, C. (2002). Professors and the practicum: Involvement of university faculty in preservice practicum supervision. *Journal of Teacher Education, 53*(1), 6–19.

Bullock, S. M. (2007). Finding my way from teacher to teacher educator: Valuing innovative pedagogy and inquire into practice. In T. Russell & J. J. Loughran (Eds.), *Enacting a pedagogy of teacher education: Values, relationships, and practices* (pp. 77–94). New York, NY: Routledge.

Bullock, S. M., & Christou, T. (2009). Exploring the radical middle between theory and practice: A collaborative self-study of beginning teacher educators. *Studying Teacher Education, 5*(1), 75–88.

Bullock, S. M., & Ritter, J. K. (2011). Exploring the transition into academia through collaborative self-study. *Studying Teacher Education, 7*(2), 171–181.

Butler, B. M. (2014). Learning to teach emerging teacher educators. In D. Garbett & A. Ovens (Eds.), *Changing practices for changing times: Past, present and future possibilities for self-study research* (pp. 41–43). Auckland, New Zealand: University of Auckland.

Butler, B. M., Burns, E., Frierman, C., Hawthorne, K., Innes, A., & Parrott, J. A. (2014). The impact of a pedagogy of teacher education seminar on educator and future teacher educator identities. *Studying Teacher Education, 10*(3) 255–274.

Butler, B. M., Cuenca, A., & Elfer, C. (2012). Metaphors of complexity: The roles of university supervisors. In J. Young, L. Erickson, & S. Pinnegar (Eds.), *Extending inquiry communities: Illuminating teacher education through self-study* (pp. 68–71). Provo, UT: Brigham Young University.

Butler, B. M., & Diacopoulos, M. M. (2016). Re/learning student teaching supervision: A co/autoethnographic self-study. *Studying Teacher Education, 12*(2), 117–134.

Conklin, H. G. (2015). Preparing novice teacher educators in the pedagogy of teacher education. *Action in Teacher Education, 37,* 317–333.

Costa, A. L., & Kallick, B. (1993). Through the lens of a critical friend. *Educational Leadership, 51,* 49–51.

Cuenca, A. (2010). *In loco paedagogus*: The pedagogy of a novice university supervisor. *Studying Teacher Education, 6*(1), 29–43.

Cuenca, A. (2011). Care, thoughtfulness, and tact: A framework for university supervisors. *Teaching Education, 21*(3), 263–278.

Cuenca, A., Schmeichel, M., Butler, B. M., Dinkelman, T., & Nichols, J. R. (2011). Creating a "third space" in student teaching: Implications for the university supervisor's status as "outsider." *Teaching and Teacher Education, 27*(7), 1068–1077.

Dinkelman, T. (2003). Self-study in teacher education: A means and ends tool for promoting reflective teaching. *Journal of Teacher Education, 54*(1), 6–18.

Dinkelman, T. (2011). Forming a teacher educator identity: Uncertain standards, practices and relationships. *Journal of Education for Teaching, 37*(3), 309–323.

Dinkelman, T., Cuenca, A., Butler, B. M., Elfer, C., Ritter, J. K., Powell, D. J., . . . Hawley, T. (2012). The influence of a collaborative doctoral seminar on emerging researcher-teacher educators. *Action in Teacher Education, 34*(2), 172–190.

Dinkelman, T., Margolis, J., & Sikkenga, K. (2006a). From teacher to teacher educator: Experiences, expectations, and expatriation. *Studying Teacher Education, 2*(1), 5–23.

Dinkelman, T., Margolis, J., & Sikkenga, K. (2006b). From teacher to teacher educator: Reframing knowledge in practice. *Studying Teacher Education, 2*(2), 119–136.

Foot, R., Crowe, A. R., Tollafield, K. A., & Allan, C. E. (2014). Exploring doctoral student identity development using a self-study approach. *Teaching and Learning Inquiry, 2*(1), 103–118.

Goodwin, A. L., Smith, L., Souto-Manning, M., Charuvu, R., Tan, M. Y., Reed, R., & Taveras, L. (2014). What should teacher educators know and be able to do? Perspectives from practicing teacher educators. *Journal of Teacher Education, 65*(4), 284–302.

Gregory, K., Diacopoulos, M. M., Branyon, A., & Butler, B. M. (2017). From skepticism to scholarship: Learning and living self-study research in a doctoral seminar. *Studying Teacher Education, 13*(3), 257–274.

Hamilton, M. L., Smith, L., & Worthington, K. (2008). Fitting the methodology with the research: An exploration of narrative, self-study, and auto-ethnography. *Studying Teacher Education, 4*(1), 17–28.

Kosnik, C., Cleovoulou, Y., Fletcher, T., Harris, T., McGlynn-Stewart, M., & Beck, C. (2011). Becoming teacher educators: An innovative approach to teacher educator preparation. *Journal of Education for Teaching, 37*(3), 351–363.

Labaree, D. F. (2004). *The trouble with ed schools*. New Haven, CT: Yale University Press.

LaBoskey, V. K. (1998). Introduction to Part IV: Case studies of collaborative self-study. In M. L. Hamilton (Ed.), *Reconceptualizing teacher practice: Self-study in teacher education* (pp. 151–155). London, England: Falmer Press.

LaBoskey, V. K. (2004). The methodology of self-study and its theoretical underpinnings. In J. J. Loughran, M. L. Hamilton, V. K. LaBoskey, & T. Russell (Eds.), *International Handbook of self-study of teaching and teacher education practices* (pp. 817–869). Dordrecht, The Netherlands: Springer.

Logan, K., & Butler, B. M. (2013). "What do we know about *elementary* social studies?" Novice secondary teacher educators on learning to teach elementary social studies methods. *Studying Teacher Education, 9*(3), 267–283.

Lortie, D. (2002). *Schoolteacher: A sociological study* (2nd ed.). Chicago, IL: University of Chicago Press.

Loughran, J. J. (2004). A history and context of self-study of teacher and teaching education practices. In J. J. Loughran, M. L. Hamilton, V. K. LaBoskey, & T. Russell (Eds.), *International handbook of self-study of teaching and teacher education practices* (pp.7–39). Dordrecht, The Netherlands: Springer.

Loughran, J. J. (2006). *Developing a pedagogy of teacher education: Understanding teaching and learning about teaching*. London, England: Routledge.

Murphy, S., McGlynn-Stewart, M., & Ghafouri, F. (2014). Constructing our identities through a writing support group: Bridging from doctoral students to teacher educator researchers. *Studying Teacher Education, 19*(3), 239–254.

Murray, J., & Male, T. (2005). Becoming a teacher educator: Evidence from the field. *Teaching and Teacher Education, 21*, 125–142.

Noddings, N. (2003). *Caring: A feminine approach to ethics and moral education* (2nd ed.). New York, NY: Teachers College Press.

Ritter, J. K. (2007). Forging a pedagogy of teacher education: The challenges of moving from classroom teacher to teacher educator. *Studying Teacher Education, 3*(1), 5–22.

Ritter, J. K. (2009). Developing a vision of teacher education: How my classroom teacher understandings evolved in the university environment. *Studying Teacher Education, 5*(1), 45–60.

Ritter, J. K. (2011). On the affective challenges of developing a pedagogy of teacher education. *Studying Teacher Education, 7*(3), 219–233.

Ritter, J. K., Powell, D., & Hawley, T. S. (2007). Takin' to the streets: A collaborative self-study into social studies field instruction. *Social Studies Research & Practice, 2*(3), 341–357.

Samaras, A. P. (2011). *Self-study teacher research: Improving your practice through collaborative inquiry*. Thousand Oaks, CA: SAGE.

Samaras, A. P., Adams-Legge, M., Breslin, D., Mittapalli, K., O'Looney, J. M., & Wilcox, D. R. (2007). Building a plane while flying it: Reflections of teaching and learning self-study. *Reflective Practice, 8*(4), 467–481.

Trout, M. (2008). The supervision dance: Learning to lead and follow a student teacher. *The New Educator, 4*(3), 252–265.

Trout, M. (2010). Social skills in action: An ethic of care in social studies student teaching supervision. In A. Crowe (Ed.), *Advancing social studies education through self-study methodology: The power, promise, and use of self-study in social studies education* (pp. 119–138). New York, NY: Springer.

Williams, J., Ritter, J., & Bullock, S. M. (2012). Understanding the complexity of becoming a teacher educator: Experience, belonging, and practice within a professional learning community. *Studying Teacher Education, 8*, 115–130.

Zeichner, K. M. (1999). The new scholarship in teacher education. *Educational Researcher, 28*(9), 4–15.

Zeichner, K. M. (2005). Becoming a teacher educator: A personal perspective. *Teaching and Teacher Education, 21*(2), 117–124.

Zeichner, K. M., & Paige, L. (2008). The current status and possible future for 'traditional' college and university-based teacher education programs in the US. In T. Good (Ed.), *21st century education: A reference handbook, Vol. 2* (pp. 33–42). Los Angeles, CA: SAGE.

CHAPTER 11

FACING PRACTICE AS TEACHER EDUCATORS

A Self-Study of Program Graduates

Jennifer L. Snow
Boise State University

Cheryle A. Dismuke
Boise State University

Julianne Wenner
Boise State University

Serena Hicks
Boise State University

As teacher educators, we have developed our practice through self-initiated communities of practice (Snow, Martin, & Dismuke, 2015) and sought venues and practices for studying teacher educator practice. However, much like other researchers have identified, we have noted the dearth of scholarly research focused specifically on teacher educators (Kosnik et al., 2011). Recognizing the need for *becoming* (Jenkins, 2008) along with the complex

Preparing the Next Generation of Teacher Educators for Clinical Practice, pages 249–271
Copyright © 2019 by Information Age Publishing
All rights of reproduction in any form reserved.

phenomenon of *being* a teacher educator (Cochran-Smith, 2012; Cochran-Smith et al., 2016), we as teacher educators also sought teacher educator professional development while we studied complexities of be(com)ing a teacher educator (Goodwin & Kosnick, 2013).

Therefore, in this chapter we examine the multiple roles we as teacher educators play. In particular, this chapter describes our inquiry sparked from an investigation geared toward continuous improvement of our teacher education programs. During a case study of program graduates, we recognized an opportunity for us to model the practice of examining student outcomes to improve teaching and learning. Through a collaborative self-study of our responses to program outcomes evidenced by new teachers (our program graduates) in their early years of teaching, we used our students' performance to inform our own professional practice. The main purpose of this study was to improve our own teacher educator practice by engaging in systematic reflection on our experiences studying outcomes of professional practice (Bullough & Pinnegar, 2007; Pinnegar & Hamilton, 2009).

Embracing the complex roles and responsibilities of being a teacher educator and studying how our participation in multiple networks of teacher education work informed not only our professional practice and program structures, but also our professional development. Teacher educators are often not purposefully prepared for the work of teacher education prior to act of engaging in it (Jacobs, Yendol-Hoppey, & Dana, 2015; Kosnik et al., 2011). Therefore, as noted in Figure 11.1, we found a space for teacher educator professional development within the cross section of our teacher education work and our focus on supporting new teacher (our former students) development. Engaging in our own teacher educator development, we were following a model we taught our program graduates as we reviewed data and artifacts of student learning to make decisions about our professional growth and effective practice in terms of knowledge, skills, and habits of mind. Our collaborative self-study was framed by the following research questions: (a) How do teacher educators experience the phenomenon of observing program graduates in their early years of teaching? and (b) What

Figure 11.1   Teacher educator professional development.

do we learn about our own practice from analyzing multiple measures of new teacher performance?

In this chapter, we will first describe the context for our collaborative self-study. Next, we will review the theoretical frameworks that underpin this self-study and methods used to highlight a model for teacher educator development that we created from our self-study process. We then share findings from our study that identify this model with categories of attitude, context, and outcomes as informing our teacher educator development in a way that embraced its complexity within multiple contexts and functions. Finally, we discuss implications of our collaborative self-study for the preparation of teacher educators and teacher educator professional development.

SITUATING THE CONTEXT FOR OUR COLLABORATIVE SELF-STUDY

Our collaborative self-study was born from work in a case study (Yin, 2018) of new educators who had graduated from our teacher education programs. While digging deeper into our reflections on this case study data and its connections to our own professional practice, we identified the multiple intersecting networks of our professional practice (e.g., teaching pedagogy courses, supervising student teachers, compiling data for accreditation systems, evaluating teacher candidate performance, supporting teacher candidate development, etc.) and how they informed our teacher educator development. We also recognized the complexity of working within an external context demanding accountability measures focusing on our graduates' impact on pre-K–12 student learning and our own desire to work from a foundation of learning from practice, in practice (Ball & Cohen, 1999).

Context of Accountability and Initial Case Study: External Forces

As accreditation bodies in teacher education now require evidence of graduate performance in the evaluation of program effectiveness and processes for continuous improvement (CAEP, 2014), we seized this opportunity to think more deeply about our practice as teacher educators. Pursuing a case study of graduate performance, we joined as four teacher educators to work closely with recent program graduates and identify areas for improvement in the teacher education programs from which they graduated. Although each of us found this investigation inherently interesting, we also recognized the standards discourse (Clarke & Moore, 2013) from which we were researching and the tensions that caused for us seeking personal development and program improvement at the same time. However, from the beginning of the initial case study, we employed a perspective of maintaining a culture for/of inquiry and continuous improvement within this accountability context (Miller, Carroll, Jancic, & Markworth, 2015).

Devising a plan for collecting multiple measures of new educator performance with hopes of connecting outcomes to program preparation, we found ourselves growing vulnerable deconstructing professional practice of our program graduates. Educational contexts where the initial case study and subsequent collaborative self-study occurred were largely framed with a "what works" agenda (Biesta, 2007; 2010) where "evidence-based practice promises a panacea for uncertainty" (Mockler & Groundwater-Smith, 2015). The accountability context pushed into not only the pre-K–12 systems where our graduates worked, but also into our own pressure in higher education for meeting new national accreditation standards. Outcomes were a prevalent discourse for pre-K–12 and our higher education context. This parallel pressure led to an emphasis on our desire as teacher educators to purposefully model working within such a context and emphasizing continued professional development across the professional life span.

The pull on documenting student performance outcomes while at the same time studying practice existed as a persistent tension. U.S. education policy calls for the evaluation of teachers by their pre-K–12 student performance; teacher educators, too, are now judged by their teacher candidate performance as new educators (Cochran-Smith et al., 2016). As Miller and his colleagues (2015) argued, it is possible to work within a high stakes assessment context and come together as teacher educators, learn from professional practice, and inform the standards discourse agenda. Peck, Galluci, and Sloan (2010) described tensions in teacher educator work when faced with high stakes assessments and compliance in implementing state mandates. As teacher educators, we explicitly dove into the tensions of accountability, studying program outcomes, and teacher educator professional development to investigate the interaction of multiple networks of teacher education work.

Collaborative Self-Study as Teacher Educator Professional Development: Internal Forces

Dinkelman (2011) claimed teacher educator professional development revolves around identity as "influenced 'out there' and 'in here'" (p. 310). Professional identity development for teacher educators involves working through internal tensions like values as a classroom teacher and professional orientations for learning and teaching as well as new external forces in positionality as a teacher educator. Deeper attention paid to the complexity of teacher educator development within multiple contexts allowed for examining dissonance as teacher educators observing new educators who had graduated from our programs. We felt vulnerability with regards to sustainability in an academy undervalued and underrepresented in the national policy context for teacher education (Cochran-Smith et al., 2016). Therefore, we recognized the significance of engaging in a collaborative self-study of our practice, interrogating the space between self and practice (Pinnegar & Hamilton, 2009). We engaged in a reflective, dialogic mode of inquiry in which we shared data and our individual responses to data such that we could interrogate experience to learn from each other and *with* each other (LaBoskey, 2007; Loughran, 2007).

Through this reflection, we identified multiple spaces where we enacted our work. We work in institutions of higher education to prepare teachers and provide further professional development. We work in pre-K–12 schools and school systems to teach professional practice (Grossman et al., 2009) with school partners who work in a parallel yet different system. To learn deeply from studying our practice, we engaged in a shared discourse of how the contradictions between our theory and practice, research and pedagogy—self *and* other—played out in an initial case study of new educator performance to inform our own professional development. For example, during observations of practice for case study data, we were sometimes shocked by what we saw. One of us noted a teacher candidate who had been a "rock star" during her time at the university was now encountering serious struggles with classroom management in her new context. As researchers *and* teacher educators, we needed to dig into what this indicated about our preparation programs as well as how we could grow as teacher educators in unraveling the complexity of the work of teacher educators.

THEORETICAL FRAMEWORKS FOR STUDYING
TEACHER EDUCATOR DEVELOPMENT

As teacher educators who embraced the process of continuous improvement (Snow, Dismuke, Zenkert, & Loffer, 2017), we also embraced the idea that we "do more than discuss good ideas" (Snow et al., 2015). We identified core pedagogies in teacher educator practice and used the following conceptual frameworks to guide our self-study: communities of practice; professional stance; and social network theory. Each of these frameworks informed our professional practice in our teacher educator programs and consideration of teacher educator professional development.

Communities of Practice Serve as Contexts for Professional Development

Studying practice in community (Lieberman & Miller, 2008; Wenger, 1998) provided opportunity to learn from self and others. Just as new educators are simultaneously teachers and learners—growing into their identities as professional educators—so are teacher educators. As teacher educators, the literature surrounding teacher communities of practice was a natural foundation for considering our own professional development. Wenger (1998) identified characteristics of communities of practice including mutual engagement, shared practice, and collaborative endeavors.

Our shared commitment deepened a community of practice while at the same time involving "legitimate peripheral participation" (Lave & Wenger, 1991) in a study of program outcomes. In their systematic review of literature including Chou's (2011); Gallagher, Griffin, Parker, Kitchen, and Figg (2011); and Keung's (2009) articles on communities of practice; Vangrieken, Meredith, Packer, and Kyndt, (2017) described formative teacher communities that improved teacher practice. Interpersonal dynamics including belief in oneself as a professional and a "shift to uncertainty" (Snow-Gerono, 2005a) allow vulnerability to exist in a community to further educator development. Again, Vangrieken and colleagues (2017) included research from Attard (2012); Jones, Gardner, Robertson, and Robert (2013); and Snow-Gerono (2005a) in pointing out "dissensus is argued to stretch people's ideas, provide learning opportunities, and enhance collaboration" (p. 55). Vulnerability and a willingness to learn more about our practice pushed us to engage in reflection on dissensus in our practice in a safe, small community of practice (Hamilton, 2009).

Professional Positioning Toward Knowledge Informs Identity Development

A framework for our teacher education programs and our professional practice includes considerations of knowledge construction. Cochran-Smith and Lytle (2001) describe three types of knowledge: knowledge-*for*-practice, knowledge-*in*-practice, and knowledge-*of*-practice. Knowledge generated by external researchers is *for* practice while knowledge practitioners generate within their own professional contexts would be *in* practice. Knowledge-*of*-practice merges considerations of both knowledge *in* and *for* practice such that this knowledge becomes a way of being, or what teacher educators in this context have considered an "inquiry stance toward teaching" (Snow-Gerono, 2005b). Dana and Yendol-Hoppey (2014) describe an inquiry stance toward teaching where "this stance becomes a professional positioning, owned by the teacher, where questioning one's own practice becomes part of the teacher's work and eventually a part of the teaching culture" (p. 9). Teacher inquiry and an inquiry stance toward teaching may be paramount to new teacher development, particularly with regard to improving classroom practice and student learning (Ball & Cohen, 1999; Hiebert, Morris, Berk, & Jansen, 2007; Windschitl, Thompson, & Braaten, 2011). It would follow that the development of teacher educator practice could also benefit from inquiry into practice and studying new teacher learning.

Teacher educators may learn from studying our practice and deconstructing knowledge *in* and *for* our practice such that our inquiry stance generates knowledge for the field of teacher education and teacher educator development. Mockler and Groundwater-Smith (2015) used practitioner inquiry as framed by "understanding and transforming practice as an ethical professional enterprise that shapes the quality of outcomes" (p. 603). These authors also identified "teacher professional learning through the seeking and embracing of 'unwelcome truths'" (p. 604). Mockler and Groundwater-Smith considered teacher learning with regard to hearing their pre-K–12 students' voices. In a similar manner, we identified our graduates' insights as a space to thoughtfully consider "unwelcome truths." A professional stance focused on inquiry emphasizes the co-construction of knowledge with openness to perspective-taking, multiple realities, and the interaction of social networks on practice.

As Dinkelman (2011) shared, "Identity turns on a mysterious interplay of external influences and an individual's internal sense-making…to sort out what about identity stems from what is 'out there' and what is 'in here'" (p. 310). By emphasizing an inquiry stance toward teaching, we recognized the external forces on our identity development (e.g., accreditation standards and higher education evaluation contexts) along with the internal forces (belief in student/teacher voice, etc.). Dinkelman acknowledged "identity is ultimately grounded in complex processes of recognition that play out in various social communities" (p. 319).

Teacher Educator Social Networks Interact to Inform Work and Development

"Teacher educator identities reflect an unstable and ever-shifting weave of personal and professional phenomena" (Dinkelman, 2011, p. 309). Each of the roles and responsibilities teacher educators take up is enacted within a social network. As the functions of different teacher educator work is informed by different contexts, the relational interaction of the people and functions involved inform teacher educator development. Therefore, social network theory informed the different communities of practice in which teacher educators took up our work to inform performance outcomes (Moolenaar, Sleegers, & Daly, 2012). We teacher educators worked within several social networks as portrayed in Figure 11.2.

Like most teacher educators, we found ourselves serving in multiple roles within professional responsibilities. Each of us served as a clinical field experience supervisor, called "liaison" in this context. We also taught pedagogy courses and served on committees and task forces involved in program evaluation and continuous improvement efforts. We each considered ourselves teacher education researchers as well as faculty who contribute to accreditation or university processes for accountability reports. Depending on the specific task or role we were playing, different parts of our work might be prioritized. In particular, working so much in pre-K–12 school contexts at the same time we worked for and within the university highlighted our role as hybrid professionals. Embracing the different networks highlighted in Figure 11.2, along with their interactions, informed teacher educator professional development such that individual actions had multiple meanings. For example, working as methods instructors to build knowledge of differentiated instruction and then building on that knowledge working with teacher candidates to enact differentiated instruction (as a liaison) was also modeled by teacher educators when we worked together to discuss candidate unit plans, analyses of student learning, and their impact on teacher candidate future performance (as a continuous improvement

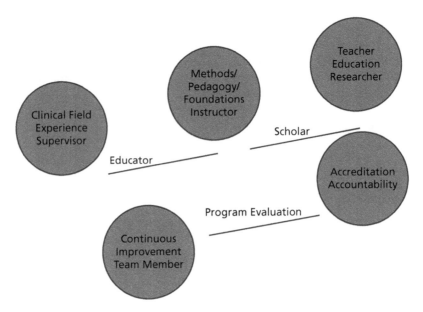

Figure 11.2 Social networks of teacher educators.

team member). The functions of the different roles and responsibilities of teacher educators could stand alone in our work within a network. However, they also interacted to inform teacher educator development.

Daly, Moolenaar, Bolivar, and Burke (2010) claimed "social capital is concerned with the resources that exist in social relationships (sometimes referred to as 'ties') between individuals as opposed to the resources of a specific individual" (p. 364). Looking at our multiple relationships connected to varied functions of being a teacher educator, we recognized the "content that flows through relationships" (p. 364). Working across our communities of practice via our social networks allowed for us as teacher educators to

> transcend the practicalities (and limitations) of discrete teaching skills and tools gained from previous teaching experience; and develop ways of thinking about and approaching teaching and learning that promote the application of a professional repertoire to a vast array of dilemmas, most of which cannot possibly be anticipated beforehand. (Goodwin & Kosnick, 2013, p. 337)

Social network theory allowed for us to study the interactions of our work in and across multiple contexts for our work. Valuing the dynamic interaction allowed for layered meaning in our analysis. For example, we recognized our emotional responses to teacher practice during our observations of new teachers while at the same time identifying space for improvement in our continuous improvement task force work.

METHODOLOGY

Collaborative Self-Study

After experiencing some dissonance as teacher educators observing new educators who had graduated from our programs, we engaged in a reflective, dialogic mode of inquiry where we shared data and our individual responses to it such that we could interrogate experience to learn from each other and *with* each other (LaBoskey, 2007; Loughran, 2007). This collaborative self-study maintained its origins in qualitative and interpretive traditions (Bullough & Pinneagar, 2007). A primary emphasis was our felt discomfort as "hybrid people" (Elijah, 2007) studying our own practice and experiencing the third party results of that practice. To learn deeply from studying our practice, we engaged in a shared discourse of how the contradictions between our theory and practice played out in the original case study of program graduates to inform our professional development as teacher educators.

Toward that end, we revisited data excerpts from a case study of program graduates' professional practice in early years of teaching and identified felt vulnerabilities in our evaluation of their practice upon program completion. The original case study data informing this self-study focused on new teacher performance data geared to respond to educator preparation program accountability demands in the United States. By researching our own experience and voice responding to new teacher performance data, we sought a more empowering vision for teacher educator professional development. Once again, our collaborative self-study was framed by the following research questions: (a) How do teacher educators experience the phenomenon of observing program graduates in their early years of teaching? and (b) What do we learn about our own practice from analyzing multiple measures of new teacher performance? Considering these questions, we mirrored the professional practice we hoped program graduates engaged as they studied pre-K–12 student learning to make decisions about their own professional growth and effective practice.

Program Context and Participants

The context of our collaborative self-study emerged from a case study (Yin, 2018) of program graduates, including monthly workshops over 1 year in which new educators engaged in the study of pre-K–12 student learning connected to work-sample artifacts, alumni surveys, and focus group interviews on felt preparedness to teach, and investigating support structures for sharing experience as new educators. Researchers also surveyed employers and interviewed administrators of new teachers and conducted classroom observations connected to a framework for teaching (FFT; Danielson, 2013), rating performance according to FFT rubrics. The data sources in this case study also built from key aspects of the preparation program.

The teacher education programs from which these new teachers graduated support a vision for candidates working in communities of practice and conducting teacher inquiry. Candidates engage in teacher inquiry projects and share their findings in a roundtable session where all teacher education faculty and community/pre-K–12 school partners attend. This project was completed in the first semester of a "professional year," referred to as an internship where candidates spent approximately 3 days per week in their placement school. The second semester of this year-long clinical field experience was full-time student teaching where candidates conducted a standard performance assessment for teaching (S-PAT) involving extensive unit planning, assessment analysis, and in-depth progress monitoring of three specific students and the entire class connected to student learning outcomes (SLOs). The inquiry project was designed to stimulate the development of an inquiry stance toward teaching during the student teaching semester and throughout their career. The S-PAT was designed to focus inquiry into specific teaching and learning outcomes and student performance data throughout an instructional unit. Candidates were also observed with formative assessments and "professional year assessments" aligned with the FFT rubrics. Our state also requires teacher candidates to develop professional learning plans to carry with them throughout their professional positions.

Each of these experiences from the teacher education programs were emulated in the follow-up case study with "studying practice and student learning" (SPSL) workshops, unit and assessment analysis with SLOs and professional goal-setting connected to feedback data and developed with an emphasis on inquiry and "problem-posing" (Dana & Yendol-Hoppey, 2014). This link from program preparation to induction structures was an important component of the case study structure. Also significant was the background and perspectives each of us as researchers and teacher educators brought both to the case study research and then to this collaborative self-study.

Jennifer and Sherry had both been working in the preparation programs for several years when the case study research was developed and implemented. Jennifer led the teacher education programs across campus and facilitated the introduction of requirements for inquiry projects across programs over the past decade and a revision of the performance assessment to align more purposefully to professional standards and learning progressions (CCSSO, 2013). Sherry also had administrative duties on campus as a program coordinator. Sherry shared that she was "a teacher educator who transitioned from 14 years of public school elementary teaching to work as teacher educator in the university" (memo, 2018). She worked across our teacher education networks as a committee leader for continuous improvement teams and task forces, a methods instructor for classroom management in the elementary program, and a liaison to multiple partner schools, to name a few of her roles. Jennifer also participated in these roles as a tenured professor and associate dean in the college.

According to Sherry,

> This study provided concrete data with which to inform and develop my personal practice in all my many roles. The voices and actions of our graduates in their first years of teaching... directed my steps and decisions and pushed me out of my comfort zone in order to meet their needs as new educators. (memo, 2018)

Likewise, Julianne was "trying to get a feel for what our graduates looked like and could do in their first year or two" (memo, 2018). Yet, Julianne was coming at this question from the perspective of someone new to this university context. She taught science methods and served as a liaison to candidates; however, she was new to this university even though she had worked as a science teacher educator and clinical supervisor in other contexts. She reflected during this study: "I'm still a new teacher educator, juggling everything that our candidates are supposed to know/be able to do, and constantly thinking about how I can get the most bang for my buck" (memo, 2018).

In the same vein, Serena came from a classroom teacher background where she had conducted several professional development workshops for teachers and was immersed in her daily classroom teaching in a middle school. She was in her first year in a university position when we conducted the case study and also used this opportunity to learn more about the programs and her potential role as a teacher educator. Serena shared, "Frankly, I was confused a lot of the time. I don't recall any formal training..." (memo, 2018). She took comfort in her expertise in the classroom: "Having worked across secondary grade levels and secondary content areas, I was familiar and comfortable applying best practices and modeling them for students" (memo, 2018).

From our reflections it was clear that we undertook this self-study together to enhance our understandings of our own practice. We found we each also wondered about formal preparation of teacher educators in any context. Self-study of practice or engaging in practitioner inquiry is a meaningful tool for engaging in professional growth with specific connections to becoming a teacher educator (Jacobs et al., 2015).

Data Sources and Analysis

Investigating the self-study questions referenced above, we kept journals connected to our experiences and from our diverse perspectives as teacher educators. We kept notes to bracket assumptions and feelings during the case study focus group interviews, classroom observations, and as a reflective space during the entire study (Pinnegar & Hamilton, 2009; Richardson, 2000). Upon initial debriefings in which we realized we were having conflicted emotions and experiences with what we were observing during case study research and what we had expected, we further coded case study data excerpts and our researcher journals with attention to our responses to data and what we were learning about our own practice from analyzing multiple measures of new teacher performance.

This new focus led to systematic memoing of data so that we could share reflections on our experiences and engage in discourse on how we grew professionally as individuals and as a team of teacher educators. In particular, as we reviewed focus group transcripts with new educators and principal interviews, we revisited our experiences during classroom observations and the workshops. We shared narrative memos and had group discussions connected to questions uncovering assumptions in our expectations and more objective data collection. We identified how we felt when we saw practice that surprised us; how we negotiated new educator needs when we had served as preparation faculty; how our practices were similar and/or different from our role as teacher educators in or after preparation programs. We coded across data sources (e.g., focus group transcripts and classroom observations, along with assessment of a teacher work sample) and wrote self-narratives about the experience. Reading and coding across each narrative, we identified shared learning for our teacher educator professional development.

TEACHING/LEARNING PRACTICE ACROSS THE PROFESSIONAL LIFE SPAN

As we engaged in our collaborative, systematic investigation of our professional practice with the outcomes evidence of our graduates' performance as new teachers, we identified a model for looking at our data. Figure 11.3 shares a model for teacher educator learning that could be used in communities of practice for teacher educator preparation or continued professional development. Framing our shared inquiry around similar tools we prepared new teachers to use, we considered professional positioning, educational contexts, and performance outcomes for our own professional development through this study. We began our journey with a learning stance—a professional positioning toward knowledge as open and shared. We also acknowledged the hybrid space we engaged within the university as teacher educators and within pre-K–12 schools as teacher educators. Our

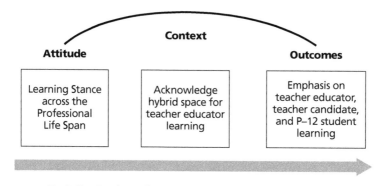

Figure 11.3 Model for teacher educator learning.

professional development model had to honor both spaces as social networks to recognize our authority and positioning within each institution. Finally, we had to emphasize the outcomes of our practice via new teacher performance and pre-K–12 learning to inform professional development.

Attitude: Finding Humility and Scaling Expectations

One of the first findings across the self-study narratives included the notion that we each, at some point, had some sense of "eating humble pie." Some of our initial researcher comments included somewhat of a defensive stance. For example, when candidates referenced an experience connected to a course one of us specifically taught, it was difficult not to provide rationale for why their situation was described as such. For example, one of us memoed data from new teachers evidencing little implementation of pedagogy learned in coursework with the following comment: "They can't transfer when there was no opportunity to teach this content area in the clinical experience. I wonder if this is also true for social studies and science" (Coding Memo, p. 13). We shared this response as preparation program faculty and observers in classrooms where certain curriculum and pedagogy was apparently privileged over others. We continued this concern with another memo:

> There isn't consistency in the experience. Some students have a great mentor and have a wonderful experience with some guided instruction. Others are thrown into teaching when they have no idea what they should be doing. Some...wander around making up things to do... (Researcher Memo, July, 2016, p. 1)

Resisting an immediate response to blame a context or structure of the program or current teaching context, we explored how to prepare new educators for where they would teach so that we could engage in improvement-aimed frameworks for programmatic and professional development. For example, based on concerns regarding inconsistencies in preparation across content areas we dug deeper and made comparisons of new teacher abilities to teach science in comparison with math and reading on the FFT and a more sensitive content specific observational instrument, the practices of science observation protocol (P-SOP; Forbes, Biggers, & Zangori, 2013). Triangulating additional data sources with our own concerns pushed us past "blaming" and gave us the data to pinpoint specific adjustments that could be made to coursework to improve consistency across content area preparation. Another specific, detailed discussion involved working with English language learners. We identified science as a space to emphasize academic language and study linguistic complexity to best support the reading, writing, speaking, and listening of all learners.

Reframing our own responses to data sources allowed for a more engaged look at what we should expect for new teacher practice. We focused on "well-started" teachers and how our work as teacher educators could engage appropriate expectations. One of us wrote in a reflective memo:

> I think it goes back to the well-started beginner thing. I need to arm my students with whatever I think is necessary for them to be well-started beginners. And rather than arming them with individual tricks or activities, I need to arm them with philosophies, ways of thinking, the "heart" of what it means to be a good teacher who values students and knows how to support all students in learning. (Researcher Memo, January, 2017)

Some of the dissonant self-study data leading to this reframing included comments like "What if I see something that isn't the greatest philosophically and both the principal and teacher think it's good?" (Data Memo, June, 2016). As teacher educators, we learned how important it was to work more purposefully with our clinical field experience partners—both to support the preparation program structure and to sustain and develop professional practice within our pre-K–12 partner schools. Our goal was reframed as one of seeking to understand and support learning in every situation.

This learning stance allowed us to engage the context and the outcomes of professional practice. One of us shared,

> I'm really torn about this because I've had a professional year student who really shouldn't be a teacher disposition-wise (she's not passionate, she doesn't take initiative, etc.), but technically, she's getting it done [scoring basic on all evaluations]. This really bothers me. (Researcher Memo, January, 2017)

Revisiting our expectations through this self-study allowed for professional development across teacher educators in the programs. We focused more on revising the rubrics for our S-PAT unit study and reflection and ensured the teaching strategies, assessment literacy, and inquiring disposition we hoped to see was also evidenced in the planning, analysis, and response to student work. As one of us wrote,

> It's like standing a baby up and getting them solidly on their feet, but it's up to the baby to walk and lean on the assistive pieces in its environment...As much as I want my students [teacher candidates] to learn content and internalize certain concepts, I'm starting to think that I'm just here to shepherd them along and point out the ways in which they can be great, the ways in which they can help students learn with the skills that they've already acquired. (Researcher Memo, January, 2017)

This reframing of expectations and our own humility in purpose as teacher educators also allowed for more careful consideration of induction supports.

Context: How to "Match" Knowledge and Application

Moving through multiple networks informing program outcomes, this collaborative self-study provided opportunities for us to push ourselves to both meet accountability standards and consider our purposes as teacher educators. One of us wrote about a principal interview where the principal emphasized the importance of "learning on the job":

> So how do you teach this [differentiation/working with individuals] when so much SPED [special education] stuff is based on the individual and the situation? We can't cop out and say that they need to learn on the job. What are the foundational pieces that would hold true, no matter the situation or individual? (Researcher Memo, January, 2017)

From our dialogue, we agreed to push ourselves to engage more with school partners and new teachers during induction and professional development so that "learning on the job" included consideration of key pedagogical practices. In particular, we emphasized differentiated instruction in our programs and, more purposefully, in a subsequent induction project. We became more deliberate about continuing teacher preparation program practices in the early years of teaching. Integration of frameworks (and social networks) in this study—teacher educator theory and practical teaching contexts—provided opportunity for considering hybrid spaces without blaming one or the other for disappointing outcomes.

A consistent theme in our memos included the idea of modeling practices we hoped our graduates would emulate as new teachers. Continuing the struggle over what it meant to be "well-started," one of us recognized the influence of multiple contexts on the attitude of continued learning. As teacher educators we needed to support teachers in their pre-K–12 teaching contexts as well as within our work from a higher education context.

> I think being a teacher educator means not focusing only on theoretical foundation or the application of practical strategies. I do think the answer is building from and with both. I do think the answer is with/in knowing who our candidates are and where they are at any given moment... Isn't that what we ask of them with their own learners? (Researcher memo, January, 2017, p. 2)

We needed to recognize our theoretical foundations and practical support while also supporting the individual teacher learner.

Each of our self-narratives focused on individual connections to programs. For example, one of us who taught elementary science methods had the most reflection on the absence of elementary science instruction in new educator practice, and those of us who emphasized the importance of writing pedagogy noted the difficulty new teachers had in practicing these skills. As we pushed across individual narratives, however, we found there was a larger theme indicating the necessity of a deeper integration across all program components. Looking at data considering what we expected new teachers to be able to do, we identified the notion that "they can tell you what the information is, but don't know how to apply it" (Researcher Memo, July, 2016, p. 1). For example, we found ourselves noting that new teachers could talk about differentiating instruction as a concept; however, when it came to applying those skills to a new teaching context (i.e., different from one where they student taught), they had difficulty. Teacher candidates who may have been "excellent classroom managers" during their professional year appeared to have "no control" in classrooms where they were first- and second-year teachers. We determined there was a "mismatch" in how new teachers took what they learned in practice to other contexts with higher stakes attached.

> The teachers are able to say what they do/use in the classroom, but not really dig into the crux of whatever it is (technology, differentiation) . . . I'm wondering if they're just seeing everything as so compartmentalized without any sort of theme or connecting piece running throughout. (Researcher Memo, January, 2017)

Simply talking about a professional positioning toward knowledge and practice as an inquiry stance may not be enough to sustain new educators in challenging early years of teaching. Considerations of quality from both an accountability (or "end") point as well as a developmental continuum became important for us. One context cannot overtake another space so that there is a loss of either theory or practice in professional development.

Learning Outcomes: Professional Development as a Lifelong Endeavor

Finally, as we studied our program graduates and their work, we were struck by the parallels between our professional stance and our graduates' professional stance. All principals highlighted new educator capacity for growth, requests for feedback, and a stance toward lifelong professional learning. While principals rated all participants between basic and proficient in all four InTASC standards groupings (CCSSO, 2013) on an employer survey included in the initial case study, "Professional Responsibilities"

TABLE 11.1 Principal Survey				
In TASC Groupings	Unsatisfactory	Basic	Proficient	Distinguished
The Learner and Learning	0%	13%	78%	8%
Content and Pedagogical Knowledge	0%	0%	97%	3%
Instructional Practice	0%	9%	86%	6%
Professional Responsibility	0%	4%	79%	18%

were highlighted with 97% rated proficient or distinguished (see Table 11.1). These strengths in non-academic qualities were elaborated in the principal interviews. They appreciated that our graduates as new teachers were "teachable," collaborative, and humble. Case study participants were confident in their skills and were willing to seek help and improve their practice. This reinforced for us that we should continue to model a professional stance towards lifelong learning.

Overlapping data sources also pointed to two areas where the development of frameworks could be strengthened in initial preparation. First, data from teachers and principals indicated the need for more explicit strategies for working with and differentiating instruction for learners with diverse needs. Another indication was including additional opportunities to teach in diverse contexts. Data from the alumni survey administered and collected within the case study measures indicated 50% of teachers rated themselves unsatisfactory or basic for InTASC grouping one, including ratings on statements such as: "I can teach in ways that support English Language Learners" and "I can teach students with a wide variety of needs" (see Table 11.2).

We noted multiple ways in which we could continue to model lifelong professional development for our teacher candidates and eventual graduates by modeling our own willingness to engage in continued professional development. First, two of the researchers in this self-study enrolled in a language acquisition class to develop our own lack of knowledge in this area. One of us also responded to the data by reflecting: "Looking across the multiple sources of data collected in this study, the notion of our students

TABLE 11.2 New Teacher Survey				
In TASC Groupings	Unsatisfactory	Basic	Proficient	Distinguished
The Learner and Learning	4%	46%	37%	12%
Content and Pedagogical Knowledge	0%	26%	56%	18%
Instructional Practice	0%	31%	60%	9%
Professional Responsibility	0%	19%	66%	16%

not being prepared to work in diverse settings comes up so often I cannot continue to ignore it" (Researcher Memo, January, 2017). In response to this data, she reestablished a clinical field experience partnership in a diverse setting that served a large number of refugee students to ensure her candidates a more diverse context. After the change in practice she wrote,

> In my gut I knew I was going to have to take my candidates and myself out of our comfort zone. This experience rocked my reality and has caused me to shed my hard and fast belief that our candidates should stay in one school. (Researcher Memo, January, 2017)

Finally, we looked for opportunities to better model professional practices we hoped to see in candidates and new educators. For example, "differentiation—ooh, boy. I know I'm doing a [poor] job modeling this for students, and I need to do it on two levels: within the structures of my course and then within the lesson-plan activities." (Researcher Memo, January, 2017)

Pushing our considerations of teacher/candidate practices allowed us to also stretch our individual and collective practice. We recognized the need to share practices around modeling and purposeful scaffolding for teacher candidates. As teacher educators, we needed to not only use practices we hoped new teachers would emulate, but we also needed to share aloud and discuss the modeling we intended through these practices.

CONCLUSIONS FOR TEACHER EDUCATOR PROFESSIONAL DEVELOPMENT

This collaborative self-study sought to answer questions related to our experiences observing program graduates, what we learned from these observations, and what we intended to do with this newfound knowledge. We learned to share our reflections on professional stance, contexts, and outcomes in a community of practice where we could develop our own teacher educator identities. As a result of this study, we sought to recalibrate our expectations to create well-started beginners and considered thematic foundations in our programs that allowed graduates to more readily transfer their foundational knowledge from context to context. We became more explicit about our modeling as teacher educators, making clear when we were practicing what we hoped our candidates would take up as new educators.

Beyond programmatic improvements, the significance of this collaborative self-study revealed the importance of scaffolding teacher educator professional development. Not only did we need our inquiry stance, community of practice, and appreciation for the multiple social networks within which we worked, we needed a model to investigate our experiences. All of us recognized we were learning to do our jobs as we did them; we were not purposefully prepared for the role of teacher educator. Doctoral programs could be a space to initiate inquiry into the professional practice of teacher education (Jacobs et al., 2015). As Jacobs and her colleagues noted, graduate students conducting inquiry into their new practice as teacher educators allowed them to grow and develop teacher educator identities. Providing specific frameworks for studying professional practice could also support the preparation of teacher educators in their early years of professional practice. We needed the "collegial tool-based practices" teacher educators have structured for new teacher development (Windschitl et al., 2011) to focus our own professional growth. Using a model of teacher development in communities of practices (see Figure 11.3), teacher educators may also engage in professional development via a community of practice where professional stance, or attitude, the professional context, and the outcomes of professional practice interact. Having a shared language or experience to deconstruct new teacher and teacher educator practice allows for deliberate teacher educator development. Practitioner inquiry and cultivating an inquiry stance toward teacher education will support the development of the next generation of teacher educators.

Discussion Questions

1. How might teacher educators best work within tensions of outcomes-based accountability contexts and a need for teacher educator professional development?
2. What does a "well-started" educator look like? How do teacher educators best support new teacher development and teacher educator expectations at the same time?
3. How might self-study and inquiry into professional practice be elevated in academic settings such that teacher educators might work within higher education contexts prioritizing research and scholarship to also engage in their own professional development?

REFERENCES

Attard, K. (2012). Public reflection within learning communities: An incessant type of professional development. *European Journal of Teacher Education, 35,* 199–211.

Ball, D., & Cohen, D. (1999). Developing practice, developing practitioners: Toward a practice-based theory of professional education. In L. Darling-Hammond, & G. Sykes (Eds.), *Teaching as the Learning Profession: Handbook of policy and practice* (pp. 3–32). San Francisco, CA: Jossey-Bass.

Biesta, G. (2007). Why "what works" won't work: Evidence-based practice and the democratic deficit in educational research. *Educational Theory 57*(1), 1–22.

Biesta, G. (2010). A new logic of emancipation: The methodology of Jacques Rancière. *Educational Theory 60*(1), 39–59.

Bullough, R. V., & Pinnegar, S. (2007). Thinking about self-study: An analysis of eight chapters. In J. Loughran, M. L. Hamilton, V. K. La Boskey, & T. Russell (Eds.), *The international handbook of self-study of teaching and teacher education practices* (Vol. 1, pp. 313–342). Dordrecht, The Netherlands: Kluwer Academic.

Council of Chief State School Officers. (2013). *Interstate teacher assessment and support consortium in TASC model core teaching standards and learning progressions for teachers 1.0: A resource for ongoing teacher development.* Washington, DC: Author.

Chou, C. H. (2011). Teachers' professional development: Investigating teachers' learning to do action research in a professional learning community. *Asia Pacific Education Researcher, 20,* 421–437.

Clarke, M., & Moore, A. (2013). Professional standards, teacher identities and an ethics of singularity. *Cambridge Journal of Education, 43*(4), 487–500.

Cochran-Smith, M. (2012). Composing a research life. *Action in Teacher Education, 34*(2), 99–110.

Cochran-Smith, M., & Lytle, S. L. (2001). Beyond certainty: Taking an inquiry stance on practice. In A. Lieberman & L. Miller (Eds.), *Teachers caught in the action: Professional development that matters* (pp. 45–58). New York, NY: Teachers College Press.

Cochran-Smith, M., Stern, R., Sanchez, J. G., Miller, A., Keefe, E. S., Fernandez, M. B.,... Baker, M. (2016). *Holding teacher preparation accountable: A review of claims and evidence.* Policy Brief. National Education Policy Center. University of Colorado, Boulder, CO.

Council for the Accreditation of Educator Preparation. (2014). CAEP Accreditation Standards. Washington DC. Retrieved from http://caepnet.org/standards/introduction

Dana, N. F., & Yendol-Hoppey, D. (2014). *The reflective educator's guide to classroom research: Learning to teach and teaching to learn through practitioner inquiry* (3rd ed.). Thousand Oaks, CA: Corwin Press, Inc.

Danielson, C. (2013). *Enhancing Professional Practice: A Framework for Teaching* (2nd ed.). Alexandria, VA: ASCD.

Daly, A. J., Moolenaar, N. M., Bolivar, J., M., & Burke, P. (2010). Relationships in reform: The role of teachers' social networks. *Journal of Educational Administration, 48*(3), 359–391.

Dinkelman, T. (2011). Forming a teacher educator identity: Uncertain standards, practice and relationships. *Journal of Education for Teaching, 37*(3), 309–323.

Elijah, R. (2007). Voice in self-study. In *International handbook of self-study of teaching and teacher education practices* (pp. 247–272). Dordrecht, The Netherlands: Kluwer.

Forbes, C. T., Biggers, M., & Zangori, L. (2013). Investigating essential characteristics of scientific practices in elementary science learning environments: The practices of science observation protocol (P-SOP). *School Science and Mathematics, 113*(4), 180–190.

Gallagher, T., Griffin, S., Parker, D. C., Kitchen, J., & Figg, C. (2011). Establishing and sustaining teacher educator professional development in a self-study community of practice: Pre-tenure teacher educators developing professionally. *Teaching and Teacher Education, 27*, 880–890.

Goodwin, L. A., & Kosnik, C. (2013). Quality teacher educators = quality teachers? Conceptualizing essential knowledge domains for those who teach teachers. *Teacher development: An international journal of teacher's professional development, 17*(3), 334–346.

Grossman, P., Compton, C., Igra, D., Ronfeldt, M., Shahan, E., & Williamson, P. (2009). Teaching practice: A cross-professional perspective. *Teachers College Record, 111*(9), 2055–2100.

Hamilton, M. L., (2009). The somehow of teaching: Small groups, collaboration, and the self-study of teacher education practices. In C. J. Craig & L. F. Deretchin (Eds.), *Teacher Learning in Small-Groups* (pp. 207–282). Lanham, MD: Rowman & Littlefield Education.

Hiebert, J., Morris, A. K., Berk, D., & Jansen, A. (2007). Preparing teachers to learn from teaching. *Journal of Teacher Education, 58*(1), 47–61.

Jacobs, J., Yendol-Hoppey, D., & Dana, N. F. (2015). Preparing the next generation of teacher educators: The role of practitioner inquiry. *Action in Teacher Education, 37*(4), 373–396.

Jones, M. G., Gardner, G. E., Robertson, L., & Robert, S. (2013). Science professional learning communities: Beyond a singular view of teacher professional development. *International Journal of Science Education, 35*, 1756–1774.

Keung, C. C. (2009). Cultivating communities of practice via learning study for enhancing teacher learning. *Kedi Journal of Educational Policy, 6*, 81–104.

Kosnik, C., Cleovoulou, Y., Fletcher, T., Harris, T., McGlynn-Stewart, M., & Beck, C. (2011). Becoming teacher educators: An innovative approach to teacher educator preparation. *Journal of Education for Teaching, 37*(3), 351–363.

Lave, J., & Wenger, E. (1991). *Situated learning: Legitimate peripheral participation.* Cambridge, England: Cambridge University Press.

Lieberman, A., & Miller, L. (2008). *Teachers in Professional Learning Communities: Improving teaching and learning.* New York, NY: Teachers College Press.

LaBoskey, V. K. (2007). The methodology of self-study and its theoretical underpinnings. In *International handbook of self-study of teaching and teacher education practices* (pp. 817–870). Dordrecht, The Netherlands: Kluwer.

Loughran, J. J. (2007). Learning through self-study: The influence of purpose, participants and context. In *International handbook of self-study of teaching and teacher education practices* (pp. 151–192). The Netherlands: Springer.

Miller, M., Carroll, D. Jancic, M., & Markworth, K. (2015). Developing a culture of learning around the edTPA: One university's journey. *The New Educator, *(11), 37–59.

Mockler, N., & Groundwater-Smith, S. (2015). Seeking for the unwelcome truths: Beyond celebration in inquiry-based teacher professional learning. *Teachers and Teaching: Theory and Practice, 21*(5), 603–614.

Moolenaar, N. M., Sleegers, P. J. C., & Daly, A. J. (2012). Teaming up: Linking collaboration networks, collective efficacy, and student achievement. *Teaching and Teacher Education, 28*(2), 251–262.

Peck, C. A., Gallucci, C., & Sloan, T. (2010). Negotiating implementation of high-stakes performance assessment policies in teacher education: From compliance to inquiry. *Journal of Teacher Education, 61*(5), 451–463.

Pinnegar, S., & Hamilton, M. L. (2009). *Self-study of practice as a genre of qualitative research: Theory, methodology, and practice.* New York, NY: Springer.

Richardson, L. (2000). Writing: A method of inquiry. In N. K. Denzin & Y. S. Lincoln (Eds.), *Handbook of qualitative research* (2nd ed., pp. 923–948). Thousand Oaks, CA: SAGE.

Snow, J. L., Martin, S. D., & Dismuke, S. (2015). "We do more than discuss good ideas": A close look at the development of professional capital in an elementary education liaison group. *Teacher Education Quarterly, 42*(2),43–63.

Snow, J. L., Dismuke, S. D., Zenkert, A. J., & Loffer, C. (2017). Re-culturing educator preparation programs: A collaborative case study of continuous improvement. *The Teacher Educator, 52*(4), 308–325.

Snow-Gerono, J. L. (2005a). Professional development in a culture of inquiry: PDS teachers identify the benefits of professional learning communities. *Teaching and Teacher Education, 21(3),* 241–256.

Snow-Gerono, J. L. (2005b). Naming inquiry: PDS teachers' perceptions of teacher research and living an inquiry stance toward teaching. *Teacher Education Quarterly, 32*(4), 79–95.

Vangrieken, K., Meredith, C., Packer, T., & Kyndt, E. (2017). Teacher communities as a context for professional development. A systematic review. *Teaching and Teacher Education, 61,* 47–59.

Wenger, E. (1998). Communities of practice: Learning, meaning, and identity. New York, NY: Cambridge University Press.

Windschitl, M., Thompson, J., & Braaten, M. (2011). Ambitious pedagogy by novice teachers: Who benefits from tool-supported collaborative inquiry into practice and why? *Teachers College Record, 113*(7), 1311–1360.

Yin, R. K. (2018). *Case study research and applications: Design and methods* (6th ed.). Los Angeles, CA: SAGE.

PART IV

REFLECTIONS ON THE FUTURE
OF TEACHER EDUCATOR PREPARATION

The first three sections of this book included chapters that took a pragmatic look at *pockets of excellence* that currently exist in preparing the next generation of teacher educators. In the final section of this book, we invited Paul Parkison, an educational philosopher and teacher educator, to problematize the current context of teacher education. Are we really preparing the next generation of teacher educators? In this chapter, he raises questions about what the future might bring to the field as we face increasing competition for scarce resources within the teacher education arena.

Parkison draws attention to the seemingly narrowing of perspectives in a time of growing scarcity of teacher candidates, professional respect, and resources. He argues that this narrowing of perspectives related to the increased emphasis on competition and commodification of preparation creates a context that dehumanizes the process of teacher preparation. He also argues that the next generation of teacher educators will need to be capable of inhabiting the diverse, heterogeneous territories and contexts that emerge in today's classrooms, schools, and communities. His chapter is shaped around three questions:

- How do we begin to overcome the structural obstacles that have been institutionalized as mechanisms of accountability across education?
- How do we engage with fellow teacher educators across preparation pathways in a manner that recognizes both strengths and limitations?

Preparing the Next Generation of Teacher Educators for Clinical Practice, pages 273–274
Copyright © 2019 by Information Age Publishing
All rights of reproduction in any form reserved.

- How do we leverage teacher educators' dispersed experience and expertise toward a common just and humane end?

In response to these questions, Parkison argues that the next generation of teacher educators will need to be nomadic teacher educators. They will need to: (a) develop ethical-aesthetic courage; (b) cross borders and learn to accompany teachers, classrooms, schools, and communities; (c) challenge the push for homogeneity that the current schooling paradigm encourages in favor of valuing heterogeneity and strength in difference; (d) become an advocate for public involvement in education; (e) carry on new forms of study, inquiry, and research, investigating new questions of effectiveness.

As a result, Parkison leaves us with some thoughts related to how teacher educators may navigate educational change and transformation. He reminds us that:

- Educational change and transformation does not come from compliance and commitment to a set of externally defined criteria.
- Educational change and the transformation of the narrative of justice and liberation cannot be imposed from an elite or privileged position.
- Educational change and the transformation of the narrative of justice and liberation will grow from nomadic and revolutionary practice in which the community includes as members nomadic collaborators to discover new pathways toward heterogeneous effectiveness together.

In response to these considerations, Parkison offers that practice-based communities, not revolutionary programs nor privileged positions, are needed to create the spaces where teacher educators can demonstrate commitment to the diversity of common good.

CHAPTER 12

THE NOMADIC TEACHER EDUCATOR
Teacher Educator's Emerging Role

Paul Parkison
University of North Florida

Teacher educators are in the midst of a transformation in the recommended ways of preparing teachers. Teacher educators now find themselves participants in the collateral processes of a competition-based paradigm that strategically scapegoats alternative pathways and programs. In this process, they stand the risk of making the individual effective teacher emerging from heterogeneous pathways into teaching, the potential collateral damage of the market and competition-based system. Good teachers become obscured and mis-recognized as they are essentialized as completers of a specific pathway. Teacher educators have become adept in their acquiescence to forms of common sense and the reified categories of effectiveness promoted by the state and accreditation. They reify the territories defined by habitual ways of doing teacher preparation and development, fetishizing concepts of implementation and outcomes relative to a given sense of effectiveness.

Preparing the Next Generation of Teacher Educators for Clinical Practice, pages 275–294
Copyright © 2019 by Information Age Publishing
All rights of reproduction in any form reserved.

Dedicated teacher educators work in the interests of not only their candidates but the potentially thousands of students those future teachers will impact. What this chapter hopes to draw attention to is the narrowing of perspectives in times of increasing professional precariousness. This context is defined by growing scarcity of teacher candidates, professional respect, and resources. This type of scarcity trap (Mullainathan & Shafir, 2013) can be informative when thinking about the need for a new role for teacher educators and the necessity of preparing for this new territory:

> Getting out of our scarcity trap first requires formulating a plan, something the scarcity mindset does not easily accommodate. Making a plan is important but not urgent, exactly the sort of thing that tunneling leads us to neglect. Planning requires stepping back, yet juggling keeps us locked into the current situation. Focusing on the ball that is about to drop makes it terribly difficult to see the big picture. You love to stop playing catch-up, but you have too much to do to figure out how. (p. 130)

Institutions and professional relationships are challenged to respond to sweeping changes taking place in education in general and with teacher preparation specifically.

The ways in which teacher educators put their knowledge to work and recognize the authentic potential present in institutional and professional relationships and common projects depends on new professional characteristics:

- capacity for empathy and cooperation, as much as for initiative and autonomy;
- capacity both to evaluate risk and to take risk; and
- ability to place actions in context, or territory, in both the long and short-term.

Precariousness is a way of being in which teacher educators need to become comfortable. Given our current context, teacher educators need to become nomads, adapting and integrating into ever changing and precarious territories.

CURRENT ENFRAMING OF TEACHER EDUCATION AND EDUCATORS

Teacher educators have been devoted to providing rich experiences for teacher candidates and graduates of higher education-based preparation programs. The intent is to help program graduates be the most professional and successful teachers in America's schools. Graduates are meant to be the best, the exemplars of what good teaching and professionalism can and should be. Graduates should win the competition of effectiveness that currently defines education and provides the metric by which teachers, programs, classrooms, and schools are judged. This competition has led contemporary teacher educators to be incentivized to engage with candidates, in-service teachers, partner schools, and the community in which the school exists in new ways, with differing relationships of power and respect. Negotiating this engagement requires planning and reflection. It will require an escape from the scarcity trap and the tunneling that binds many teacher educators to habitual ways of being grounded in tradition and the past. Teacher educators have become advocates for the constructs, processes, and outcomes that these programs are created to fulfill. As a result, teacher educators have also become competitive and have adopted the ideological framework of competition with other programs and emerging teacher preparation pathways outside the university.

By structuring education for teachers within an ideological framework of competition teacher educators fail to leverage the collective strength which comes from a commitment to the democratic and humanistic perspectives that value and acknowledge diverse expressions of ways of being that emerge when providing educative experiences within schools. Competition obscures the common enterprise of preparing teachers that all teacher educators share. The collective graduates of both traditional and alternative pathway programs are future colleagues within America's community schools. These teachers have the strengths of their experiences, education, and mentors. They also carry the limitations of their experiences, education, and mentors from specific pathways into the profession. Competition interferes with and dis-incentivizes any relationship of accompaniment, co-operation, or collaboration that is not winner-take-all.

The enframing of education for teachers as a competition between alternative pathways into the profession hides the purpose and goal of schooling—to provide educative and socially generative experiences for all K–12 learners. Among teachers in the school setting, the route to the position as teacher taken by each individual plays only a subconscious role in daily actions and interactions. The route to the classroom utilized by the teacher across the hall, on grade-level team, or within a discipline-based department is of consequence only if teachers stop to consciously compete with each other. Competition encourages an investigation of points of difference that can then be used to categorize, stigmatize, and exclude those who come by a different pathway. Consideration of shared experiences as teachers, learners, and human beings gets subsumed when teacher educators and teachers adopt this competition lens. The sense of professional community that crosses the boundaries of preparation programs is lost in the competition to win. Considerations of being a teacher and what it means to be a teacher are bracketed within a competition frame.

Martin Heidegger (1977) proposed that our way of being human and the way the world is for us are cast historically through a fundamental ontological questioning. An ontology is a formal naming and definition of the types, properties, and interrelationships of the subjects that exist in a particular territory or context of discourse. An ontology compartmentalizes the interactions that are possible within a specific context and establishes the relationships between them. Humanity's way of being, its ontological state according to Heidegger, is to inquire and seek common understanding. For Heidegger, to bracket the consideration of our way of being, to not ask the fundamental ontological questions, is to bracket our humanity, our potentiality for becoming, and our sustainability. By falling back on the rules and metrics of competition between preparation pathways or between and among teachers, teachers and teacher educators essentially bracket the human experience of education. The competition paradigm discourages the ontological process of inquiry and searching for common understanding that is humanity's way of being in the world. Teachers and teacher educators seek to win, not inquire toward common understanding.

By structuring education for teachers within an ideological framework of competition teacher educators fail to leverage their collective strength in providing educative experiences within schools for all K–12 students. A contemporary approach to the preparation of teacher educators needs to focus on a search for common understanding rather than on imposing an understanding. Current teacher educators within institutions of higher education, individuals who have acquired extensive expertise through research and focused study, are threatened with marginalization by alternative route preparation programs like Teach for America (TFA), Transition to Teaching (T2T), or lateral entry program like educator preparation institutes (EPI). At the same time, the aesthetic and often political ethic that motivates alternative route programs is marginalized by the asset specificity accumulated by higher education faculty. Framing each other as competitors obscures the shared mission of education for all. The sustainability of education in classrooms, schools, and communities is put at risk in this process as teachers become just another commodity in the education market (Parkison, 2016). The next generation of teacher educators needs to be capable of inhabiting the diverse, heterogeneous territories and contexts that emerge in today's classrooms, schools, and communities. The next generation of teacher educators need to develop the ethical-aesthetic courage to engage the dominant, hegemonic ideology of competition from a position of authentic values and beliefs, seeing the beauty and value of each classroom, school, and community in its authenticity.

Competition permeates education as a hegemonic paradigm. Today's teacher educators are not immune to this way of being. Competing leads down the path to standardization, exclusion, and homogeneity that stifles innovation and does not capitalize on the creativity and generativity of diversity and heterogeneity. Preparing the next generation of teacher educators needs to build from a belief in the strength that comes from commitment to the democratic and humanistic perspectives that seeks the diverse and heterogeneous expression of values that emerge through relationships and community.

Current schooling and education for teachers within the competition-based context require that we learn to think differently about what it means to be a teacher educator—to break free of the competitive framing of teachers and preparation routes to re-engage with the human experience of education. Learning to think differently requires the formation of new habits of inquiry, interacting, and preparation. New habits that break free of the confined and restrictive ways in which teacher educators think about themselves as individuals separate from other educators who have arrived by divergent paths are required in order to create sustainable programs and pedagogies that are both educative and generative for teacher candidates, novice teachers, and in-service professionals.

Reframing the preparation of the next generation of teacher educators requires that the following questions serve to open a space for dialogue:

- How do we begin to overcome the structural obstacles that have been institutionalized as mechanisms of accountability across education?
- How do we engage with fellow teacher educators across preparation pathways in a manner that recognizes both strengths and limitations?
- How do we leverage teacher educators' dispersed experience and expertise toward a common just end? An end that sees the beauty and value of each classroom, school, and community in their authenticity and heterogeneity.

OVERCOMING THE CURRENT STRUCTURAL OBSTACLES IN TEACHER PREPARATION

Problematizing the Competition-Based Framework

The competitive frame currently imposed on and, to a troubling degree, adopted by traditional university-based teacher educators, creates a significant stumbling block to thinking in a different and sustainable way. How is a revolutionary consciousness fostered in a population of teacher educators that has ceased, or failed, to think of themselves as a political and oppressed or trapped group? How do teacher educators prepare to think other than competitively? How do the next generation of teacher educators develop a revolutionary consciousness, a consciousness that asks the ontological questions, inquiring into diverse ways of being, and seeking common understanding? Teacher educators are in the process of adapting themselves to the oppressive environment of competition between preparation routes—they are accepting the oppressive environment of competition. This position has generated cynicism and for many teacher educators this cynicism has become the standard explanation for the perennial problem of teachers' failure to revolt against an authoritarian and narrowed schooling system and curriculum. Current teacher educators struggle to understand the compliance they see in in-service teachers, classrooms, and schools to the rules and metrics of the competition paradigm. While cynical about teachers' ability to transform the system, today's teacher educators do not always see the same self-protecting compliance at work in themselves.

This cynicism reflects how teacher educators are failing to see their interest in collective terms. It is the collective view that allows teacher educators to recognize that schools and society would be better off if the competitive frame that sets teacher against teacher and preparation route against preparation route were halted or reversed. Teacher educators continue to prioritize their self-interests, fueled by the desire to win the competition. Since this situation exists, it is important to face that it exists because it is desired. Confronting this desire and its origins challenges each teacher educator. A revolutionary consciousness is needed as the next generation of teacher educators are prepared. Recognizing the competitive ideological framework as an obstacle to educative experiences, the next generation of teacher educators will need to cross borders and learn to accompany teachers, classrooms, schools, and communities rather than transforming them in an effort to win. This is a nomadic consciousness that inhabits diverse territories and crosses borders to accompany the indigenous residents.

Teacher educators have seen their role shift as policies and expectations were refined and as classroom contexts shift under the pressures of the competition-based mechanisms of accountability that have been embedded in legislation throughout the United States. In this same time period, the needs of teacher candidates, novice teachers, and in-service professional teachers have become magnified under the microscope of accountability based on value-added measures that utilize high-stakes standardized testing as the pivotal benchmark. This statutory context has led to the diversification of teacher preparation programs and pathways into the teaching profession (Parkison, 2016). Legislation in many states now recognizes teaching academies like EPI, T2T pathways for career changers, and lateral entry local education agency (LEA) provided programs as teacher preparation on par with programs offered by institutions of higher education. Combined with the significant shortening of the median tenure of service of teachers this competition-based context has generated a professional development void. Professional development has been homogenized and provided to all candidates, novices, and in-service professional teachers in the same manner as if they all have the same needs (Jacobs, Burns, & Yendol-Hoppey, 2015; Yamagata-Lynch & Haudenschild, 2009).

Renewing the preparation of teacher educators requires challenging this hegemonic perspective by considering the capitulation that is embedded in adopting this competition-based ideology. Hegemony is the domination of a diverse society by a ruling class who manipulate beliefs, explanations, perceptions, values, and mores so that their worldview becomes the universally accepted and valid dominant ideology. By adopting the stance of advocate for a specific program and program graduates, teacher educators are abdicating their power as political actors. They become captive of the competitive system fueled by the impulse of standardization (standardization in the form of a specific way of doing teacher preparation) which obliterates alternative potentialities and modes of counter-embodiment of teachers that might emerge. Rejecting the potentiality of the singular, the individual effective teacher emerging from heterogeneous pathways into teaching, the competition-based and standardizing impulse of teacher preparation takes as its essential mode of production the reification of common sense, or the territorialization of thought related to teacher preparation and development according to the given beliefs, explanations, perceptions, values, and mores. This homogenization seeks to stabilize patterns of teacher production by capturing preparation and development in orders of meaning and dominant regimes of competition-based narratives. Teacher educators come to embrace the mechanisms of accountability, standards, and ratings utilized by the hegemonic competition-based ideology as measures of their effectiveness. This compliance grants the hegemony a degree of legitimacy.

What We Are Losing: An Example of Competition's Foreclosure

To be educated and to work in a profession dedicated to the education of others should mean to pursue the risky business of considering our being in the world. Inquiry into the fundamental questions of what is given, of how individuals exist (become) in the world, or how they are oriented toward the being of others provides a foundation for all education. Though complicated, how people experience the world, how individuals find a sustainable position from which to view the world and experience it requires conscious attention. Finding a position, and continuing to orient that position, in relation to essential ontological concepts and each other would seem critical to occupying a sustainable position or territory.

In order for teacher education and nomadic teacher educators to be part of something good, we have to reclaim some critical terms: education, reform, dialogue, and public. For the past 30 plus years (since *A Nation at Risk* if not earlier) these concepts have been co-opted by the hegemonic competition-based ideology as part and parcel of the ideological façade of the system. They have served to conceal a reality of intensely personal experiences that have grown increasingly disheartening as this ideological enframing has solidified its hegemony. These words and concepts have become part of the official incantations of "reformers" to justify and hide their actions and intentions as they continue to do whatever they want—pillaging public education for profits while sacrificing our most vulnerable fellow citizens.

The word "education"—much like the words "reform," "dialogue," and "public"—has been reduced to serving as one rung on the ladder up which clever individuals clamber and as a stick for beating those who stand at the margins. Can we wonder that "education" evokes feelings of distrust, skepticism, ridicule, and revulsion among citizens? This is not distaste for education as such: It is distaste for the ideological structure of lies into which the concept has been integrated (Biesta, 2009; 2014; Giroux, 2012; Kumashiro, 2009; Parkison, 2015).

I teach a course on Social Studies Methods for Elementary Teachers. It is a course that I have taught numerous times. Most recently we were embedded in one of our professional development schools. The school faces many of the challenges that confront schools: teacher turn-over, high student mobility, limited resources, and shotgun style professional development. A conversation with my students raised the issue of scripted lessons and the purpose of rigid out-of-the-box curricula. I found myself falling back on the argument that the school and district found these tools necessary to accommodate the limited preparation of many of the new teachers. I even asserted that my students were simply victims of this context since their preparation made them more professional. Struck by the ease with which I adopted this response, I have worked to problematize this view of alternative route teacher preparation and the assumed norm of preparation through institutions of higher education.

To be part of something good teacher education and nomadic teacher educators must acknowledge the perpetual state of becoming that is our being and the nature of education. To seek a clean, neat, and certain conclusion is to set ourselves up for frustration and to follow the dystopian path we should be resisting. The Czech political activist and eventual president of the Czech Republic Vaclav Havel said it best:

It is the tragic story of a "mental short circuit": Why bother with never ending, genuinely hopeless search for truth when a truth can be had so readily, all at once, in the form of an ideology or a doctrine? Suddenly it is all so simple. Think of all the laborious existential tasks from which our minds are freed once and for all! The essence of this short circuit is a fatal mistake: The tacit assumption that some ingenious, universally applicable artefact—and is a doctrine or an ideology ever anything more than a human artefact?—can lift from our shoulders the burden of the incessant, always unique, and essentially inalienable question and utterly transform man from a questioning being into an existing answer. This is the illusion that the demanding, unending, and unpredictable dialogue with conscience or with God can be replaced by the clarity of a pamphlet, that some artefact, like a set of pulleys freeing us from physical effort, can liberate us from the weight of personal responsibility and timeless sorrow. (1986, p. 174)

Teacher education, like all education, is a search, guided by a utopian ideal that does not have a conclusion. Its outcome is not certain nor is it defined by a determined set of standards. Embracing our common journey through and in education is how we become part of something good.

As teacher education opens to a perspective guided by heterology, diverse programs become spaces that draw upon "temporary stabilization" in the form of academic disciplines, literacies, and numeracies in order to unhinge the hegemonic competition-based ideology that oppresses diverse programs (IHE, EPI, T2T, or TFA pathways) and differentiates teacher candidates based upon arbitrary criteria (preparation pathway).

ENGAGING WITH FELLOW TEACHER EDUCATORS ACROSS PREPARATION PATHWAYS

Crossing the Borders of Preparation Programs

Teacher educators have been staunch advocates for the clinically rich preparation of teachers through programs implemented by institutions of higher education. These programs have diverse forms—traditional academic majors and minors, master's level degrees, post-baccalaureate certificates, and even accelerated residency programs. The common trait within this model of teacher preparation is the reliance upon a combination of highly trained, research-based faculty, advanced degree holding and experienced teachers, and experienced clinical coaches and mentors. Competition develops over the criteria and metrics that are used to identify these expert teacher educators. For tenure-track faculty at the university level, this is significant as they build their dossier for tenure and promotion review. What counts as valued teaching, scholarship, and service? Contemporary programs also compete over where and for whom these experts should work. Should teacher educators be employed by universities or schools and school districts? Should teacher educators spend most of their work time on the university campus, online, or in schools? Is there one model that should be adopted by all teacher educators? As the next generation of teacher educators are prepared it is important to have responses to these questions.

An alternative framework to the hegemonic competition-based ideology requires that teacher educators investigate the rules, the standards, by which all programs for the education of teachers are measured. Beginning by problematizing what it means to be "standardized" opens the dialogue regarding the potentialities that flow through educative settings—with primary interest focused on curriculum and pedagogical strategies used in the education of future teachers. The standardization of curriculum and desired teacher candidate proficiency outcomes has made possible the limiting and bonding of teacher preparation and teacher educators. By prescribing the outcomes to be achieved by teacher preparation programs, whether in the form of licensure tests required by the states or through accreditation and program approval self-studies, teacher preparation is contained and normed to the standards of the hegemony. Standardization is mythologized as the positive continuity of endless repetition, the eternal return of the same. It creates the territory teacher education is trapped within and inhabits. Standardization frames the disciplinary order of teacher preparation stripped of its ambiguity and diverse potentialities in an effort to maintain the status quo—it establishes a playing field or territory within which programs compete.

In many ways, teacher educator's good intentions to provide rigorous preparation programs as defined by the standards have worked against real progress. The reticence to speak out with courage, to truly educate peers and colleagues when confronted with misinformation and propaganda, is a problem within teacher education. When these discussions are seen as ideological confrontations, teacher educators miss out on the opportunity to listen to diverse perceptions and to achieve new common sense through educative dialogue. Teacher educators need to set aside their reluctance to educate due to a prevailing mood of caution, distrust, and uneasiness derived from the competition-based system. They need to embrace the instances in which some piece of heartening experience exposes the areas in which their peers and colleagues working in alternative pathways or programs agree with them or have a similar reluctance due to their own cautions or ignorance.

Entering the Competition's Locker Room

As a former coach and athlete the imagery and processes of sport help me conceptualize, problematize, and understand much of what I do within the competition-based enframing. Within the field of teacher education there has been an effort from policymakers to establish competition between traditional teacher education programs founded upon an academic major delivered by institutions of higher education (IHE) and alternative pathway "preparation" programs like EPI, T2T, and TFA. It is important to recognize that these pathways into the teaching profession have been framed as competing in order to expand the law of the market ideology into teacher education. The creation of competition is supposed to incentivize the efficient and effective preparation of teachers so that every child has the teacher they deserve and to sacrifice inefficient and ineffective providers to the market. This mythology is open to challenge even though we seldom engage in the opportunity.

A recent experience working with a competing preparation provider (TFA) has led me to reflect upon what this competition thematic is doing to the way in which teachers experience education and are educated. There seems to be an underlying assumption that we know what effective teachers need to know, that we can standardize the knowledge, skills, and dispositions needed by teachers no matter the school or student cultures in which those teachers will engage (Council of Chief State School Officers [CCSSO], 2013; National Board for Professional Teaching Standards, 2014). This normalization through competition raises critical questions. As I interacted with and helped a group of 120 TFA Core Members (first and second year teachers) struggle with their experience of responsive practices, challenges of scripted/prescribed curricula, and school cultures unlike the ones they had experienced as successful students at often prestigious institutions of higher education, it became clear that the framework of competition was itself a liability.

As we worked through a phenomenological exercise that required the TFA Core Members to reframe a critical experience as a fairy tale, it became evident that their experiences were the same experiences that troubled the graduates from my IHE program. As they probed the ontological questions and inquired into their being as teachers in the school territory in which they found themselves, these novice teachers were able to recognize and acknowledge the need for human relationships within the classroom. As they flipped their fairy tale narratives and retold their story for the point of view of their antagonist, they surfaced their role as obstacle to educative experiences for the students. The impact of inquiry like this is not limited to a specific program. Crossing borders and inquiring with individuals in the process of becoming is a nomadic exercise.

By structuring education for teachers within a framework of competition we fail to leverage our collective strength in providing educative experiences within schools. Teacher educators within institutions of higher education, individuals who have acquired extensive expertise through research and focused study, are marginalized by EPI, T2T, and TFA style preparation programs. At the same time, the aesthetic ethic that motivates EPI, T2T, and TFA programs is marginalized by higher education. Framing each other as competitors obscures the shared mission of education for all. The question we are left with involves the inquiry into what kind of pedagogy might we adopt and employ to ignite a revolutionary attitude founded on new ways of thinking about being a teacher educator? We have to move away from the competitive frame provided and enforced by the hegemonic ideological paradigm. If interests are born of desire, then to change the way in which we approach teaching, our profession, and the mission of education we have to address our desires. As educators, whether teachers or teacher educators, we must embrace thinking differently in order to facilitate the process which seeks to turn teachers as professionals-to-come into co-investigators, thus eliminating the competitive lens and the distinction between preparation pathways.

Nomadic teacher education will require teacher educators to come to terms with the heterogeneity that the current schooling paradigm is producing. Coping with the excesses, the leftovers—or left-behinds—of the current schooling paradigm requires a nomad's participatory impulse. It is for this reason that a practical counter-framework for teacher education is necessary.

LEVERAGING TEACHER EDUCATORS' DIVERSE EXPERIENCE AND EXPERTISE

A counter-teacher educator, the next generation teacher educator who crosses boundaries and inhabits diverse territories within education, takes on the function of the nomad. The origin of the word "nomad" is not a romanticized image of actual nomadic peoples, but based, rather, Immanuel Kant's claim that outside of philosophy is a wasteland fit only for nomads (Deleuze & Guattari, 1987). In one of Kant's more concise and accessible manuscripts, *Idea of a Universal History from a Cosmopolitan Point of View*, his fourth thesis asserts: "The means employed by Nature to bring about the development of all the capacities of men is their antagonism in society, so far as this is, in the end, the cause of a lawful order among men" (Kant, 2018). In an explanation of the oppositions that exist among individuals and the drive to enter society, Kant opens a space for the discussion of transgressing boundaries, crossing into the territories established by others, and developing within this relation to others.

> This opposition it is which awakens all his powers, brings him to conquer his inclination to laziness and, propelled by vainglory, lust for power, and avarice,

to achieve a rank among his fellows whom he cannot tolerate but from whom he cannot withdraw. Thus are taken the first true steps from barbarism to culture, which consists in the social worth of man; thence gradually develop all talents, and taste is refined; through continued enlightenment the beginnings are laid for a way of thought which can in time convert the coarse, natural disposition for moral discrimination into definite practical principles, and thereby change a society of men driven together by their natural feelings into a moral whole. (Kant, 2018, p. 4)

The process pointed to by Kant is the beginning of a nomadic process of engagement with others. Within Kant's thought this would lead to a consideration of reciprocal hospitality that also informs being a nomad.

The concept of the nomad captures a tendency towards de-territorialization that can be found to some degree in all phenomena. Within teacher education the nomadic teacher educator would advocate for teaching and teachers, not a particular program. Gilles Deleuze and Felix Guattari point toward the difference between a royal science and a nomadic science, and though they freely admit that the nomadic science creates structures and processes that are prone to collapse, they also celebrate its ability to open creative opportunities for heterogeneity. Advocating for those individuals capable of opening spaces for the creation of new habits of thought and action aligned to the current difficulties and challenges of classrooms and schools (generating new pedagogies to address emergent themes and polemics designed to transform the educational setting and processes) is the emergent role of a nomadic teacher educator. The nomadic teacher educator's project consists in identifying this tendency toward pedagogical innovation and responsiveness wherever it can be located and finding ways of amplifying it.

Being a nomadic teacher educator means becoming an advocate for public involvement in education to the extent that space is created beyond competition-based interventions in the preparation and development of teachers. The idea is to ring-fence educational spaces (A concept borrowed from business that describes a process of segregating a company's singular asset or liability in order to bracket or mitigate the risk of liquidation). Each teacher, classroom, and school regardless of preparation, development, or philosophy is protected and accompanied by the nomadic teacher educator as an exemplar of the heterogeneous nature of teachers and teaching, pedagogic content knowledge acquisition and development, and teacher effectiveness. A nomadic teacher educator focuses on the ways in which the de-territorialization of schools, classrooms, and communities can happen and inquire into the unique attributes they embody.

Becoming a nomadic teacher educator requires ethical-aesthetic courage. Breaking loose of our acquiescence to the common sense of education policy and accreditation standards and outcomes will require nomadic teacher educators to recognize the social nature, the developmental social needs, and social indebtedness of every member of the classroom, community, and school. Nomadic teacher educators must be willing to engage the hegemonic competition-based ideology from a position of authentic values and beliefs grounded in their personal experiences and their generative education. These teacher educators will come to see the beauty and value of the classroom, school, and community in its authenticity (Makiguchi, 1989). By working to protect or ring-fence educational spaces from the hegemonic pressures of competition-based requirements, the nomadic teacher educator must be prepared to put forward a view of the end in mind, a shared notion of the good that constitutes the form of life the classroom, school, and community could pursue. The means to that end will need to be framed by and with the classroom, school, and community. This bracketed territory, ring-fenced to mitigate the risk it both confronts and presents, will function by a nomadic science of inquiry that celebrates its heterogeneity within structures and processes that are subject to collapse.

Nomadic teacher educators facilitate a politics of self-defense and self-actualization in which local classrooms, schools, and communities that do not want to remain complicit with the competition-based paradigm are de-territorialized. Standing up for the diverse needs and goals of teachers, classrooms, schools, and communities against the punitive and homogenizing values mechanized within accountability systems is part of this politics of self-defense. Social change and the transformation of education do not come from compliance and commitment to a mode of teacher preparation and development. Many traditional programs and ways of doing teacher preparation and development represent a commitment to an elite or privileged pathway. Social change and the transformation of education cannot be imposed from such an elite or privileged position. Social change and the transformation of education will grow from nomadic and revolutionary practice in which the classroom, school, and community work with nomadic teacher educators to discover new pathways toward heterogeneous effectiveness together. Practice-based communities, not revolutionary programs nor privileged pathways, represent spaces of commitment to the diversity of common goods in which we gain the moral and intellectual habits that make us independent, singular, practical educators.

Thinking Differently About Our Colleagues

Thinking differently is facilitated through what Paulo Freire called "problem-posing" (Freire, 1990), which would seek to turn teachers and teacher educators as professionals-to-come into co-investigators, thus eliminating the competitive lens and the distinction between preparation pathways and educational roles. Whereas the competitive model that currently dominates leaves all teachers and teacher educators as inert, commodified objects to be manipulated and oppressed by mis-educative norms of narrowed curriculum, scripted lessons, high-stakes testing, and accountability, problem-posing opens up a being-affirming alternative. Teachers and teacher educators are positioned not merely as co-investigators in a project of providing educative and socially generative experiences, but as active agents in whose hands the shape of schooling actually rests.

The potential realized through heterogeneous teacher education programs, potential which is typically classified as useless, unproductive, and ineffective within a competition-based enframing (this is the language of marginalization), should be understood to have a nomadic existence valid and valuable in itself. Georg Bataille would frame these heterogeneous programs as sovereign and thus of worth as an expression of sacramental sacrifice by either the collective education community or the individual program and its nomadic faculty (Bataille, 1985). His explanation of this type of heterogeneous sacrament is helpful:

> The reality of heterogeneous elements is not of the same order as that of homogeneous elements. Homogeneous reality presents itself with the abstract and neutral aspect of strictly defined and identified objects (basically, it is the specific reality of solid objects). Heterogeneous reality is that of a force or other in a more or less abstract fashion, almost as if the change were taking place not in the world of objects but only in the judgments of the subject. The preceding aspect nevertheless does not signify that the observed facts are to be considered as subjective: thus, the action of the objects of erotic activity is manifestly rooted in their objective nature. Nonetheless, in a disconcerting way, the subject does have the capacity to displace the exciting value of one element onto an analogous or neighboring one. In heterogeneous reality, the symbols charged with affective value thus have the same importance as the fundamental elements, and the part can have the same value as the whole. It is easy to note that, since the structure of knowledge for a homogeneous reality is that of science, the knowledge of a heterogeneous reality as such is to be found in the mystical thinking of primitives and in dreams: it is identical to the structure of the unconscious... (Bataille, 1985, p. 143)

In the schooling context, examples of homogeneous reality can be found in the manner in which students are categorically classified and differentiated. The paradox for heterology is that a new perspective does not eliminate the useless and left-behind, it can only change its perception, form and expression which affect teachers' and teacher educators' understanding of this population of learners, programs and various other experiential factors. Homogeneity asserts one outcome, alternate frames recognize the diversity within teacher preparation while resisting the impulse to "differentiate" according to standardized, or normalized, criteria.

Thinking about colleagues as a professional-to-come means valuing learning as a process of transformation, the process of teachers' and teacher educators' coming to think differently from the norm of narrowed curriculum, scripted lessons, high-stakes testing, and accountability that dominate in the hegemonic competition-based ideology. Learning to think differently provides a route to become other in the process of interactions. Nomadic teacher educators, by supporting thinking differently, transform schools and professional development, producing a diverse range of critical and creative ideas, and experience the joy of expressing each educator's capacity for transformative pedagogy.

If teacher education, within the current hegemonic paradigm, is to be successful, it is assumed that the derivative waste or surplus that gets left behind or is at-risk will be minimized and eventually eliminated through competition among diverse pathways. Heterology takes an alternative and conceptually more positive view of diverse outcomes. Heterogeneity as excess is perceived as the source of innovation and asset rather than the source of stagnation and deficit.

Learning is an encounter with the unknown, the uncanny, the disturbing. It conditions experience and provides a still-contingent arbitrary ontology and nomadic science (Hawking & Mlodinow, 2010). Standardization of teacher education releases candidates and teacher educators from this encounter and rigs the outcomes of classroom experiences. By focusing upon learning as an encounter, nomadic teacher educators working in courses and programs based in heterologic curriculum, address questions rather than supply answers.

CONCLUSION

The enduring interest in the world, the political choice of what is important and valuable, is what characterizes inclusive, heterogeneous teacher education and grants meaning to life (Arendt, 1954, 1972; Benhabib, 1986; Habermas, 1987; Husserl, 1965). When we become disengaged from the educational and democratic process and the dialogue that is brought forward within a diverse and inclusive space, we cease to fully engage in the process that is meant to facilitate teacher learning and development. Capitulation to the exclusive leads to an orientation that fits a "participatory subject" rather than a critical "democratic citizen" (Almond & Verba, 1963). Deterritorializing teacher education, crossing cultural borders, the borders of exclusivity, helps to facilitate the type of inclusive education (Kymlica, 1995) that is necessary within a pluralist, democratic culture.

In a recent dialogue with a group of future teachers, the topic of recognition and the affective outcomes to be achieved in a classroom emerged.

The topic is one that comes up a lot in today's teacher education context. In a context in which teachers and teacher educators are encouraged to focus on limiting the deficit perspective they bring to the classroom and the motivation to facilitate the development of a "growth mindset," (Dweck, 2016) it is challenging to see the student sitting in the classroom and inhabiting the school and community. To recognize them as an individual, to treat each student with respect, dignity, and sacredness is to love them. This group of teachers in preparation wanted to discuss the relationships that should be developed within a classroom so that each student and adult in the classroom community feels loved and desires to be part of what the class is trying to accomplish together. This topic of discussion is one in which there are diverse answers—factors of common and disparate experiences, cultural diversity, and social continuity in a mobile student and teacher population all influence the response teachers, classrooms, schools, and communities can give.

In many ways this discussion is the core of nomadic teacher education. These learners were asking each other how do we care about and love each other and how do we buy into a future yet to come. The conversation was a moment in which individuals really learn. These are moments of problematization in which individuals are "unlearning" what is anticipated as given, common sense. They are escaping standard methods, curricula, and what is already known to inquire together—to study as a journey outside what is anticipated knowledge into the relational experience of thinking in new ways.

Nomadic teacher education and nomadic teacher educators acknowledge and embrace the search for pathways of recognition, love, and shared affect within heterogeneous classrooms, schools, and communities. This will require a joyful rampage—the creative destruction of the way things are expected to be done. This emergent form of nomadic teacher education involves nomadic teacher educators carrying on new forms of study, inquiry, and research, investigating new questions of effectiveness to rampage through the old models that have been homogenized. Teacher education in this paradigm is one that passes from one struggle to next, one context and group to the next, and is a joyful process of recognition, love, and community buy-in built on heterogeneous relationships.

Discussion Questions

1. How is our approach to the preparation of teachers based on an inclusive, generative, and risk-tolerant process of exploration and inquiry?
2. When we look at the accountability metrics and systems that we work within as teacher educators, how are we able to be responsive,

innovative, and creative of new habits or ways of teaching both with our teacher candidates and our community partners?

3. Do we limit our actions in the face of competition from other preparation routes and programs?
    – How do we begin to overcome the structural obstacles that have been institutionalized as mechanisms of accountability across education?
    – How do we engage with fellow teacher educators across preparation pathways in a manner that recognizes both strengths and limitations?
    – How do we leverage teacher educators' dispersed experience and expertise toward a common just end? An end that sees the beauty and value of each classroom, school, and community in their authenticity and heterogeneity.

Where and how should teacher educators work?
    – What counts as valued teaching, scholarship, and service?
    – Should teacher educators be employed by universities or schools and school districts?
    – Should teacher educators spend most of their work time on the university campus, online, or in schools?
    – Is there one model that should be adopted by all teacher educators?

In what ways is teacher educator preparation grounded in a nomadic science of inquiry?
    – Is candidate work useful and productive?
    – Is cooperation and collaboration between candidates and with mentor teachers part of preparation?
    – How is inquiry embedded throughout the preparation process?
    – Is preparation centered upon children's learning interests and curiosity?

REFERENCES

Almond, G. A., & Verba, S. (1963). *The civic culture: Political attitudes and democracy in five nations.* Boston, MA: Little, Brown and Company.

Arendt, H. (1954). *Between past and future: Eight exercises in political thought.* New York, NY: Penguin Books.

Arendt, H. (1972). *Crisis of the republic.* New York, NY: Harcourt, Brace and Company.

Bataille, G. (1985). The psychological structure of fascism. In *Visions of excess: Selected writings, 1927–1939* (pp. 137–160). Minneapolis: University of Minnesota Press.

Benhabib, S. (1986). *Critique, norm, and utopia: A study of the foundations of critical theory.* New York, NY: Columbia University Press.

Biesta, G. J. (2009). Good education in an age of measurement: On the need to reconnect with the question of purpose in education. *Educational assessment, evaluation and accountability, 21*, 33–46.

Biesta, G. J. (2014). *The beautiful risk of education.* Boulder, CO: Paradigm.

Council of Chief State School Officers. (2013, April). *InTASC model core teaching standards and learning progressions for teachers 1.0.* Retrieved from https://ccsso.org/sites/default/files/2017-12/2013_INTASC_Learning_Progressions_for_Teachers.pdf

Deleuze, G., & Guattari, F. (1987). *A thousand plateaues: Capitalism and schizophrenia* (B. Massumi, Trans.) Minneapolis, MN: University of Minnesota Press.

Dweck, C. S. (2016). *Mindset: The new psychology of success.* New York, NY: Ballantine Books.

Freire, P. (1990). *Pedagogy of the oppressed.* New York, NY: Continuum.

Giroux, H. (2012). *Education and the crisis of public values: Challenging the assault on teachers, students, & public education.* New York, NY: Peter Lang.

Habermas, J. (1987). *The theory of communicative action.* Cambridge, England: Blackwell.

Havel, V. (1986). An anatomy of reticence. In V. Havel & J. Vladislav (Eds.), *Living in truth* (pp. 164–195). London, England: Faber and Faber.

Hawking, S., & Mlodinow, L. (2010). *The grand design.* New York, NY: Bantam Books.

Heidegger, M. (1977). *The question concerning technology, and other essays* (W. Levitt, Trans.) New York, NY: Harper & Row.

Husserl, E. (1965). *Phenomenology and the crisis of philosophy: Philosophy as rigorous science and philosophy and the crisis of European man* (Q. Lauer, Trans.). New York, NY: Harper Torchbooks.

Jacobs, J., Burns, R., & Yendol-Hoppey, D. (2015). The inequitable influence that varying accountability contexts in the United States have on teacher professional development. *Professional Development in Education, 41*(5), 849–872.

Kant, I. (2018, April 11). *Idea for a universal history from a cosmopolitan point of view.* Retrieved from www.marxists.org/reference/subject/ethics/kant/universal-history.htm

Kumashiro, K. (2009). *Against common sense: Teaching and learning toward social justice* (Revised ed.). New York, NY: Routledge.

Kymlica, W. (1995). *Multicultural citizenship: A liberal theory of minority rights.* New York, NY: Oxford University Press.

Makiguchi, T. (1989). *Education for creative living: Ideas and proposals of Tsunesaburo Makiguchi* (D. M. Bethel, Ed., & A. Birnbaum, Trans.). Ames: Iowa State University Press.

Mullainathan, S., & Shafir, E. (2013). *Scarcity: The new science of having less and how it defines our lives.* New York, NY: Picador.

National Board for Professional Teaching Standards. (2014). *The teacher leadership competencies.* Retrieved from http://www.nbpts.org/sites/default/files/teacher_leadership_competencies_final.pdf

Parkison, P. (2015). Catharsis in education: Rationalizing and reconciling. *Curriculum and Teaching Dialogue, 17*(2), 121–135.

Parkison, P. (2016). Teacher as commodity: Controlling the supply chain. *The Education Forum, 80*(1), 107–123.

Yamagata-Lynch, L., & Haudenschild, M. (2009). Using activity systems analysis to identify inner contradictions in teacher professional development. *Teacher and Teacher Education, 25*(3), 507–517.

CHAPTER 13

CONCLUDING THOUGHTS

Looking Across the Chapters

Diane Yendol-Hoppey
University of North Florida

Nancy Fichtman Dana
University of Florida

David Hoppey
University of North Florida

The chapters within this book collectively demonstrate that the nature and responsibilities of teacher educators who work in programs requiring strong clinical practice are shifting and expanding. These shifting and expanding practices necessitate a rethinking of how to prepare university and school-based teacher educators for their work in clinical settings. We have seen this no more candidly stated than in the words of McCoy and Nickens, shared in Chapter 5 of this book:

> Many professors in campus-based teacher education programs have classes on two or three days each week. They focus primarily on teaching, scholarship,

Preparing the Next Generation of Teacher Educators for Clinical Practice, pages 295–300
Copyright © 2019 by Information Age Publishing

and service to the university and to the profession of education; prepping and grading for classes, corresponding with and meeting with students, answering endless emails, doing committee work and participating in scholarly endeavors. They work very hard. As the launch of our clinical model neared realization, our faculty had a realization of their own: this work was going to be even harder. On top of all of the existing faculty obligations, our clinical program requires faculty members to keep one foot on campus, teaching college courses to college students and one foot in the public schools, supervising teacher candidates' growth across two years. A new type of program that is significantly different requires a new type of faculty member and we learned that not all university-based teacher educators could make the transition. Nor did all of them want to make this transition. (p. 99)

This reflection portrays the experiences of many teacher educators as they have began their careers or transitioned to teacher education that includes strong clinical practice. In fact, many academics hired in teacher education have not been prepared for, expected to, or even want to help bridge the university research to school-practice divide. Our school-based partners, although so committed to mentoring new teachers, also struggle to understand and enact the expanding responsibilities that they face. These remarks prompt the question, how can we better prepare the next generation of university and school-based teacher educators for this complex work?

As seen throughout the chapters, re-envisioning, implementing, and sustaining teacher education programs that are more clinically integrated requires much more than just more time in schools. This work necessitates university and school-based teacher educators becoming intentional and systematic about the linkages they desire. For example, quality clinically intensive teacher education means disciplinary knowledge, theory, and research are all woven into practice. This requires cultivating university–school relationships and knowledge networks strong enough to connect research and theory to practice and vice versa. This complex work demands that teacher educators address the variability and unpredictability of the teaching and learning processes within constantly changing clinical contexts. To do this requires developing the capacity of teacher educators to fully assume expanded responsibilities that go well beyond what is traditionally referred to as subject, content or disciplinary knowledge.

We believe that the scholars of teacher education who have shared their work and experiences within this book offer insight to others related to the expanding responsibilities of teacher educators. Collectively, their insights provide a set of guide points to others. To these ends, in the conclusion to this text, we offer an analysis of what we learn in looking across the chapters. First, we suggest *what* this next generation of teacher educators need to be effective and second, we describe *how* the next generation of teacher educators can learn the knowledge, skills, and abilities needed to navigate teacher education that values strong and integrated clinical practice.

WHAT DO TEACHER EDUCATORS NEED TO BE EFFECTIVE?

As we integrate the clinical components of teacher education throughout preparation programs, teacher educator work requires the ability to purposefully connect theory, research, and practice. These connections gradually scaffold teacher candidate learning. Throughout the chapters, our authors point to important knowledge, skills and dispositions that teacher educators will need to utilize as they cultivate the clinical context and scaffold learning. For example, authors noted that in addition to possessing important disciplinary knowledge, university and school-based teacher educators must be able to design and implement field-based courses, establish relationships with key players in clinical settings, provide feedback on teaching, support action research, address barriers, tensions, and concerns, support mentor development, navigate the school context, utilize clinical pedagogy, as well as assess the developmental needs of the PK–12 learner and teacher candidates. These skills are needed to enact six overarching practices that are becoming increasingly recognized as responsibilities of teacher education: coaching, evaluation, partnership, course configuration, program leadership, and research practices. These practices are central to the work of those who are responsible for integrated and cohesive clinical practice (Hoppey & Yendol-Hoppey, 2018).

In addition to these skills, the authors of these chapters noted that effective teacher educators also benefit by possessing some specific *dispositions*. For example, Norman et al. (this volume) noted in Chapter 2 that the stance of an "educative mentor" is that of a co-learner. Being a co-learner requires respect and appreciation for the expertise of classroom teachers, willingness to work alongside classroom teachers, embrace collaboration, and willing to seek to understand practices in schools. A part of being a co-learner requires a disposition of persistence and willingness to negotiate as they work through tensions related to program and personnel development. These teacher educators who have chapters in this book negotiated many differences including conflicts presented by the very institutional systems in place. Across the chapters, much evidence suggests that teacher educators need to possess an inquiry disposition to their practice of teacher education. In many cases, teacher educators used their inquiry disposition or stance to make connections between their research *on* teacher education with the practice of being a teacher educator.

HOW DO THEY LEARN?

One of the primary contributions this text makes is the identification of multiple vehicles that can be used for systematically and intentionally developing teacher educator knowledge, skills, and dispositions. Figure 13.1 provides an overview of several vehicles that show promise for building future university and school-based teacher educator development. For example, multiple authors presented intentionally scaffolded doctoral candidate development through a *doctoral course coupled with or followed by an*

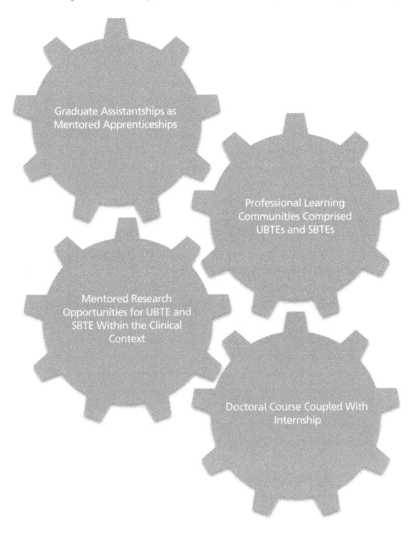

Figure 13.1   Vehicles for preparing teacher educators.

internship that develops the boundary spanning skills (e.g., coaching, mentoring, partnership, clinical coursework, research) of a teacher educator. Critical to moving the field forward was how these linked graduate student experiences helped future teacher educators learn to navigate the tension between studying teacher education and learning how to be a teacher educator. Others described the use of *professional learning communities* as a vehicle that brought together teacher candidates, mentor teachers, and administrators to learn from one another. The PLCs provided a supportive, risk-free structure to assist teacher education doctoral students as well as school-based partners with their ongoing development. In these cases, highly skilled university-based teacher educators thoughtfully and intentionally created opportunities for graduate students to participate with their school-based partners in teaching, scholarship, program innovation, and professional learning, as well as many other activities associated with the partnership.

Opportunities for *highly mentored graduate assistantships,* designed with intentionality, also provided future teacher educators an apprenticeship for learning partnership work. In many cases, the nature of mentoring doctoral students was strikingly different from university doctoral advising that often focuses primarily on traditional coursework and more traditional research projects. Rather, doctoral students and junior faculty benefitted from the support they received by working side by side multiple mentors as they learned to navigate teaching, research, and partnership in relation to clinical practice. Clinical programs require faculty members to mentor doctoral students as they are learning how to keep one foot in the university while simultaneously placing the other foot in the public schools supervising teacher candidates as they develop their classroom practice.

Providing *mentored research opportunities* are equally important in the preparation of university and school-based teacher educators. These experiences help those new to the field cultivate an inquiry stance toward studying their teacher education efforts and important problems of practice experienced in the schools. Dredsen et al. (see Chapter 3) discussed how an on-site doctoral course that heavily involved ongoing dialogue with school faculty about the school's needs, issues, and concerns led to initial research ideas. The experience began to shape the doctoral student's understanding of doing research as a teacher educator with school partners. Self-study helped teacher educators better understand and improve their practices while maintaining teacher education as the core of their research. Self-study research led to more informed decisions about pedagogical decision-making, identity and practice, as well as cultivating collaborative communities. Future and current teacher educators benefit greatly by opportunities to conduct research that is a part of their practice and engage in reflective practices that cultivate an inquiry stance.

CONCLUSION

Many of the teacher educators who shared their stories within this volume alluded to the challenges they faced in confronting institutional norms as they tried to establish institutional recognition of the depth and breadth of their faculty expertise as teacher educators. In navigating institutional expectations of scholarly expertise, the authors confronted the difficulty of establishing their identities as teacher educators within a context that seemed to more highly value certain parts of the teacher educator role (e.g., content specialist/disciplinary knowledge) more than others (e.g., partnership, research to practice, clinical pedagogy).

Likely one of the most important lessons we can learn from this text is that the solution to creating strong teacher preparation that links theory, research, and practice isn't to value *either* teacher educators with content specialist/disciplinary knowledge *or* emphasize the importance of teacher educators with clinical pedagogy, program, and partnership expertise. Important to developing quality teacher education will be institutional recognition that *both* specialized clinical pedagogy, partnership, and program design knowledge *as well as* content/disciplinary knowledge are essential to creating high quality, clinically based teacher candidate learning. This requires assisting junior faculty in crafting annual review as well as promotion and tenure narratives that highlight their teaching, research, and service work that is tightly coupled with high quality clinical teacher education (Yendol-Hoppey, Hoppey, Morewood, Hayes, & Graham, 2013). Also requiring institutional recognition is the importance of bringing university and school-based teacher educators together to create seamless preparation programs with strong, relevant, and coherent clinical components. Our teacher candidates and the students whom they will teach, deserve that each preparation program authentically bring together, value, and integrate the expertise needed to build quality preparation programs.

REFERENCES

Hoppey, D., &. Yendol-Hoppey, D. (Eds.). (2018). *Outcomes of high quality clinical practice in teacher education*. Charlotte, NC: Information Age.

Yendol-Hoppey, D., Hoppey, D., Morewood, A., Hayes, S., & Graham, M. (2013). Micropolitical and identity challenges influencing new faculty participation in teacher education reform: When will we learn? *Teachers College Record, 115*(7), 1–31.

ABOUT THE EDITORS

Diane Yendol-Hoppey, PhD, is a Professor and the Dean of the College of Education and Human Services at the University of North Florida. Diane's research specifically focuses on understanding practice-based teacher education, preservice and in-service job-embedded teacher learning (e.g., teacher inquiry, coaching, mentoring, PLCs), and teacher leadership. Prior to her current position at the University of North Florida, she held positions at the University of Florida, and West Virginia University. Her leadership related to working with schools has helped develop and sustain several nationally recognized school/university partnerships. Diane has co-authored four books as well as published over 50 studies which have appeared in such journals as *Educational Researcher, Teachers College Record* and *Journal of Teacher Education*. During Diane's first 13 years in education, she taught Pk-5 in Pennsylvania and Maryland.

Nancy Fichtman Dana, PhD, is a Professor in the School of Teaching and Learning in the College of Education at the University of Florida. At both the Pennsylvania State University and the University of Florida, she led the development of clinically-based award-winning teacher education programs. Her research focuses on wrapping the continual learning of teacher candidates, practicing teachers, and teacher educators around the learning of PK-12 students through practitioner inquiry. Nancy has published ten books and over 100 articles and book chapters related to teachers', teacher candidates', administrators', and teacher educators' professional learning through inquiry in clinical settings. She has also worked extensively in supporting schools, districts and universities in implementing powerful pro-

Preparing the Next Generation of Teacher Educators for Clinical Practice, pages 301–302
Copyright © 2019 by Information Age Publishing
301

grams of job-embedded professional development across the United States and in several countries, including China, South Korea, Belgium, Portugal, The Netherlands, Slovenia, and Estonia.

David Hoppey, PhD, is an Associate Professor and Director of the Doctoral Program in Educational Leadership at the University of North Florida. He received his PhD from the University of Florida. Prior to arriving at UNF, David held faculty positions at West Virginia University and the University of South Florida. Previously, he worked as an inclusion specialist and district administrator for Alachua County Public Schools in Gainesville, FL and started his career as a middle school special educator in Orlando, FL. David has taught courses to both special education and elementary education majors on best inclusive practices to meet the needs of students with disabilities as well as doctoral seminars on teacher education and special education. He also has worked extensively redesigning undergraduate and doctoral programs to include more clinically rich teacher preparation components. David's scholarship examines inclusive teacher education, special education policy, and school university partnerships, including providing quality pre-service teacher education, and ongoing in-service teacher professional development. Dr. Hoppey's research has been published in *The Journal of Special Education, Teachers College Record,* and *Learning Disabilities Research and Practice,* as well as in book and handbook chapters.

ABOUT THE CONTRIBUTORS

Melissa A. Baker, PhD, is a clinical assistant professor of Middle Level Education at the University of South Carolina. Her scholarship focuses on professional development school partnerships, teacher education, family engagement experiences, and elementary to middle school transitions.

Brandon M. Butler is an Associate Professor of Teaching and Learning at Old Dominion University in Norfolk, VA. He received his doctorate from the University of Georgia, and before entering higher education was a middle school social studies teacher in Lawrenceville, GA. His scholarship focuses on the spaces in which teaching and teacher education is learned and enacted, with specific attention paid to methods instruction, clinical supervision, and doctoral student learning. He has publications in such journals as *Theory and Research in Social Education, Studying Teacher Education, Action in Teacher Education*, and *Teaching and Teacher Education*.

Elizabeth Currin is a doctoral candidate in Curriculum, Teaching, and Teacher Education. She serves as coordinator of the elementary education doctoral program. A former high school English teacher, Elizabeth currently supervises interns (local and distant) in the Unified Elementary Proteach program and teaches undergraduate courses on the sociology and history of education. Elizabeth's research interests include practitioner inquiry, the history of education, and representations of teaching and learning in popular culture.

Rocio Delgado is as associate professor of Education at Trinity University. She is the director of the special education and bilingual/ESL certification

Preparing the Next Generation of Teacher Educators for Clinical Practice, pages 303–309
303

areas in the Master of Arts in Teaching program. She is a former bilingual special education teacher from Juarez, Mexico who taught in Las Cruces Public School and the Texas Schools for the Deaf and Blind in Austin. She currently works with professional development schools in San Antonio ISD. Her research and practice revolve around the preparation of teachers to work with culturally and linguistically diverse populations with and without disabilities and collaboration between school, families, and communities.

Pooja Dharamshi is an Assistant Professor of Teacher Education in the Faculty of Education at Simon Fraser University. Her previous experiences as a classroom teacher in linguistically and culturally diverse communities of New York City sparked her research interests in the area of critical literacy and teacher education. She holds a doctoral degree from the Ontario Institute for Studies in Education, University of Toronto.

Cheryl (Sherry) Dismuke is a Clinical Assistant Professor at Boise State University where she coordinates the Elementary Education program, teaches methods courses, and serves as a university liaison to partner schools. Her research interests focus on teacher education, writing instruction, and new educator induction.

Janna Dresden is a clinical professor in the early childhood program in the Department of Educational Theory and Practice, and the Director of the Office of School Engagement (OSE) at the University of Georgia. In her role as director of the OSE she is responsible for coordinating the partnership between the College of Education and the local Clarke County School District. Her teaching and scholarship are focused on examining school-university partnerships from a variety of perspectives and exploring the ways in which clinically-intensive settings create opportunities for learning at all levels.

Sara L. Hartman is an Assistant Professor of Early Childhood Education in the Gladys W. and David H. Patton College of Education at Ohio University. Under an early childhood umbrella, Dr. Hartman's research interests are situated within themes pertaining to the clinical model of teacher preparation and school-community-university partnerships in rural settings. Dr. Hartman also works closely with local schools, serving as the faculty coordinator for early childhood teacher candidates who are working in the field.

Lara Hebert earned her PhD in Curriculum, Aesthetics, and Teacher Education from the University of Illinois in Urbana-Champaign in 2012. Her research centers on networked professional learning systems for beginning teachers, and she has published in *Action in Teacher Education, Best Practices* *in Mentoring for Teacher and Leader Development*, and Past, Present, and *Future Research on Teacher Induction*.

Sara R. Helfrich is an Associate Professor of Literacy in the Gladys W. and David H. Patton College of Education at Ohio University. Her major research interests pertain to the clinical model of teacher preparation and school-community-university partnerships, reading teacher preparation and pre-service and in-service teacher self-efficacy related to teaching literacy.

Serena Hicks is Clinical Faculty in the Department of Curriculum, Instruction, and Foundational Studies at Boise State University. Her research focuses on mentor teacher experiences, secondary teacher education, and collaboration in higher education.

Lindsayanne (Annie) Insana is currently the Director of Literacy for Educator Preparation and Induction Programs at the Tennessee Department of Education. She supports higher education institutions across the state of Tennessee with various literacy initiatives. Prior to coming to Tennessee, Annie served as the Assistant Director of Teacher Education in the College of Education and Director of the Illinois New Teacher Collaborative at the University of Illinois at Urbana-Champaign. Her research involves understanding teachers' adaptive decision-making processes in the complex environment of the classroom. Annie is dedicated to teacher development and education at the preservice and inservice levels. She taught elementary school for seven years and has taught teacher candidates in Early Childhood, Special Education, and Elementary programs.

Jennifer Jacobs is currently an Associate Professor at the University of South Florida. She serves as coordinator of the elementary education doctoral program. Her research is situated within the context of teacher education or the continuum of professional learning that begins with preservice teacher education and moves through induction and inservice teacher career learning. Specifically, her research agenda within teacher education focuses on the development of equity-centered or equity literate teachers by understanding and building contexts that facilitate teacher learning and studying process that support teacher learning for equity. Her work has been published in *Action in Teacher Education, The Journal of School Leadership, The New Educator, School University Partnerships*, and *Professional Development in Education*.

Alexis Jones is an Assistant Professor in the Department of Teaching, Learning, and Foundations at Eastern Illinois University. She received her doctorate from the University of Illinois at Urbana-Champaign. Prior to her doctoral work, Dr. Jones was a grant and staff development coordinator in a Central Illinois school district, applying for state and federal funding for professional development workshops and programs for new teacher mentoring. Her research areas include the moral dimensions of teaching and teacher education, including the ways teachers notice and respond to youth, and how teachers' emotions are constantly at play in their decision-making. Dr. Jones uses self-study and narrative to analyze her own practice, and she has published in *Issues in Teacher Education* (in press) and the *Journal of Inquiry and Action in Education*.

Meghan Kessler is an Assistant Professor in the Department of Teacher Education at The University of Illinois Springfield. She received her PhD from the University of Illinois at Urbana-Champaign. Prior to beginning her doctoral program, Dr. Kessler was a high school and middle school social studies teacher in Illinois. Her research interests include preservice teacher education and evaluation measures, teacher education policy, and social studies education.

Clare Kosnik is Professor at the Ontario Institute of Studies in Education/University of Toronto and is the Director of the Dr. Eric Jackman Institute of Child Study. She has systematically studied many aspects of teacher education including a study of 28 literacy teacher educators in four countries and a longitudinal study of 40 teachers over 10 years.

Courtney Lynch is currently Director of EDUCATE at the Pennsylvania State University. She earned her PhD in Curriculum and Instruction with an emphasis in Mathematics Education from the Pennsylvania State University. Her doctoral work focused on the collaboration between school- and university-based teacher educators in planning for an elementary mathematics methods course. Her research interests include the boundary-crossing work of hybrid teacher educators, the role of video technology in supervision, and supporting preservice teachers as they navigate new standards for teachers and teaching.

Ann C. McCoy, PhD is professor and chair of the Department of Elementary and Early Childhood Education at the University of Central Missouri. Prior to working in higher education, Dr. McCoy taught for 22 years at the elementary and middle school levels. Her research interests include studying the impact of clinical models on the development of preservice teachers. She is also interested in the effect of the use of elementary mathematics specialists on student achievement in elementary mathematics.

Lydia Menna is an Assistant Professor of Language and Literacy in the Department of Elementary Education at the University of Alberta. Her research interests are in the areas of teacher education, multiliteracies, critical literacy, and teacher identity construction. She completed her doctorate in the Department of Curriculum, Teaching and Learning at the Ontario Institute for Studies in Education, University of Toronto.

Nicole Nickens, PhD is a professor of Educational Psychology and has worked as a behavior specialist in special education and mental health prior to entering higher education where she has been a teacher educator for more than 20 years. Her research interests focus on educational measurement and assessment including performance assessment of student teaching, evaluation of clinical partnerships, and impact of clinical practice.

Patricia Norman, PhD, is an associate professor in the Department of Education at Trinity University. She coordinates the elementary Master of Arts in Teaching program. In addition, she serves as the university liaison at Lamar Elementary in San Antonio ISD, one of Trinity's Professional Development School partners. Her research interests focus on field-based teacher education across an educator's learning to teach developmental continuum.

Ashley S. Nylin, EdS was a sixth-grade science teacher in metro Atlanta before beginning her doctoral studies. Her research interests include professional development schools, teacher empowerment, and service-learning. She was recently recognized as an Emerging PDS Leader by the National Association of Professional Development Schools and hopes to continue and extend her work within PDSs upon graduation.

Audra Parker, PhD, is an Associate Professor and Academic Program Coordinator in Elementary Education at George Mason University. Her primary research interests include clinical teacher preparation and young adolescents' school experiences. In addition to teaching courses in elementary methods and management, she also serves as a boundary spanning teacher educator at a professional development school site in Fairfax County Public Schools. Her work has appeared in *The New Educator, School University Partnerships,* and *Teacher Education and Practice.*

Paul Parkison is an associate professor and Chair of Childhood Education, Literacy, & TESOL at the University of North Florida. His primary research interests focus on teacher identity and the politics of schooling. His recent publications address issues related to the politics of assessment, accountability, and curriculum alignment to standards.

Seth A. Parsons, PhD, is an associate professor in the College of Education and Human Development at George Mason University. He teaches courses in the Elementary Education, Literacy, and Research Methods program areas. His research focuses on teachers' instructional adaptations, teacher education and development, and students' motivation and engagement. His work has appeared in numerous journals including *Review of Educational Research, Elementary School Journal, Teaching and Teacher Education, The Journal of Educational Research, Journal of Literacy Research, The Reading Teacher,* and *Language Arts.*

Sara A. S. Sherwood is an assistant professor of clinical practice in elementary education at Trinity University. She teaches undergraduate and graduate education courses and supervises the fieldwork for Master of Arts in Teaching students at the Advanced Learning Academy, where she serves as the university liaison and a governing board member. Her research focuses on preservice teachers' beliefs about play, educator preparation program improvement, and the university's role in first year teacher induction into the teaching profession.

Melissa Siller is a PhD candidate at the University of Texas at San Antonio and adjunct faculty member in the Department of Education at Trinity University. Her research focuses on teacher education, curriculum and inquiry as well as beginning in-service teacher induction support.

Kajal Sinha is a doctoral candidate in the College of Education Department of Educational Theory and Practice. Kajal has worked with teacher educators and teacher education programs in India focusing on professional learning workshops and the development of curriculum. Building on her experiences in India and in the United States, she is inquiring into the everyday practices of teacher candidates and the contexts that make them possible. Her dissertation explores the subject positions produced for teacher candidates in these two contexts.

Larina I. M. Sisson earned a Bachelor of Science degree in Early Childhood Education from Ohio University. She is a graduate student in The Gladys W. and David H. Patton College of Education at Ohio University studying Reading Education.

Jennifer L. Snow serves as the Associate Dean for Teacher Education and coordinates all teacher education programs at Boise State University. She also works closely with preK–12 school partnerships and clinical field experiences. Her scholarly interests focus on school-university partnerships, teacher leadership, and educational policy and programming.

Katherine F. Thompson is a clinical professor of middle grades education in the Department of Educational Theory and Practice at the University of Georgia (UGA). She serves as a Professor-in-Residence at Hilsman Middle School in Athens-Clarke County as part of the professional development schools partnership between UGA and the Clarke County School District.

She is also the Georgia state director of the Title II-Part A Improving Teacher Quality program. Dr. Thompson has authored numerous publications and other scholarly contributions focused on the education of young adolescents, community-engaged teaching and learning, and professional development school partnerships.

Julianne Wenner is an Assistant Professor for the Department of Curriculum, Instruction, and Foundational Studies at Boise State. Dr. Wenner's research focuses on teacher leadership, elementary science teacher education, and schooling contexts/systems that support/hinder equitable science instruction and outcomes.

Kristien Zenkov, PhD, is Professor of Education and the Academic Program Coordinator for the Secondary Education (SEED) program at George Mason University (GMU). He is the author and editor of more than one hundred fifty articles and book chapters and six books, focusing on teacher education, literacy pedagogy and curricula, social justice education, school-university partnerships, and Professional Development Schools. Dr. Zenkov is a long-time boundary-spanning educator and school-university partnership facilitator. He currently collaborates as a co-teacher at TC Williams High School in Alexandria, Virginia and conducts numerous project-based clinical experiences with youths and preservice and inservice teachers at TC Williams and Northern Virginia schools. He co-directs *Through Students' Eyes,* a Youth Participatory Action Research and photovoice project where youths document with photographs and writings their beliefs about citizenship, justice, school and literacy.

CPSIA information can be obtained
at www.ICGtesting.com
Printed in the USA
BVHW040516211219
567395BV00006B/32/P